Black Protest in the Sixties

Black Protest in the Sixties

Edited with an Introduction by

August Meier,
John Bracey, Jr. and
the late Elliott Rudwick

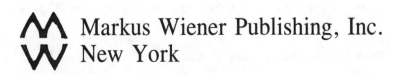 Markus Wiener Publishing, Inc.
New York

First Markus Wiener Publishing, Inc. edition 1991

For information write to:

Markus Wiener Publishing, Inc.
225 Lafayette Street, New York, NY 10012

Library of Congress Cataloging-in-Publication Data

Black protest in the sixties / edited by August Meier, Elliot
  Rudwick, John Bracey, Jr. — 2nd updated and enl. ed.

    Includes bibliographical references and index.
    ISBN 1-55876-031-8:
    ISBN 1-55876-032-6 (pbk.):
    1. Afro-Americans—Civil rights. 2. Black power—United States.
3. Afro-Americans—History—1964- 4. United States—
-History—1961–1969. I. Meier, August, 1923- . II. Rudwick,
Elliott M. III. Bracey, John H.
E185.615.B5472   1990
322.4′0973—dc20   90-13071
                                                         CIP

Cover photo courtesy of Urban Archives Center, Samuel Paley
Library, Temple University, Philadelphia, PA.

Printed in the United States of America

Contents

Introduction   *1*

Addendum for 1991 Edition   *23*

1. The Ascendancy of Nonviolent Direct Action   *25*

Negroes in South in Store Sit-down   *28*

Progress—by Moderation *and* Agitation   *29*
     by Eric F. Goldman

Two Ways: Black Muslim and N.A.A.C.P.   *37*
     by Gertrude Samuels

Sheriff Harasses Negroes at Voting Rally in Georgia   *46*
     by Claude Sitton

Negro Queue in Mississippi Is Symbol of Frustration
in Voter Registration Drive   *53*
     by Claude Sitton

Racial Strife   *62*

Rights Pact   *65*

For Rights   70

Status of Integration: The Progress So Far Is
Characterized as Mainly Tokenism   74
    by Claude Sitton

Their Text Is a Civil Rights Primer   79
    by Pat Watters

Mississippi Factions Clash Before Convention Panel   89
    by E. W. Kenworthy

Negro Party Set to Push Its Drive   93
    by John Herbers

Why the Negro Children March   96
    by Pat Watters

"The Wonder Is There Have Been So Few Riots"   107
    by Kenneth B. Clark

After Watts—Where Is the Negro Revolution Headed?   116
    by C. Vann Woodward

2. The Ascendancy of Black Power

A Negro Psychiatrist Explains the Negro Psyche   129
    by Alvin F. Poussaint

The Story of Snick: From "Freedom High" to Black Power   139
    by Gene Roberts

An Advocate of Black Power Defines It   154
    by Charles V. Hamilton

The Full and Sometimes Very Surprising Story of Ocean Hill,
the Teachers' Union and the Teacher Strikes of 1968   169
    by Martin Mayer

The Call of the Black Panthers   230
    by Sol Stern

The Black Studies Thing   *243*
    by Ernest Dunbar

Odyssey of a Man—and a Movement   *262*
    by Paul Good

Dr. King's March on Washington, Part II   *277*
    by José Yglesias

"No Man Can Fill Dr. King's Shoes"—but Abernathy Tries *294*
    by Paul Good

"We Can't Cuss White People Any More. It's in Our Hands
Now"   *312*
    by Walter Rugaber

There Is No Rest for Roy Wilkins   *325*
    by Martin Arnold

A Strategist Without a Movement   *339*
    by Thomas R. Brooks

3. Epilogue: The Ascendancy of Political Action   *355*

For a Black Vice President in 1972   *356*
    by Andrew M. Greeley

Suggested Reading   *363*

Index   *365*

A Note on the Editors   *375*

Introduction

DURING THE 1960's the black protest movement underwent momentous changes. When the now-famous four young college students sat-in at a Woolworth lunch counter in Greensboro, North Carolina, on February 1, 1960, the National Association for the Advancement of Colored People (NAACP) was the pre-eminent civil rights organization, and its technique of legalism was the most widely used method of attacking American racism. But the action of these four young men precipitated a chain of events that made nonviolent direct action the leading tactic of the civil rights movement for half a dozen years. Then, in the latter part of the decade, nationalist tendencies and the rhetoric of violence, bracketed together under the phrase "Black Power," became the new rationale for action.

I

The NAACP was founded in 1909 by a group of white Progressives and Socialists and black militants, at a time when the status of Negroes in the United States was at low ebb. Blacks lived under a race system which involved disfranchisement, Jim Crow laws, plantation sharecropping, and lynch law in the South, segregation by custom in much of the North, and extreme job discrimination in all parts of the country. White public opinion demanded—and the most influential black leaders acquiesced in —the practice of segregation or racial separatism. In contrast, the founders of the NAACP believed in a direct frontal attack on the system of racial segregation and discrimination through lobbying for civil rights legislation and, more important, fighting in the courts for the enforcement of the Reconstruction amendments. Over the years the NAACP, hacking away at one barrier after another in its long upward battle against disfranchisement and segregation, piled up an impressive series of victories in the United States Supreme Court. By mid-century the Court had outlawed discriminatory voting procedures, legal devices promoting residential segregation, and segregation in interstate transportation, in publicly owned recreational facilities, and in public institutions of higher education. In 1954, in the epochal Brown decision, it declared segregation in public elementary and high schools unconstitutional.

Although the NAACP with its legalistic tactics occupied the center of the stage in the black protest movement for some fifty years, nonviolent direct action was not unknown. Techniques in the arsenal of nonviolent direct action, as it was developed by Gandhi in India, included mass marches, boycotts, picketing, sit-downs or sit-ins, and civil disobedience. Certain of these techniques—particularly the boycott and what would today be called sitting-in—had been sporadically used by Negroes during the nineteenth and early twentieth centuries in fighting transportation and school segregation, and during the 1930's in attacking job discrimination, particularly in white-owned stores—though the term nonviolent direct action was not used to describe these efforts. The first conscious use of the nonviolent direct-action philosophy, based upon the Gandhian model, occurred about the time of World War II, with the first March on Washington Movement of 1941, and the forming of the Congress of Racial Equality (CORE) in 1942. The March on Washington Movement was the fruit of a proposal by the noted black labor leader A. Philip Randolph, who threatened a mass march on the nation's capital by the black laboring classes in order to press President Franklin D. Roosevelt to act against flagrant job discrimination in the rapidly expanding war industries. Though the March was never held, the threat of it did secure the creation of a wartime Fair Employment Practices Commission.

CORE was founded a year later by James Farmer and other black and white pacifists interested in applying Gandhian techniques to the solution of problems of racial conflict in the United

States. In its early years CORE focused mostly on desegregating places of public accommodation and recreation in the Northern states; by the middle of the century it was active in the border states; as early as 1947 it had sponsored a precursor of the 1961 Freedom Ride, known as the Journey of Reconciliation. The interracial teams who participated in the Journey tested Supreme Court compliance with the 1946 *Morgan v. Virginia* decision, obtained by NAACP, in which the Supreme Court had held that state laws requiring segregation on interstate transportation were an undue burden on interstate commerce. The Journey, limited to the Upper South, demonstrated that the bus and train companies still practiced segregation. It also precipitated some instances of mob violence from angry whites, and resulted in three of the testers (including Bayard Rustin) spending twenty-two days on a North Carolina road gang.

It was not CORE, however, but the Montgomery, Alabama, bus boycott of 1955–1956 that captured the imagination of the nation and of the Negro community in particular, and was chiefly responsible for the rising use of direct action in the late 1950's. In no small part this came about because the boycott, a local action, catapulted into national prominence the one person in the civil rights movement who most nearly achieved charismatic leadership, Rev. Martin Luther King, Jr. Like the founders of CORE—but unlike the great majority of civil rights activists, who have regarded nonviolence as a convenient tactic—King professed a Gandhian belief in the principles of pacifism. Elsewhere in the South there were other nonviolent direct-action campaigns during the late 1950's. Even before a court decision obtained by NAACP attorneys in November 1956 had desegregated the Montgomery buses and spelled victory for the Montgomery Improvement Association, a similar movement had started in Tallahassee, Florida, and afterward one developed in Birmingham, Alabama. In June 1957 the Tuskegee Civic Association undertook a three-year boycott of local merchants after the state legislature gerrymandered nearly all of the black voters outside of the town's boundaries. This campaign achieved success when, as the result of a suit filed by the NAACP Legal Defense Fund, the Supreme Court ruled the gerrymander illegal. These events were widely heralded as indicating the emergence of a new sort of black man in the South—militant, no longer fearful of white hoodlums, police, or jails, and ready to use his collective weight to achieve his ends. Seizing upon this new mood, King in 1957 established the Southern Christian Leadership Conference (SCLC) to coordinate direct-action activities in Southern cities.

Far more deeply rooted in the black experience than the practice of nonviolent direct action were nationalist tendencies. While one can describe Negro social thought as ranging along a continuum of ideologies from complete biological amalgamation and cultural assimilation with members of the dominant society at one extreme, to complete withdrawal from American society and the creation of independent black states at the other, most Afro-Americans have been characterized by an ethnic dualism. Thus between the two extremes have been a great variety of ideologies recognizing Negroes as American citizens, yet emphasizing their distinctiveness as an ethnic group. These intermediate categories have included the advocacy of attaining constitutional rights through self-help and racial solidarity, an insistence upon racial equality combined with preference for separate clubs and churches, and the espousal of all-Negro communities within the United States. This ethnic dualism, this ambivalence, which has been produced by the contradiction between the values of American democracy and the facts of race discrimination, was best articulated by W. E. B. Du Bois. In an essay written early in this century, he said: "One ever feels his two-ness,—an American, a Negro; two souls, two thoughts, two unreconciled strivings; two warring ideals in one dark body, whose dogged strength alone keeps it from being torn asunder. . . . He simply wishes to make it possible for a man to be both a Negro and an American, without being cursed and spit upon by his fellows, without having the door of opportunity closed roughly in his face."

In general, nationalist ideologies have been weakest in periods when the black man's status seemed to be improving, when there appeared to be hope for the achievement of equality in American society. Nationalist ideologies have been strongest in periods of deteriorating conditions, or when, as in the latter part of the 1960's, Negro expectations far outran actual gains, with consequent frustration and disillusionment. Yet despite the ebb and flow in the relative ascendancy of integrationist and nationalist ideologies in the thinking of American Negroes, it should be emphasized that in no case have Negroes, even those most completely favoring integration and assimilation, been able to forget their connection with an oppressed group. From this very alienation came the thrust for separate institutions operated without white interference, such as the church and the mutual benefit societies, the calls for race pride and a cultural pluralism, and, most recently, the demands of the black power advocates. The gap between ideal and practice in American society has meant that black men not only wanted to be a part of that society but that they also found it desirable to develop their own group life within it.

II

Nonviolent direct action became popular only in part because of the effectiveness of Martin Luther King's leadership. The fact was that the older techniques of legal and legislative action had proved themselves limited instruments. Impressive as it was to cite the advances made in the fifteen years after the end of World War II, in spite of state laws and Supreme Court decisions something was clearly wrong. Though in the twelve years after the outlawing of the white primary in 1944 the NAACP and other groups had raised the total number of Negroes registered in Southern states from about 250,000 to nearly a million and a quarter, black people were still disfranchised in most of the South. Supreme Court decisions desegregating transportation facilities were still largely ignored there. Discrimination in employment and housing abounded, even in Northern states with model civil rights laws. Beginning in 1954 the Negro unemployment rate moved steadily upward. Finally there was the Southern reaction to the Supreme Court's 1954 decision on school desegregation: attempts to outlaw the NAACP, intimidation of civil rights leaders, "massive resistance" to the Court's decision, the forcible curtailment of Negro voter registration, and the rise of hostile White Citizens' Councils.

At the very time legalism was thus proving to be of limited usefulness, other events were bringing about a change in Negro attitudes: black people were gaining a new self-image as a result of the rise of the new African nations; King and others were demonstrating that nonviolent direct action could succeed in the South; and new state anti-discrimination laws and Supreme Court decisions, Communist Russia's successful attempt to embarrass the United States by pointing to its racist violations of its democratic pretensions, and the evident drift of American white public opinion had developed in black Americans a new confidence in the future. In short, there had occurred what has appropriately been described as a "revolution in expectations." Negroes no longer felt they had to accept the humiliations of second-class citizenship, and consequently these humiliations—somewhat fewer though they now were—appeared to be more intolerable than ever. Ironically, the NAACP's very successes in the legislatures and the courts, more than any other single factor, led to this revolution in expectations and the resultant dissatisfaction with the limitations of the NAACP's program. This increasing impatience accounted for the rising tempo of nonviolent direct action in the late 1950's, culminating in the student sit-ins of 1960 and the inauguration of what is popularly known as the "Civil Rights Revolution" or the "Negro Revolt."

III

Although the importance of the Montgomery bus boycott cannot be overestimated, the really decisive break with the pre-eminence of legalistic techniques came with the college student sit-ins that swept the South in early 1960. In dozens of communities in the Upper South, the Atlantic coastal states, and Texas, student demonstrations secured the desegregation of lunch counters in variety and drug stores. Arrests numbered in the thousands, and police brutality was only too evident in scores of communities. In the Deep South the campaign ended in failure, even in instances where hundreds had been arrested, as in Montgomery, Alabama, Orangeburg, South Carolina, and Baton Rouge, Louisiana. But the youths had captured the imagination of the black community and to a remarkable extent of the whole nation. The civil rights movement would never be the same again.

The Southern college student sit-ins set in motion waves of events that shook the power structure of the black community, made direct action temporarily the most popular civil rights technique, ended NAACP hegemony in the civil rights movement, speeded up incalculably the whole process of social change in race relations, all but destroyed the barriers standing against the recognition of the Negro's constitutional rights, and ultimately turned the black protest organizations toward a deep concern with the economic and social problems of the masses. Involved was a steady radicalization of tactics and goals: from legalism to direct action and ultimately to black power; from participation by the middle and upper classes to mass action by all classes; from guaranteeing the protection of the Negro's constitutional rights to securing economic policies that would insure the welfare of the culturally deprived in a technologically changing society; from appeal to white Americans' sense of fair play to demands based upon power in the black ghetto.

The successes of the student movement in desegregating hundreds of lunch counters threatened the leadership arrangements of the black community far more profoundly than had the Montgomery boycott and the rise of King and SCLC. A spirited rivalry ensued among all civil rights organizations, and a new major protest group—the Student Nonviolent Coordinating Committee—was born.

The NAACP, CORE, and SCLC all attempted to identify themselves with the student movement. The organizing meeting of the Student Nonviolent Coordinating Committee, at Raleigh, North Carolina, in April 1960, was called by Martin Luther King. The SNCC platform expressed the same ideas of religious pacifism as did King himself. But within a year the youth had come to consider King as too cautious, and not dedicated enough to the cause, and had broken with him and SCLC. The NAACP, which had previously engaged in demonstrations only in a peripheral way, decided to make direct action a major part of its strategy. In many cases eager youths pushed reluctant NAACP adults into backing direct action. The young demonstrators, especially in the NAACP branches, depended heavily on the legal and financial aid that adult citizens supplied. CORE, which was still unknown to the general public, installed James Farmer as national director in January 1961 and moved to the front rank of civil rights organizations with the famous Freedom Ride to Alabama and Mississippi that spring. Designed to dramatize the persistence of segregated transportation in those states, the Freedom Ride eventuated in a bus-burning and the beating of riders in Alabama, hundreds spending a month or more in Mississippi prisons, and partial state compliance with a new order from the Interstate Commerce Commission desegregating all facilities used in interstate transportation.

Disagreements over strategy and tactics inevitably became intertwined with rivalries between personalities and organizations. The clashes between individuals and organizations both nationally and locally were often severe, and the lack of unity was frequently deplored. Actually, down to about 1964 the overall effect of the competition was to stimulate activity as organizations attempted to outdo each other in city after city. On the other hand, even among the strictly direct-action organizations, there developed differences in style. SCLC appeared to be the most cautious and to engage chiefly in a few major projects. From the beginning SNCC staff workers lived on subsistence allowances and appeared to conceive of going to jail as a way of life. More than any of the other groups, SNCC workers were "True Believers."

Direct-actionists often criticized the NAACP for being dominated by a conservative black bourgeoisie wedded to a program of legal action and gradualism. Actually the NAACP's program became the most highly varied of all the protest organizations. It retained a strong emphasis on court litigation. Acting in part through the Civil Rights Leadership Conference, consisting of more than one hundred Negro and interracial organizations interested in promoting civil rights legislation, the NAACP maintained an extraordinarily effective lobby in the nation's capital. It also engaged in many direct-action campaigns. Some branches disdained direct action, but other branches enthusiastically adopted the tactic.

IV

After the surge of Southern demonstrations in 1960–1961, conducted mainly by the college youth affiliated with either the NAACP or SNCC, there was something of a lull in direct-action activity, the major exceptions being demonstrations in Maryland and two major campaigns in Albany, Georgia. The next major wave of direct action came in the spring and summer of 1963. Using the slogan "Freedom Now," activists in black communities throughout most of the South demanded complete desegregation of places of public accommodation and of privately and publicly owned recreational facilities. They also demanded employment in nonmenial positions in downtown stores. In addition to the escalation of demands, the demonstrations differed from the 1960 sit-ins in that they involved masses of citizens, from schoolchildren to adults, for the first time, and in the widespread use of the technique, tried earlier on the Freedom Ride and at Albany, Georgia, of filling the jails with hundreds of arrestees who refused to accept bail. Usually these people were arrested in mass marches conducted in the face of the authorities' refusal to grant permission for such a demonstration.

In a number of cities, such as Danville, Virginia, Gadsden and Birmingham, Alabama, and Plaquemine, Louisiana, these demonstrations provoked some of the worst police brutality in the history of the movement, including the use of powerful water hoses, police dogs, and electric cattle prods. The most famous of these demonstrations, led by Martin Luther King, was the one in Birmingham in April–May 1963. In many places desegregation was materially advanced; but in the Deep South there was, again, failure, or, as in the case of Birmingham, a compromise victory which was later overturned by local whites. But this wave of demonstrations, particularly the one in Birmingham, riveted national attention on the South as never before. They thus paved the way for the extraordinary turnout of a quarter-million people of both races at the 1963 March on Washington.

The March aimed chiefly at securing legislation that would guarantee the black man's civil rights in the South—and it influenced the passage of the Civil Rights Act of 1964, which outlawed discrimination in places of public accommodation, instituted a modest program for guaranteeing the Southern Negroes' right to vote, created a federal fair employment practices agency with modest enforcement powers, and—potentially most significant of all—gave the President the power to withdraw federal funds from state and local agencies that discriminated against Negroes. The demonstrations at Birmingham and elsewhere in the South during the spring of 1963 dramatized more effectively than ever the technique of nonviolent direct action, and paved the way for its extensive application to the problems of the Northern ghettos in 1963–1964.

The Civil Rights Law of 1964 settled the public accommodations issue in the South's principal cities. Its voting section, however, promised more than it accomplished. Again Martin Luther King and SCLC dramatized the issue, this time at Selma, Alabama, and on a massive interracial march from Selma to Montgomery in early 1965. Yet, as President Lyndon B. Johnson pointed out in his address to Congress and the nation urging passage of the voting rights act of 1965, beyond the protection of constitutional rights lay the still unsolved problems of the poor.

V

Where Birmingham had made direct action respectable, the Selma march, drawing thousands of white moderates from the North, made direct action fashionable. Nevertheless, as early as 1964 it was becoming evident that, like "legalism," nonviolent direct action was a limited instrument. This was the result of two converging developments.

One of these was the failure of the sit-ins of 1960–1961 to desegregate public accommodations in Deep South states like Mississippi and Alabama, and the realization, first grasped by Robert Moses of SNCC, that without the leverage of the vote, demonstrations there would be failures. Beginning in 1961, Moses, with the cooperation of CORE and the state NAACP as well as SNCC, established voter-registration projects in the cities and county seats of Mississippi, under the banner of a coalition known as the Council of Federated Organizations (COFO). In the summer of 1964 the program broadened to include community centers, which would offer recreational and cultural facilities to the black communities and, more notably, Freedom Schools for the youth. By then COFO had registered only a handful of blacks, but it created the Mississippi Freedom Democratic party which at the 1964 Democratic party convention challenged the seating of the regular delegation on the grounds that blacks were unconstitutionally disfranchised in Mississippi. The Democratic party would not agree to seat the MFDP delegation, but it did offer to seat two of its representatives as delegates-at-large. MFDP rejected this compromise.

Direct action also failed when applied to the difficult economic and social problems facing Negroes in the black ghettos of the North. Inferior schools, rat-infested slum housing, discrimination by the building-trades unions, and police brutality proved invulnerable to an attack of this kind. Street demonstrations did compel employers, ranging from banks to supermarkets, to add many blacks to their work force. But technological innovation was bringing a steady decline in the number of unskilled jobs available, and the masses of Negroes, half of whom had not gone beyond the eighth grade, were unable to qualify for positions requiring higher skill and education. As a result, while the Negro "job mix" changed because of new hiring policies on the part of business, the basic pattern of mass unemployment remained.

Meanwhile, there had been a steady radicalization among many civil rights activists. As the excitement of the earlier demonstrations dissipated, and as it became evident that many places of public accommodation remained firmly segregated, more dramatic forms of direct action proved essential. It became quite obvious that the unmerited suffering of the direct-actionists did not transform the hearts of the oppressors. Rather, it was the economic pinch created by the sit-ins and boycotts, the publicity obtained through mass arrests, and the national and international pressure generated by the violence of white hoodlums and police that forced social change. At the same time there occurred a secularization of those Southern Negro activists who remained in the movement for any length of time. Few of them had ever been pacifists in the first place; yet an important reason for the initial attraction of non-violent direct action had been its consonance with their Christian faith. But as early as 1963, instead of speaking in terms of love and Christianity, activists were coming to talk in terms of power. They thought less of convincing the white man of the moral righteousness of their aspirations and more of forcing him to change his policies through the power of black bodies to create social dislocation.

A major factor leading to the radicalization of the civil rights movement was unemployment and poverty—and an important force awakening the protest organizations to this problem was the meteoric rise of the Black Muslims to national prominence. More than any other factor, the growing problem of black unemployment, combined with the rapidly rising expectations of the masses, produced an environment in which the Black Muslims flourished. To those willing to submit to its rigid discipline, the Nation of Islam gave a sense of purpose and destiny. Its program offered them four things: an explanation of their plight (white devils); a sense of pride and self-esteem (black superiority); a vision of a glorious future (black ascendancy); and a practical program of uplift (working hard, saving money, and uniting to create Negro enterprises and prosperity). With this Puritan ethic the Muslims appealed to an upwardly mobile group of lower-class blacks. Ironically, until split by internal dissension and the departure of their charismatic spokesman Malcolm X, the Black Muslims were a distinct help to the civil rights organizations, for their talk of violence and their hatred of blue-eyed devils frightened white people into becoming somewhat more amenable to the demands of the integrationists.

Paradoxically, the trials and successes of the integrationist protest movement after 1960, by producing heightened self-esteem among black men, encouraged other nationalist tendencies. For one thing, as Negroes grew in racial pride they displayed a sharply rising interest in black history. Another nationalistic manifestation was the call for black leadership within the civil rights movement, based upon the belief that Negroes could, through their own power, bring about drastic changes in American society. As early as 1963 there were proposals for the formation of an all-black political party. At the same time others proposed self-help and racial cooperation in order to attack the economic needs of the rural and urban poor. Finally, a group of writers expressed their alienation by questioning the values of middle-class white America and militantly calling for preservation of the unique aspects of the Negro subculture. Subsequently, after 1965, this cultural pluralism was to become a widely held ideology, described by the phrase "black consciousness."

VI

Ironically, at the very time white support for the civil rights movement was rising, its most militant black members felt increasingly isolated from the American scene. By 1964 people in this radical left wing of the movement, consisting of SNCC and many in CORE, were growing disdainful of American society and the middle-class way of life, cynical about liberals and the leaders of organized labor. Any compromise, even if a temporary tactical device, had become anathema to them. They talked more and more of the necessity for "revolutionary" changes in the social structure, even of violence. They became increasingly skeptical of the value of white participation in the movement, racially chauvinistic in their insistence that black power alone could compel concessions from the "power structure" of capitalists, politicians, and bureaucratic labor leaders. The black nationalist Malcolm X, after his assassination in 1965, became a symbolic hero for the militants. At the extreme left wing of the movement, Marxism and nationalism coalesced into a truly revolutionary ideology.

In contrast, the "conservative" wing, mostly an older group of individuals, appreciated the civil rights legislation of 1964 and 1965, the public stands taken by Presidents Kennedy and Johnson, and other signs of racial progress. They were keenly aware of new opportunities in business, in government, and in the academic world for those with training to fill them. Civil rights activity in general, and the NAACP in particular, had become so respectable that even famous protest leaders achieved high public office. The most notable example was the elevation of the NAACP's brilliant chief counsel, Thurgood Marshall, to the Supreme Court. NAACP leaders, who could be described as moderates, did not believe that the millennium had arrived, but changed conditions had prompted a reorientation of their strategy. Impressed by the degree of social change, many of them came to view their role as exercising influence within established institutions rather than fighting them from the outside. These men did not, it should be emphasized, rule out overt protest. In fact, effective publicity of Negro grievances—if necessary, direct action—would often be the best means of compelling reluctant public officials to act.

Between these two poles of thought was a group who recognized the new willingness of the nation's decision-makers to move toward greater racial justice, but perceived also that powerful pressure would be needed to push them in that direction. Consisting of many in the NAACP and CORE, and with their point of view best articulated by the long-time activist Bayard Rustin, A. Philip Randolph, and Martin Luther King, this group held that Negroes, as a dispossessed minority, could not hope to achieve their goals purely through their own actions. They based their strategy on a coalition of blacks with white liberals, organized labor, and white clergy such as had developed during the plans for the March on Washington. Though this theory was not officially a part of the NAACP platform, the Association, through the Civil Rights Leadership Conference, actually based part of its strategy upon it. Ultimately the centrists hoped that a Negro-liberal-church-labor alliance, acting as a political force, would compel the federal government to eliminate poverty in America for whites and blacks alike. But they still favored direct action—even mass civil disobedience—where it was needed to create the kind of social dislocation that would bring action from political authorities.

Between 1964 and 1966 the black protest movement became increasingly fragmented and ineffective. Fundamentally the growing disunity was rooted in the frustration of radically heightened expectations and in the extraordinary problems involved in achieving genuine equality for the black poor. In the face of these circumstances, the various segments of the movement became increasingly divided on how to tackle the situation.

The 1964 Democratic party convention foreshadowed this trend. Events there, in the eyes of the militants, thoroughly discredited both the Democratic party establishment and white liberal elements in the interracial coalition who backed the national civil rights legislative program. The black militants not only rejected the party's compromise offer of two delegates-at-large for the Mississippi Freedom Democratic party, but their growing distrust of the white liberals became complete when many of the latter, having originally supported the Mississippi challenge, in the end favored the compromise. Finally, the Negroes themselves were deeply divided, with SNCC and CORE refusing to approve the compromise, while NAACP elements in the Freedom Democratic party and men like Rustin and King argued for its acceptance.

The war in Vietnam exacerbated the growing cleavages. Some believed that the war diverted attention and funds from the country's leading domestic problem. Others went further and regarded the war as cut from the same cloth as domestic racism, charging that both involved an attempt by the American "white power structure" to keep a colored race in a colonial status. A number of people who had devoted their full energies to fighting racial discrimination were diverted to working against the war in Vietnam. At the opposite pole were those who held that the Vietnam issue was irrelevant as far as the black protest was concerned, and that to mix the two issues was tactically dangerous, since it would lose some support for the Negroes' cause. The Urban League and the NAACP refused to identify themselves with the Vietnam issue. King, previously a key figure in the coalition strategy, openly attacked United States policy in Vietnam, as did SNCC and CORE. White supporters of the coalition were similarly split, with organized labor particularly endorsing the war program.

The anti-poverty act, passed in 1964, had several effects on the protest movement. It accelerated the shift, already evident, from an emphasis on a national legislative program to local community action led by grass-roots people from among the poor themselves. The struggle within the black community over who would administer the community action programs exacerbated the polarization between the more moderate middle-class leaders and the more radical types. Finally, the anti-poverty program unintentionally served to increase frustration and discontent among the black poor by further escalating their expectations—but failing to deliver anything substantial. Yet one legacy of the War on Poverty was the feeling that the government should allocate resources to the ghetto for programs initiated and administered by the ghetto-dwellers themselves. Thus, paradoxically, the Office of Economic Opportunity projects, while not solving the problems of the poor, led to a heightened militance among them.

VII

The average Negro was on a dreary treadmill. Without much education, he found it difficult to obtain a decent job; without adequate work and something for his children to aspire to, it was not likely that they would be motivated to seek an adequate education even if it were available. The feeling of frustration, of hopelessness, was reflected in the riots at Los Angeles, Newark, Detroit, and the more than four hundred disorders of varying degrees of seriousness between 1964 and 1969. Paradoxically, these outbreaks were born of a sense of powerlessness and at the same time a sense of power derived from the knowledge that "whitey" now felt afraid or guilty and was unlikely to fight back.

Beyond the seething discontent that tended to erupt into overt racial warfare in the urban ghettos during the long, hot summers, the theme of retaliatory violence was evident in various forms in the thinking of the most militant elements in the black protest movement. First, the Black Muslims suggested that Negroes should fight back against the vicious "slavemasters," and their eschatology included a violent end to white domination. Then small numbers of Marxist-nationalists appeared at the fringes of the black protest movement in the early 1960's, the most vocal of whom was Robert F. Williams. Dismissed as president of the Monroe, North Carolina, branch of the NAACP in 1959 for his open advocacy of violence against the oppressive white community, Williams was later charged with kidnapping a white couple and forced to flee abroad to Cuba and China, where he issued a monthly bulletin urging blacks "to wage an urban guerrilla war of self-defense." While in exile, he was named chairman of the Revolutionary Action Movement (RAM), a tiny group of college-educated youth in a few Northern cities, two of whose members were sentenced to prison in 1968 for conspiring to murder Roy Wilkins, executive director of the NAACP, and Whitney Young, executive director of the National Urban League.

Williams, RAM, and the better known Black Muslims were on the fringes of the Negro protest in the early 1960's. Subsequently, violence and propaganda for violence moved closer to the center of the race relations stage. Among many of the more militant individuals in the nonviolent direct-action organizations, there was an increasing use of revolutionary vocabulary and a rising skepticism about the value of nonviolence. By 1964 and 1965 at least some of them, especially in SNCC, were toying with the idea that revolutionary violence might be necessary. At the same time there was considerable publicity about the Deacons for Defense, organized in Louisiana to protect blacks and CORE demonstrators of both races from white attackers.

Beyond the wave of summer riots that began in 1964, the incendiary statements of the Rap Browns and the Stokely Carmichaels became familiar TV and newspaper fare for millions of white Americans. The Oakland, California, Black Panthers, and other local groups espousing a nationalist and revolutionary rhetoric, thrived and received national publicity. As has often been pointed out, there is no evidence that the race riots of the 1960's had any direct relation to the teachings of Williams, of these various groups, even of the SNCC advocates of armed rebellion and guerrilla warfare. But both the statements of these ideologists and the spontaneous actions of the masses had much in common. For both were the product of the frustrations resulting from the growing disparity between the black man's status and the rapidly rising expectations induced by the civil rights revolution and its earlier successes.

VIII

Disillusionment with the national administration and with white liberals, the fragmentation of the Negro protest movement, the enormous difficulties that stood in the way of overcoming the problems of the black masses, and the riots that erupted spontaneously in 1964 and 1965 as a consequence of the anger and frustration of the urban slumdwellers—all set the stage for the dramatic appearance of the black power slogan in the summer of 1966.

Black power first articulated a mood rather than a program—disillusionment and alienation from white America, race pride, and self-respect or "black consciousness." The precipitating occasion was the June 1966 freedom march of James Meredith, whose enrollment at the University of Mississippi in 1962 had triggered a riot that brought two deaths, hundreds of injuries, federal intervention, and the presence of thousands of troops. Four years later Meredith decided that a dramatic way to interest more Mississippi Negroes in voter registration was to demonstrate that it would be possible for him to walk unharmed through Mississippi to Jackson during primary election week. Hardly had he begun when a would-be assassin's bullet wounded him. National civil rights leaders rushed to Memphis, and Martin Luther King and Stokely Carmichael, chairman of SNCC, resumed the march amidst harassments and taunts from jeering whites. The two men soon revealed to the world a leadership schism of major proportions. While King continued to preach nonviolence and racial integration to Mississippi blacks, Carmichael electrified the crowds with cries of "Black Power": "The only way we gonna stop them white men from whuppin' us is to take over. We been saying freedom for six years and we ain't got nothin'. What we gonna start saying now is black power. . . . Ain't nothin' wrong with anything all black 'cause I'm all black and I'm all good. Now don't you be afraid. And from now on when they ask you what you want, you know what to tell them." The crowd replied in unison, "Black power! Black power! Black power!"

The slogan expressed tendencies that had been present for some time and had been gaining strength in the black community. As it became a household phrase, the term generated intense discussion of its real meaning, and a broad spectrum of ideologies and programmatic proposals emerged. In politics, black power meant independent action—Negro control of the political power of the rural Southern Black Belt counties and of the black ghettos, and the use of this control to improve the condition of farm laborers and slumdwellers. It could take the form of organizing a black political party or controlling the political machinery inside the ghetto without the guidance or support of white politicians. Where predominantly Negro areas lacked Negroes in elective office, whether in the rural black belt of the South or in the urban centers, black power advocates sought the election of Negroes by voter-registration campaigns, and by working for the redrawing of electoral districts. The basic belief was that only a well-organized and cohesive bloc of black voters could provide for the needs of the black masses. Even some Negro politicians allied to the major political parties adopted the term "black power" to describe their interest in the Negro vote. In economic terms, black power meant creating independent, self-sufficient Negro business enterprise, not only by encouraging Negro entrepreneurs but also by forming Negro cooperatives in the ghettos and in the predominantly black rural counties of the South. In the area of education, black power called for local community control of the public schools in the black ghettos. Throughout, the emphasis was on self-help, racial unity, and, among the most militant, retaliatory violence, the latter ranging from the legal right of self-defense to attempts to justify looting and arson in ghetto riots, guerrilla warfare, and armed rebellion.

Phrases like "black power," "black consciousness," and "black is beautiful" enjoyed an extensive currency in the Negro community, even within the NAACP and among relatively conservative politicians. Expressed in its most extreme form by small, often local, fringe groups, among the national organizations the black power ideology became most closely associated with SNCC and CORE.

Generally regarded as the most militant among the leading Negro protest organizations, CORE and SNCC had different interpretations of the black power doctrine. Though neither group was monolithic in its viewpoint, broadly speaking it can be said that SNCC called for totally independent political action outside the established political parties, as with the Black Panther party in Lowndes County, Alabama; questioned the value of political alliance with other groups until Negroes themselves built a substantial base of independent political power; applauded the idea of guerrilla warfare; and regarded riots as rebellions. CORE, while not disapproving of the SNCC strategy, advocated working within the Democratic party to overthrow the established machine leadership, and forming alliances with other groups. It sought to justify riots as the natural explosion of an oppressed people against intolerable conditions, but it urged violence only in self-defense. While CORE favored cooperatives, it was more inclined toward job-training programs and developing a Negro entrepreneurial class based upon the market within the black ghetto.

The popularity of the term "black power" represented both a sense of power produced by the earlier successes of the movement, and an escape into the rhetoric of power caused by the powerlessness to achieve more rapid progress toward full equality. The slogan emerged when the Negro protest movement was slowing down, when it was finding increased resistance to changing goals, when it discovered that nonviolent direct action was no more a panacea than legal action, when CORE and SNCC were declining in activity, membership, and financial support. Unable to make fundamental changes in the life of the masses, the advocates of black power substituted a separatist program for the platform of integration. Ironically, although the goal of equality was still far off, this occurred at the very time that Negroes were closer to the goal of integration than ever before. Sixty years earlier the themes of racial unity and separatism had functioned primarily as part of an ideology of accommodation, while the black radicals demanded integration; now, among the latest generation of black radicals, integration was decried as a white man's strategy of tokenism aimed at holding Negroes in a subordinate position. Racial separatism had become part of a platform of radicalism and militance, while the erstwhile radical program of integration was now denounced as conservative, and sometimes as downright racist.

With CORE and particularly SNCC greatly weakened, the banner of Black Power and Black Nationalism passed to other groups, mostly locally based. Black caucuses appeared in the predominantly white professional and church organizations. There was a general surge of community organization—of a spirit of self-help and racial solidarity, of uniting ghetto residents for concerted action, culturally, economically, and politically. Far better known—because far more dramatic and extreme—were such Marxist-oriented revolutionary movements as the Black Panthers, founded in Oakland, California, in 1966, and the Republic of New Africa, founded in Detroit the following year. Both advocated forms of territorial separatism. The Black Panthers, who took their name from the abortive SNCC-sponsored Lowndes County, Alabama, Black Panther party of 1965–1966, espoused black control of the central cities; the Republic of New Africa proposed a separate all-black sovereign state in the Deep South. More significant was the rapid proliferation of Afro-American societies and Black Student unions on predominantly white college campuses, with their demands for greater black representation in the student body, in the faculty, and in the curriculum on the one hand, and for separate dormitories, recreational centers, courses, and even separate colleges within the universities, on the other hand. These groups, which often espoused revolutionary violence, were frequently led by middle-class student intellectuals. But they flourished largely because the black students from the ghettos who were entering the major colleges and universities under liberalized and compensatory admissions policies, faced serious problems in adjusting to the academic and social norms of a middle-class or upper-middle-class environment, for which neither their background nor their schooling had prepared them. With the rise of nationalism the pressures for public school integration lessened, especially in the North. Local community, or neighborhood, control of the schools became a lively issue—often advocated by those who had organized the boycotts for integrated schools in 1963–1964. Most pervasive was the widespread revival of cultural nationalism, which enjoyed an enormous popularity among all social classes. There was more interest in Negro history than ever before; countless local groups devoted to black art, literature, and drama sprang up, and a national magazine like *Ebony*, heretofore devoted largely to chronicling the achievements and social life of the black bourgeoisie, became a leading popularizer of "black consciousness." At the same time there occurred an unprecedented renaissance of black creativity in art, literature, and the theater.

IX

Black nationalism, black separatism, and black revolutionary rhetoric seized the headlines. But important as the enthusiasm for various forms of black nationalism became after 1966, especially among Northern ghetto youth, it must be stressed that full participation in American society on an integrated basis is still the goal of the great majority of black Americans. Public opinion polls demonstrate this fact, even though they also indicate that nationalist sentiment is growing. Neither SCLC nor NAACP has adopted a nationalist program or ideology. Martin Luther King's last months before his assassination in 1968 were spent in developing a major project intended to show the continuing viability of the nonviolent direct-action strategy—the Poor People's Campaign that brought thousands to Washington during the summer of 1968 to demonstrate for greater justice to the economically deprived. In what was probably his last published article, King still articulated the dream of "black and white together." And the NAACP vigorously counterattacked against the black separatists, denouncing them as segregationists who undermined the very things the black protest movement had sought for so many years to accomplish.

Nationalist tendencies, which are especially strong among the youth, may become the dominant mode in black protest. Yet the history of Negro thought and protest indicates that integration will remain a central theme, and that the prominence of nationalism is likely to be a temporary phenomenon. Or, if a white backlash of serious proportions develops, a mood of passivity and resignation may become widespread. Predictions are risky; only one thing is certain, and that is that the future course of the black protest movement is uncertain.

August Meier and Elliot Rudwick
Kent, Ohio
February 1970

Addendum to the 1991 Edition

BLACK PROTEST of the 1960's has had some incontrovertible consequences. Perhaps the most significant is that blacks now vote without restriction. Several mechanisms have been employed to reduce the strength and effectiveness of this vote: redistricting, the holding of dual primaries, and the institution of technical impediments to voter registration. There is general agreement, nevertheless, that the black vote is a permanent and significant factor in the nation's politics.

Black activism has now largely shifted from the streets to the ballot box. At local, state, and national levels, the number of blacks has increased significantly. Of particular importance is the election of black mayors in major cities—including Los Angeles, Chicago, New York, Atlanta, New Orleans, and Birmingham—as well as the recent election of Douglas Wilder to the governorship of Virginia. Black congresspeople have also achieved more power; they are organized in an increasingly effective Black Caucus, and are expanding their legislative influence.

The political militancy of the sixties has led to other important *de facto* and *de jure* developments. The protest of blacks on university campuses has become institutionalized. Black student organizations continue to function as a significant presence, while Black Studies programs are not only surviving, but experiencing a resurgence of interest and support. In primary and secondary schools too, the African-American experience, as well as African history and culture, now have an established place in the curriculum.

In the last twenty-odd years, discrimination in public accommodations has virtually been eliminated. Significant gains have also been made in the area of employment, encouraged by judicial and administrative implementation of the Equal Opportunity section of the 1964 Civil Rights Act. The Reagan years, however, have seen many setbacks. During the 1980's a more conservative federal judiciary has slowed or even reversed the flow of progress in the area of job discrimination. During this era, the chief beneficiaries of non-discriminatory attitudes and policies among government officials, corporate leaders, and education professionals have been those blacks best positioned by education or circumstances to take advantage of newly opened opportunities. The result has been substantial growth in the black middle class. There remains, though, a vast black underclass which has been unable to obtain the necessary education or vocational training to advance.

The long-range struggle for full acceptance into U.S. society goes on in the face of complex changes in racial attitudes on the part of the white population. The overwhelming popularity of such figures as Eddie Murphy, Bill Cosby, Magic Johnson, Michael Jackson, and Michael Jordan contrasts with the shift to the right of the federal executive and judiciary, and with sporadic outbursts of anti-black violence.

Meanwhile the enormity and persistence of the problems of thwarted economic advancement, decay of the urban schools, and the proliferation of the drug culture, with its concomitant black-on-black crime and gang violence, have made many of the sixties debates appear irrelevant. In addition, the greater possibility for intellectuals and activists to function in the institutions of the larger society has generally resulted in some form of accommodation to the needs and priorities of those institutions. The intense, sometimes violent ideological disputes of the 1960's over integration and nationalism, and over the meaning of those terms, have subsided. Formerly fierce antagonists now agree on many of the divisive issues raised in these essays.

August Meier and John Bracey
Amherst, Massachusetts
October 1990

Part 1

THE ASCENDANCY OF NONVIOLENT DIRECT ACTION

ALTHOUGH NONVIOLENT direct-action techniques were being used more and more in the late 1950's, no one, either in the movement or out of it, was prepared for the surge of activity precipitated by the Greensboro, North Carolina, sit-ins of February 1, 1960. The Greensboro sit-ins themselves were first covered in the *New York Times* in the form of a brief, unobtrusive UPI dispatch, describing the second day of demonstrations carried out at the Greensboro lunch counters by students from North Carolina A. and T. College. The students' spirit as reported in this article—their determination to continue "until we get served," and their strong religious orientation—were typical of the early phase of the nonviolent direct-action movement of the 1960's.

Slightly over fifteen months after the Southern college student sit-in movement began, the Freedom Ride electrified the nation in the spring and summer of 1961. Eric Goldman gives historical perspective to its significance by comparing it with earlier cases of successful nonviolent direct action. His article is also important because it explains why this kind of militant action is successful at certain points in history, but not at others.

Contemporaneous with the dramatic use of nonviolent direct action in the South during the early 1960's, the nationalist Black Muslims flourished among a number of upwardly mobile, lower-class blacks in the urban ghetto slums, particularly in the North. Gertrude Samuels' article, comparing the Nation of Islam with the NAACP, gives a succinct summary of the ideology and program of both organizations at the time the nonviolent direct-action movement was reaching its crest.

From 1962 to 1964 an extensive voter-registration campaign, financed by a few foundations and administered by the interracial Southern Regional Council, was conducted in the Southern states by all of the major civil rights organizations. In the hard-core areas of the Deep South—Mississippi, Alabama, most of Louisiana, and large parts of Georgia and Florida—voter registration became a form of nonviolent direct action because it was so fiercely resisted by Southern whites. Claude Sitton's articles from Sasser, Georgia (1962), where the voter-registration drive was conducted by SNCC workers, and from Canton, Mississippi (1964), where it was conducted by CORE staffers under the umbrella of the COFO organization, illustrate the intimidation by white lawmen and the spirit of the local black citizens who participated in these campaigns, which were largely futile in the most resistant areas of the South.

In 1963 the nonviolent direct-action phase of the black protest movement reached its zenith. To illustrate the two most famous demonstrations that year—SCLC's Birmingham campaign and the March on Washington—we have selected summary descriptions from the *New York Times*'s "News of the Week in Review." The March on Washington symbolized both the progress that had been made and the unfinished work that lay ahead; as Claude Sitton indicates in his discussion of the "Status of Integration" right after the March, from the black perspective this progress proved to be largely "tokenism."

One of the most heroic, and poignant, phases of the nonviolent direct-action movement in the South was the attempt to register black men to vote and to run for office in Mississippi in 1962–1964. Three articles in this section illustrate COFO's work in Mississippi—Claude Sitton's description of a voter-registration campaign in Canton, Mississippi, early in 1964; Pat Watters' description of a Freedom School in Ruleville, Mississippi, located in Sunflower County, the home of the notorious Senator Eastland, and the community from which the famous Mrs. Fannie Lou Hamer came; and two *New York Times* news articles describing the work of the Mississippi Freedom Democratic party and the appearance of its delegates before the Democratic party credentials committee at the convention in Atlantic City in August 1964. Though COFO collapsed shortly afterward, the campaign for voter registration continued; Martin Luther King made it the central issue for his next crusade, at Selma, Alabama, in the spring of 1965; Pat Watters' article on Negro children deals with one aspect of this famous demonstration.

The Selma demonstration and the Watts riot of 1965 together seemed to mark the end of an era. It had become clear, as the articles by Kenneth Clark and C. Vann Woodward indicate, that all the victories of the nonviolent direct-action campaigns of the early 1960's had left many basic problems unsolved. As Woodward pointed out, it was a question as to how effective even the new legislation would be, and, as Clark expressed it, "The wonder is there have been so few riots."

Negroes in South in Store Sit-down

GREENSBORO, N.C., Feb. 2 (UPI)—A group of well-dressed Negro college students staged a sit-down strike in a downtown Woolworth store today and vowed to continue it in relays until Negroes were served at the lunch counter.

"We believe since we buy books and papers in the other part of the store we should get served in this part," said the spokesman for the group.

The store manager, C. L. Harris, commented:

"They can just sit there. It's nothing to me."

He declined to say whether it was the policy of the store not to serve Negroes.

The Negroes, students at North Carolina Agricultural and Technical College here, arrived shortly after 10 A.M. and sat at two sections of the lunch counter.

At 12:30 P.M., the group filed out of the store and stood on the sidewalk in this city's busiest downtown street. They formed a tight circle, threw their hands into a pyramid in the center and recited the Lord's Prayer.

The spokesman said that "another shift" of students would carry forward the strike and it would continue "until we get served. . . ."

From the *New York Times,* February 3, 1960, copyright © by The New York Times Company.

Progress—
by Moderation
and Agitation

by Eric F. Goldman

THE BUSES that have been carrying Freedom Riders into the South have confronted Americans with an old and endlessly tortuous problem: How do you achieve genuine social progress in a democracy? Is it better simply to pass the laws and let them grind away or should the legal processes be supplemented, and run ahead of, by the fire of dramatic agitation and direct action? Do the explosions generated by dedicated individuals really advance a cause or do they, in the long run, throw it back because of the fears and resentments they create?

Of course, gradualism is often the argument or rationalization of those who want no change, gradual or otherwise. For decades, a good many Southerners and more than a few Northerners have been talking this way about Negro rights, extolling the virtues of step-by-step reform all the while they accepted few if any steps at all. But the gradualist argument is not confined to enemies of change. In the specific area of Negro rights, it has been made by men whom few would accuse of wanting to impede the Negro's advance toward equality.

The other day Harry Truman told the Freedom Riders that they were just so many meddlesome intruders. "They ought to stay here [in the North] and attend to their own business," working "in an orderly and legal manner" through the organizations devoted to the Negro's welfare. Their activities, far from speeding desegregation, were "stirring up trouble." Pointedly, Mr. Truman added that the nineteenth-century anti-slavery agitators "did their part in bringing about the Civil War."

Attorney General Robert F. Kennedy, all the while he was sending Federal marshals to Alabama to protect the Freedom Riders, had his own words of moderation. He called on both sides to show "restraint," recommended "a cooling off period" of no Freedom Riding until "an atmosphere of reason and normalcy has been restored."

The Attorney General went on to make the argument that usually accompanies a plea for moderation—the argument of higher considerations. President Kennedy was about to go to Europe on "a mission of great importance." The demonstrators as well as the segregationists should avoid doing anything which could bring "discredit on our country" at such a time.

Apparently the Attorney General not only talked but acted moderation. According to one of the Freedom Riders, the Rev. William Sloane Coffin Jr., Chaplain of Yale University, "people in high places in the Attorney General's office did ask us—most circumspectly—to reconsider our decision to make the trip."

Liberal Southerners of both races criticized the Freedom Riders. These men maintained, in the words of one pro-Negro white, that "plenty of Southerners have been brought over because they recognized the justice of the [past Negro] protests. But for persons just to test and challenge is too much like baiting. They don't appeal to any underlying sympathy among Southerners. This becomes a dare, not a protest," and antagonizes the white moderates on whom the Negro must depend. A Southern Negro leader agreed, adding: "What concerns me is what may happen to Southern Negroes after the Freedom Riders return to the safety of their homes outside the Deep South."

The gradualists can appeal to American history itself to support their argument. A little more than a half-century ago the United States was a land of enormous extremes in wealth and status, with its political machinery largely controlled by a moneyed élite, its industrial workers and farmers scrounging along at near-subsistence levels, and all its religious and ethnic minorities denied the privileges of real acceptance.

Year after year, scores of groups peacefully, and with relatively little drama, kept pressuring away for laws and for the enforcement of laws. The result was an almost steady advance toward the extraordinarily leveled American society of the Nineteen Sixties—a society which is the more securely leveled because it has so few of the bitter memories which mark nations changed by turbulence and force.

Yet everything has not been moderation and legality. After all, the United States became an independent nation because fire-eating nationalists thumbed their noses at the legal tie to Britain and went hell-bent through the colonies summoning men to revolt. Slavery was abolished in America not by the coos of persuasion but by one of the bloodiest wars in history.

Before and after the Civil War, endless bands of dedicated individuals with some utopia in their pockets turned to the dramatic and the spectacular, often to the illegal. They tried everything in the ancient arsenal of agitation—picketing, hunger strikes, badgering the mighty, stormy cavalcades and ominously silent demonstrations. Some of these attempts were abysmal flops and undoubtedly hindered the cause they were seeking to advance. But others were resounding successes.

A striking example was provided by the American suffragettes of the early twentieth century. For years women's organizations had been pleading and maneuvering for the vote but by 1912 only six states had granted enfranchisement. A Federal woman's suffrage amendment seemed far away. The newly elected President of the United States, Woodrow Wilson, ardent reformer that he was, had only sniffish disdain for petticoat voting. About this time a delicate, soft-voiced young Quaker, Alice Paul, and a little group of suffragettes decided to put some fire into the movement, and fire there was.

The militants staged massive parades and kept them marching while the women were subjected to obscene insults, spat upon, slapped in the face, tripped up and pelted with burning cigar stubs. Early in 1917, Alice Paul launched her most belligerent effort—the day-after-day picketing of the White House with purple-white-and-gold banners shrilling: MR. PRESIDENT, HOW LONG MUST WOMEN WAIT FOR DEMOCRACY? For eighteen months the pickets kept to their stations. At times mobs ripped the banners and mauled the women while police looked the other way. During one period, the police took to arresting the pickets. Convicted, the women refused to pay the fines. Jailed, they went on hunger strikes.

Before long the headlines reported still another Alice Paul spectacular. She installed a "watch-fire" in an urn on the sidewalk of the White House. Every time Wilson made a speech in which he used the word "freedom," a copy of the document was duly burned.

A powerful wing of the women's movement openly repudiated the "extremists"; they were doing "much more harm than good." President Wilson spoke for a large section of progressive-minded opinion when he wrote that the Alice Paul group seemed "bent upon making their cause as obnoxious as possible." After the United States entered World War I, scores of commentators denounced the pickets for, in the words of one Senator, "a selfish and silly disregard of the grave national need for unity."

To all such criticism, Alice Paul replied: "If a creditor stands in front of a man's house constantly demanding the amount of the bill, the debtor has either to remove the creditor or pay the bill." The more the pickets marched, the more women flocked to the purple-white-and-gold; the more money flowed into the militants' treasury; the more men began saying, as one New York politician put it, "By God, we'd better do something to satisfy these hellions."

When the suffrage amendment finally won Congressional approval in 1919—and now with President Wilson behind it— few impartial observers doubted that the hellions had a good deal to do with slamming over the victory.

Two decades later, angry American workers offered another example of the efficacy of turbulence. In 1935 President Franklin Roosevelt signed into law the Wagner Act with its guarantee of the right of collective bargaining. But as the months dragged by, it was clear that many large-scale employers, including the automobile titans, were far from ready to accept unionization. Early in 1937 the newly invigorated United Automobile Workers demanded recognition from General Motors and were given a brushoff. They answered by striking all seventeen G.M. plants—and by the startling, frightening technique of the sit-down.

The sit-downers went at their operation with whole-hearted zeal. Food and other supplies were brought in by a tightly organized system. No liquor was permitted in the buildings. Union patrols ranged the plants and their word was law. Efforts to dislodge the strikers were met by unabashed violence. When the police tried to rush Fisher Body Plant No. 2, they were driven back by a hail of coffee mugs, pop bottles, iron bolts and heavy automobile door hinges.

The police returned to the attack with tear gas only to be scattered by torrents of water from the plant hoses. "The Battle of the Running Bulls," the workers jeered and girded for the next assault.

Pretty plainly the sit-downs were illegal (in time they were declared to be so by the courts) and the din of criticism was terrific. The Senate of the United States resolved that the strikes were "illegal and contrary to public policy." Scores of pro-labor leaders spoke the usual arguments of moderation. No less than William Green, president of the American Federation of Labor, declared: "Both personally and officially, I disavow the sit-down strike." It had "grave implications detrimental to labor's interests." The "temporary advantages gained through sit-downs will inevitably lead to permanent injury."

The workers added to their repertoire of songs,

> *Old man Green is off his nut*
> *Let him choke on his useless butt,*

and went on sitting.

After forty-four days, General Motors capitulated and recognized the U.A.W. Already thousands of other workers had turned to the sit-down and before long a half-million Americans had been involved in the defiant technique.

Woolworth clerks stood behind their counters blandly refusing to wait on customers; pie bakers lounged in front of their ovens with arms crossed; Philadelphia electrical workers sat so long that two bridegrooms sat out their honeymoons. More and more unions won recognition. Labor power surged forward.

And when, with the increasing acceptance of the Wagner Act, the sit-downs petered out, it was difficult to discern William Green's "permanent injury" to organized labor.

Why do some spectacular agitations forward their cause and others do not? How determine the efficacy of the explosive demonstration as opposed to the gradual processes of legalism?

Generalizations about this are as rickety as most dicta about human affairs but certain observations do suggest themselves. The all-out agitators, to be successful, must be moving with history. They cannot appear on the scene too soon. They cannot represent a cause that cuts counter to where things are going anyhow. They seem to be powerful only as instruments of the inevitable, providing the final push in toppling over an obstacle that has been increasingly undermined.

Militant suffragettes or sit-down strikers in the days of Rutherford B. Hayes would have been merely pathetic. But by the second decade of the twentieth century, feminism had been infiltrating one area after another of American life. Similarly, the sit-down strikes were only a climax to decades of mounting labor victories.

Above all, an American agitation which is going to work seems to require a particular kind of cause. The cause cannot be simply and crassly economic; it cannot represent a raw lunge for power. It must touch some larger, deeper issue, some aspect of democracy or religion and morality—and ideally, it touches some fusion of the two. It must raise the kind of issue which has immemorially moved Americans, giving inner strength to the agitators and deeply embarrassing their enemies.

When Alice Paul burned the "freedom" speeches of Wilson, she was striking the authentic note. Refusing votes to women *was* undemocratic. Opposition to woman suffrage could be—and decidedly was—associated with all the minions of immorality, whether the liquor interests who feared the female vote or the corrupt political bosses who, with one hand, opposed child-labor legislation and, with the other hand, battled the suffrage amendment.

One of the most striking aspects of the sit-down strikes was that they were rarely waged in the name of economic issues. They were called with the demand for recognition of the union and for the recognition of the union as an assertion of the dignity, the democratic and moral dignity, of the individual worker.

The head of the U.A.W., youthful Homer S. Martin, was a former Baptist minister and he brought to the automobile sit-downs a near revivalistic tone. His answer to the charge of property violations was an instinctive fusion of appeals to democracy and morality: "The most sacred of all property rights is the right to your job and your right to have it on terms fit for a free man."

On the basis of these considerations, the Freedom Riders and the whole present-day Negro movement of passive resistance seem likely to prove one of those agitations which genuinely pushes ahead the cause. The timing is perfect. The National Association for the Advancement of Colored People was founded in 1909 and since then the drive for Negro equality has been steadily winning specific victories and almost as steadily adding allies in the white population.

The Freedom Riders not only have behind them a solid foundation; they also represent the clear trend of affairs. The Supreme Court school-desegregation decision of 1954 was the great watershed and after that only the most purblind could fail to see the flow of American opinion with respect to the Negro. Plainly, incontestably, the Freedom Riders have the great strength of riding with history.

They take on added strength from the nature and tone of the movement. It cannot be stressed too much that most of the leaders of the drive are ministers and its principal fortresses are churches; that its slogans invariably catch up the themes of democracy; that it moves along on the passion of the thousands joining religious fervor and democratic aspirations as they chant:

> *Freedom! Freedom!*
> *God's Own Freedom!*
> *Amen, Amen.*

Theirs is the Kingdom, the Power and the Glory—to keep their own ranks zealous and to make the most obdurate of their enemies feel at least a bit uncomfortable.

The Freedom Riders have on their side still another fact which few similar agitations have been able to muster. One of the most damaging arguments made against such demonstrations has been that they are a selfish pursuit of a group interest, quite ready to disrupt the community, create contempt for law, and hurt the whole nation for the gain of a relative few. This charge has certainly been flung at the Freedom Riders but it is difficult to make it stick.

On the contrary, it is easy for supporters to argue effectively the opposite proposition, as they have been repeatedly doing. The Freedom Riders ride against segregation, and after years of cold war only the most ignorant man does not know that the existence of segregation in the United States is a tremendous liability to all Americans in the East-West struggle.

The Freedom Riders ride to get a program like that of the N.A.A.C.P. carried out quickly. More and more, thoughtful Americans are coming to realize that unless such a program is executed swiftly, many of the 18,000,000 Negroes may well lose faith in it, may well lose patience with any rational approach, and endanger the very social peace of the United States by turning to hate organizations like the Black Muslims.

During a lull in the Freedom Rider agitation, reporters made their rounds in Montgomery, Ala. They heard again everything they had been hearing for days—the spleen of the all-out segregationists, the worries and criticisms of the gradualists. But now other notes were sounded. The appeal of the Freedom Riders to moral and democratic sensitivities was having its effect.

One newspaper man, Claude Sitton, noted the reports that some segregationists were beginning to say: After all, the Negro demand for civil rights is "human and just." An Alabama state investigator mused, "If I were in their place, I would do the same thing."

Along a tree-shaded street in the trim new brick houses where the upcoming young executives live, the trend of American history, prodded along by the Freedom Riders, was producing its own results. A civic leader there told Sitton that his neighbors had become quite aware of the "implications" of the race friction. The bus incidents "had driven home to them the inevitability of desegregation."

This spokesman of tomorrow added: "Cautiously and quietly we are talking over what we must do to make the change as smooth as possible."

Two Ways: Black Muslim and N.A.A.C.P.

by Gertrude Samuels

THROUGHOUT THE American Negro community—nearly 20,000,-000 people, or one-tenth of the nation—there is a growing bitterness over the slow pace of progress on civil rights. On all sides the frustrations have been deepening since the historic Supreme Court decision of 1954, banning segregation in schools. Today, nine years after that decision, less than 10 per cent of Negro students are in nonsegregated schools in the South. Opportunities for Negroes generally remain bound by the shackles of race. As Dr. C. Eric Lincoln, who teaches sociology at Clark College in Atlanta, writes: "Every intelligent Negro experiences a feeling of quarantine when he ponders his future and the avenues of creative existence open to him."

On these beliefs—that equality must come, and that it must come more quickly—the Negro community is united. But it is deeply split over how it should proceed: whether it should continue to move democratically though more militantly; or whether it should alienate itself completely from American white society.

This schism shows up in the diametrically opposed approaches of two main groups: the National Association for the Advancement of Colored People—N.A.A.C.P.—for fifty years the best-known group identified with Negro aspirations, and considered moderate; and the radical Black Muslims, who oppose integration and for months have been increasingly active in their challenge to the N.A.A.C.P.

The Black Muslims

This is a religion of protest and rebellion, which preaches black union against the white man. It rejects Christianity. It preaches that the black man is "divine" and that all whites are "devils." An Islamic sect, it believes that it alone has the answer for the Negro masses who are groping for social dignity and for social action. Its avowed goal is to separate from America, to set up its own state with its own flag.

The Muslims reject integration as vehemently as do Mississippi's Gov. Ross Barnett and Senator Eastland. They contemptuously reject the Negro moderates who are fighting for integration as "Toms" and "white man's niggers." They appeal deliberately to the Negroes at the bottom of the social totem pole —the lower working class, the poor and the illiterate. They identify with Moslems overseas, and obey the rules that forbid smoking, gambling, drinking and the eating of pork. They are secretive about their membership, estimated at 100,000.

Their doctrine of black supremacy is offering a minority people, confined in racial ghettos, the escape of fantasy—a "nation" of their own—to counteract the the reality of their despair. This is what the Muslims recognize and exploit.

The movement began back in 1930, when a peddler—who may have been an Arab and who was known by various names but chiefly as W. D. Fard, Professor Ford and "The Prophet"—appeared in Detroit and shocked his listeners with denunciations of Christianity. He taught slum Negroes that their enemy was the white man. He set up a temple of Islam, and appointed Elijah Muhammad (born Elijah Poole in Georgia) as his "Messenger." Then, in the way of prophets, he "disappeared." Under Muhammad, who lives in a mansion in Chicago's South Side, the sect thrived.

Temples now abound in various cities. Muslim real-estate holdings and commercial enterprises have grown. Many members were recruited in prisons. The most flamboyant of these and

Muhammad's chief lieutenant is the New York leader Malcolm X. Minister Malcolm X is today both personal magnet and political threat, a fascinating study in human contradictions.

In Temple 7 Restaurant in Harlem, one of the many Muslim holdings, you meet Malcolm X under a large framed portrait of "The Honorable Elijah Muhammad, Messenger of Allah." No-smoking signs abound in the well-appointed restaurant where white-jacketed waiters serve well-dressed diners. A mural of the Sphinx fills one wall. Even the juke box seems toned down. It is like a stage set.

For three and a half hours, Malcolm X virtually mesmerizes the listener with his ingratiating manners, an endless flow of ideas, Biblical quotations, boyish smiles and bland insults. He is tall (6 feet 3 inches), a light-brown, 37-year-old, ruggedly handsome man with coldly appraising eyes behind horn-rimmed glasses. With pauses for phone calls or to sip water (he is on a monthly three-day fast), he roams widely over religious, economic, cultural and racial subjects on which he has educated himself.

He never got beyond a formal eighth-grade education. He attributes "all that I am and all that I know" to his teacher, Mr. Muhammad. When he pronounces the name, it is with the same awe that Catholics refer to St. Peter, or Jews to Moses.

He was born Malcolm Little in Omaha, Neb., one of 11 children and the son of a Baptist minister. He tells you he was 6 years old when the Ku Klux Klan burned his home to the ground; later his father was found killed. These terrible memories have never left him. The family broke up and Malcolm went to a boys' institution. Eventually, he moved East and into the underworld. Known as "Big Red," he went to prison for larceny in Massachusetts on an 8-to-10-year sentence, and served seven years. In prison he began to absorb the Muslim religion and to correspond with Muhammad. He likes to say that "Christianity took me to prison and Islam brought me out."

"This Elijah," he tells you, "is teaching us that just as Moses solved the problem of the Jews by taking them to a land of their own, this Moses, our Elijah, will lead us to a land of our own."

"Where?" (Some reports have identified the sites as three Southern states.)

Malcolm X flashes his smile. "Moses never told the Jews where it was to be. It was part of the Mosaic strategy politically just to lead them out toward the 'promised land.'

"The reason that Muslims don't want integration with the white man," Malcolm X continues, "is because we see what's coming to the white man, what's in store for him. It's a sinking ship.

"We're not anti-white. We're anti-oppression, and the oppressor is white. That's why I say there is a guilt complex among the whites.

"The N.A.A.C.P. is not a Negro organization, so Roy Wilkins [N.A.A.C.P. executive director] is not a Negro leader. As long as Arthur Spingarn is the president, it's a Jewish organization. And it's the same with the Urban League, CORE, the N.A.A.C.P. Legal Defense Fund—all those are white organizations.

"When Negroes in those organizations open their mouths to speak words of praise, it's always for white people—the good liberals, the good Jews, the good white folks. When they say anything good about Mr. Muhammad, it's always with reservations to let people know that 'I'm not a Muslim.' These are statements by scared men."

Asked whether he feels his racism is comparable to Hitler's he replies blandly: "Uncle Sam was practicing racism and white supremacy before Hitler was born. Hitler learned from Uncle Sam. Kennedy exploited the Negro to get in office and since then he bucked everyone on this earth—U.S. Steel, Khrushchev, Castro, everybody—but he won't buck the Southern segregationists. Tokenism—minimum integration—is a political trick."

But is not race irrelevant? Shouldn't man be judged as a human being, not on his color?

"It's too late to undo the chain reaction of events that has been set in motion by the white supremacists. There is some Muslim in a whole lot of Negroes. The only movement with mass appeal today is the Muslim movement. Why? Because Negroes are fed up. The most dangerous thing that confronts whites today is the white man's attempt to minimize the intense dissatisfaction among Negroes."

Malcolm X likes to say that he has no political ambitions, yet like other Muslim ministers, he is constantly recruiting—on speaking tours, at outdoor rallies, on college campuses, in pool halls, prisons and drugstores—inviting Negro Christians to attend lectures at the mosque.

So strong is Malcolm X's drawing power in Harlem today that Congressman Adam Clayton Powell, a Baptist preacher, has begun to link himself to the Muslims.

The other week, at a huge, outdoor rally in Harlem Square, the Congressman declared:

"I tell you again and again, we are not going to get anything more in this life except that which we *fight* for and *fight* for with all our power. Unless we can seize completely the administration of our national Negro organizations, then we must say there is no hope there for us. This may sound like black nationalism. If it is, then what is wrong with it?"

Powell added that he did not agree with "some things" that Malcolm X preached, but he said Malcolm X was his "friend." In wrathful tones that won loud approval, he attacked on racist grounds such nonviolent, interracial groups as N.A.A.C.P. (of which he happens to be a life member), the Urban League, CORE, and the Rev. Martin Luther King's Southern Christian Leadership Conference. They had, he said, white people in leadership positions.

Malcolm X rose at the same meeting to declare: "We won't get our problems solved depending on the white man." Both speakers obliquely singled out for attack those leaders with Jewish names.

The leading Negro press has been scathing in reaction to the attacks on the N.A.A.C.P. But in Harlem, the Muslims and Powell have been given a curious boost by the writings of James Hicks, executive editor of The Amsterdam News, a Harlem Negro weekly. Hicks has been trying to paint N.A.A.C.P. leaders and Negroes high in government as in league with "the enemy," calling them "stupid." (His paper, paradoxically, has been advertising that its "great" columnists are the very men he is criticizing—Roy Wilkins and Dr. King.)

During the newspaper strike, when reaction was necessarily mute, the paper charged that "Jews control New York's top jobs." Recently, Hicks wrote that he was "fed up" with leaders who criticized Malcolm X for "fighting the wrong war in the wrong place at the wrong time."

"Who is the enemy?" asked Mr. Hicks.

The N.A.A.C.P.

The enemy, answers N.A.A.C.P., is race hatred—whether it comes from men with white skins or black skins.

The N.A.A.C.P. rejects segregation or, as the Muslims call it, "separation." It is bi-racial. It was founded fifty years ago by liberal whites and Negroes. N.A.A.C.P. fights in three nonviolent ways—legal, legislative and educational—to help Negroes break out of their ghettos. It is trying to teach all people that race is irrelevant, that man must be judged as man.

In contrast with the Muslims, N.A.A.C.P. seeks to bring about complete integration in all phases of American life. It wants equal justice under the law, the right to vote (Muslims discourage voting), personal security against mob and police violence, and nondiscriminatory treatment in housing and all public facilities. It is the largest civil rights organization in the nation with some 400,000 paying members and probably millions of supporters, Negro and white.

For traditional reasons, all presidents of N.A.A.C.P. have been white. The board of directors, which sets policy, numbers 60, of whom 11 are whites. The board has included such public figures as Mrs. Eleanor Roosevelt, Ralph Bunche, Gov. Herbert Lehman, Rabbi Stephen S. Wise, Walter Reuther. Arthur Spingarn, 85-year-old Jewish lawyer, who heads N.A.A.C.P., was for nearly a quarter-century the association's entire "legal department," serving on a no-fee basis.

Today the N.A.A.C.P. Legal Defense Fund, a separate, nonprofit group, works for civil rights through legal actions. Its nine lawyers (six of whom are Negro) have 121 cases pending in the Southern states. Of these, 66 are school segregation cases; six involve admission of physicians to hospital staffs and patients to treatment facilities; the remainder are sit-in and Freedom Rider cases.

N.A.A.C.P. is also encouraging the economic boycott—what it calls "selective buying." Negro purchasing power is estimated at $15 billion a year; N.A.A.C.P. reports that planned boycotts of certain merchants and retail stores in Jackson, Miss.; Savannah, Ga.; Macon, Ga., and St. Petersburg, Fla., are "effective" and that the idea is spreading.

The chief legal counsel until recently was Thurgood Marshall, a Negro who is now a Federal judge. When asked to comment on the appointment of Jack Greenberg, his successor as director-counsel (now under attack by the Muslims and Congressman Powell), Judge Marshall said: "As those who are fighting discrimination, we cannot afford to practice it."

Urbanity is the word for Roy Wilkins, N.A.A.C.P.'s graying executive director, who looks younger than his 62 years. The son of a Methodist minister, tall, lean, known as a cool strategist, Wilkins worked his way through the University of Minnesota (as a redcap and a railroad dining-car waiter). He was managing editor of The Call, a Negro weekly in Kansas City, Mo., until he joined the association some thirty years ago. At N.A.A.C.P. headquarters in mid-Manhattan the other day, Wilkins discussed Powell and spoke with contempt of the Muslims and their hate philosophy.

"What is Adam Clayton Powell doing in Congress," asked Wilkins, "if he doesn't believe in integration? Logically, if he's given up on the system, or doesn't support what most Negroes want—integration—he ought to resign.

"I don't think that there's any doubt that Negroes are frustrated, bitter and impatient, but I don't see that as identical with the Muslim objectives. This Muslim group is a cult. The first point of departure is its anti-Christianity which gives them the cult aspect and is attention-getting. But Christianity has been for the American Negro part and parcel of his development and his life. So when he is asked to get rid of it and to adopt Islam and Allah, well, it is bound to get attention.

"And, let's face it," he went on coolly, "the white community brought it on themselves. The whites are responsible for the seeds of this cult being even an inch high—their rebuffs to the Negro, their rejection of his worthiness no matter how worthy.

"The supreme push to this defeatist Muslim philosophy was given by the tolerated defiance of the Supreme Court decision. Negro citizens had a right to believe that once the Supreme Court in 1954 had affirmed that segregation was unconstitutional, things would change. But instead of progress, there has been token integration—driplets of compliance. Of course, the Muslims capitalize on all this.

"But for all his frustrations, the Negro is still an American. This is his country. He's sore about a lot of things. But most

Negroes—the vast majority—have decided to fight it out, fight for what is their due. The Negro is convinced that he can do something about it. If he didn't believe it, you wouldn't have the steady membership in N.A.A.C.P., the personal following of Martin Luther King, the kneel-ins at the churches, the sit-ins at the lunch counters, and the demonstrations."

What is the meaning of the present schism for the Negro community and for America?

Many people believe that the influence of the Muslims is growing. They seem to have plenty of money. Their code, emphasizing race pride and individual decorum, is helping to shatter the Negro stereotype of shiftlessness and lawlessness and has undeniable appeal. As one non-Muslim Negro put it: "No one can calculate the psychological and emotional impact throughout the nation." Though their political power is latent, it is a threat. The immediate danger is that, through them, a growing number of colored people are beginning to experience a real sense of alienation from American society.

Partly in reaction to the rise of the Muslims but mostly because of its own impatience with the slow progress on civil rights, the N.A.A.C.P. and other moderate groups are being forced into more militant positions. The militancy, especially of the young Negro American, has been dramatized in recent days by the various "freedom walks" and the hundreds of arrests of young Negroes in Birmingham, Ala., in the demonstrations against segregation. Some believe that the very existence of the Muslims points to a failure of the N.A.A.C.P. to reach the grass roots where the cult is having success.

As Roy Wilkins moves about the South, he encounters redcaps, porters and bellhops who keep abreast of events, reading the papers and watching TV. They are apt to ask him: "How're things going? You think those folks are going to act down there in Washington?"

"I think so," Wilkins replies, "if you keep up the pressure."

"We're going to do it," they answer, "but sometimes—" and they shake their heads—"I don't know . . . I don't know. Adam flies off the handle—but he gets white folks *told*."

The warnings are clear. The Muslims exist and their influence will remain potent so long as they are able to give the Negro masses something that articulates their pent-up frustrations.

Dr. Kenneth B. Clark, professor of psychology at City College, chief of HARYOU (the Federally supported Harlem Youth Opportunities Unlimited) and himself a target of the Muslims, puts it this way:

"The danger of the Muslim movement is that it exploits chaos. It is really the other side of the White Citizens' Councils of the South. It can put terror into people and intimidate the responsible elements. The anti-Semitism is part of the demagoguery. The Muslims have again demonstrated the ease with which masses of human beings can be aroused by hatred. There is no reason to believe that Negroes are any more immune to this type of hate appeal than are whites."

It is the disease of racism and discrimination that must be attacked. Negro leaders are warning that the whites must open their eyes to some painful realities they have been trying desperately not to see. The racial confrontation in America now exists and cannot be postponed. Gradualism and tokenism are no longer acceptable to the Negro people.

At the highest level of government, it is felt, there must be wider understanding of the sense of urgency. The racial crisis is upon us.

"It must be resolved positively now," Kenneth Clark concludes, "or we run the risk of stagnation, moral dry-rot or worse. No Negro leader in America today can ask the masses to wait for rights which are enjoyed by the newest American citizen who is white."

Sheriff Harasses Negroes at Voting Rally in Georgia

by Claude Sitton

SASSER, GA., July 26—"We want our colored people to go on living like they have for the last hundred years," said Sheriff Z. T. Mathews of Terrell County. Then he turned and glanced disapprovingly at the thirty-eight Negroes and two whites gathered in the Mount Olive Baptist Church here last night for a voter registration rally.

"I tell you, Cap'n, we're a little fed up with this registration business," he went on.

As the 70-year-old peace officer spoke, his nephew and chief deputy, M. E. Mathews, swaggered back and forth fingering a hand-tooled black leather cartridge belt and a .38-caliber revolver. Another deputy, R. M. Dunaway, slapped a five-cell flashlight against his left palm again and again.

The three officers took turns badgering the participants and warning of what "disturbed white citizens" might do if this and other rallies continued.

Sheriff Fred D. Chappell of adjacent Sumter County, other law enforcement officials and a number of the disturbed white citizens clustered at the back of the sanctuary. Outside in the black night, angry voices drowned out the singing of the crickets as men milled around the cars parked in front of the little church on the eastern edge of this hamlet in southwestern Georgia.

On the wall was an "All-American Calendar" advertising a local funeral home. It displayed pictures of President Kennedy and past Presidents.

The concern of Sheriff Zeke Mathews, "twenty years in office without opposition," is perhaps understandable.

Terrell County has 8,209 Negro residents and only 4,533 whites. While 2,894 of the whites are registered to vote, only fifty-one Negroes are on the rolls, according to the Secretary of State's office.

On Sept. 13, 1960, Federal District Judge William A. Bootle handed down the first decision under the Civil Rights Acts of 1957 and 1960, which guarantee Negro voting rights.

The judge enjoined the Terrell County Board of Voter Registrars from making distinctions on the basis of race or color, illegally denying Negroes their rights under state and Federal laws and administering different qualification tests for the two races.

Judge Bootle refused a request from the Justice Department that he appoint a voter referee to oversee the registration. But he retained jurisdiction in case further court directives might become necessary.

Nevertheless, Negroes contended that because of fear and intimidation, subtle and not so subtle harassment and delaying tactics, they still found it difficult to register. Many of them are illiterate. This presents a further barrier since they are required by state law to pass a difficult qualification test.

Another source of the sheriff's concern is the fact that field secretaries for the Student Nonviolent Coordinating Committee, an Atlanta-based civil rights organization, began a voter registration drive in the county last October.

Sheriff Mathews said the racial crisis in nearby Albany also had aroused local whites and had brought the "agitators" to Sasser.

Two workers of the student committee active in Terrell County were present as the meeting opened with a hymn, "Pass Me Not, Oh Gentle Saviour."

They are Charles Sherrod, 25, from Petersburg, Va., a Negro, who took part in the sit-in demonstrations in 1960 against lunch-counter segregation, and Ralph Allen, 22, a white student at Trinity College, from Melrose, Mass.

Some of the participants said they had driven here from adjoining Lee and Daugherty counties to encourage others by their presence. Among them were two other workers in the student committee, Miss Penelope Patch, 18, of Englewood, N.J., a white student at Swarthmore College, and Joseph Charles Jones, 24, a Negro from Charlotte, N.C.

After the hymn, Mr. Sherrod, standing at the pine pulpit on the rostrum, led the Lord's Prayer. The audience repeated each line after him.

Overhead, swarms of gnats circled the three light globes and now and then one of the audience would look up from the pine floor to steal a fearful glance at the door.

Mr. Sherrod then read from the Scriptures, pausing after completing a passage to say:

"I'm going to read it again for they're standing on the outside."

The sound of voices around the automobiles parked beside the church could be heard as license numbers were called out. And the faces of the audience stiffened with fear.

A group of thirteen law officers and roughly dressed whites clumped through the door at this point. One pointed his arm at three newspaper reporters sitting at the front and said:

"There they are."

"If God be for us, who can be against us," read Mr. Sherrod. "We are counted as sheep for the slaughter."

With the exception of Deputy Dunaway, who stood smoking a cigarette at the rear, the whites withdrew to confer among themselves.

Mr. Sherrod began another prayer.

"Give us the wisdom to try to understand this world. Oh, Lord God, we've been abused so long; we've been down so long; oh, Lord, all we want is for our white brothers to understand that in Thy sight we are all equal.

"We're praying for the courage to withstand the brutality of our brethren."

And, in this country where Negroes have frequently fallen under the club, the blackjack and the bullet, no one appeared to doubt that the brutality of which he spoke would not be long in coming.

Nevertheless, the audience swung into a hymn with gusto, singing "We Are Climbing Jacob's Ladder." The deputy in the doorway swung his flashlight against his palm and looked on through narrowed eyes.

Lucius Holloway, Terrell County chairman of the voter registration drive, stood up.

"Everybody is welcome," he said, "This is a voter registration meeting."

Sheriff Mathews trailed by Deputy Dunaway burst into the sanctuary and strode to the front. Standing before the reporters, but looking away from them, he began to address the audience.

"I have the greatest respect for any religious organization but my people is getting disturbed about these secret meetings," he said.

"I don't think there is any colored people down here who are afraid. After last night the people are disturbed. They had a lot of violence in Albany last night."

The sheriff and chief deputy introduced themselves to the reporters and shook hands. Negroes had said they had been warned that the rally would be broken up, but the law officers seemed taken aback by the presence of the newsmen.

Sheriff Mathews then turned to the Negroes, saying that none of them was dissatisfied with life in the county. He asked all from Terrell to stand.

"Are any of you disturbed?"

The reply was a muffled "Yes."

"Can you vote if you are qualified?"

"No."

"Do you need people to come down and tell you what to do?"

"Yes."

"Haven't you been getting along well for a hundred years?"

"No."

The sheriff then said he could not control the local whites and that he wanted to prevent violence.

"Terrell County has had too much publicity," he said. "We're not looking for violence."

Chief Deputy Mathews then expressed his viewpoint.

"There's not a nigger in Terrell County who wants to make application to vote who has to have someone from Massachusetts or Ohio or New York to come down here and carry them up there to vote," he said.

The sheriff turned to Ralph Allen.

"Ralph," he said, "I'm going to have to ask you to stay out of this county until this thing quiets off.

"I don't appreciate outside agitators coming in here and stirring up trouble and it's causing us a lot of trouble. I've helped more colored people than any man in the South, I reckon.

"Would you mind telling me who pays you?" he asked Mr. Allen.

The student replied that he received a subsistence allowance from the committee.

"They give you your orders?"

"They place me."

The chief deputy took over the questioning.

"Then you got Terrell County—that's your project, huh?"

A long exchange of forceful questions followed. After that, Deputy Mathews turned to the others and told them:

"There is a prohibit to register between now and December."

Under Georgia law, registration goes on throughout the year, although only those registered at various specified times prior to the primaries and elections may vote in them.

Sheriff Mathews then pointed to the crowd of whites at the back of the sanctuary.

"Gentlemen," he said to the reporters, "those are all of them.

"The people have lost faith and respect in the coordinating bunch. They don't have to have it, Cap'n. They don't have to have it."

Deputy Mathews informed the Negroes that it would not be "to your interest" to continue the meeting.

"You don't have to have nobody from Massachusetts to come down here and help you the way to the courthouse," he said.

In another reference to Mr. Allen, he commented:

"I don't think he's got any business down here, to tell you the damn truth."

Deputy Mathews turned to Deputy Dunaway and ordered him to take the names of all those present.

"I just want to find out how many here in Terrell County are dissatisfied," explained Sheriff Mathews.

Turning to a local Negro and pointing at Mr. Allen, the Chief Deputy then said:

"He's going to be gone in two weeks, but you'll still be here."

As the names were collected, Deputy Mathews began pressing questions on Mr. Sherrod and interrupting him sarcastically as the Negro tried to reply.

He turned to Mr. Allen again. Shaking a finger in his face, he said:

"You couldn't get a white person to walk down the street with you."

When Deputy Dunaway asked the names of five Negro youths sitting on a bench with Miss Patch, they refused to give them.

"I wouldn't either," said Deputy Mathews.

As the Sheriff walked away, he said to reporters:

"Some of these niggers down here would just as soon vote for Castro and Khrushchev."

The Negroes began humming a song of protest popularized during the sit-in demonstrations, "We Shall Overcome." And as the law officers withdrew to the outside, the song swelled to a crescendo.

The business meeting then got under way. Miss Patch reported on her work in Lee County. Mr. Allen told of having been knocked down twice last Saturday, beaten and threatened with death by white men in Dawson, the county seat.

Charles Jones asked Mr. Holloway if anything had been heard from the Justice Department regarding an investigation into the dismissal of a Negro teacher.

"No," replied the chairman.

Shortly after 10 o'clock, the Negroes rose and joined hands in a circle. Swaying in rhythm, they again sang, "We Shall Overcome." Their voices had a strident note as though they were building up their courage to go out into the night, where the whites waited.

Lucius Holloway prayed.

"Our concern is not to destroy," he said. "Our concern is not to displace or to fight, but to build a community in which all our children can live and grow up in dignity."

The Negroes then filed out the front door past the group of law officers.

"I know you," said one officer to a Negro. "We're going to get some of you."

Flashlight beams slashed through the darkness to spotlight the face of Miss Patch as the white student climbed into an automobile with some Negroes from Lee County. The whites standing by cursed but made no move toward the car.

Miss Patch and her companions pulled out behind the station wagon in which the newsmen were riding. But the air had been let out of the right front tire of the wagon, forcing it to stop close to the church. The other car stopped, too.

Carloads of whites roared past again and again while the tire was being changed. A deputy stopped and said with mock solicitude, "Help you, Cap'n?" He drove away grinning.

Five whites in an automobile trailed the station wagon and the car in which Miss Patch was riding to Albany, eighteen miles away. Newsmen stopped to take the license number but the plate had been bent over to conceal it. The whites swerved into a side street and sped away.

A mechanic who examined the station wagon today found that quantities of sand had been poured into the gasoline tank, causing untold damage to the engine. He found no evidence of a puncture on the tire, only a knife mark on the valve where the air had been released.

Negro Queue in Mississippi Is Symbol of Frustration in Voter Registration Drive

by Claude Sitton

CANTON, MISS., Feb. 29—A drama symbolic of the Negro's fight for voting rights in the Deep South is unfolding here beneath the magnolias on the lawn of the Madison County Courthouse.

Yesterday and again today long lines of Negroes, some wrinkled and bent with age, waited patiently before the white-columned entrance of the century-old brick building for their turn to apply for registration.

Some were afraid that this challenge to white political supremacy might cost them their jobs or worse. All knew it would likely prove futile.

Only one Negro applicant at a time is permitted in the registrar's office. Of the more than 260 who waited outside Friday and the more than 50 there Saturday, only seven finally got inside to take the test.

Those seven must have sensed the futility anew as they passed through the office door of L. F. Campbell, the circuit clerk and voter registrar. On its glass window is a red, blue and gray sticker bearing a Confederate battle flag and the message, "Support Your Citizens' Council," a militantly segregationist organization.

The futility must have been reinforced as they read the complex constitutional interpretation test that Mississippi has imposed on prospective voters since Negroes joined their ranks.

Outside in a chill wind, the waiting Negroes stood stiffly on the concrete walkways or along the black, wrought-iron fence that was set in place 106 years ago when the courthouse was built.

A sheriff's deputy in a black leather jacket, black slacks and black Western boots paced up and down the lines, an automatic carbine swinging in his left hand and a wooden club dangling from his belt. A bone-handled revolver rode loosely in a holster on his left hip.

Now and then, the Negroes were joined by others who had walked there by·two's seven and a half blocks from pleasant green Holiness Church, staging area for this "Freedom Day" sponsored by the Congress of Racial Equality in cooperation with the National Association for the Advancement of Colored People and the Student Nonviolent Coordinating Committee.

Police auxiliaries in blue helmets and makeshift uniforms mounted a shotgun guard along the route. Sheriffs and deputies from Madison and surrounding counties wearing 10-gallon hats and driving white cars with as many as three radio antennae patrolled the streets.

City policemen armed with nightsticks, revolvers and a variety of shotguns and rifles snapped orders at the Negroes as they shepherded them through a crosswalk to the courthouse grounds. Occasionally, law enforcement officers clustered in the entrance spoke derisively to prospective applicants whom they knew.

State and local officials in plainclothes photographed Negroes, newsmen, agents of the Federal Bureau of Investigation, observers from the National Council of Churches and, sometimes, other plainclothesmen. Spotters with field glasses watched over the activity from second-floor windows. The State Highway

Patrol manned a police radio network set up in a command post in the courthouse.

White spectators muttered sullenly along the sidewalks and in the stores around the square. But there was no violence, a tribute, perhaps, to the efforts of the city's few moderates and responsible segregationists and to the policy of the new Governor, Paul B. Johnson, of avoiding racial violence.

This does not mean, however, that Negroes will now have equal access to the ballot box in most of Mississippi any more than it foretells voting equality for them in much of Alabama and Louisiana or a large area in Georgia.

The long lines outside the Madison County Courthouse are, in fact, suggestive of the failure of the Civil Rights Acts of 1957 and 1960.

Further, there is little evidence that the situation will improve substantially in the near future even if the United States Senate passes the voting section of the civil rights bill already approved by the House. This conclusion is based on interviews with whites and Negroes here, the heads of the Southern Regional Council's Voter Education Project in Atlanta and Justice Department officials in Washington.

The basic objection raised to the new legislation is that the task of eliminating discriminatory practices would still be left to the Federal courts. Thus, it represents no departure from the underlying principle of the Civil Rights Acts of 1957 and 1960.

"This judicial approach is strictly a long-range proposition," asserted Leslie W. Dunbar, executive director of the Southern Regional Council. "It's a matter of years and years."

Mr. Dunbar and other students of the voting problem argue that it is so entwined with the over-all system of segregation that a narrow-gauge campaign through court action alone would lose much of its force at the local level.

"The reality is that, to the Negro in Mississippi, the law is still the law as enforced by the sheriff, not the law that comes out of Washington," he said.

Strong supporting evidence for this argument is seen in the situation in Madison County, which is typical in many important respects of the Deep South area at which the voting section of the proposed Federal civil rights bill is aimed.

Madison County stretches northward from the outskirts of Jackson, the state capital, for 40 miles between the Pearl and Big Black Rivers. It is a succession of wooded swamps, rolling pasture land and highly productive cotton and soybean fields of brown loam, bounded on the west by the Delta and on the east by the hills.

The Western dress of many residents underscores the fact that Madison is the second largest cattle county in Mississippi. Canton, a city of 10,000 persons, has experienced some industrial growth in recent years and produces wood products, coarse yarn, ski belts, tents, chemicals, automobile springs, electrical appliances and furniture.

The Natchez Trace, the road through the wilderness from Nashville, Tenn., to the Mississippi River, ran along the county's eastern edge. But its chief commercial artery now is the Illinois Central Railroad, whose famed engineer Casey Jones ended his final run in a wreck just across the Big Black in Yazoo County.

At one time, Madison's Negro residents—now 72 per cent of its population of 32,904 persons—were among its most prized assets. But industrialization and agricultural mechanization have all but eliminated the need for their labor. Most whites say they would like to see the Negroes leave.

In keeping with the custom of most rural Deep South counties in which Negroes outnumber whites, politics here is viewed as "white folks' business" by most. A leading white citizen of Canton said that despite the proposed voting legislation there would be no marked increase in Negro participation "until Bobby [Robert F.] Kennedy comes down here with some Federal marshals."

As many as 475 Negroes were once on the voting rolls. But this high point was followed quickly by the defeat of the registrar who put them there.

Because of the refusal of county officials to release information, the latest statistics available are those filed by the Justice Department in a voting suit against the state and six other counties. These show that 121 Negroes, or 1.1 per cent of those in Madison County of voting age, were registered in 1962. The corresponding figure and percentage for whites that year was 5,458 and 97 per cent.

This first serious challenge to white political supremacy in the county began last June. A Negro voter registration drive was started then under the banner of the Council of Federated Organizations. Known as C.O.F.O., the group is a Mississippi alliance comprised of the N.A.A.C.P., CORE and the Student Nonviolent Coordinating Committee.

David Dennis, a soft-spoken 23-year-old Negro from Jackson, who is C.O.F.O.'s assistant program director and a CORE field secretary, heads the drive. Eight other CORE workers and four student committee members are on the staff.

The registration campaign has met with little success, according to Edward S. Hollander, a 23-year-old white CORE field secretary from Baltimore. He said 1,000 attempts to register had been made, only 30 of them successful.

The Negroes opened a boycott against 19 white merchants last January that now threatens some of them with financial ruin. The objectives are "more courteous treatment" for Negro customers, and, Mr. Hollander conceded, pressure by the white merchants on county officials to accept Negro voter applicants.

Instead, the boycott has divided the city into warring camps and brought a campaign of harassment, intimidation and violence. Each side accuses the other of various criminal acts but the Negroes appear to be suffering the most by far.

A Citizens' Council chapter has been revived. Virtually every business establishment in the city has a council sticker on its door or in its front windows. Some were placed there despite the objections of the proprietors.

Even the State Legislature has taken a hand in the crisis. Several measures passed by one or both houses appear to conflict, at least in their intent, with constitutional rights.

One bill would impose a penalty of six months' imprisonment and a $500 fine for printing or circulating boycott literature. Before it was adopted by the House, a representative objected that "some of our friends might be arrested" under its provisions.

Although he did not say so, the boycott has been a traditional weapon of the Citizens' Councils against Negroes or whites who challenge the white supremacist dogma.

The reply to this criticism came from Representative Thompson McClellan of West Point.

"If one of our friends is arrested, if he is tried in Mississippi before a Mississippi jury, I don't have any doubt about how he would come out," he said.

In the opinion of Mr. Campbell, the county voter registrar, the wide-ranging dispute here is much fuss about nothing. Any Negro who can pass the complex interpretation test will be placed on the rolls, he said.

Mr. Campbell agreed to the interview with reluctance.

"I don't give out any information—that's just my policy," he replied when asked how many Negroes were registered.

He then said with a smile of recollection that he did not know the answer because records were not kept by race.

In its efforts to investigate Negro complaints of discrimination by Mr. Campbell, the Justice Department was forced to appeal to the Supreme Court for an order opening his records. The documents were finally photographed last June but results have not been announced.

The opposition to Negro registration that is apparent here is common throughout most of Mississippi, large areas of Alabama and Louisiana and in southwestern Georgia.

Sometimes this opposition takes the form of discriminatory practices by registrars. Individual accounts of such acts fill page after page of the documents filed by the Justice Department in a suit against the registrars of six Mississippi counties, not including Madison, and the State Board of Election Commissioners.

Other local officials are involved. This week, for example, a Federal District Court in Jackson held that Sheriff A. P. Smith of adjoining Holmes County had prevented Negroes from voting simply by refusing to accept their poll-tax payments.

Negroes who seek to register or encourage others to do so may run the risk of violence against their persons or property. They may be threatened with the loss of their jobs.

Voter registration drives, understandably, have made little headway under these circumstances. Wiley A. Branton, project director of the Southern Regional Council's Voter Education Project, said he and other project officials had become so discouraged over the situation in Mississippi that they had withdrawn financial support from the registration campaign in the state.

In the period from April 1, 1962 through last Dec. 31, according to Mr. Branton, the project spent $51,345 in backing the drive being conducted by the Council of Federated Organizations. Some money went for voter education purposes.

He said the most optimistic estimate of the results showed that only 3,228 new voters had been added to the rolls in the state as a whole. Estimates of the total number of Negro voters registered in Mississippi range from 20,000 to 28,000.

In the same 21-month period, the voter project spent $52,958 in Georgia, Mr. Branton said. This financed effort is credited with adding 46,347 new registrants and saving 5,000 more Negroes from being purged from the voting lists.

"We don't think you are going to get any significant results in Mississippi until the Justice Department gets meaningful [court] decrees, enjoining both discrimination and intimidation, followed by vigorous enforcement of those decrees," Mr. Branton declared. "I'm disillusioned by the fact that they've had several decrees that have not been vigorously enforced."

The Justice Department has filed in 58 cases, under the acts of 1957 and 1960, 13 involving intimidation and 45 discrimination. Its officials are far from satisfied with the results.

They say that their experience in implementing the acts has disclosed serious inadequacies. Lengthy and often unwarranted delays have taken place in court proceedings.

In one case cited by department officials only 725 of 16,000 Negroes of voting age in a county are registered, while the suit to enforce their right to vote has been pending for more than two years.

The case against the six Mississippi registrars and the State Election Commissioners, at present the department's chief hope for a significant breakthrough in this state, was filed two years ago. It has yet to receive a full hearing.

The misuse of literacy and other tests is another problem, according to department officials. All too frequently, they say, the tests given Negroes are far more difficult than those given whites.

Even when the tests are uniform, discriminatory standards are used in judging the answers.

"Thus, barely literate white people have been registered while well-educated Negroes have been rejected for the most trivial of errors," the Justice Department has said.

The problem of court delays is attributed in part to the segregationist viewpoint of some Federal District judges. In the November issue of The Yale Law Journal, Stephen R. Field pointed out that of eight judges appointed by President Kennedy in Georgia, Alabama, Louisiana and Mississippi, "four have indicated a considerable reluctance to follow the letter and spirit of the prevailing law in the civil rights area."

To eliminate this barrier, the Federal civil rights bill proposes that, upon the application of the Attorney General, the chief judge of the Circuit Court of Appeals would appoint a three-judge District Court to hear the case. Any appeal would go directly to the Supreme Court.

Observers note that the Federal courts in the Deep South are already overloaded. A further delay, not covered by the bill's provision, stems from the fact that massive resistance is forcing the Justice Department to attack voting discrimination on virtually a county-by-county basis.

Discriminatory testing procedures would be covered under the proposed legislation by a requirement that registrars apply uniform standards in registering voters for Federal elections. Where literacy tests are used, they would have to be in writing, except where state law permits and the applicant requests an oral test.

Further, if an applicant with a sixth-grade education were disqualified on literacy grounds and subsequently brought suit, the registrar would be required to prove that the applicant was illiterate.

The proposed bill's testing limitations, however, would fail to eliminate the discrimination that observers contend is frozen into the system even where tests are administered honestly. This is borne out by the situation here.

Mr. Campbell contended that all whites who registered during his eight years in office were literate. He conceded this was not true of all of those accepted before that period.

Virtually all whites of voting age, including illiterates, are already on the rolls in Madison County. Only those now coming of age are required to take the constitutional interpretation test, which is considered difficult even by college graduates.

On the other hand, educated Negroes, who might have registered in the past had they not been prevented from doing so, must now submit to the test.

One of the civil rights bill's greatest shortcomings, in the opinion of full-time workers in registration campaigns and their supporters, is its failure to provide protection for them.

A suit, which was filed against Attorney General Robert F. Kennedy and J. Edgar Hoover, F. B. I. director, by eight registration workers in Mississippi, seeks a court order compelling the Federal Government to provide protection for demonstrations in support of registration drives and to prosecute state officials and others who interfere with these drives.

Another difficulty encountered in the effort to eliminate voting discrimination is the lack of an adequate legal and clerical staff in the Justice Department.

The department's civil rights division, headed by Assistant Attorney General Burke Marshall, has only 12 lawyers.

David Norman, an assistant who oversees the preparation of voting cases, said a suit involving, for example, a county of 6,000 persons required six weeks of work by an experienced lawyer. He said there were eight lawyers in the division capable of handling one.

Mr. Kennedy and Mr. Marshall have requested that Congress increase the number of lawyers in the civil rights division to 116 if the new civil rights bill is passed. But most would be assigned to work on enforcement of the proposed ban on discrimination in public accommodations and on school desegregation matters.

Most persons here, in Atlanta and in Washington with whom the voting problem was discussed expressed doubt that the Federal civil rights bill could bring its solution in the near future. Some said this might take five to 10 years.

Despite this prospect, Negroes voice optimism over the largely symbolic advancements that they have made in the Deep South.

The Rev. B. Elton Cox, a CORE field secretary from High Point, N. C., who is taking part temporarily in the registration drive here, contended it was highly significant that Negroes had been permitted to line up in front of the courthouse.

"This is a milestone, not just a stepping stone, in Mississippi," he declared.

Racial Strife

"I STAND ALONE in the middle of two opposing forces in the Negro community. One is the force of complacency. . . . The other force is one of bitterness and hatred and comes perilously close to advocating violence. It is expressed in the various black nationalist groups."

The words are Dr. Martin Luther King's. He was explaining why he has resorted increasingly to direct but non-violent action in his leadership of the Negro drive for equal rights. The weapons are sit-ins, demonstrations, boycotts, protest parades, freedom rides.

It is Dr. King's belief—and the view is shared by a number of Negro leaders—that if moderate Negro leaders do not provide effective channels of Negro action, more and more Negroes will heed the extremist voices. One of the problems, however, is that Southern opposition even to non-violent Negro action constantly raises the danger that demonstrations will get out of hand.

Last week there were crises in relations between Negroes and whites in two areas of Alabama. One involved the integration ferment in the city of Birmingham. The other involved the aftermath of the martyrdom the week before last of a white who had been protesting against segregation.

Since more than a month ago, Birmingham has been the focus of the direct-action campaign. The city is almost totally segregated; not only in the schools, but in stores, restaurants, parks, swimming pools and other public facilities, and in local hiring policies.

Dr. King, who went to Birmingham last month to lead the direct-action campaign, was arrested two weeks ago along with scores of his followers for demonstrating in the city streets. He is now free pending appeal of a sentence of five days in jail and a $50 fine. Last week, as he resumed leadership of the Birmingham campaign, the size of the demonstrations and the number of arrests swelled.

On Thursday the demonstrators were mostly youths in their teens, some even younger. They formed a series of parades composed of groups of 50 or more, and tried to march to the city hall. They sang the integration hymn, "We Shall Overcome." The police threw up barriers at key points and began to arrest the demonstrators in droves. There was no resistance by the laughing, singing youngsters. Some of the marchers fell to their knees and prayed when the police stopped them. Others ran almost joyfully to the buses that were used to transport the marchers to jails or detention centers. About 700 were arrested.

On Friday the mood grew uglier. Again there were demonstrations on the city streets but the participants were older than the previous day—mostly adults. The police used fire hoses and police dogs to break up the parades. Some Negroes threw stones and bottles at police from the roofs of buildings. At least three Negroes were bitten by the dogs, and several others suffered minor injuries from the hoses. Two firemen were injured by the hail of stones and bottles. About 250 were arrested, bringing the total taken into custody since the demonstrations began last month to well over 1,000.

Yesterday about 1,000 Negroes demonstrated in Birmingham. Fire hoses were used again, and again there were arrests. The Justice Department sent two officials to Birmingham to confer with both sides. . . .

As the Birmingham events demonstrated, however, many Negroes have become impatient with the slow process of the integration battle in the courts. Dr. King recently pointed out that eight years after the Supreme Court decision, only 7.8 per cent of the Negro students in the South are attending integrated schools. "At this pace," Dr. King said, "it will take 92 more years to integrate the public schools of the South."

A plea for moderation, combined with a recognition of the acute state of Negro resentment, was made by Attorney General Robert Kennedy last week. Mr. Kennedy appealed to Negro and white leaders in Birmingham to enter into "good faith negotiations" to redress injustice rather than try to settle the matter "in the streets." He said:

"I believe that everyone understands that [the Negroes'] just grievances must be resolved. Continued refusal to grant equal rights and opportunities to Negroes makes increasing turmoil inevitable."

Rights Pact

BIRMINGHAM, after weeks of turmoil in its streets, was quiet as last week drew to a close. Whether it will remain quiet is uncertain. And even if it does there will still be the large question that the events in Birmingham have brought into focus—the question of where the race struggle in the United States is heading.

In Birmingham itself, five weeks of demonstrations against discrimination have won for the Negroes at least the promise of concessions. Their leader, Dr. Martin Luther King, called this their "most significant victory" in the Deep South.

Still there is no assurance that diehard segregationists will allow the promises to be carried out peacefully. If not, race relations will surely take a turn for the worse, not only in Birmingham but elsewhere, North as well as South. Negro unrest was evident last week even in cities where opposition to integration is relatively moderate—Nashville, Tenn., Raleigh, N.C., and Atlanta, Ga.

It is apparent that Negro bitterness over the slow pace of the drive against discrimination is rising. Negro militancy is growing, and some Negroes are turning to racist extremists for leadership.

As a result, some hard decisions may be ahead for the Kennedy Administration. It has counseled moderation for integrationists—reliance on the courts, the ballot box, persuasion—and the Federal Government has brought its own power fully to bear only as a last resort, as it did at the University of Mississippi last year. Now crises of that kind may occur more frequently, as Negro militancy runs up against the rock of segregationist resistance in the Deep South.

It was nine years ago this Friday—on May 17, 1954—that the Supreme Court of the United States unanimously outlawed segregation in public schools. To the American Negro that ruling was long enough in the coming: Lincoln freed the slave, and gave him some hope of equality, a century ago this year.

Since 1954 substantial progress—but far from enough progress to satisfy Negro expectations—has been made. In border areas—Washington and St. Louis, for example—the walls of school segregation came down swiftly. But as the struggle reached deeper and deeper into the South, white resistance was stiffer and stiffer. In 17 states with a history of segregation, fewer than 8 per cent of the Negroes in public schools in the 17 states sit side by side with whites. "Tokenism" has become anathema to many Negroes.

The Negro resentment extends beyond discrimination in education. Jobs also are involved, and not only in the South. The rate of unemployment among Negroes has been more than double that among whites.

In this situation rivalries have sprung up among Negro leaders. The N.A.A.C.P., the biracial body that carried the successful fight against segregation to the Supreme Court and has litigated extensively since, has come under questioning. There have been complaints that the N.A.A.C.P.'s accomplishments have been too few, subject to too many delaying tactics by segregationists.

One result has been the emergence of advocates of direct but nonviolent action, the most prominent of whom has been Dr. King, head of the Southern Christian Leadership Conference. Another result has been a rise of Negro extremist groups. The most conspicuous of these is the Black Muslims, a frankly racist group. The Black Muslims scorn whites as "devils" and reject what they call "the white man's religion," Christianity, in favor of Islam; oppose integration and advocate separation of the races, with Negroes given part of the country for their own; and claim they oppose violence except in defense of Negro rights.

The importance of the "battle of Birmingham" stems in part

from the effect it may have on the competition for ascendancy among Negro leaders.

Birmingham is Alabama's largest city; its population of 341,-000 is about 40 per cent Negro. It has been described as the most segregated large city in the nation. Segregation applies in its schools, stores, restaurants, theaters and other public facilities, and in the hiring policies in its businesses and its extensive industries.

The initial Negro demonstrations in Birmingham, beginning April 3, seemed to be following a pattern that has become familiar in one community after another in the South. There were protest marches by a few score or a few hundred Negro adults; warnings by the police against unauthorized parades; defiance by the Negroes and arrests of some of them.

Then the week before last the pattern began to change. The protests seemed to become a rallying of the whole Negro community. Negroes gathered by the thousands at what had become the staging area for the demonstrations—the 16th Street Baptist Church overlooking a park in the Negro section near downtown Birmingham.

Large numbers of them were schoolchildren, some younger than 10. To criticism of the exposure of the children to possible danger, Dr. King replied, "Children face the stinging darts of segregation as well as adults." A Negro mother said, "These younger people are not going to take what we took."

Singing "We Shall Overcome" and chanting slogans, the demonstrators filed out of the church in groups, taking different routes toward City Hall. Most were quickly arrested, and they piled into the paddy wagons or school buses in an almost festive mood. Some crowds were dispersed by the police with fire hoses and dogs.

Last Tuesday, the demonstrations got out of control of the Birmingham police, and apparently of the "movement's" leaders also. Swarms of Negroes overwhelmed the police lines and swept through the downtown area. Some, evidently bystanders to the demonstrations and thus not coached to avoid violence, pelted the police with stones. State troopers were called in to help the city police. Public Safety Commissioner Eugene (Bull) Connor said of the Negroes, "We were trying to be nice to them but they won't let us be nice." Birmingham seemed to be on the brink of a racial explosion.

In this situation negotiations on the Negro demands took on growing urgency. The talks were held in secret between the Negro leadership and members of Birmingham's "white power structure"—civic and business leaders. For the Federal Government the role of mediator was played by Burke Marshall, Assistant Attorney General in charge of the Justice Department's civil rights division. He kept in close touch with Attorney General Robert F. Kennedy in Washington, who in turn kept the President informed.

Wednesday came the first hint of a break. In Birmingham Dr. King and other Negro leaders announced a 24-hour truce, pending the completion of an agreement. A few minutes later in Washington President Kennedy opened his news conference with a statement saying he was "gratified" by the "responsible efforts" on both sides to deal with the "very real abuses too long inflicted on the Negro citizens" of Birmingham. Gov. George C. Wallace of Alabama, a strong segregationist, quickly got out a statement saying the trouble was caused by "lawless Negroes."

In Birmingham the agreement was finally nailed down Friday afternoon and announced by Dr. King and the Rev. Fred Lee Shuttlesworth, leader of the anti-discrimination movement in Alabama. The Negroes settled for less than their original demands. The agreement provided for (1) desegregation within 90 days of lunch counters, rest rooms and the like in large downtown stores (the Negroes had sought immediate desegregation); (2) non-discriminatory hiring and promotion, including specifically the hiring of Negroes as clerks and salesmen in the stores within 60 days, and the appointment of a fair employment committee; (3) release of all arrested Negroes on bond or personal recognizance (the Negroes had demanded dismissal of all charges); (4) creation of a biracial committee to maintain a "channel of communications" between the races.

There were doubts about whether the agreement would be implemented. The political leadership in city and state disavowed the negotiations while they were going on. Mayor Arthur J. Hanes called the white negotiators "a bunch of quisling, gutless traitors." And yesterday Commissioner Connor urged a white boycott of merchants who had agreed to desegregation in their stores. "That's the best way I know," he said, "to beat down integration in Birmingham."

Moreover, doubts were cast on the possibility of progress as a result of a change of city administration in Birmingham. The city recently elected a new administration headed by Albert Boutwell, who was called a "moderate" on racial matters. But the present administration contested the right of the new regime to take office; the state Supreme Court will hear the case this Wednesday. There has been speculation that the Boutwell regime, if placed in control, would move to meet Negro demands. But Mr. Boutwell issued a statement Thursday saying he had "no commitment" on any matter being negotiated.

There were reports that white-supremacy groups such as the Ku Klux Klan were applying pressure behind the scenes. This pressure was a big reason for the caution that was evident among moderates.

Thus there is considerable uncertainty about what the Negro drive in Birmingham will prove to have achieved. If the concessions prove to be genuine and not just paper agreements, some observers say, they can be regarded as substantial gains.

Whether Negroes in general will regard the gains as substantial is another matter. The demonstrations in Birmingham evidently have had a great impact on Negroes throughout the country. The N.A.A.C.P. called for demonstrations in 100 cities in support of "the movement." Several nationally known Negroes —among them Dick Gregory, the comedian, Jackie Robinson, the former ball player, and Floyd Patterson, the former heavyweight champion—were in Birmingham or planning to go. If the hopes thus raised turn out to have been disappointed, the influence of moderates such as Dr. King may suffer a blow.

Evidence that the more militant Negroes will not be easily satisfied came from Malcolm X, the New York leader of the Black Muslims, who arrived in Washington Thursday to take on the additional task of leading the branch there, where more than half the population is Negro. Malcolm X spoke scornfully of the Negro leadership in Birmingham. "Real men," he said, "don't put their children on the firing line."

For Rights

"THE DAY WAS important in itself and what we do with this day is even more important."

Thus did Negro author James Baldwin sum up the great civil rights demonstration in Washington last Wednesday.

The *importance of the day* was that it brought 200,000 Negroes and whites to the nation's capital—by far the biggest demonstration the city has ever seen—in a fervent plea whose twin refrains were "Freedom!" and "Now!"

Millions watched on TV and the consensus around the country was that the orderly and peaceful demonstration had helped the Negroes' cause. There was disagreement, however, on whether it had changed any votes in Congress on pending civil rights legislation.

What Negroes *do with the day* will be determined in the weeks and months ahead. Negro leaders said the demonstration would give new impetus to the direct-action campaign and the struggle for equal rights in all parts of the country. But the nature and intensity of that struggle seem certain to be strongly influenced by what Congress does on civil rights.

The day began quietly. Washington's streets in the early hours had the deserted look of a Sunday morning as thousands stayed home from their jobs. At 10 A.M., an hour and a half before the scheduled start of the march, there were about 40,000 persons on the slopes near the Washington Monument. In the next hour and a half, the number swelled to 200,000 as Negroes and whites —the ratio was estimated at between 5 to 1 and 3 to 1—poured into Washington by train, bus, plane and private car. These were the highlights of the dramatic day:

The Marchers. The march began spontaneously about ten minutes before its scheduled start as thousands of persons began moving away from the Washington Monument down the mall on either side of the Reflecting Pool toward the Lincoln Memorial. By noon the mall was a solid mass of people. The ranks were informal and the march had the atmosphere of a stirring demonstration, a revival meeting, and a picnic outing. There were songs as the marchers flowed along: the solemn cadences of "We Shall Overcome," hymns, spirituals, the catchy rhythm of folk tunes, and clapping in unison.

The Slogans. Thousands of placards spelled out the purpose of the demonstration and the Negroes' demands. "We demand freedom—Now!" "We demand an end to bias—Now!" "We march for integrated schools—Now!" "We demand decent housing—Now!" At the Lincoln Memorial, the marchers chanted in swelling crescendo—"Pass that bill! Pass that bill!"

The Speakers. The list of speakers was long, the messages were similar: Go back to your communities and redouble your efforts; the road to be traveled is "still long and steep." The high point and climax of the day, it was generally agreed, was the eloquent and moving speech late in the afternoon by the Rev. Dr. Martin Luther King Jr., president of the Southern Christian Leadership Conference. As he rose, a great roar welled up from the crowd. When he started to speak, a hush fell. In cadences that rang of the Bible and the great pronouncements on human liberty down through the ages, he spoke of his "dream chiefly rooted in the American dream." Over and over again he intoned, "I have a dream . . ." and the crowd, deeply stirred, roared its response— a dream of equality, of brotherhood between whites and blacks, of justice and opportunity for all.

The Confrontation with Congress. In the morning prior to the march, the demonstration leaders conferred with Senator Mike Mansfield of Montana, the Democratic leader; Senator Everett McKinley Dirksen of Illinois, the Republican leader; Speaker John W. McCormack, Democrat of Massachusetts; Representative Charles A. Halleck of Indiana, House Republican leader; and

Representative Carl Albert of Oklahoma, House Democratic leader. Courtesy and restraint marked the conferences. "There was no pressure, there was no insistence," Mr. Dirksen reported.

The Conference with the President. After the ceremonies at the Lincoln Memorial, the leaders of the demonstration went to the White House for a conference with President Kennedy. His principal message, they said afterward, was of the need for strong bipartisan support for the civil rights bill.

In a formal statement, the President praised the "deep fervor and quiet dignity" of the demonstration and declared:

"The cause of 20,000,000 Negroes has been advanced by the program conducted so appropriately before the nation's shrine to the Great Emancipator, but even more significant is the contribution to all mankind."

What did the demonstration accomplish and what was the reaction to it?

One unmistakable result was the effect the demonstration had on the participants themselves. The great turnout, the chanting in unison, the sense of solidarity clearly had given the participants a tremendous moral uplift, a feeling of renewed faith and dedication to their struggle. A Negro woman from Alabama said: "If I ever had any doubts before, they're gone now. . . . I'm ready to march on Montgomery or even march in Birmingham again. When they march, I'm going to march."

One widespread reaction throughout the country was praise for the manner in which the march was conducted. There had been fears and predictions in some quarters prior to the demonstration that there might be disorder, ugly incidents, violence, that a "howling mob" might take over the nation's capital. The orderly, temperate, good-natured atmosphere of the demonstration was in sharp contrast to those predictions, and the feeling was that this had helped the Negro's cause.

As for whether the demonstration changed any prospective votes on Capitol Hill, there was disagreement. Speaker McCormack said he thought the demonstration "would be helpful" in stimulating more activity and support in Congress for civil rights legislation. Senator Hubert H. Humphrey, Democrat of Minnesota, said, "I think it may lead people at home to put pressure on their Congressmen and that's where you'll get the muscle."

On the negative side were Senator Dirksen, who said the civil rights bill would be decided on its merits independent of any demonstrations or pressures, and Senator John Stennis, Democrat of Mississippi, who said: "I think it [the demonstration] will backfire."

Status of Integration:
The Progress So Far
Is Characterized
as Mainly Tokenism

by Claude Sitton

ATLANTA, Aug. 31—The march on Washington, whether successful or not in generating new support among Congressmen for
civil rights legislation, had other significant results.

More Americans than ever before have some understanding
of what the Negro means when he speaks of freedom and
equality. More are aware of the distance the nation yet must
travel if all citizens are to enjoy those ideals.

At least a few whites undoubtedly are asking if the long-range
penalties of racial privilege, to the nation and thus to themselves,
may not outweigh whatever short-term personal gains it has
brought them.

And some Negroes may have been led to consider whether
orderly, though militant, pleas and protests are not more persuasive than those that embrace the violence and racism displayed by some of their opponents.

The demonstration before the memorial to Abraham Lincoln,
who saved the nation from the divisive effects of an earlier racial

crisis, underscored the multiplicity of the issues that are undermining its unity again.

The chief national problems, as Negroes see them, include discrimination in hiring, education and housing. Those that are principally found in the South are denials in the fields of voting, public accommodations and the administration of justice.

"We want employment," said Roy Wilkins, executive director of the National Association for the Advancement of Colored People, "and with it we want the pride and responsibility and self-respect that go with equal access to jobs. Therefore, we want an F.E.P.C. bill as a part of the legislative package."

Unemployment statistics offer the most readily available indication of discrimination in this field. The Negro, who makes up less than 10 per cent of the nation's work force, accounts for 20 per cent of its unemployment.

Other evidence shows that the denial of equal opportunity also extends to the restriction of Negroes to lower-paying positions, wage differentials based on race, vulnerability to automation and exclusion from training and upgrading programs.

Negroes and their supporters contend that the employment issue is crucial. "We will not solve education or housing or public accommodations as long as millions of American Negroes are treated as second-class economic citizens and denied jobs," Walter P. Reuther, president of the United Automobile Workers and head of the Industrial Union Department of the A.F.L.-C.I.O., told march participants.

The situation is complicated by the fact that there are more workers than jobs. Some 5 per cent of the nation's whites are unemployed. But Negroes still would not receive a proportionate share of wages if all discrimination were erased. The principal reason is their generally lower skill level, a reflection of the poorer education available to them. Segregation—by law in the South, by custom elsewhere—is a primary factor, according to their leaders.

Despite the 1954-55 Supreme Court decisions against public school segregation, only some 8 per cent of the Negro students in the 17 Southern and border states and the District of Columbia attend classes with whites. This gives only a partial picture. No percentages are available for other regions, although it has been demonstrated that they also have considerable segregation.

One aspect of this situation, according to civil rights advocates, is that school districts tend to provide poorer facilities and teaching staffs for lower income neighborhoods and for Negro neighborhoods.

Even if a Negro obtained a good education and thus equipped himself for a highly paid job, he still would face insurmountable handicaps in buying a home in many of the nation's more desirable communities. Further, surveys of the problem indicate that he must often pay more than whites for a given housing unit. And when he is a renter he frequently finds that his landlord is more careless about maintenance than when the renter is white.

Despite widespread progress in the South, Negroes still encounter considerable difficulty in registering to vote in some areas. Moreover, efforts by the Justice Department and the Federal Courts to eliminate discrimination in this field have led to increasingly sophisticated practices by resisting whites. However, observers generally concede that apathy is by far the greatest problem in the region as a whole.

Discrimination in public accommodations is highly irritating to Negroes because it not only offends their dignity but also causes them considerable inconvenience. For example, a Negro traveling through the South frequently has difficulty in finding a decent place to eat or sleep in many sections. The fact that some desegregation has taken place in this field helps but little since he often has no way of knowing what facilities are open to him.

The elimination of police brutality, which to the Negro is symbolized by the fire hoses and police dogs of Birmingham, Ala., carries a high priority in the civil rights movement. One reason is that it has been employed to intimidate demonstrators and thus to impede the struggle for equality. Another is that many Negroes have had an unpleasant experience with the police at one time or another in their lives.

Police brutality seems to be one area where Federal action promises least, a situation Negroes find hard to understand. "It is simply incomprehensible to us here today and to millions of others far from this spot that the United States Government, which can regulate the contents of a pill, apparently is powerless to prevent the physical abuse of citizens within its own borders," asserted Mr. Wilkins.

The growing militancy of the Negro and the crisis this has produced have forced whites in and out of government to devote an increasing amount of time to the controversy. Considerable progress has been made as a result of their efforts but it falls far short of the demand for change.

Actions of the Kennedy Administration have virtually eliminated segregation in public transportation, with the notable exception of some Mississippi and Alabama areas. Advances of equal magnitude seem likely to come in the relatively near future in the field of voting rights, both because of pressure from the Federal executive and judiciary and because of the various voter registration drives under way in the South.

Washington's influence also is becoming more apparent in employment, particularly among industries with Government contracts. One handicap here is the lack of applicants with the requisite skills.

Some state and local governments also have accomplished material progress in improving job opportunity. In a few cases, chambers of commerce and individual concerns have taken the initiative.

Housing remains one of the hardest problems to solve in both the South and North. And in some Southern cities that once had an over-all pattern of mixed neighborhoods, the trend is toward more segregation.

Racial ghettos lead, in turn, to school segregation even in areas where it is not official policy. And no plan satisfactory to all sides has yet been developed for eliminating the resulting racial imbalance in the schools.

Token school desegregation has spread throughout the South, and, with the exception of Mississippi, every state will have taken some step toward compliance with the Supreme Court's 1954 decision by the end of next week. However, the outlook for widespread progress in this field is dimmed by the evolving pattern of housing segregation coupled with continued white resistance.

Public accommodations, perhaps, is the most promising area of change. Recent experience in the South has shown that businessmen often are willing to lower racial barriers if the threat of retaliation from segregationists is not too great and if the step has the support of local officials and civic leaders.

Some Southerners have expressed the belief that this more or less voluntary progress may stop or even be reversed if Congress refuses to enact legislation designed to eliminate discrimination in this field.

However, the mere end of segregation and discrimination will not bring the millennium for Negroes. Dr. Philip M. Hauser, one of the nation's noted sociologists and the director of the University of Chicago's population research and training center, emphasized this point recently.

"Even if the Negro achieved every objective for which he is striving in terms of the legality of this situation, the sad fact would remain that he would still have high unemployment, low wages, poor housing and low social status for a long time, and that time would be measured in generations," he said.

Dr. Hauser and many others who have studied the problem contend that the Federal Government must make a special effort to raise the economic and educational level of the Negro.

Few persons now question the need for urgency in attacking the issues raised by the civil rights crisis. Those who do might consider the remarks made at the march ceremony by the Rev. Dr. Martin Luther King Jr., president of the Southern Christian Leadership Conference.

"There will be neither rest nor tranquillity in America until the Negro is granted his citizenship rights," he said. "The whirlwinds of revolt will continue to shake the foundations of our nation until the bright day of justice emerges."

Their Text Is a Civil Rights Primer

by Pat Watters

RULEVILLE, MISS.

DECEMBER HAD BROUGHT the first severe cold, a sudden sinking of the temperature to 24 degrees. The fireplace in the Ruleville Freedom School was smoking; it certainly was not heating the classroom. The toilet was frozen. Moreover, one of the staff members had just been given a traffic ticket by police who had been following his integrated car through a neighboring town. And there was a rumor (false, as it turned out) that the owner of the building which houses the school insisted it be vacated the next day. The climate of adversity was undoubtedly different from what it had been during Mississippi's summer of tensions and violence—but it was still there.

The Ruleville Freedom School is run by the Council of Federated Organizations (COFO, pronounced "Cofoe"), which is a local alliance of four civil-rights groups: the Student Nonviolent Coordinating Committee (S.N.C.C., pronounced "Snick"), the Congress of Racial Equality (CORE), the Southern Christian Leadership Conference (S.C.L.C.) and the National Association for the Advancement of Colored People (N.A.A.C.P.).

Last summer, when 700 volunteers flocked in from across the nation to help run them, there were 47 such schools throughout the state. There still are 34, including the one here, though enrollment is sharply down from the summer peak of 2,000 Mississippi Negroes. About 150 volunteers work in the schools alongside some 200 paid staff members of the civil-rights organizations.

With the passing months, the curriculum of the schools has changed, too. It began with emphasis on the three R's—to enable Negroes to pass voter-registration tests. There was also an effort to help them to understand themselves, and thereby to understand their society and the need to change it. Now this aspect, rather than straight academic work, has come to receive primary emphasis. The idea is to teach Negro Mississippians to take themselves seriously, to articulate their ambitions and their discontents—in short, to instill political awareness.

The program has come under fire recently from sources other than its constant segregationist critics. Newspapers reported dissension among COFO organizations, and quoted F.B.I. reports of "subversive" infiltration. COFO denied both. Friendly observers praise the program and volunteers generally, and express the hope that COFO does not leave itself open to damage. Their big concern is that all possible be done to help Negro Mississippians realize their potential.

A visit to the Ruleville school suggests why this is so important. The town, deep in the cotton-growing Delta, is in Senator James Eastland's cotton-plantation homeland, Sunflower County. Population is 934 whites and 961 Negroes.

The school itself is not the largest, and COFO spokesmen say it is not necessarily the best, though it is better organized than most. (There is, they insist, no typical school.)

It has a kindergarten every morning (the local public schools have none), with 4 to 12 children attending. Each afternoon, it offers a supervised-play session for grade-schoolers (there was a brief effort to give the children formal classes, but they seemed too tired after regular school to benefit). On Monday and Wednesday nights, there are discussion sessions for young people, which attract 15 to 20; on Tuesday and Thursday nights, classes for adults, attended by half a dozen to 14, depending on the weather. Mass meetings, with all the Negro community invited, are held on Friday nights.

Linda Davis, 20, one of three white workers at Ruleville, is in charge of the school. She is short and pretty, with brownish blond hair. She was a sophomore last year at Oberlin College in Ohio, worked as a summer volunteer in Ruleville, and stayed on for at least a year as a paid ($10 a week) S.N.C.C. worker. Her father, a Winnetka, Ill., attorney, visited her recently in Ruleville. "He was very impressed," she said. "He met some people he'll never forget."

The two other white volunteers are John Tillotson, 21, a University of Minnesota drama student, slim and tall, his brown hair crew-cut, who arrived in Mississippi in mid-November, and Kathy Ruble, 23, a pretty brunette with short hair, who came in September from Los Angeles where she had been doing clerical work. Both say they will stay as long as they can take it. Kathy said her father urged her not to come. Her reply: "Oh— Daddy!"

Another assistant is Cephus Smith, 19, of Ruleville, a Negro. He wants to organize a course in Negro history before leaving to start college next month.

Charles McLauren, called "Mac," a Negro who directed COFO activities in Sunflower County during the summer, also is attached to the staff while waiting to start college in January. He wears the sophisticated clothes, dark glasses and confident air of a veteran S.N.C.C. worker. He was one of the very first in Mississippi.

The school is at present housed in a building on Quiver Street, a highway near the edge of town. The rear door, the only one used, opens into a heatless hall containing a pay telephone, a citizens-band radio, a duplicating machine and an old sewing machine with a typewriter on top. There are civil-rights and election posters on the walls, and a bulletin board covered with newspaper and magazine clippings.

The hall opens into the room with the smoky fireplace. The fireplace is augmented by a portable electric heater. The ceiling has been insulated with cardboard from boxes. Three walls and the mantel are lined with books. There are Degas and Gauguin prints and posters with maps and information about various states, and two maps of the United States. The floor is covered with speckled linoleum. The fireplace bricks have been chalked red, green and purple. Shades are left up during the day, but drawn at night. This is where classes and activities are held.

An adjoining room is for reading. It is similarly decorated and lined with books, but not heated. The books are all classified, with tags on the shelves. They have been donated, and sent on by the central COFO office.

The afternoon recreation program begins at 3:30. Four grammar-school boys appeared for it on the first day of the cold snap. Some days the schedule calls for basketball or some other game; this time it was drum practice. The drums were made from metal cans, about a foot high, brightly painted. Each had lettered on it the initials of a civil-rights organization: S.N.C.C., CORE, S.C.L.C. The boys had whittled drumsticks.

The drums would be too loud inside, everyone agreed, so they moved out to the front porch where they pounded away. Neighbors looked over, one old Negro lady seeming to scowl. John kept telling them they needed to play together, instead of doing all that good, but uncoordinated, banging. Finally, they settled into a simple beat in unison.

Inside, Kathy was reading before the fire to two little children who had slipped in, a girl about 5, with tight pigtails, and a smaller boy in a blue overcoat, his eyes still watering from the outdoor cold. The drummers came in and joined them, and listened to a story about a princess and her suitors.

The little girl hid her face in a teddy bear when a stranger tried to talk with her. One of the boys, an 11-year-old, said his father works on a cotton plantation. He didn't know what kind of work he wanted to do. Would it be the same as his father? "No." Another, 10, said he hoped to go to college. He added that he would like to live in St. Louis, where a brother is. (A major goal of the Freedom Schools is to change the common desire of young Negroes to leave Mississippi.)

Two more boys, 11 and 12, joined the reading circle. As Kathy finished one story, someone would hurry to get another book. It began to grow dark; the shades were pulled, and Linda began making arrangements to get the children home for supper.

The COFO staff avoids Ruleville's segregated white restaurants and its Negro bars. They are left with the one Negro restaurant. It is operated by James King, a young man whose chief trade is that of plumber, and who has lost business to white competitors since his identification with the movement.

He said he got "interested in feeding the people" when the

summer volunteers first came. "I think it's right to feed people, regardless of who they are. People are human beings, no matter the color. I never saw any people nicer than these."

He put Johnson-Humphrey posters in the restaurant window during the Presidential campaign—probably the only merchant in Ruleville to do so. A brick was thrown through the window, and later a pellet gun was fired into it. The holes are still there. "I try to do right, regardless of the consequences," Mr. King said. "When I learn better, I do better. If I know better, I do better. If a person learns better, but doesn't do better, something's wrong."

After dinner that cold night, five girls and 11 boys came for the youth class. They included grammar-school children (the four drummers were there), as well as high-schoolers.

Linda and John led the discussion. A high-school girl said they felt discouraged. She waved a hand at those present. "This is all the kids we'll get for a long time," she said.

They talked of how—until this year—Negro children had been expected to pick cotton for one day each year to raise money for their public school. Linda asked if white students had ever had to do this. No, the group said. Where does school money come from? The superintendent, they answered her. Where does he get it? From the government. Where does the government get it? From taxes. What does "taxes" mean? Giggles. Do you pay a sales tax? Four cents on the dollar. Do your parents pay taxes? House taxes.

"So all the money comes from the people," Linda said. "If you pay money for schools and you don't like the way the schools are run, why can't you do something and change things?"

She asked what they would change if they had the power. Answers included providing free lunch, a better library, more subjects, a business course, a larger science lab.

A high-school girl said: "Those teachers—they don't know how to teach. If they get a good teacher, she doesn't stay long. They go somewhere else for more money. I was learning to type real good. I could do 30 or 40 words a minute without looking at the keyboard. Then that teacher left." Her family picks cotton for a living.

Would it be a good idea to fight for better things at the white schools as well as at the Negro ones? Yes, came the answer.

Why? "We don't do people like they do us." And there was a murmur: "Do unto others . . ."

Linda suggested another reason: They could go to the white schools. "Why aren't you there now?" she asked. "If somebody was to go there," a grammar-school boy said, "he wouldn't make it back unless someone drug him." You mean he'd be beaten up? Why would they beat you up? "Because you're a Negro," the boy said.

Would anyone help you? "No one outside you-all." Who is we-all? "You're the only somebodies I see here will do it." John said the President would send United States marshals to help them, because "the law says you have every right to go to that school."

Soon he closed the meeting, promising next time "some ideas about what you might be able to do. So you won't be discouraged . . ."

He asked for someone to help clean up. A thin little girl, about 10, wearing blue jeans under her dress, said softly to a girl about 7: "Come on, let's get a broom and sweep." They did, very thoroughly.

Linda showed some themes the class had written. When she had overheard some of the youngsters talking about why they did not trust their teachers, she had asked them to write about it. Most of the papers concerned failures of the teachers to keep confidences. One high-school girl wrote: "I would like to have some teachers I could go to and discuss my personal problems and they will try to help me and not make fun of me."

There were also themes about picking cotton. A 15-year-old boy wrote: "You sea white people ride by and laft and say look at that Negro picking that cotton and getting sun burnt."

An 11-year-old girl wrote: "I was 6 years old when I started picking cotton. Picking cotton is a nasty job. In the morning the dew be on and you have to go out there and get wet. The worms are mashed up and that nasty green stuff be coming out. Up in the day it be very hot and you be sweating away. . . ."

Linda told of pictures the adults had painted—a bird, a duck, a tree with bright red apples. She sent one of a cotton field to an artist friend in Italy. Kathy said the women had felt silly at first about painting. Then they came to love it. One had cried out, like a kindergartener: "More paper. More paper."

The kindergarten was there in full force the next morning—eight children, including a girl of 4 in a wonderful purple cap full of flashing spangles and frills. It was still cold, the room still full of smoke. They danced the hokey-pokey, putting their left shoulders in, left shoulders out, shake it all about. Then, sitting in their winter wraps on the linoleum floor, they pasted dyed rice onto construction paper in their versions of circles and squares. There was a bit of rice-throwing, and even some dancing on spilled rice, but a lot of conscientious effort to sweep up and put back a spilled jar of it.

A girl of 5 went out to wash paste off her hands, using a spigot on the porch whose leaking during the night had left big formations of ice. She came back in with her hands wet and, uncomplaining, let them dry in the air of the smoky room.

"Linda, put our names on them," they cried when they had finished the dyed-rice creations. Then they clamored for their walk. Down the dirt roads of the neighborhood in the sparkling sun they went, skipping and running, Linda in their midst, skipping and running too. They passed a house with its front yard fenced with plastic bleach containers—red, yellow and green. They passed a big Negro man climbing into his truck. "Hup, hup," they shouted. "Hup, hup, hup," he called after them, laughing.

They skipped and ran to a filling station, and had cookies in silence inside it, Linda paying the white proprietor. Then they skipped and ran back to the Freedom School. "I got some red shoes," cried a girl. "Look at that big old truck," yelled a boy. "Oh, oh, oh, oh." With the toe of her shoe one girl broke the ice in the open drainage ditch running in front of the houses.

That night, because of the cold and smoke, the adult class met in a nearby church, the Williams Street Chapel. It is an old structure, ark-shaped, with two pictures of Jesus and an American flag behind the pulpit. An attempt to bomb it was made shortly after the summer volunteers arrived.

Linda's hair was neatly combed, and she wore makeup, tiny earrings, and a skirt and blouse for this meeting. The 14 women who had come sat with her in a circle. Most were old, wearing glasses. They turned solemn eyes above wide humorous mouths on Linda and John, also spruced up for the occasion. They took turns reading aloud from The Freedom Primer, a mimeographed COFO publication intended for the November elections, which had arrived late in Ruleville. The primer, with humorous line drawings, describes the Freedom Vote campaign whereby Mississippi Negroes are urged to participate in mock elections. It says this is necessary because they are not allowed to vote in regular elections. It lays the blame for this on the "regular Democratic party" in the state, and then traces the history of Reconstruction Negro suffrage and the development afterward of methods of Negro disfranchisement. The primer says the Freedom Democratic party will show people everywhere "that Negroes are working together again all over Mississippi— just like after the Civil War."

The ladies read all of it. Their voices were rhythmical and musical—eloquent reproach sounding when they came to the parts about violence to prevent Negroes from voting.

"What if every Negro in Mississippi could vote?" Linda asked. "We would outvote them." What would that mean? "We could change the system." What would that mean? "We could elect who we want. We could elect some Negroes in office." A middle-aged woman continued in a metallic, almost bass voice. "Some could be judge. Some could be sheriff. Some could be . . . could maybe be President."

Mac took the floor at this point with announcements, about voting in a county agriculture committee election, about a petition to replace the Negro policeman in town because Negroes were displeased with him, about a mock election of county officers coming in January. He read to them from a Citizens' Council document, making fun of it. The ladies seemed relieved to laugh with him.

At the session's end, Linda passed out workbooks for improvement of handwriting, and suggested that at the next meeting they might paint Christmas cards to send to the volunteers who had gone home. The old women, still in their circle, looking to this 20-year-old girl, all nodded, smiling. The idea pleased them. They sat awhile longer in silence, seeming to hate to leave.

Only a few Negro families in Ruleville have anything to do with the Freedom School, said Mayor Charles M. Dorrough, who is also president of the Mississippi Municipal Association. He sat at his desk in City Hall, having just ordered some bulbs for the annual town Christmas lighting, and he spoke what might be regarded as the prevalent white attitude—even a little moderately. "We don't see a need for what they're doing. The big thing that is needed is to create ambition in Nigras." He said that at a local Negro school with an enrollment of 1,300 the average daily attendance is 1,100. "They think nothing of staying out of school."

He said any Negro who could pass the test could vote, and that more money went into Negro schools locally than white ones, because Negro enrollment is higher. He also spoke of the need for improvement of education for both races.

"They've sent some of the trashiest people down here," he went on. "Those two little girls over there now don't represent American womanhood. . . . Wallowing around Negro men who need a bath is degrading to their sex."

Asked about a training program for Negroes held in Ruleville for two local sewing plants, he said its results were disappointing. Of 11 Negroes who enrolled, only four qualified, and only two of them are still working. He did not discuss the burning of a cross before his home, apparently because of the training program. There was some little criticism, he said, but he blamed it on COFO's presence and the hardening of attitudes it has caused. The Williams Street Chapel hadn't been bombed, he said, just burned with a little gasoline—by COFO itself. He said COFO was killing the old good relations, where white people wouldn't let Negroes freeze or starve. "Now each can must stand on its own bottom. If they can't stand, they'll have to go."

Linda said that there has been no real communication with the local white people, even though she banks in the town and shops there. On the few occasions when local whites have tried to talk with the workers at the Freedom School, police have appeared and sent them away.

Negro reception is harder to gauge. Obviously, the classes attract few Negroes. The "mass" meetings pull more, usually 60 or 70. The Freedom Democratic vote, which is a less perilous way for Negroes to show support, was 400 in Ruleville on Election Day. The COFO workers and Negroes in the movement say that many others would like to join them but are afraid to because they live on plantations or otherwise are economically vulnerable in this area of intense Negro poverty. Still others have just become discouraged, they said.

Another dimension of Negro response is evident in the homes

where the white volunteers live with Negro families. Kathy's hostess, a middle-aged widow, commented on this dangerously novel kind of living arrangement in Ruleville: "There's nothing bad about it. We stay in they houses from sun to sun anyhow when we work for them. People tell you things to frighten you. But we needed help and if we don't let these young people stay with us, they can't stay. If they blow us away for it, we'll just have to go."

She was sitting at an ancient foot-pedal sewing machine, making star patterns for a quilt she will sell to Northerners through COFO. Kathy, who worries about the danger she may bring, had tensed up. The Negro woman laughed and laughed. "Why, you know if I'd believed that when they said about bombing us, I'd of waked you right then and said, 'Let's go,' " she said. The laughter went on, and Kathy finally smiled.

Such moments demonstrate, among other things, just who on many occasions in the Mississippi movement is taking care of whom, and how learning and teaching are reciprocal. That seems to be what the Ruleville Freedom School is really all about.

Mississippi Factions Clash Before Convention Panel

by E. W. Kenworthy

ATLANTIC CITY, Aug. 22—The Credentials Committee of the Democratic National Committee listened today with rapt attention to an emotion-laden confrontation between the regular delegation of the State of Mississippi and the challenging biracial delegation of the Freedom Democratic party.

The committee postponed decisions on the Mississippi contest and a challenge to the Alabama delegation until tomorrow afternoon.

A reason for the postponement was that David L. Lawrence, former Pennsylvania Governor, who is chairman of the committee, was trying to work out a formula to avoid a bruising floor battle in front of the television cameras. The chances for such a compromise were believed to be fairly good tonight.

The Freedom party contests the right of the regular delegation to represent Mississippi Democrats on the ground that Negroes were systematically denied the right to take part in the process of selecting delegates from precinct meetings to the state convention.

It was an emotional session. Witnesses for the Freedom party, led by its chairman, Aaron Henry of Clarksdale, told in quiet voices of the brutality and terror they said they had experienced while trying to register and vote.

The chief spokesman for the regulars, State Senator E. K. Collins of Laurel, defended the right of his all-white delegation to be seated with an argument that relied heavily on the overwhelming support traditionally given the Democratic party in Mississippi.

Then, toward the end, the counsel for the Freedom party, Joseph L. Rauh Jr. of Washington, told the Credentials Committee that its decision on the seating challenge would determine the course of society in Mississippi.

"If the Freedom party is once seated, Mississippi will change," Mr. Rauh said. "The regulars come here and sweet-talk you to keep the Freedom party from the seats, because if they get the seats they'll go back and build a new Mississippi that the Democratic party will be proud of."

Mr. Rauh read some bitter comments from leading Mississippi politicians on President Johnson and the national Democratic party. "Is this what we are going to approve here?" he asked.

In contrast, Mr. Rauh said, he had received his loudest applause in a speech to the Freedom party convention when he had spoken of supporting President Johnson.

"Are you going to throw out of here the people who want to work for Lyndon Johnson, who are willing to be beaten and shot and thrown in jail to work for Lyndon Johnson?" he asked in a dramatic voice. "Are we for the oppressor or the oppressed?"

Mr. Rauh predicted that the Mississippi Democratic convention would come out for Senator Barry Goldwater, the Republican nominee, next month.

Mr. Collins indicated that he could not predict what the party in Mississippi would do. He pledged that he himself would support the national ticket.

Providing that the members of the regular Mississippi delegation give satisfactory assurances of their own loyalty, it is believed a formula can be devised to avoid an open floor fight like the one in 1948, when all of the Mississippi delegation and half of the Alabama delegation walked out to protest a civil rights plank.

These are the main provisions of the formula under discussion:

First, the regular Mississippi delegation would be accredited, but the Freedom party delegates would be given seats on the floor.

Second, there would be a statement commending the Freedom party for its efforts to break down the racial barriers in the Democratic party in Mississippi.

Third, guidelines would be drawn up for changing the convention rules to make clear that, in the future, deliberate discrimination in party affairs would be a basis for challenging the acceptability of a delegation.

In the public session held in the ballroom of Convention Hall, the drama was provided by the testimony of witnesses for the Freedom party.

Each side was allowed one hour to present its case.

Mr. Rauh concentrated on drawing a picture of Mississippi society and the actions of its officials in preventing the registration and voting of Negroes.

He called up a stream of witnesses ranging from the wife of a Negro sharecropper, who told a story of how she had been jailed and beaten for attempting to register Negroes, to the Rev. Dr. Martin Luther King Jr.

Dr. King said that no state in the union had gone to "such extremes" as Mississippi to prevent Negro participation in political life.

Turning to the Freedom delegation, which is made up largely of Negroes, he said:

"You cannot imagine the anguish and suffering they have gone through to get to this point."

What, he asked, was the alternative for the Negro—the regular Democratic party in Mississippi?

"This is the party which allows an atmosphere of violence and lawlessness," he said.

"If you value your party, if you value your nation, if you value the democratic process," Dr. King cried, "you must recognize the Freedom party delegation."

The wife of the sharecropper, Mrs. Fannie Lou Hamer of Ruleville, said that after she had led a group of 26 Negroes to register, the "plantation owner" had said to her:

"If you don't go down and withdraw your registration, you will have to go."

She told how, on a later occasion, she and others who were engaged in the registration campaign were arrested, jailed and beaten.

One officer, she related, said to her, "You're going to wish you was dead."

She was ordered to lie down on a bunk bed, she said, and two Negro men were ordered to beat her with blackjacks.

"Is this America, the land of the free and the home of the brave," she concluded, "where we are threatened daily because we want to live as decent human beings?"

Mrs. Rita Schwerner, wife of one of three civil rights workers murdered near Philadelphia, Miss., told briefly how she and her husband had been threatened.

Mrs. Schwerner, a slight woman with a pale, drawn face under black hair, said she had tried several times to see Gov. Paul B. Johnson Jr. after her husband's murder but was told "the Governor is unavailable."

"The State of Mississippi and the County of Neshoba have not even sent me a copy of the death certificate," she said.

The Rev. Edwin King, who is the white chaplain at Tougaloo College, said that, because of his activities on behalf of Negroes, "I have been imprisoned, I have been beaten, I have been close to death.

"The Freedom party is an open party," he said. "They [the regulars] are a closed party of a closed society."

At this point, Mr. Lawrence suggested that the witnesses for the Freedom party confine themselves to the legal issue before life in Mississippi."

the committee and not expatiate on "the general subject of general

Mr. Rauh demurred, saying that the testimony of what life was like there was pertinent to the point that the Negro was deprived of participation in the Democratic party.

Negro Party Set
to Push Its Drive

by John Herbers

JACKSON, MISS., Oct. 7—The Freedom Democratic party, which provided the only real contest at the Democratic National Convention, plans another challenge in January.

The group that sought to unseat the regular Mississippi Democrats at the Atlantic City convention will attempt to have the state's Senators and Representatives in Congress removed on the ground that they were chosen through a discriminatory voting procedure.

Meantime, party leaders are working for the election of President Johnson next month, even though they blame him for their failure to win full recognition at the convention.

And they have under way several projects designed to give the new organization some political muscle in the future. One is an ambitious plan to solicit the support of poor whites who, along with the Negroes, can outvote every other faction on every level in the state.

The party was organized last spring by the Council of Federated Organizations, a coalition of civil rights groups in Mississippi, claiming to speak for thousands of Negroes who have been denied the right to vote.

It claimed Mississippi's seats at the national convention on the

From the *New York Times*, October 11, 1964, copyright © 1964 by The New York Times Company.

ground Negroes were denied participation in the regular Democratic party, which controls all levels of government in the state.

The Credentials Committee proposed a compromise that would seat the regular Democrats, provided they signed loyalty oaths, but also would admit two Freedom Democratic leaders as delegates at large. The compromise called for establishment of a committee to see that all delegates to the convention in 1968 be chosen through processes that would not exclude Negroes.

All but three of the regular delegates and the entire Freedom group rejected the compromise.

A spokesman for the Freedom Democrats said the new party would have won in a floor fight, but "massive pressure from the White House" kept the issue from going to the floor of the convention.

Nevertheless, leaders of the party considered Atlantic City a victory and a foot in the door toward national recognition. The group returned to Mississippi and began campaigning for the Democratic ticket. Aaron Henry of Clarksdale, the chairman, has been making speeches in Northern states for President Johnson.

The group is faced with a state court injunction barring it from acting as a party on grounds it does not meet legal requirements. Three of its leaders—Mr. Henry, Mrs. Fannie Lou Hamer of Ruleville and Mrs. Annie Devine of Canton—have been attempting to get on the November ballot as independent candidates for Congressional seats. The State Board of Election Commissioners has turned them down.

The group plans a mock election to run from Oct. 31 to Nov. 3 open to everyone of voting age. The ballot will carry the Democratic and Republican Presidential tickets and the regular and Freedom Democrats for Congressional seats.

"Since 94 per cent of Mississippi's Negroes of voting age are not registered," the party said in a statement, "the Freedom Democratic party can offer only token support for candidates in the regular election. Instead, its efforts will focus on the Freedom group, where anyone can vote."

The mock election is designed to show that most Negroes would vote if they were encouraged to do so and the outcome of the regular election would be "radically different" if they did.

"The party hopes to have more votes cast for its candidates in the Freedom vote than are cast for the opposition candidates in the regular election," the statement said.

This information will be used in the attempt to unseat members of the Mississippi Congressional delegation. If this fails, as it is expected to, the party will then ask the Democratic caucus "to strip all Mississippi Representatives of their seniority."

That maneuver, like the one in Atlantic City last summer, is designed more to attract the attention of the nation to its cause than for practical results.

The Council of Federated Organizations last week announced a "white folks program" to prevent the party from remaining predominantly Negro.

Why the Negro Children March

by Pat Watters

SELMA, ALA.

THE NEGRO BOY of 10 leaned his arms on the pew ahead of him and slid far to the side to get a better view of Dr. Martin Luther King Jr., who was telling the mass meeting: "Sheriffs and troopers over the South have brutalized and beat us . . . Slumbering giants of discontent and even violence threaten to rise up in us . . . But there is another way."

A little girl of no more than 4, seated with her shiny black shoes straight out, stared transfixed as a stray beam from television lights caught and played upon a square of deepest scarlet in one of the church's stained-glass windows, and Dr. King continued: "The tragedy is that the state of Alabama does not believe in the First Amendment." A girl of 13, in a blue coat, her round brown face soft under a high pompadour hairdo, moved and showed the title of the textbook under her arm. It was "Civics."

A boy of 15, hair close-cut, his head in profile lean and long at the rear, narrowed his eyes, and grinned, as Dr. King said with finality: "We will not obey the state's ban on night marches."

The practical course in race-struggle civics there in Brown's Chapel African Methodist Episcopal Church was like many another absorbed by Negro children caught up in the direct-action

From the *New York Times Magazine*, March 21, 1965, copyright © 1965 by The New York Times Company.

movement. Amid such words and the meaning of such a meeting, the presence of the children (and of childhood's own special meaning) there with all the grown-ups always carries its shock of incongruity, and its reminder of a terrible reality. For the meaning of the meeting is not just absorbed by the children; they act upon it.

High-school and college students were, of course, the driving force of the sit-ins and freedom rides. But younger boys and girls, grade-schoolers and occasionally even a preschool tyke, become deeply and actively involved in the kind of campaign Selma has undergone, where all segments of the Negro community are involved in a prolonged siege of demonstrations and mass meetings, day after day, week after week.

The first of this kind of campaign was in Albany, Ga., in 1961 and 1962, and children marched and went to jail then. They were with the marchers last summer in St. Augustine, Fla., when nightly they took bloody beatings from a Klan-led mob. They are in the school strikes and other forms of direct action in the North. In Birmingham, in 1963, the children followed older demonstrators against the fire hoses and police dogs—and the nation was shocked sufficiently to begin action on the Civil Rights Law.

In Selma, the youngsters have demonstrated and also gone to jail; they were among the marchers bloodied by state patrol bludgeoning as they took part in the intensified voter-registration campaign started this year when Dr. King's Southern Christian Leadership Conference joined forces with a 2-year-old outpost of the Student Nonviolent Coordinating Committee.

In one spectacular episode, 165 of them were singled out by Dallas County Sheriff James G. Clark and his "posse" of deputized citizens for a forced march on a country road, two and one-half miles of running and fast walking. Witnesses said the sheriff and his men rode in cars, taking turns getting out to set the fast pace and to force the youngsters along with electric cattle prods and blows from clubs. "God sees you," a 15-year-old boy said to a deputy, and was clubbed in the mouth.

One shudders and knows shame to see the young boys and girls, hand in hand, with tight grins, stepping lightly along with adults who walk more heavily toward the danger and even death of racial confrontations. America has not before seen its worshipped children so engaged in its forms of adult conflict. The spectacle often angers white Southerners; the most moderate elements in Selma condemn use of the children as the worst feature of the campaign. A moderate preacher calls it "sinful."

Are the children exploited, and being taught, as these moderates believe, to hate white people? Or are they, as Dr. King and John Lewis, chairman of S.N.C.C., put it in almost the same words in separate interviews at Selma, being given the opportunity to express creatively their discontent with the injustice that begins at birth? Are the children needlessly exposed at a tender age to physical and psychological danger, or are they rising above an environment and a society that are far more dangerous than the demonstrations to their bodies and minds? How much do they understand of the philosophical and political content of the direct-action movement; how much of their participation is a lark or an outlet for childhood destructiveness?

Interviews with a number of the movement's children in Selma suggest answers to such questions, and suggest also sources of the shame and anger with which they fill adults.

Louis Miller is 12, and in the seventh grade, a light-skinned, large-eyed boy with prominent front teeth. Yes, he said, he had marched. It was on a Friday. "What happened? I got stuck with a cow prod. That's what they did to me. On the leg here." He bent and showed.

Did it hurt? "It hurt a little. It stung. We were getting on the bus, after we were arrested. They said hurry. And used the cow prod."

Was he scared? The only time was when a man started lining them up at the prison camp, "with our noses on each other's shoulders." The man said "he was going to skeet us with water hoses. He said everything, and started cursing. We laughed. And trembled a little, too."

He had been in the movement only three or four weeks, he said. His parents and sisters attended the meetings, too, but hadn't marched. He collects coins, plays football and basketball, and likes history and math in school. He wants to be a doctor. If he must do military service, he wants to be a marine.

He didn't know he was going to march that day until the time came to do it. Then he said to himself he didn't care what his father or his uncle said, he was going to do it. When he finally got out of the prison camp at 10:30 of the night of his arrest, and got home to his family, "they laughed at me." He said it so you knew that it was fond laughter. His sister had told the family where he was; they hadn't been worried.

Why did he march? "For freedom." What is freedom? "To go where you want to go, to do what you want to do, say what you want to say. I think we'll get it."

Would he march again? "I hope to."

Reginald Moton is 10, in the fifth grade, a wiry fellow in a sweat shirt and trousers tattered and splattered from play. He marched, he said, "I think it was the first of February. We stood up and held signs. 'Let our teachers vote.' 'Let us vote.' And then we said our prayers, and went back." What were the prayers? "Each said his own."

Why did he march? "To get my freedom. Freedom means for your mother to get a better job, and for us to get better homes."

Reginald, though he had been assured by a movement official that the interview was "all right," looked frightened and answered reluctantly until the questions were broken off and he was given a real explanation of what they were for. Then he relaxed and talked easily. After the interview, he slipped away, and returned shortly, grinning, with an older boy, his brother, Cliff, 13. "He wants to talk, too," said Reginald.

Cliff was short and dark, and spoke bashfully, looking away, but with good command of his words. He was in the forced march, he said, and was in jail another time when two boys "fell out" in a faint. He was stuck with a cattle prod on a bus going to jail. "It stings—right then."

The forced march made him mad—"but I couldn't do nothing. The leaders told us not to run. But the rest of them were running, so I did. You'd be beat if you didn't." Was he frightened? "No suh."

Why did he march? "Freedom is to be what you want to be. I want my parents to be able to get better jobs. I want them to pay Mama the same as they pay others, when she does the same amount of work. When I grow up, I want to be a carpenter. And be able to vote. I want my children not to have to be in this mess like we are in now."

He said his mother had told him not to march, but that he had done it the first time "because I knew that it was right. The Lord told me it was right." He told his mama this when he got home from jail the first time. He said his mama never said anything that night. But then the next morning "she told me it was all right to march. She had been scared she would lose her job. But she said that was all right. She said go on."

He turned to his little brother. "We'll march again, whenever they want us to."

He never smiled. Not all were so serious, or so eloquent. Martha Griffin, 12, a sixth-grader, wearing a pretty tan jacket with freedom slogans written on it in black ink ("We Want Our Freedom Now" . . . "Jim Clark Must Go"), laughed and said she didn't want to answer questions, but finally agreed to.

"I've marched three or four times. I haven't been in jail but twice." On her last arrest, they took the young people to a former National Guard armory. How were they treated? *"Bad!"* she declared, opening her eyes wide and drawling the word, a way of Southern feminine speech quite familiar, more often associated with the white belle. In the same manner, she went on: "They gave us cookies to eat. We had to sleep on the cement, with no cover. And all those *things* [the guards] around there!"

Would she march again? "I'll be right there. I ain't scared of those old things. Some people are scared of them, but I'm not. They ain't nothing. They stuck my sister in the head with a pole and everything, but I'm not scared of them."

The time the two boys fainted in jail was described in more detail by Morris Jackson, 12, another sixth-grader. It happened at Camp Selma, another prison. He said, "They put us in a room. It was real hot. We were real close together. The two boys fainted and they laid 'em out on the floor." And what then? "They just cursed us." Was he scared? "Yes, sir."

He had been in the movement since it started. (S.N.C.C. first set up operations in Selma in the fall of 1962.) Why did he march? "I wanted my freedom like all the rest of the kids. If they'd let our parents vote and let us come in places, the movement would stop."

David Calhoun, 13, a seventh-grader, also spoke of how important it was for his parents to be able to vote, and how he hoped that some day "black and white will be mixed together, and we will be free to have jobs like white people." Then he added another reason, that he thought it was "fine—not a bad feeling" to be involved in the movement.

"One day," he said, "if I have children, I can tell them all about this that has happened."

Sometimes in jail it can be funny. Linda Blackman, 14, a ninth-grader, described something that made nearly all of the youngsters who mentioned it smile or laugh. "There was one man there at Camp Selma, a guard, who said he was 'Bugger Bear.' A big old man, going around hollering, 'I'm Bugger Bear.'" She got through laughing about this attempt to scare them ("Bugger Bear" is an old Southern equivalent of "bogyman") and about how the attempt underestimated their sophistication. Then she recalled how he had told them they had to line up against the wall and push it, as though they were trying to push it down, and laughed some more. "Bugger Bear!"

She told, too, how on the bus going to the camp, she had called out to the others, "Let's sing. Let's sing 'We Love Everybody.'" She said one of the men stuck her with a cattle prod, "on the coat."

"He said, 'You don't love everybody.' I said, 'Yes I do.'" Then she described how bad the food was, and laughed some at that.

She was one of the few among the girls who would talk about her beliefs about the movement. Things should be, she said, so that "if I was qualified for office and could hold it, I could run for it and they wouldn't hold my color against me . . . When I grow up, you know, I want to be Secretary of State. I had a dream about that. No kidding. My little brother—he's 9—says he wants to be sheriff. He says he wants to take Sheriff Clark's place. Then he'll treat white folks like they treat us."

She smiled about this, and then said: "When Sheriff Clark was in the hospital, I wanted him to get well as soon as possible, because when we demonstrate, he lets the whole world know how bad it is here."

One of the more touching moments of the Selma campaign came when Sheriff Clark was hospitalized with a respiratory ailment and the youngsters marched in the rain and prayed for him at the courthouse, carrying signs: "Get well in body and mind." Andrew Marrisett, 24, an S.C.L.C. staff member who works with the youngsters, said some cheered a little when they first heard of his illness.

"I told them that even though Clark is our enemy and we hate his ways, we do not advocate violence or rejoicing over his being sick. I said, 'I think we should pray for Brother Clark.' I talked to them about Christ crucified, and they said they were willing to march in the rain. They were real enthusiastic about hating what the man does but not hating the man, but loving him as a human being."

He told, too, how when they were coming back from that march, a white lady called out her car window at the youngsters: "You son-of-a-bitches."

The philosophy of nonviolence is in the youngsters, he said. They talk a lot about violence, but in the act of demonstrating, they are organized and disciplined. "They are real good people to work with."

As in other crisis cities, the Selma teen-agers and younger children were organized into a distinct unit during the voter campaign. They held meetings of their own, separate from the adults, and attended "nonviolence workshops." Classes on Negro history, local history and "political education" were being planned.

Leaders emerge from the ranks of the youngsters in such a process. In Selma, Charles Mauldin, a soft-spoken youth of 17, is the newly named president of the student movement. He was described as hard-working and effective at organization and inspiring confidence. After a march, he told the youngsters: "I'm proud of you. I used to wish I was white. Now I wish I was blacker."

A S.N.C.C. veteran said teen-agers are usually the first to join the movement when a civil-rights organizer comes into a town like Selma. They are around—in the Negro ice-cream parlors or bars, on the street corners—some of them free after school, some of them dropouts with nothing but time.

Younger children cluster around a movement headquarters after school, he said, following the teen-agers, curious, eager to be part of something exciting, always willing to do chores, to help out. Likewise, when the civil-rights workers canvass the Negro neighborhoods asking for support, it is the youngsters who are first and most willing to join in. They are free from the concerns that might hold back their parents. The S.N.C.C. spokesman said, "Kids like that just believe in what we're doing."

After the March 7 beating and tear-gassing by the state patrol of the Selma Negroes trying to march to Montgomery, the youth group held a special meeting while adults were trying to decide whether to violate a Federal court order against further marches. They agreed to march regardless of what the adult leaders decided.

A young S.N.C.C. leader talked to them about their decision. They could sing and clap in unison, he said, but if they marched, each had to move on his own, knowing why he did it. Why would they march? For freedom, they answered.

What—deeper than answers to interview questions—are the life, culture, hope and fear of these Selma youngsters, these well-dressed, bright-faced children, many of whom walk in giggling, chattering bunches from the mass meetings to homes in nearby decrepit shacks? (Most of them, as the sociologists tell us, must struggle with such other problems as the tendency of their society to be matriarchal, denigrating the men.) Glimpses into this world behind the interviews came when three of them talked among themselves about questions they had been asked, and about growing up in Selma.

They were older teen-agers: John Henry Suttles, 16, who had told how he was arrested at age 14 for "nothing," and had straightway joined the movement so that the next time it would be for something, and when that came, he had been put in solitary confinement, where you just "sit down every day, and pray every day"; and Bernard Sims, 16, who had said he was hit in the head by a deputy last summer while testing a theater for civil-rights-law compliance, and who admitted that even in something like that, because you could see you were making the sheriff and deputies mad, "it was *fun . . .*"; and William King, 17, who had contributed the opinion that it is not Sheriff Clark who is so brutal, "it's the power behind him, the Citizens' Council and all."

Bernard said he liked the movement, even if it did get pretty rough sometimes. "It proves that we're not scared." Before he got in the movement, he had been scared of white people. "I'd watch those policemen go by the house and my heart would go blap-blap-blap." He hit his chest. "We expect to prove, too," he added, "that our parents aren't scared." And:

"When I marry and have kids, I can look back and tell them about all this. It will make them think their father was quite a man."

He also said, "The whites down here are very hard to understand. If a white boy is with me and he is my age, he wants me to say, 'Yes, sir.' If someone is real old, that's the time to say, 'Yes, sir.' But somebody around 30, it's proper to say yes and no. We're all just human beings."

John and William both recalled how when they were little, they played with white boys. "We'd go to the creek and swim and catch crawfish," John said.

William said that on such an outing, when he was 9, one of the white boys said to him, "I know what you are, William." " 'What?' I asked him. 'What am I?' 'You're a nigger,' he said. I said, 'How you know?' He said, 'My mama told me.'

"That night I asked my daddy. He said, 'That's what we're called.' I said, 'No. No. I'm not. I'm not that.' He said, 'Yes, you are.'

"I cried and carried on. Ever since, I've sort of hated that word. Not sort of—I hate it."

William said he still sees some of those white boys he used to play with, "and they don't even know me."

Two scenes in Selma seem to suggest, if grotesquely, the past and present of the racial struggle. Amid the tension as the youngsters formed their line for a dusk march, all of a sudden a white horse came galloping up the road in front of the church. Riding it was a Negro teen-age boy, wearing an old army coat and a black fur cap, the get-up and his gallop somehow comic. He waved and shouted and laughed as he rode by, and the youngsters laughed back, and he went on out of sight.

Later, in the dark of late night, on a street corner of the downtown area, an old Negro man stood, drunk or demented, howling a wordless song at the top of his voice. He was moving slowly along, shouting the song, and 15 minutes later, a block further on, the inevitable police car stopped and got him. The past which produced him and his song is gone; the laughing youth on his white horse is galloping on.

Where is it taking him? Many whites, apprehensive moderates as well as segregationists, believe or fear that a generation of Negro Americans is being conditioned to hate whites, scorn authority and take the law in their hands. Friends of the movement make the point that such criticism would come better from a society that had not used law and authority to suppress and thwart the previous Negro generations.

The tone of what the Selma youngsters say—an entirely unsparing, unfooled, yet somehow forbearing attitude toward whites —is consistent with attitudes still miraculously found among Negroes across the South. Certainly no one has to indoctrinate Negro youngsters about the injustices and inequities of their lives. And the miracle of their generally nonviolent, mainly constructive, responses can't be expected to last indefinitely.

What of the criticism that it is wrong for children to endure the trauma of demonstrations, the tension, fear and physical and psychological abuse? Dr. Robert Coles of Harvard University, a psychiatrist who has studied Southern Negro youngsters in desegregated schools and the movement for several years, has remarked on how unscathed psychologically they have remained.

He wrote in the winter, 1964, American Scholar the following about youngsters like those in the direct-action movement: "By 7 or 8, most Negro children know the score, and I have seen them draw only faintly disguised pictures of the harsh future awaiting them. Yet such a future can be either harsh and purposeless or harsh but at least with some promise that the pain endured will contribute to the eventual end of its causes."

There are indications that full-time staff workers in the tensions of the Negro movement, many of them in their teens or just out of them, as in Mississippi, have fared less well. Dr. Coles and others have noted the symptoms of combat fatigue among them. Some of them, too, undoubtedly struggle with various other devils —black nationalism, an aimless, perhaps destructive brand of radicalism, and, indeed, hatred of whites, or at least of white society. But the interviews with the Selma youngsters are just one of the many reassurances that such peripheral sicknesses have not attacked the mass of the followers in the movement—certainly not in the South.

Whether they will, whether the dire predictions will come true about the future of today's children of the direct-action movement, still, of course, depends on America's continued ability to improve its racial situation.

The beating of the Selma marchers is one kind of destructive influence. Another might be found in an investigation of the condition today of the Negro youngsters who marched in other cities —St. Augustine, Birmingham, Albany. It would show, despite the Civil Rights Act and the War on Poverty, and because of a failure so far of the Negro movement to consolidate all its gains, something less than what the children dream of when they march.

The nation and the Negro movement, in this, confront the same question. It is the ancient one that the bravery and the belief of children raise: Can we live up to them?

Meanwhile, in Selma, at a youth meeting that was discussing whether to try to march again to Montgomery, a boy cried out: "We're going, and nothing can stop us," and the rest of the boys and girls picked it up and chanted over and over, louder and louder: "Nothing. Nothing. Nothing. . . ."

"The Wonder Is There Have Been So Few Riots"

by Kenneth B. Clark

IT IS ONE measure of the depth and insidiousness of American racism that the nation ignores the rage of the rejected—until it explodes in Watts or Harlem. The wonder is that there have been so few riots, that Negroes generally are law-abiding in a world where the law itself has seemed an enemy.

To call for reason and moderation, to charge rioters with blocking the momentum of the civil-rights movement, to punish rioters by threatening withdrawal of white support for civil rights may indeed ease the fears of whites and restore confidence that a firm stern hand is enforcing order.

But the rejected Negro in the ghetto is deaf to such moral appeals. They only reinforce his despair that whites do not consider equal rights for Negroes to be their due as human beings and American citizens but as rewards to be given for good behavior, to be withheld for misbehavior. The difficulty which the average American of goodwill—white or Negro—has in seeing this as a form of racist condescension is another disturbing symptom of the complexities of racism in the United States.

It is not possible for even the most responsible Negro leaders

From the *New York Times Magazine*, September 5, 1965, copyright © 1965 by The New York Times Company.

to control the Negro masses once pent-up anger and total despair are unleashed by a thoughtless or brutal act. The prisoners of the ghetto riot without reason, without organization and without leadership, as this is generally understood. The rioting is in itself a repudiation of leadership. It is the expression of the anarchy of the profoundly alienated.

In a deeper sense such anarchy could even be a subconscious or conscious invitation to self-destruction. At the height of the Harlem riots of 1964, young Negroes could be heard to say, "If I don't get killed tonight, I'll come back tomorrow." There is evidence these outbreaks are suicidal, reflecting the ultimate in self-negation, self-rejection and hopelessness.

It was the Negro ghetto in Los Angeles which Negroes looted and burned, not the white community. When white firemen tried to enter the ghetto, they were barred by Negro snipers. Many looters did not take the trouble to avoid injury, and many were badly cut in the looting orgy. So one cannot help but wonder whether a desire for self-destruction was not a subconscious factor. Of the 36 people killed in the Los Angeles riot, 33 were Negroes, killed in the campaign to restore law and order. The fact of their deaths—the senseless deaths of human beings—has been obscured by our respectable middle-class preoccupation with the wanton destruction of property, the vandalism and the looting.

Appeals to reason are understandable: they reflect the sense of responsibility of Governmental and civil-rights leaders. But they certainly do not take into account the fact that one cannot expect individuals who have been systematically excluded from the privileges of middle-class life to view themselves as middle class or to behave in terms of middle-class values. Those who despair in the ghetto follow their own laws—generally the laws of unreason. And though these laws are not in themselves moral, they have moral consequences and moral causes.

The inmates of the ghetto have no realistic stake in respecting property because in a basic sense they do not possess it. They are possessed by it. Property is, rather, an instrument for perpetuation of their own exploitation. Stores in the ghetto—which they rarely own—overcharge for inferior goods. They may obtain the symbols of America's vaunted high standard of living—radios, TV's, washing machines, refrigerators—but usually only through usurious carrying costs, one more symbol of the pattern of material exploitation. They do not respect property because property is almost invariably used to degrade them.

James Bryant Conant and others have warned America it is no longer possible to confine hundreds of thousands of undereducated, underemployed, purposeless young people and adults in an affluent America without storing up social dynamite. The dark ghettos now represent a nuclear stockpile which can annihilate the very foundations of America. And if, as a minority, desperate Negroes are not able to "win over" the majority, they can nevertheless effectively undermine what they cannot win.

A small minority of Negroes can do this. Such warnings are generally ignored during the interludes of apparent quiescence and tend to be violently rejected, particularly when they come from whites, at the time of a Negro revolt.

When Senator Robert Kennedy incisively observed, after Watts, "There is no point in telling Negroes to observe the law. . . . It has almost always been used against [them]," it was described by an individual who took the trouble to write a letter to The New York Times as an irresponsible incitement to violence. The bedeviling fact remains, however, that as long as institutionalized forms of American racism persist, violent eruptions will continue to occur in the Negro ghettos. As Senator Kennedy warned: "All these places—Harlem, Watts, South Side—are riots waiting to happen."

When they do happen, the oversimplified term "police brutality" will be heard, but the relationship between police and residents of the ghetto is more complicated than that. Unquestionably, police brutality occurs. In the panic probably stemming from deep and complex forms of racism, inexperienced policemen have injured or killed Negroes or Puerto Ricans or other members of a powerless minority. And it is certainly true that a common denominator of most, if not all, the riots of the past two summers has been some incident involving the police, an incident which the larger society views as trivial but which prisoners of the ghetto interpret as cruel and humiliating.

In spite of the exacerbating frequency of police racism, however, the more pertinent cause of the ghetto's contempt for police is the role they are believed to play in crime and corruption within the ghetto—accepting bribes for winking at illegal activities which thrive in the ghetto. The police, rightly or wrongly, are viewed not only as significant agents in exploiting ghetto residents but also as symbols of the pathology which encompasses the ghetto. They are seen matter-of-factly as adversaries as well as burdens. The more privileged society may decide that respect for law and order is essential for its own survival, but in the dark ghettos, survival often depends on disrespect for the law as Negroes experience it.

Thus the problem will not be solved merely by reducing the frequency of police brutality or by increasing the number of Negro policemen. It will require major reorganization and reeducation of the police and a major reorganization of the ghetto itself. To say as Police Chief William Parker did of the Los Angeles Negroes, "We are on top and they are on the bottom," is to prove to Negroes that their deep fears and hatred of established law and order are justified.

While the riots cannot be understood by attempts to excuse them, neither can they be understood by deploring them—especially by deploring them according to a double standard of social morality. For while the lawlessness of white segregationists and rebellious Negroes are expressions of deep frustrations and chronic racism, the lawlessness of Negroes is usually considered a reflection on all Negroes and countered by the full force of police and other governmental authority, but the lawlessness of whites is seen as the primitive reactions of a small group of unstable individuals and is frequently ignored by the police—when they are not themselves accessories. Moreover, rarely do the leaders of a white community in which white violence occurs publicly condemn even the known perpetrators, while almost invariably national and local Negro leaders are required to condemn the mob violence of Negroes.

As long as these double standards of social morality prevail, they reflect the forms of accepted racism which are the embers of potential violence on the part of both Negroes and whites. And it should be obvious also, although it does not appear to be, that the violence of the Negro is the violence of the oppressed while the violence of white segregationists seeks to maintain oppression.

It is significant that the recent eruptions in Negro communities have not occurred in areas dominated by more flagrant forms of racism, by the Klan and the other institutions of Southern bigotry.

They have occurred precisely in those communities where whites have prided themselves on their liberal approach to matters of race and in those states having strong laws prescribing equal opportunity, fair employment and allegedly open housing. (Some observers see a relationship between the defeat of the open housing referendum in California and the Los Angeles outbreak, but it would seem misleading to attempt to account for the riot by any single factor.)

It is revealing to hear the stunned reaction of some top political officials in Los Angeles and California who are unable to understand that such a thing could happen in Los Angeles. Here, they said, whites and blacks got along fine together; here, as reporters constantly pointed out, ghetto streets are lined with palm trees, some with private homes surrounded by tended lawns.

Americans are accustomed to judging the state of people's minds by the most visible aspects—the presence of a TV antenna indicates affluence and a neat lawn a middle-class home. The fact is a ghetto takes on the physical appearance of the particular city—in New York, rat-infested tenements and dirty streets; in Los Angeles, small homes with palm trees—but in many a small home live numerous families and in every house live segregated, desperate people with no jobs or servile jobs, little education, broken families, delinquency, drug addiction, and a burning rage at a society that excludes them from the things it values most.

It is probably not by chance that the Federal Civil Rights Act of 1964 and the Voting Rights Act of 1965 were followed by violence in the North. This was important legislation, but it was more relevant to the predicament of the Southern Negro than to Negroes in Northern ghettos.

It may well be that the channeling of energies of Negroes in Southern communities toward eliminating the more vicious and obvious signs of racism precludes temporarily the dissipation of energy in random violence. The Northern Negro is clearly not suffering from a lack of laws. But he is suffering—rejected, segregated, discriminated against in employment, in housing, his children subjugated in *de facto* segregated and inferior schools in spite of a plethora of laws that imply the contrary.

He has been told of great progress in civil rights during the past 10 years and proof of this progress is offered in terms of

Supreme Court decisions and civil-rights legislation and firm Presidential commitment. But he sees no positive changes in his day-to-day life. The very verbalizations of progress contribute to his frustration and rage. He is suffering from a pervasive, insensitive and at times self-righteous form of American racism that does not understand the depth of his need.

Not the civil-rights leaders who urge him to demonstrate, but the whites who urge him not to "in the light of present progress" contribute to the anger which explodes in sudden fury. He is told by liberal whites *they* contribute to civil rights causes, *they* marched to Washington and journeyed to Selma and Montgomery to demonstrate their commitment to racial justice and equality.

But Negroes see only the continuing decay of their homes, many of them owned by liberal whites. He sees he does not own any of the means of production, distribution and sale of goods he must purchase to live. He sees his children subjected to criminally inefficient education in public schools they are required to attend, and which are often administered and staffed by liberal whites. He sees liberal labor unions which either exclude him, accept him in token numbers or, even when they do accept him en masse, exclude him from leadership or policy-making roles.

And he sees that persistent protest in the face of racism which dominates his life and shackles him within the ghetto may be interpreted by his white friends as a sign of his insatiability, his irrationality and, above all, of his ingratitude. And because this interpretation comes from his friends and allies it is much harder to take psychologically than the clear-cut bigotry of open segregationists.

It is precisely at this point in the development of race relations that the complexities, depth and intensity of American racism reveal themselves with excruciating clarity. At this point regional differences disappear. The greatest danger is an intensification of racism leading to the polarization of America into white and black. "What do they *want?*" the white man asks. "Don't they know they hurt their own cause?" "Get Whitey," cries the Negro. "Burn, baby, burn." At this point concerned whites and Negroes are required to face the extent of personal damage which racism has inflicted on both.

It will require from whites more than financial contributions to civil-rights agencies, more than mere verbal and intellectual support for the cause of justice. It will require compassion, willingness to accept hostility and increased resolve to go about the common business, the transformation and strengthening of our society toward the point where race and color are no longer relevant in discussing the opportunities, rights and responsibilities of Americans.

Negroes, too, are confronted with difficult challenges in the present stage of the civil-rights struggle. The bitterness and rage which formed the basis for the protests against flagrant racial injustices must somehow be channeled into constructive, nondramatic programs required to translate court decisions, legislation and growing political power into actual changes in the living conditions of the masses of Negroes. Some ways must be found whereby Negro leadership and Negro organizations can redirect the volatile emotions of Negroes away from wasteful, sporadic outbursts and toward self-help and constructive social action. The need for candid communication between middle-class Negroes and the Negro masses is as imperative as the need for painful honesty and cooperation between Negroes and whites.

These demands upon whites and Negroes will not be easy to meet since it is difficult, if not impossible, for anyone growing up in America to escape some form of racist contamination. And a most disturbing fact is the tendency of racism to perpetuate itself, to resist even the most stark imperatives for change. This is the contemporary crisis in race relations which Americans must somehow find strength to face and solve. Otherwise we will remain the victims of capricious and destructive racial animosities and riots.

The key danger is the possibility that America has permitted the cancer of racism to spread so far that present available remedies can be only palliative. One must, however, continue to believe and act on the assumption that the disease is remediable.

It is important that all three branches of the Federal Government have committed themselves to using their power to improve the status of Negroes. These commitments must be enforced despite overt or subtle attempts to resist and evade them.

But this resistance must be seen not only in the bigotry of segregationists. It must be recognized in the moralizing of Northern whites who do not consciously feel themselves afflicted with the disease of racism, even as they assert that Negro rioting justifies ending their involvement in the civil-rights cause. It must be recognized in the insistence that Negroes pull themselves up by their own bootstraps, demonstrating to the liberal and white communities they have earned the right to be treated as equal American citizens. These are satisfying, self-righteous arguments but they cannot disguise the profound realities of an unacknowledged racism.

If it is possible to talk of any value emerging from the riots it would be this: They are signals of distress, an SOS from the ghetto. They also provide the basis for therapeutically ventilating deeply repressed feelings of whites and Negroes—their underlying fear and the primitive sense of race.

In the religiously oriented, nonviolent civil rights movement in the South, courteous, neatly dressed Negroes carrying books fitted into the middle-class white image more adequately than the vulgar whites who harassed them. The middle-class white, therefore, identified with the oppressed, not the oppressor. But empathy given as a reward for respectable behavior has little value. Understanding can only be tested when one's own interests are deeply threatened, one's sensibilities violated.

These feelings of hostility must be exposed to cold reality as the prelude to realistic programs for change. If under the warmth of apparent support for civil rights lies a deeply repressed prejudice, no realistic social change can be effective.

It would be unrealistic, of course, to expect the masses of whites and Negroes who have grown up in an essentially racist society suddenly to love one another. Fortunately, love is not a prerequisite for the social reorganization now demanded. Love has not been necessary to create workable living arrangements among other ethnic groups in our society. It is no more relevant to ask Negroes and whites to love each other than to ask Italians and Irish to do the same as a prerequisite for social peace and justice.

Nevertheless, real changes in the predicament of previously rejected Negroes—changes compatible with a stable and decent society—must be made, and soon.

The Negro must be included within the economy at all levels of employment, thereby providing the basis for a sound family life and an opportunity to have an actual stake in American business and property.

The social organization of our educational system must be transformed so Negroes can be taught in schools which do not reinforce their feeling of inferiority. The reorganization, improvement and integration of our public schools is also necessary in order to re-educate white children and prepare them to live in the present and future world of racial diversity.

The conditions under which Negroes live must be improved—bad housing, infant mortality and disease, delinquency, drug addiction must be drastically reduced.

Until these minimum goals are achieved, Americans must accept the fact that we cannot expect to maintain racial ghettos without paying a high price. If it is possible for Americans to carry out realistic programs to change the lives of human beings now confined within their ghettos, the ghetto will be destroyed rationally, by plan, and not by random self-destructive forces. Only then will American society not remain at the mercy of primitive, frightening, irrational attempts by prisoners in the ghetto to destroy their own prison.

After Watts—
Where Is the Negro
Revolution Headed?

by C. Vann Woodward

IN JUDGING THE progress of a revolution, much depends on
whether the bottle is seen as half full or half empty; whether one
concentrates on what has been done or on what remains to be
done. From the Negro's point of view, a good deal depends on his
class and region. It matters whether one belongs to the small urban
middle class pictured in Ebony or the poverty-locked mass in
Mississippi or Harlem or Watts; whether one is Southern and
senses tangible advances from a low starting point, or non-
Southern and disillusioned with gains yet to be achieved down
South.

The mass of recent Federal legislation on civil rights has been
directed primarily at conditions in the South—at racial discrimination in public schools, public accommodations and voting
rights. Insofar as Federal laws are capable of coping with these
knotty problems, Congress has just about fulfilled its role.

The result is one of the most impressive achievements in Congressional history. Within the past year, under Administration
pressure, Congress has put more teeth in the law and more law

on the books than it has in the whole period since 1875. It was as if the first Reconstruction had been endowed with the 14th and 15th Amendments, the Reconstruction Acts, the Freedmen's Bureau, the Civil Rights Acts and the Ku Klux Klan Act by one session of Congress. The Civil Rights Act of July, 1964, was the great breakthrough, and the new Voting Rights Act rounds out the remarkable year.

It remains to be seen how effective the new laws will be. Compliance with public-accommodation provisions has been surprisingly prompt, though less than complete, in Southern cities. In public-school desegregation and voting rights the prospects are less clear. Much of the progress will have to come in the Deep South where the going is rough. Given the ingenuity at evasion and delay displayed in the past, school desegregation may tend to be an expansion of tokenism and voter registration to be less than sensational.

Granting the limited character of these gains, optimists point out that in absolute terms the last two decades witnessed the most rapid advance of Negro Americans since emancipation. Much of this progress had nothing directly to do with the Negro revolution. It was the product of an expanding economy and the mass migration of Negroes from the rural South to the cities, North and South. The newcomers shared to some extent at least the relatively higher urban standards of living, health and education.

The gains are registered in numbers of high-school and college graduates, in expanding opportunities for those few qualified for professional and clerical jobs, in purchasing power, savings accounts and insurance policies. In politics, the new status is evident in the appointment of scores of Negroes to high-level Federal posts, as well as their capture of more than 280 elective offices, including six Congressmen and 90-odd state legislators— 10 of them in Georgia.

In view of all these gains, why the mounting Negro impatience, bitterness and anger; the slogan that yesterday was too late and the atmosphere that leads to such insane explosions of violence as that on the West Coast? One reason is that many of these gains are limited to a very small class. Another is that they are measured in absolute, not relative, terms. The important difference is that the Negro is now measuring his advance, not by what he once *was,* but by what the white man now *is;* not by outgrown scarcity, but by surrounding abundance; not by old expectations, but by new possibilities.

For all his gains, the Negro has not begun to close the gap between the races in many areas and he sees it widening in several. He therefore feels himself to be losing out, not only in comparison with other Americans but with the emerging African nations. Northern and Western Negroes even feel at times they are losing out in comparison with Southern Negroes, who get the bulk of attention, enjoy greater relative gains and take key positions of leadership.

The discontented point to several ugly paradoxes that have accompanied progress in civil rights. The inch-by-inch retreat of *de jure* segregation in Southern schools has been ironically paralleled elsewhere (and in parts of the South as well) by a rapid advance of *de facto* segregation of schools. The exploding population of urban Negro ghettos and the white stand on the neighborhood-school principle largely account for this. Racial "imbalance" and "resegregation" are growing, not declining, features of urban schools. The result is that Negroes now have less contact with whites in schools than they did a generation ago, and that more Negroes are attending *de facto* segregated schools now than when the Supreme Court handed down its schools decision in 1954.

Another paradox of progress is that the Negro's rise in legal and social status has been accompanied by an increase in residential segregation in American cities to peak levels. It is now painfully clear that the late President Kennedy's Executive order against housing discrimination has proved ineffective. In fact Federal public-housing and urban-renewal programs have often enhanced the trend to segregation. State laws and private action have not made substantial progress in this field. Segregated housing is deeply rooted in our society, is still spreading and seems destined to remain with us for the foreseeable future. The relation of this type of segregation to problems of the school, the slum and economic opportunity endows housing with a wide significance.

Even more difficult to reconcile with optimistic assessments of the Negro revolution is the Negro's current economic plight and prospects. According to Herbert Hill of the N.A.A.C.P., "the great mass of Negroes, especially in the urban centers, are locked in a permanent condition of poverty." Since 1951 the gap between the median incomes of white and Negro workers has been widening. Automation was wiping out some 40,000 unskilled and semi-skilled jobs in a week in 1964, and since Negro workers are disproportionately employed in such jobs they are bearing the brunt of technological displacement.

The unemployment gap between races has been growing. The Labor Department reported that Negroes constituted 20.6 per cent of the unemployed last year, though they accounted for only 10 per cent of the population. They are effectively excluded from key industries by traditional racial discrimination within organized labor. Prof. Thomas F. Pettigrew of Harvard estimates that at the rate of employment gains from 1950 to 1960, Negroes would not arrive at a proportional representation among clerical workers until the year 1992, among skilled workers until 2005, among professionals until 2017 and among business managers and proprietors until 2730 A.D.

Few Negro spokesmen any longer accept the idea that removal of artificial barriers of racial privilege and discrimination would result in the integration of the Negro in American life. They impatiently reject the suggestion that with the guarantee of civil rights their experience will repeat that of various European ethnic groups who made their way up the social ladder from lowly immigrant beginnings in previous generations. They point out with some asperity that the analogy is lacking in realism.

There is a growing conviction that civil rights alone are not enough, that the movement has outgrown this demand and that the phrase "civil rights" is itself a misleading description of the movement. As important as they are, and as far from full realization, civil rights and desegregation—so many feel—are not the way to full equality. Even in complete possession of his civil rights, the Negro would still face automation, urban decay, family deterioration, entrapment in slums and *de facto* segregation in schools. These are social and economic failures that transcend racial injustice and minority grievances. They call for more drastic remedies, and there are doubts among the more radical leaders that such remedies can be found within existing political and economic institutions.

No two revolutions are alike and none is wholly rational. This one has some remarkable peculiarities. No movement is a revolution in the classical sense that derives overt support from the established government, that strives to realize rather than destroy traditional values, that seeks to join rather than overthrow the social order.

The movement has had its apostles of violence and its violent upheavals, but so far this revolution has been mainly nonviolent, predominantly conservative and not wholly Negro.

Nevertheless, it does share some attributes of the classical type of revolution. One of these is that it feeds on hope, not despair. Another is that the closer it approaches its goals, the more intolerant it is of frustration—and the more inclined it is to raise its sights and expand its goals. It responds radically to a widening gap between rising aspirations and actual achievements.

Whatever their differences, Negro leaders are generally agreed that their revolution has reached a turning point, but they are not agreed on which way it should turn. The spectrum of opinion runs from radical right to ultra left. In the center, occupied by the N.A.A.C.P. and the National Urban League, there is public adherence to traditional goals of wider opportunity through legal action and pressure for full rights through existing institutions. Martin Luther King, striving to maintain a viable leadership of factions from center to the left, keeps his organization in working contact with the liberal establishment, but talks of boycott weapons and more and better Selmas. On the radical right, the black nationalists continue to reject all integration with "white devils" and seek to build black middle-class enclaves.

Innovation comes mainly from the left. So far, little effective impact is being made by organized Communists with allegiance to Moscow, Peking or Havana. The old Communists have declined to a new low in numbers, and the "Trots," the Maoists, and the W. E. B. Du Bois Clubs are even weaker. Some of them have infiltrated the Negro movement, but their influence is minimal. Ex-Communists and fellow travelers of the thirties—or their children—usually regard all Communists as "progressive," any criticism of them as "Red-baiting" and reject the idea of alliances with liberals, organized labor or any established forces of society. Their significance is also marginal.

More important are the radicals variously known as the Young, Student or Spontaneous Left. They are unorganized and difficult to define. They pride themselves on their militancy, their intransigence and their refusal to compromise. Their heart is in Mississippi or Harlem, not in Moscow or Peking, but they often profess a profound alienation from American society, refuse to ally themselves with labor, liberals, and church groups, reject established civil-rights leaders and despair of established institutions generally. They proclaim no specific program but hint at a coming upheaval of black and white oppressed people against the whole society and speak darkly of guerrilla tactics.

As it impinges on the Negro movement, the Spontaneous Left is perhaps best exemplified by the Student Nonviolent Coordinating Committee. S.N.C.C. has its authentic martyrs and the prestige of bloody frontline encounters with sheriffs, state troopers and Klansmen. Its workers are predominantly Negro and they address themselves to the grass roots, to "the little people." They not only shun liberals and labor and the establishment in all its guises, but the Negro middle class as well. They scorn "image" talk and decline to discuss Communist infiltration.

They have worked mainly in the Black Belt at the community level among Negroes of the most impoverished, deprived and disfranchised classes. There is more than a touch of agrarian romanticism in their rebellion against "the system." "The movement's strength," writes Tom Hayden, one of their leaders, "comes from the humanism of rural people who are immune to the ravages of competitive society." They fight automation as well as bureaucracy.

S.N.C.C. appeals less to rational self-interest based on material needs, such as liberals and Marxists stress, than to psychological deprivations, needs for expression, recognition and fellowship. Its workers insist they have not come to impose leadership or dictate programs. They have none themselves. They seek only to allow the voiceless to find their voice, the apathetic to discover their power, to express their own needs in their own way and demand participation in all decisions affecting themselves. (Students for a Democratic Society, also of the Spontaneous Left, apply much the same approach in the urban slums of the North.)

By means of freedom schools, cooperatives and people's conventions, S.N.C.C. encourages the deprived to assert themselves. Their hope is that the spirit engendered will spread and eventually work a revolutionary regeneration in American society.

Most of the great movements of social protest in American history, movements such as the anti-slavery crusade or the agrarian revolt, have not been able to find full expression in the major political parties. Their left wings have eventually found partial or temporary outlets in third parties such as the Liberty party and the Populist party. One candidate for this role in the Negro revolution is the Mississippi Freedom Democratic party, a movement that owes much of its inspiration to S.N.C.C.

The M.F.D.P. burst dramatically upon the national scene last summer at the Democratic National Convention in Atlantic City. Its delegates, including Aaron Henry and Fannie Lou Hamer, demanded equal treatment with the white delegation on the ground that Negroes were deprived of the ballot. They refused the offer of two "honorary" seats as tokenism. Their posture then was that they were more loyal to Johnson and his program than were the "regularly" elected white-supremacy delegation. Today, the prospects of the Freedom Democrats keeping the peace with Johnson and gaining full acceptance in the regular party are not good. Nor are the prospects of their drive to unseat the Congressmen from Mississippi. One alternative is a third-party revolt.

The Freedom Democrats are spreading out into other states and hoping their movement will catch on like wildfire. The odds are against them. They appeal to the historical precedent of Populism and strive for an interracial alliance of the oppressed like that of the nineties. But their appeal to the poor whites has generally met with rebuff in the South.

Furthermore, the demographic base of the movement is shrinking as the Cotton Belt shrinks and the automation of cotton-growing displaces pickers and choppers. Last year, 81 per cent of the cotton in the Mississippi Delta region was harvested by machine, compared with 27 per cent in 1958. Seventy-four per cent of Negro Americans now live in cities, and rural Negroes are fewer every year. Agrarian radicalism in the Negro revolution is in some measure a revolt of the past against the future.

Negro leaders of more maturity and experience, including some on the left, are critical of the Young Left for its lack of realism and what they call its "no-win" philosophy. They point out that a minority consisting of a mere 10 per cent of the population that spurns all allies is really preaching despair and defeatism. These critics of the Young Left share its belief in a radical refashioning of the economy and an all-out attack on poverty, slums and unemployment. But they seek coalitions and adhere to democratic processes as the only hope of a disadvantaged minority.

The most articulate spokesman of this growing school is Bayard Rustin, who organized the March on Washington in 1963. Rustin believes that the civil-rights struggle is "evolving from a protest movement into a full-fledged social movement," and declares flatly, "We need white allies." He calls for a "coalition of progressive forces which becomes the *effective* political majority in the United States." He would include trade unionists, liberals and religious groups, and such elements as staged the March on Washington and passed the Civil Rghts Act of 1964 and the Voting Rights Act of 1965. He is ready to compromise and make concessions to win larger concessions and believes that the leader who declines to do so "reveals not his purity, but his lack of political sense."

Rustin and his followers do not, like the Young Left, dismiss the Civil Rights Act as an "opiate." They regard it as a necessary prologue to a new phase of action. They point out that the most serious problems confronting the Negro are no longer civil-rights problems but economic and social problems—mainly in employment, housing and education. They call for a massive attack on poverty with budgets of wartime proportions, a war that might cost $100 billion. Among their proposals are $5 billion a year for the elimination of slums and the creation of jobs, a minimum wage of $2 per hour, repeal of Section 14b of the Taft-Hartley Act that permits state right-to-work laws, and full implementation and expansion of the Economic Opportunity Act.

Along with these demands they would continue to push programs more specifically concerned with Negroes, such as voter registration and the campaign against police brutality. But they strive to find national policies that will benefit and attract the support of labor, liberals and the white dispossessed as well.

Martin Luther King has in recent speeches given voice to more and more of this program. He chose Rustin to head a week's training school held in Atlanta for some 600 students recruited in the North for his summer project called SCOPE—Summer Community Organization and Political Education. The students are working in 60 counties in six states and stressing voter registration. This marks a departure for King's organization, which has been accused of lacking a grass-roots program.

The work of SCOPE is similar to that headed by S.N.C.C. in Mississippi last summer—but with notable differences. The volunteers are more conventionally dressed, relatively beardless and indoctrinated in a "friendly" approach. They will not shun, but will work with, local church, school and labor organization. Dr. King is very much a church man and would agree with his lieutenant Wyatt Tee Walker that "whatever you want to do in the Negro community . . . you've got to do it through the Negro church, or it doesn't get done." The political education that the volunteers conduct is calculated to stimulate participation in the established political parties—not in the Freedom Democratic party.

The success of the King-Rustin strategy of working through established local institutions and the existing political structure depends on many things. If Lyndon Johnson continues his strong support for his domestic program; if the liberal consensus sustaining it does not deteriorate over foreign issues; if the executive, legislative and judicial branches continue to work in harmony; and if the business community responds with enough concessions to prevent social dislocation, then there is reasonable hope for a peaceful absorption of the Negro revolution and the substantial realization of its goals.

The future American society envisaged in the Negro revolution will differ from the present in more ways than in providing full equality for the Negro. In order to achieve that equality, Negroes maintain that social, economic and political changes will have to be made that will affect the whole society profoundly. Already, they point out, the civil-rights phase of the revolution has acted as a powerful social catalyst. It has touched off the campaign against poverty, inspired attacks on urban decay, delinquency and unemployment, and provoked a reassessment of our whole public-school system. Further impact on established institutions and their failings is to be expected.

In the years ahead, several changes in the movement seem probable. Protest will continue, perhaps intensify, but unless the movement disintegrates in explosions of big-city slum insurrection, the trend will be, as Rustin suggests, from protest to politics.

As civil rights diminish in importance, the shift from status politics to economic politics will increase. Changes in tactics will accompany changes in objectives—sit-ins and picketing will give way to boycotts and rent strikes, for example. Housing discrimination and school imbalance will be much slower to yield ground than discrimination in public accommodations or even jobs. Lower-income Negroes, never vitally concerned over access to restaurants, theaters or golf courses, are likely to become more active participants in the revolution as the emphasis shifts to minimum-wage laws, job opportunities and rent strikes.

The drift to the left is already apparent and may become stronger. But it is likely to take several forms and adopt no one ideology. The radical populism astir in the Black Belt will intensify, though with poor prospects of national significance or of white converts. Coalition with whites comes easier in Piedmont Region cities, though the whites are more likely to be upper class than lower (the pattern of interracial alliance in the urban North is another thing again). Pluralism is likely to be as strongly characteristic of the politics as it was of the protest phase of the Negro revolution. In the future, it is likely to become more difficult for all leaders to compose their differences on ceremonial occasions.

Resistance and reversals should not be underestimated. The poor showing of Barry Goldwater in 1964 was no real measure of the white backlash. A truer indicator was the two-to-one vote for Proposition 14 against fair housing in California. And the Los Angeles explosion can only be expected to intensify racial animosity. More trouble may be expected when and if fair-employment enforcement really begins to tell against traditional trade-union discrimination and the better jobs cease to be a white monopoly. More violence is likely in the cities—and it need not all originate in the ghettos. The Deacons for Defense and Justice, a semi-secret Negro organization armed for self-defense, has spread from Louisiana into Mississippi and Alabama and plans to expand throughout the South.

Troubles may also be expected within the Negro community. No revolution can sustain zeal and idealism indefinitely, and a decade of continuous high-pitched emotion has put a strain on most revolutions in the past. A. Philip Randolph recently expressed concern over a "crisis of relaxation" in the movement and deplored what he regarded as "a tendency of the civil-rights revolution to lapse into a state of relaxation, as shown by a loss in membership and a deficit financial condition of civil-rights organizations." The Negro community is divided by lines of class and region and temperament, and some elements are prone to be more quickly satisfied or bored or disenchanted than others.

After the recent eruption of violence and bloodshed in California, no one can dismiss the danger of lawlessness and social dislocation. But the greatest danger that faces America in the Negro revolution is not violence in the streets or infiltration by subversives or escalation of Negro demands and hopes. The real danger is that an opportunity that came once in a century—that never really came before—may be passed up by default, dissipated by neglect, tragically missed. So far there is little evidence that white America, or for that matter the mass of black America either, has any real conception of the changes in their society that will be necessary to forestall that danger.

Part 2

THE ASCENDANCY
OF BLACK POWER

IF THE SPIRIT of redemptive love seemed to characterize black protest during the first half of the decade, a spirit of rage seemed to be the hallmark of the second. Psychiatrist Alvin F. Poussaint's article explains some of the psychological mechanisms that helped to set the stage for the nationalist militancy of the latter 1960's. No organization better exemplified the history of this transition than did SNCC, a story told in the essay by Gene Roberts.

Black power assumed many forms, some of which are illustrated in this book. A reformist version of black power is to be seen in Charles V. Hamilton's essay on the subject. One effort to secure local black community control over an important institution within it is described in the article on the Ocean Hill–Brownsville experiment in school decentralization. A treatment of a revolutionary version of black power is to be seen in Sol Stern's description of the Black Panthers, written about a year after the organization was founded. A striking manifestation of the new mood was the rebelliousness of Black students on college and university campuses, a theme which is illustrated here by Ernest Dunbar, "The Black Studies Thing."

Yet many civil rights leaders—including many of the former direct-actionists—remained wedded to their older philosophy. This was true even among some who had been active in SNCC, as Paul Good's article about John Lewis, a former chairman of SNCC, demonstrates.

Martin Luther King, at the time he was assassinated, was planning a Poor People's Campaign in Washington, D.C., for the summer of 1968—an attempt to use the techniques of nonviolent direct action to attack the problem of poverty; and his successor, Ralph Abernathy, basically carried on in King's tradition. (See Jose Yglesias, "Dr. King's March on Washington, Part II,"and Paul Good,' " 'No Man Can Fill Dr. King's Shoes'—But Abernathy Tries.") The articles by Walter Rugaber on the black Mississippi leader Charles Evers, and by Martin Arnold on the NAACP executive director Roy Wilkins, illustrate the stability of the NAACP's strength and program into the early 1970's. The final article, on the long-time activist, CORE founder, and former pacifist Bayard Rustin, describes how this important figure, who for years acted in the interstices of the movement rather than as an organizational leader, until his death played an important role even though the nature of the black protest movement has changed so much.

A Negro Psychiatrist
Explains the Negro Psyche

by Alvin F. Poussaint

IN RECENT YEARS social scientists have come to attribute many of the Negro's social and psychological ills to his self-hatred and resultant self-destructive impulses. Slums, high crime rates, alcoholism, drug addiction, illegitimacy and other social deviations have all been attributed in part to the Negroes' acting out of their feelings of inferiority. Many behavioral scientists have suggested that the recent urban Negro riots are a manifestation of subconscious self-destructive forces in black people stemming from this chronic feeling of self-denigration. Noted psychologist Dr. Kenneth B. Clark has even speculated that these riots are a form of "community suicide" that expresses the ultimate in self-negation, self-rejection and hopelessness.

Given the self-hatred thesis, it is not surprising that many people, both white and Negro, champion programs intended to generate a positive self-image in the Negro "masses" as a panacea for all black social problems: "Teach Negro history and our African heritage in the schools so those cats won't be ashamed of being black!" A Negro friend says, "Help those boys develop pride in being black and the riots will stop."

The self-hatred thesis appeals on the one hand to racists, who reason that if Negroes develop enough "self-love" they might wish to remain complacently segregated and stop trying to "mongrelize" the white society, and on the other to Negro militants, including the Black Muslims and Black Power advocates, who scream from soapboxes, "We must undo the centuries-old brainwashing by the white man that has made us hate ourselves. We must stop being ashamed of being black and stop wanting to be white!" There is also talk of building a Negro subculture based on "a positive sense of identity." Some militant Negroes seek too boost their self-esteem by legitimizing being black. Last year after a sit-in demonstration in Mississippi, a Negro civil-rights worker said to me: "White racism has made me hate white people and hate myself and my brothers. I ain't about to stop hating white folks, but I'm not gonna let that self-hatred stuff mess me up any more!"

No one denies that many Negroes have feelings of self-hatred. But the limitations of the thesis became apparent when one realizes that a Negro with all the self-love and self-confidence in the world could not express it in a system that is so brutally and unstintingly suppressive of self-assertion. Through systematic oppression aimed at extinguishing his aggressive drive, the black American has been effectively castrated and rendered abjectly compliant by white America. Since appropriate rage at such emasculation could be expressed directly only at great risk, the Negro repressed and suppressed it, but only at great cost to his psychic development. Today this "aggression-rage" constellation, rather than self-hatred, appears to be at the core of the Negro's social and psychological difficulties.

Consider the following. Once last year as I was leaving my office in Jackson, Miss., with my Negro secretary, a white policeman yelled, "Hey, boy! Come here!" Somewhat bothered, I retorted: "I'm no boy!" He then rushed at me, inflamed, and stood towering over me, snorting, "What d'ja say, boy?" Quickly he frisked me and demanded, "What's your name, boy?" Frightened, I replied, "Dr. Poussaint. I'm a physician." He angrily chuckled and hissed, "What's your first name, boy?" When I hesitated he assumed a threatening stance and clenched his fists. As my heart palpitated, I muttered in profound humiliation, "Alvin."

He continued his psychological brutality, bellowing, "Alvin, the next time I call you, you come right away, you hear? You hear?" I hesitated. "You hear me, boy?" My voice trembling with helplessness, but following my instincts of self-preservation, I murmured, "Yes, sir." Now fully satisfied that I had performed and acquiesced to my "boy status," he dismissed me with, "Now boy, go on and get out of here or next time we'll take you for a little ride down to the station house!"

No amount of self-love could have salvaged my pride or preserved my integrity. In fact, the slightest show of self-respect or resistance might have cost me my life. For the moment my manhood had been ripped from me—and in the presence of a Negro woman for whom I, a "man," was supposed to be the "protector." In addition, this had occurred on a public street for all the local black people to witness, reminding them that *no* black man was as good as *any* white man. All of us—doctor, lawyer, postman, field hand and shoeshine boy—had been psychologically "put in our place."

The self-hate that I felt at that time was generated by the fact that I and my people were completely helpless and powerless to destroy that white bigot and all that he represented. Suppose I had decided, as a man should, to be forceful? What crippling price would I have paid for a few moments of assertive manhood? What was I to do with my rage?

And if I, a physician in middle-class dress, was vulnerable to this treatment, imagine the brutality to which "ordinary" black people are subjected—not only in the South but also in the North, where the brutality is likely to be more psychological than physical.

Let us briefly look at the genesis and initial consequences of this oppressive behavior and the Negroes' responses to it. The castration of Negroes, and the resulting problems of self-image and inner rage, started more than 350 years ago when black men, women and children were wrenched from their native Africa, stripped bare both psychologically and physically, and placed in an alien white land. They thus came to occupy the most degraded of human conditions: that of a slave, a piece of property, a nonperson. Families were broken up, the Negro male was completely emasculated, and the Negro woman was systematically sexually exploited and vilely degraded.

Whites, to escape the resultant retaliatory rage of black men and women, acted to block its expression. The plantation system implanted a subservience and dependency in the psyche of the

Negro that made him dependent upon the goodwill and paternalism of the white man. The more acquiescent he was, the more he was rewarded within the plantation culture. Those who bowed and scraped for the white boss and denied their aggressive feelings were promoted to "house nigger" and "good nigger."

It became a virtue within this system for the black man to be docile and nonassertive. "Uncle Toms" are exemplars of these conditioned virtues. If black people wanted to keep some semblance of a job and a full stomach to survive, they quickly learned "Yassuh, Massa." Passivity for Negroes became necessary for survival both during and after slavery, and holds true even today.

For reinforcement, as if any was needed, white supremacists constructed an entire "racial etiquette" to remind Negroes constantly that they are only castrated humans. In their daily lives, Negroes are called "girl" and "boy"—this in spite of the fact that such "girls" and "boys" as domestics are capable of managing a household with an efficiency and physical endurance that their white middle-class employers seem no longer to possess. Negroes are also addressed by their first names by whites no matter how lowly, but are in turn expected to use courtesy titles when addressing whites. It was sickening for me to hear a Southern white dime-store clerk address a Negro minister with a doctoral degree as "Jimmy," while he obsequiously called her "Miss Joan." If the Negro minister rejected these social mores he would probably be harassed, punished or in some way "disciplined." White racists through the centuries have perpetrated violence on Negroes who demonstrate aggressiveness. To be an "uppity nigger" was considered by white supremacists one of the gravest violations of racial etiquette.

Nonetheless, the passivity to which the black community has been so well conditioned is frequently called apathy and self-hate by those who would lay the burden of white racism on the black man's shoulders. The more reasonable explanation is that Negroes had little choice but to bear the severe psychological burden of suppressing and repressing their rage and aggression.

Nonassertiveness was a learned adaptation to insure survival. For example, the whole system of Southern legal justice has been designed—and still functions—to inflict severe and inequitable penalties on Negroes showing even minor aggression toward whites. In both the North and South, Negroes who dare show their anger toward whites are usually punished out of proportion. Negroes who are "too outspoken" about racial injustices often lose their jobs or are not promoted to higher positions because they are considered "unreasonable." The recent unseating of Congressman Adam Clayton Powell and the use of guns and bullets by police and National Guardsmen on rioting Negro college students (white college-age rioters are seldom even tear-gassed) are examples of this inequitable white retaliation.

Black people have learned their lesson well. Both in the North and in the South it is not uncommon to hear young Negro mothers instructing their 2- and 3-year-old children to "behave, and say, 'Yes, sir,' and 'No, sir' when the white man talks to you."

Similarly, various forms of religious worship in the Negro community have fostered passivity in blacks and encouraged them to look to an afterlife for eventual salvation and happiness. Negroes have even been taught that they must love their oppressor and it is "sinful" to hate or show appropriate anger. It is significant that the civil-rights movement had to adopt passive resistance and nonviolence in order to win the acceptance of white America. But, alas, even in nonviolent demonstrations there was too much "aggression" shown by Negroes. Whites recoiled and accused civil-rights groups of "provoking violence" by peaceful protest.

The lack of self-assertion has had devastating consequences in terms of Negro social behavior and psychic responses. It has been found for instance that Negroes are less likely to go into business than are members of other ethnic groups. The most obvious explanation for this (and one missed by Glazer and Moynihan in their "Beyond the Melting Pot") is that central to the entrepreneurial spirit is assertiveness, self-confidence and the willingness to risk failure in an innovative venture. A castrated human being is not likely to be inclined in any of these ways.

A trained incapacity to be aggressive would also account in large part for Negroes' below-par achievement in school. Negro girls, who are not so threatening to whites and therefore not so systematically crushed as are Negro boys, have been found to exceed boys in achievement in elementary schools. The pattern of behavior set for the young Negro, especially the male, is directly opposed to that upheld as masculine for the rest of American youth. With our country's emphasis on individualism and the idealization of the self-made man, brutalization into passivity leaves the Negro with a major handicap.

Of course, this is also conveniently protective for the white racist, because Negroes who are nonassertive will be afraid to compete with him for education, jobs and status. Studies have reported that even when Negroes are given objective evidence of their equal intellectual ability they continue to feel inadequate and react submissively. Thus their low aspirations may be due primarily to a learned inability to be normally aggressive and only secondarily to an inferiority complex.

Many psychiatrists feel that self-denigration is secondary to the more general castration of the black man by white society. Some believe that the self-hatred should be viewed as a rage turned inward rather than as a shame in being black and a desire to be white. Both my white and Negro colleagues agree that central to whatever specific emotional problems their Negro patients exhibit is how they deal with their feelings of hostility and rage. (This problem is particularly relevant to their behavior in the presence of whites.)

Of course, Negroes react and adapt to the stresses of white racism in a myriad of ways depending upon socioeconomic level, family life, geographical location, etc. Yet the fact remains that Negroes as individuals must deal with the general effects of racism. Since individual Negroes share the common experiences of Negro castration, rage and self-hatred, group trends can frequently be discerned.

What happens then to the accumulated rage in the depths of each Negro psyche? What does the black man do with his aggression?

The simplest method for dealing with rage is to suppress it and substitute an opposing emotional attitude—compliance, docility or a "loving attitude." A colleague told me about the case of a Negro graduate student he was treating for anxiety. The student was engaged to a white girl and circulated primarily in white social circles. He had a reputation for being very ingratiating and accommodating with his white friends, who described him as a "sweet guy" and a "very loving person." The student took a great deal of pride in this reputation and "acceptance" by whites, although he frequently encountered degrading racial prejudices among them. He attempted to deal with bigoted whites by being "understanding" and hoping that they would begin to see him as "just another human being."

At the beginning of treatment, he painted a rosy picture of his social life and particularly of his engagement to the white girl, although her parents had disowned her. He consistently denied holding any angry feelings toward whites or bitter feelings about being Negro. As therapy progressed and his problems were explored, more and more anger toward whites in general and toward his white friends in particular began to emerge. He became less tolerant of the subtle racial bigotry which he saw in his fiancée and began to quarrel with her frequently. For many weeks he became so overwhelmed by rage that he developed nausea and could not face his white friends for "fear of what I might do." He also became quite guilty about his acquiescence to white racial prejudice and slowly recognized that perhaps he himself had anti-Negro feelings. He began to avoid seeing his fiancée, feeling completely alienated from white people. The engagement was finally broken. The student left treatment to take a job in another city and shortly thereafter it was reported to his therapist that he had become a "black nationalist."

As this student exemplified, the greater the repressed rage, the more abject the pretense of love and compliance. Thus feet-shuffling, scraping and bowing, obsequiousness and Uncle Tomism may actually indicate inner rage and deep hatred.

Sometimes rage can be denied completely and replaced by a compensatory happy-go-lucky attitude, flippancy or—a mechanism extremely popular among Negroes—"being cool."

Or the aggression may be channeled into competitive sports, music, dance. Witness the numbers of Negroes who flock to these activities, among the few traditionally open to them by white society. Negro males in particular gravitate to sports as a means for sublimating their rage and aggression.

Another legitimate means of channeling rage is to identify with the oppressor and put all one's energy into striving to be like him. The most obvious example of this is the Negro who feels that the most flattering compliment his white friends can pay him is, "You don't act like all the other Negroes," or "You don't seem Negro to me." Such blacks usually harbor strong, angry anti-Negro feelings similar to those of the white racists. They may project their own self-hatred onto other Negroes. This mechanism is indicated in the high incidence of impulsive violence of Negroes toward each other: assaults and homicides by Negroes are more often against Negroes than against whites.

It is also legitimate and safe for the oppressed to identify with someone like himself who for one reason or another is free to express rage directly at the oppressor. This phenomenon would account for the immense popularity among Negroes of Congressman Adam Clayton Powell and Malcolm X. They were both willing to "tell the white man like it is" and did so, for a while at least, with apparent impunity—something which many of their followers could never do.

Another technique for dealing with rage is to replace it with a type of chronic resentment and stubbornness toward white people—a chip on the shoulder. Trying to control deep anger in this way frequently shows itself in a general irritability and it always has the potential of becoming explosive. Thus the spreading wave of riots in Negro ghettos may be seen as outbursts of rage. Although these riots are contained in the ghetto, the hatred is usually directed at those whom the rioter sees as controlling and oppressing him economically, psychologically and physically—store owners and policemen.

The same hostility which is expressed in a disorganized way by a collection of people in a riot can be expressed in an organized way in a political movement. In this connection the Black Power movement is relevant.

In this South I observed many civil-rights workers struggling with suppressed rage toward whites until it culminated in the angry, assertive cry of "Black Power!" I remember treating Negro workers after they had been beaten viciously by white toughs or policemen while conducting civil-rights demonstrations. I would frequently comment, "You must feel pretty angry getting beaten up like that by those bigots." Often I received a reply such as: "No, I don't hate those white men, I love them because they must really be suffering with all that hatred in their souls. Dr. King says the only way we can win our freedom is through love. Anger and hatred have never solved anything."

I used to sit there and wonder, "Now, what do they really do with their rage?"

Well, after a period of time it became apparent that they were directing it mostly at each other and the white civil-rights workers.

Violent verbal and sometimes physical fights often occurred among the workers on the civil-rights projects throughout the South. While they were talking about being nonviolent and "loving" the sheriff that just hit them over the head, they rampaged around the project houses beating up each other. I frequently had to calm Negro civil-rights workers with large doses of tranquilizers for what I can describe clinically only as acute attacks of rage.

As the months progressed and Negro workers became more conscious of their anger, it was more systematically directed toward white Southern racists, the lax Federal Government, token integration and finally the hypocrisy of many white liberals and white civil-rights workers. This rage was at a fever pitch for many months before it became crystallized in the "Black Power" slogan. The workers who shouted it the loudest were those with the oldest battle scars from the terror, demoralization and castration which they experienced through continual direct confrontation with Southern white racism. Furthermore, some of the most bellicose chanters of the slogan had been, just a few years before, exemplars of nonviolent, loving passive resistance in their struggle against white supremacy. These workers appeared to be seeking a sense of inner psychological emancipation from racism through self-assertion and release of aggressive, angry feelings.

Often the anxiety, fear and tension caused by suppressed emotion will be expressed in psychosomatic symptoms. Tension headaches, diarrhea and low back pain are conditions frequently linked to repressed hostility. Whether these symptoms occur more frequently among Negroes than among whites is an important question that has yet to be explored.

Rage is also directed inward in such deviations as alcoholism, drug addiction and excessive gambling. These escapist expressions are very prevalent among poorer Negroes and often represent an attempt to shut out a hostile world. In psychiatric practice it is generally accepted that a chronic repressed rage will eventually lead to a low self-esteem, depression, emotional dullness and apathy.

It appears that more and more Negroes are freeing themselves of suppressed rage through greater outspoken release of pent-up emotions. Perhaps this is an indication that self-love is beginning to outbalance self-hate in the black man's soul. A report this June by the Brandeis University Center for the Study of Violence said: "Although most Negroes disliked violence and had mixed feelings about its effect, even moderates were shifting to the opinion that only intense forms of social protest would bring relief from social injustice."

The old passivity is fading and being replaced by a drive to undo centuries of powerlessness, helplessness and dependency under American racism. It is not uncommon now to hear Negro civil-rights leaders as well as the teen-ager in the ghetto say such things as, "White America will have to give us our rights or exterminate us." James Meredith echoed the sentiments of many Negroes after his "march against fear" in Mississippi when he said, "If Negroes ever do overcome fear, the white man has only two choices: to kill them or let them be free."

The implication of all this seems to be that black people can obtain dignity only through continued assertive social and political action against racism until all of their just demands are met. It also appears that old-style attempts to destroy the natural aggression of the black man and to fail to give him his full rights can only provoke further outbreaks of violence and inspire a revolutionary zeal among Negro Americans.

The behavior of young Negroes today implies their recognition that racial pride and self-love alone do not fill the bellies of starving black children in Mississippi. Nor does being proud of one's African heritage alone bring jobs, decent housing or quality education. Perhaps the emphasis by social scientists on self-hatred problems among blacks is just another thesis that is guilt-relieving for whites and misguides the Negro. It's as if many white Americans are saying, "From now on when we oppress you, we don't want you to hate being black, we want you to have racial pride and love each other."

For the fundamental survival problems of black Americans to be dealt with, a variety of social, economic and political forces controlled primarily by whites must be challenged. "Positive-sense-of-identity" programs are relevant only insofar as they generate greater constructive aggressiveness in Negroes in their struggle for full equality. Since this assertive response appears to be growing more common among Negroes, the implications for American society are clear: stop oppressing the black man, or be prepared to meet his expressed rage.

The Story of Snick: From "Freedom High" to Black Power

by Gene Roberts

DURING ONE OF the many rallies that accompanied the civil-rights march through Mississippi in June, Willie Ricks, a 23-year-old member of the Student Nonviolent Coordinating Committee, stood on the back of a flat-bed truck and harangued a crowd of nearly a thousand Negroes.

Ricks is known within the committee as "The Reverend" for his ability to thunder in the manner of a fundamentalist preacher, and that night, at the fairgrounds in Yazoo City, he talked of "white blood flowing," yelled "black power" several times and otherwise warmed up to the subject of how he, as a Negro, was tired of white society. While he was talking, the Rev. Dr. Martin Luther King Jr., the Nobel prize-winning civil-rights leader, made his way through the crowd to the flat-bed truck. The crowd surged around Dr. King, elderly women pushing each other in an effort to touch him and Negro men in overalls struggling to press callused brown hands into his.

When it was Dr. King's turn to speak, he sailed into the Student Nonviolent Coordinating Committee—or "Snick" as it is commonly known—and declared that he was tired of hearing talk of violence and black power. He said the only way to overcome violent enemies was with nonviolent love, and that the Negro should never sink to his enemies' level by trying to kill them or by emphasizing racial differences. Dr. King is an eloquent man, and he was particularly eloquent that night. Soft murmurs of "Listen, listen" and "Speak on" and "Can't he talk, Lord, can't he talk" ran through the audience.

None of the adoration came from Snick members, however. They nudged each other and chuckled about how "de Lawd," as they call Dr. King, obviously was going to preach the "same old jazz" about nonviolence until the day he dies. That day, they speculated, would not be long in coming because some redneck was almost certain to love him back with a shotgun full of "double-ought" buckshot and that would be the end of Dr. King and nonviolence.

Finally, one member of Snick had enjoyed as much of Dr. King as he could. From the edge of the crowd, he pointed to Dr. King and yelled in derision, "Blessed Jesus!" To what almost certainly was his chagrin, no one in the crowd laughed and a few even looked at him approvingly as if he were completely sincere. Rank-and-file Negroes in the South frequently call Dr. King "our own Moses" and could easily understand someone who had become carried away by Dr. King's voice and thought of him in even loftier terms.

Though the rally at Yazoo City underscored the long-standing split in the civil-rights movement between militants and moderates, it was more significant for pointing up the prevailng mood of Snick, which in recent weeks has jolted the civil-rights movement and a great many white liberals by developing a philosophy of "black consciousness" and popularizing the chant "Black power, black power, black power."

To be a Snick member in good standing these days, you have to be simultaneously angered, amused and frustrated by the society around you. It also helps if you are a Negro and can quote at length from "Malcolm X Speaks," a collection of speeches given by the late black nationalist in the year preceding his assassination. It is almost imperative that you digest "The Wretched of the Earth," by Frantz Fanon, a psychiatrist and native of Martinique who, before his death in 1961, worked with the Algerian rebels and became convinced that Western man is decadent and therefore not to be emulated by colonized peoples. Fanon believed it was therapeutic for the oppressed to fight physically for their freedom and Snick, which looks upon the problem of the American Negro as one of "internal colonialism," believes the message may be applicable in this country.

Whatever the philosophy of the moment, the majority of Snick members believe it deeply. On the day after Labor Day, when Atlanta police shot and wounded a fleeing Negro who was suspected of auto theft, Stokely Carmichael, the 26-year-old chairman of the organization, rushed to the scene and found Negroes preparing to demonstrate. He then announced that he would be back soon and "tear this place apart." True to his word, he sent in more than 10 Snick workers and a sound truck. When Mayor Ivan Allen Jr. showed up on the scene to ask Negroes to go home, Snick members followed him and urged the Negroes to ignore the Mayor.

The result was a riot. Atlanta police were convinced that it would not have happened without Carmichael and his organization, and arrested the Snick leader and several associates on charges of public disorder. Subsequently they were among 14 Negroes indicted by a grand jury and, if convicted, face up to a year in prison. The Student Nonviolent Coordinating Committee, Atlanta Police Chief Herbert Jenkins charged on the day after the riot, "is now the Non-student Violent Committee."

Carmichael, meanwhile, had gotten across two points that he previously had been making only in conversation: The organization wants an "eye for an eye" when violence is done to Negroes; and Snick, once loosely knit, can move on command and with precision in paramilitary fashion.

Little more than a year ago, the group had a different set of ground rules. Then it was a "must" that you be able to quote Albert Camus, especially "The Rebel," and distrust all organizations, including Snick. Robert Moses, a former teacher at Horace Mann in New York City with a master's degree from Harvard, proposed quite seriously that Snick members abolish all committees and offices, walk out the door of Snick headquarters and "go where the spirit say go, and do what the spirit say do." Looking back on all this, Snick members call this their "freedom high" period, which is a way of saying that they were drunk on freedom.

For all the controversy it has provoked, Snick is a small organization: about 135 members, some one-third in office and clerical jobs and the rest engaged in field work and in otherwise spreading the gospel. It has an influence far out of proportion to its size, however, partly because all its members are full-time staff workers and partly because it has been in the forefront of civil-rights activity since it was brought into being in 1960 (ironically, by none other than the Rev. Martin Luther King, who wanted an organization to coordinate the sit-ins that were sweeping the South).

After the sit-ins and the Freedom Rides had run their course, Snick began dispatching staff workers into the Deep South to carry on voter registration drives and to live in segregationist backwaters as nonviolent guerrilla fighters. It paved the way for the confrontation with segregationists in Albany, Ga., in 1962 and 1963. It led the "Mississippi summer" of 1964 when segregation in that state was challenged for the first time on a massive scale. It was busily organizing Negroes in Selma, Ala., two years before Dr. King joined in and helped make it a major civil-rights battleground in early 1965.

Today, the average Snick member is a veteran of many civil-rights campaigns but is in his early or mid-20's. He spurns all the trappings of affluent America except for a transistor radio, which he will switch on during a spare moment in the Mississippi countryside or on the weatherbeaten porch of a shack in a Southern ghetto. A person can join Snick only by becoming a full-time member of its staff, which just about means taking an oath of poverty. The average staffer gets between $20 and $35 a week in subsistence pay, although some are budgeted for $10, and one for $85. The amount is often academic, however, since Snick often goes for long periods without being able to meet a full payroll.

None of this particularly bothers the organization's field secretaries (grass-roots organizers), who appear content to go on forever sharing collard greens and pig neckbone with the poor and urging black men on street corners of city ghettos to join with others to control their own destiny. But in its impatience to revolutionize society, Snick is using its field secretaries less in the field and more in propaganda activities in the hope of reaching more people, faster. Its Atlanta presses roll almost continually, turning out "Black Power" bumper stickers decorated with a lunging black panther, Negro history pamphlets which devote considerable space to the philosophy of Malcolm X, and Snick's angry and intermittent newspaper, the Nitty Gritty.

In contrast to the past, an average day now will find only a third to a half of the 75 or 80 field secretaries out organizing (the remaining Snick members hold staff or clerical jobs), while the rest of the field workers are on the rally circuit or in Atlanta spinning off ideas and spreading the new Snick gospel.

Snick staffers, however, remain dedicated as ever, no matter what the assignment. When, for example, they are assigned to clerical or fund-raising jobs in Atlanta headquarters or in Northern offices in Boston, New York, Philadelphia, Washington or Los Angeles, they often accept night-time or weekend jobs in order to donate the regular work day to Snick. For relaxation give the Snick worker his transistor radio or a long philosophical argument in the Lovin' Spoonful, his favorite Atlanta coffeehouse. Then, let him read himself to sleep on whatever happens to be the book of the moment.

While the books may vary, there is a certain monotony to the magazines and newspapers found in Snick offices during the last two or three years. Rarely is a Snick office without a handful of copies of such publications as The Worker or People's World, both organs of the Communist party; Freedomways, a Marxist magazine: The Militant, a Trotskyite newspaper; The National Guardian, which is oriented toward both the Soviet Union and Communist China.

The reading list, of course, delights segregationists who are likely to look on it as proof of their suspicions that the civil-rights movement is a Communist front. It also disconcerts white liberals, although many liberals have defended Snick by observing that most of its members are young and it is difficult to be young and to care about social justice without flirting with various left-wing "isms."

"Everyone always says there are no Communists in positions of influence in the movement," Pat Watters of the liberal Southern Regional Council wrote a year ago. "But how they know this is hard to say. Clearly there is no reason why some skilled undercover man couldn't become a leader; indeed, in S.N.C.C. such a fellow would seem to have found a perfect setup.

"The point is that nobody really knows; nobody produces proof of anything," he went on, "and the legacy of McCarthyism . . . has created such an absurd context that it is almost impossible to think logically within its framework."

"Would to God there were Communists in Snick," Charles Morgan of the American Civil Liberties Union once quipped. "They would be a moderating influence."

"People will not stop talking about us," said Elizabeth Sutherland, a white member of the Snick staff in New York. "A few months ago, it was the Red scare. Now it's the black scare."

Comments like Miss Sutherland's are unusual. Snick's official position is to say nothing in explanation of its actions and slogans. "We don't have to explain anything to anybody," says Stokely Carmichael, the civil-rights veteran who became chairman of Snick in May and popularized the phrase "black power" within a month. "Your job," he says to white liberals, "is to understand us."

Snick's response to talk about Communist influence is cheerfully provocative. The organization refers to its three chief officers as the "troika" and its chief policy-making body as the "central committee." Some Snick members drop the word "troika" in the presence of outside visitors, then watch wryly to see whether it will bring a smile or a frown. It is difficult to know which expression they prefer to see.

About the only group label which friends, enemies and Snick itself can agree on is "radical." There are traces of nihilism about Snick's desire to shatter existing society; traces of syndicalism in its fascination two years ago with "parallel institutions" as a first step toward doing away with existing ones; traces of the old Wobblies—members of the Industrial Workers of the World—in their meanderings through the byways of poverty, telling the poor to rise up and they will be saved. Laced into it all, however, is a sort of earthiness as peculiarly American as Harlem and the cotton fields of Mississippi. Unlike most radical organizations, which developed from a distinct philosophy, Snick grew willy-nilly out of the sit-ins and has been searching for a philosophy ever since.

Nowadays the organization's attempt to articulate a credo resembles an exercise in "group think," in which members almost interminably debate civilization's oldest questions: Who are we? Where do we come from? Where are we going? They constantly arrive at what they think are the answers, and then quickly abandon them. It is all breathtaking and confusing to many white liberals, some of whom have formed a cult of "Snick understanders," and whose pursuit has proven inordinately time-consuming and unproductive.

Last year, two Snick members—Scott B. Smith and Jesse Harris—began to wear necklaces of bones fastened with rawhide and the word quickly circulated that perhaps some new philosophy had developed in Snick. Conversations with Harris, Smith and their friends weren't very enlightening, though, as they were likely one day to say that the bones represented the remains of Jefferson Davis, and the next day explain that they were part of a voodoo ritual, or brought good luck. Just as some whites were beginning to wonder if Harris and Smith didn't herald an American answer to the Mau Mau, both men took jobs in the Federal antipoverty program and are now looked upon by some Snick members as middle class.

About the only thing predictable about Snick is that its disillusionment with the old world grows more pronounced with each discussion session. In the beginning, the college students who helped create Snick simply wanted to participate more fully in the fruits of the society around them. Nonviolent protest was their weapon and Gandhi was their prophet. (They once expelled a member who was arrested in southwest Georgia for packing a pistol.) Integration was their goal and the hero during the early days of Snick was Bill Hansen, a white member who married a Negro girl and went to work for the organization in Arkansas to organize Negroes and to defy local marriage customs.

The organization now considers integration to be "irrelevant." Overalls and blue denim work shirts long ago replaced rep ties and cashmere sweaters as the Snick uniform. And guns can be found readily in Snick outposts in the South.

At least some of the changes began in 1961, when Northern activists began flocking to the newly born Southern civil-rights movement. Many of them came with a message that the Northern pattern of race relations, which then appeared to be the goal of the Southern student, was in fact hypocritical and the Southern movement should go after more revolutionary social and political changes. James Forman, a Chicago schoolteacher and aspiring novelist who threw it all over in the fall of 1961 to become Snick's executive secretary at a salary of $60 a week, was particularly convinced of the need for a new, radical set of goals.

Albert Bigelow, the skipper who sailed his Golden Rule into an atomic testing area to protest nuclear warfare, was down South during the 1961 Freedom Rides, preaching pacifism. Jake Rosen, a leader in the Maoist Progressive Labor Movement, spent months in Atlanta talking to Snick workers and anyone else who might lend an ear. Tom Hayden, a founder of Students for a Democratic Society—one of the new left organizations most militantly opposed to the war in Vietnam—worked with Snick in McComb, Miss., in 1961 and 1962. Then, in the summer of 1964, children of well-known Communists and radicals became Snick volunteers. And before his assassination last year, Malcolm X, who had become a symbol of black nationalism, was in Selma saying that the time had come when the Negro must fight back with more than nonviolent protest.

Far more important, perhaps, in shaping Snick's present mood, was its reception by Southern Negroes. Although the organization persuaded thousands to join the civil-rights movement it encountered lethargy, and at times bitterness, from Negroes who had worked out at least a tenuous accommodation with the white man. And often when Snick succeeded in arousing a community to action, local Negroes coalesced only around the presence of Dr. King, who mobilized not only the lower class, but the middle class as well, by emphasizing brotherly love. The worker's overalls Snick staffers wear have failed to be a match for King's skill as a man of religion and the realization has often left the members of Snick frustrated and bitter.

At times, the anger of the poor has turned against Snick intellectuals. Recently, for example, Bill Ware, a Negro who is Snick's project director in Atlanta, attempted to drive a white social worker out of the Vine City slums in Atlanta by calling him "white Jesus." Poor Negroes surrounded Ware's sound truck and almost turned it over. Students of Russian radicalism find parallels between Snick and the reformers of Czarist times who grew increasingly bitter and desperate when they failed to find understanding from the peasants and workers they wanted most to help.

Another reason for Snick's alienation from society, and one which has had a great impact, is the violence and abuse aimed at its members during six years of civil-rights campaigns. During the Mississippi summer of 1964, for example, Snick and its supporters endured at least 1,000 arrests, 35 shooting incidents, eight beatings and six murders. When the summer was over, Dr. Robert Coles, the Harvard psychiatrist, concluded that the effects of the experience were something to be considered seriously. "They are clinical signs of depression," he wrote. "They constitute 'battle fatigue.' They indicate exhaustion, weariness, despair, frustration and rage. They mark a crisis in the lives of those youths who experience them, and also one in the cities which may experience the results, translated into action, of such symptoms."

There was, by this time, an increasing tendency in Snick to wonder if white civilization wasn't inherently evil. When Snick held elections this year and formally adopted its black-consciousness philosophy, some members already were calling themselves "black nationalists." Ware, a native of Natchez, Miss., and former University of Minnesota student who carries a photograph showing his face after one severe beating by whites, and Fred Meeley, who is being sought by Philadelphia police on charges of possessing dynamite, announced at one point in the meeting that they no longer wanted to be in the company of whites.

It could be argued, of course, that many whites were stanch supporters of civil rights and that Snick itself had been integrated from the start. The advocates of black consciousness had prepared for this argument, however, with a lengthy position paper which declared, among other things, that whites couldn't "relate" to Negroes, tended to prevent Negroes from developing into decision-makers, and thus should be barred from working directly with the Negro masses.

And, they asked, wasn't it true that whites diluted the strength and anger of the movement? Remember how Negroes began to organize the March on Washington in 1963, and then white labor leaders, politicians and church leaders joined in and immediately began "toning things down." Remember how John Lewis, who was chairman of Snick then, wanted to ask President Kennedy, "Which side is the Federal Government on?" but the white march leaders thought the challenge was too radical, and made him take it out of his speech.

What's more, the argument went on, Snick had devoted all of last fall to fighting for increased school integration without noticeable results. Why not emphasize black consciousness, tell Negroes to forget about integration and concentrate instead on seizing political power? Bob Mants, a slender and bespectacled man from Atlanta, opposed the shift by contending, "One thing you never have to tell a Southern Negro is that he is black." Charles Sherrod, another veteran Snick member, also opposed the policy shift and withdrew from active participation in Snick to lead a racially integrated voter registration project in southwest Georgia. John Lewis, who was defeated in the election for Snick chairman, argued against black consciousness but favored black leadership of civil-rights organizations; he withdrew from the organization to return to school.

In the end, advocates of black consciousness won the day with only one concession: the election of one white member to a policy-making office.

In recent weeks, however, it has become apparent that the elevation of the lone white, Jack Minnis, to the central committee was only a technical promotion. He has far less power than when he was head of Snick's research department and a member of its finance committee. He was removed from these posts, according to one Snick member, after some complaints that Snick was perpetuating "paternalism" in allowing a white man to supervise Negroes and to sign expense vouchers turned in by Negro members. Minnis once was among the first to arrive and the last to leave the Snick headquarters in Atlanta each day; now he puts in only a brief appearance each morning.

One white secretary also works in Atlanta. With the exception of Bill Hansen, who remains in Arkansas with his Negro wife, about 20 other whites work in Northern offices at fund-raising and clerical tasks. The whites are reluctant to discuss Snick's black-consciousness philosophy, and when they do, it is only to say that Negroes are searching for their identity and that it is the white's job to remain loyal and try to understand them.

Advocates of black consciousness also argued that they had very little to lose financially in cutting themselves off from whites. Contributions had dropped off drastically since 1964 when, largely because of the dramatic impact of the Mississippi Freedom Summer project, they totaled about $700,000. Snick's attacks on the Democratic party for refusing to oust the entire all-white Mississippi delegation to the 1964 Democratic convention accounted for some of the dollar shrinkage. Its vocal opposition to the war in Vietnam accelerated the trend. By late last fall, the organization was missing more payrolls than it was meeting, but proving to itself that it could exist on a shoestring.

During the prosperous days of 1964, Snick had accumulated a down payment on an Atlanta warehouse which members converted into an office building. The warehouse was equipped with printing presses for propaganda purposes and which could also be used, as they now are, for commercial printing to help defray the overhead. By refusing to take on large numbers of summer volunteers, who had once numbered more than 300, and by slashing the size of the staff to about 135 from its 1964 peak of 225, Snick could manage on as little as $150,000 a year or less. (Allowing for still more disaffections because of the black-consciousness issue, that is what Snick expected to receive this year, mainly from a steadily dwindling list of longtime supporters. According to some sources, it is proving to be a reliable estimate.)

Snick is, of course, and always has been, a complex organization and the election of Stokely Carmichael as chairman exemplifies its moodiness, brilliance and contradictions. Only a year ago, Snick was at war against what it called "charisma" and the "cult of the personality." Robert Moses, perhaps the most mystical, magnetic and puzzling member of Snick, became so worried that he might become another Martin Luther King that he changed his name to Robert Parris and moved from Mississippi to Alabama in a conscious effort to battle the effects of his own charisma. Suddenly, Snick voted in Carmichael, its most charismatic remaining member, as chairman.

Although Carmichael is known for his slogan of "black power," his election represented only partly a philosophical victory. Ironically, for an organization that shuns anything that smacks of middle-class America, it was a victory for "old school ties."

Snick, in the past, had periods when it was dominated by the Nashville Student Movement, centered around Fisk University, and the Atlanta Student Movement, based at Atlanta University. In May, the Washington, D. C., movement, which had Howard University as its hub, had, through attrition of the other power centers, become one of the most powerful cliques in the organization.

The "Washington clique," as it is known by foes in the organization, includes Snick workers such as Courtland Cox and Bill Mahoney, who were close friends of Carmichael's at Howard and were active together with him in the Nonviolent Action Group (NAG), the Washington-based student movement that helped open up the restaurants along Route 40 to Negroes in the early sixties. Cox, a staunch believer in "freedom high," once came close to being expelled from Snick when he insisted on accounting to no one for his movements. Subsequently, Cox got back in step, invented the "Black Panther" label for Snick's independent political party in Lowndes County, Ala., and is now a member of the policy-making central committee. Mahoney, the leader of NAG, is now a Snick press relations officer, wears his hair Che Guevara style, and worries not just about white Americans but all Western society, which he is convinced is inherently bigoted. Asiatic in appearance, Mahoney was often frustrated in the days of the lunch-counter sit-ins when waitresses would serve him, but not his darker companions. *"Je noir* [I black]," he would scrawl on tablecloths to dumbfounded waitresses.

In addition to the former Washington students, Carmichael also had the support of Ivanhoe Donaldson, a New Yorker who attached himself to the Washington group and became the new head of Snick's New York office as his post-election reward. Another Carmichael backer was Willie Ricks, who joined the civil-rights movement as a high-school student in Chattanooga a few years ago and is now Snick's chief jester. Members chuckled at the all-black wardrobe Ricks purchased after "black power" came into vogue and he keeps the laughter going with his speeches and tactics in the field, where laughter is a rarity.

During a voter registration drive in Tuskegee, Ala., earlier this year, Ricks saw an elderly Negro women talking to herself as she collected scraps of paper from the streets. Offering his arm, he squired the puzzled woman into the office of the voter registrar and said: "I brought you a fine lady, Mr. Registrar. I want you to register her up just like the law says." The registrar grimaced and then accepted her into the line of waiting Negroes.

Although Carmichael is the public spokesman for the organization, all his key supporters have major voices in Snick. So does Jim Forman, a nonsupporter who only last year was under heavy fire from Carmichael and several others for his stanch opposition to "freedom high." This year, however, Forman decided against running for another term as executive secretary of Snick and instead embraced the Washington clique. The decision insured him continued influence in the student movement and, as a close advisor to his successor as Snick's executive secretary, Ruby Doris Smith, he is still extremely influential. "He'll say do something and they'll do it," says John Lewis, "or don't do something and they won't do it."

Although the influence of Robert Parris is philosophical, not political like Forman's, the schoolteacher turned mendicant also helps shape the destiny of Snick. He is no longer active in the organization, largely because he still believes in "going where the spirit say go," but his latest conclusions about life and the Negro make their way back to Snick and have an impact. As a sort of high priest of black consciousness, he refuses to speak to whites, largely on the grounds that the Negro has to withdraw into himself to develop his own identity. He currently is trying to organize Negroes around this philosophy in Alabama and Mississippi.

For all his advisers, Carmichael is highly influential, too, of course, partly because he articulates what many of the members feel, and partly because of his reputation as Snick's best organizer. He refused to leave Lowndes County even after two civil-rights workers were shot to death there, and has succeeded in making it the one county where Snick has a real chance to seize political power through its Black Panther party.

Carmichael was born in Trinidad on June 21, 1941, moved to New York with his parents when he was 11 and grew up in a predominantly white neighborhood in the Bronx. Later, he read Marx and dismissed him as a "stale guy." His debut as an activist was as a Freedom Rider in 1961, when he spent 49 days in the Mississippi state penitentiary. Thereafter, Carmichael divided his time between the South and Howard University until he graduated in 1964 with a degree in philosophy.

Traces of his background are immediately apparent in his speaking style, which already has become legendary among the faithful. In one well-constructed sentence and without pausing for breath, he can shift from the clipped tones of the British West Indies, to a sort of guttural Bronxese, to the soft and poetically ungrammatical drawl of the Southern Negro field hand. His eyes gleam, his brilliant white teeth flash, and his dark hands flail the air. One minute he is shaking with mocking laughter, the next with rage. Then, when the speech is over, he walks away with stoop-shouldered grace, his face wrapped in a friendly smile as if he did not think the speech was anything more than an exercise in rhetoric.

"Stokely likes to scare the hell out of the white folks," explains Lewis, whom Carmichael succeeded as chairman. If scaring whites is an art, Carmichael seems well on his way to becoming a master. Within minutes after mounting a speaker's platform, he has whipped up a crowd of Negroes into screaming, "Black power, black power," their hands raised in the same three-fingered salute that rioters in Watts used as they cried, "Burn, baby, burn." In the same vein, he has praised an outfit known as the Revolutionary Armed Movement (R.A.M.), which distributes leaflets prepared in Cuba that urge American Negroes to arm themselves with Molotov cocktails and surplus war weapons.

Often, after such speeches, white liberals or newsmen will draw Carmichael aside and ask if "black power" is really an antiwhite philosophy, and often Mr. Carmichael will say, of course not. "I have never said anything antiwhite in my life," he adds. "I am pro-black, I'm not antiwhite." Then he will declare that the Negro has become so dominated by the white man's culture that many Negroes have come to despise their own God-given looks. Negroes have become so accustomed to letting white men make decisions, he goes on, that they are politically lethargic even though they now have the right to register and vote.

"Black power" means nothing more than a way to help Negroes develop racial pride and use the ballot for educational and economic advancement. Carmichael is so sincere and convincing during these private explanations that many of his questioners come away believing that they completely missed the point of his public utterances.

After one such conversation, Carmichael rushed off to Cleveland for a rally of the Congress of Racial Equality. Next day he was quoted as saying, "When you talk of 'black power,' you talk of bringing this country to its knees. When you talk of 'black power,' you talk of building a movement that will smash everything Western civilization has created. When you talk of 'black power,' you talk of picking up where Malcolm X left off. When you talk of 'black power,' you talk of the black man doing whatever is necessary to get what he needs. . . . We are fighting for our lives."

One white was so puzzled by these contradictions that he recently asked a Snick worker for a "frank and confidential discussion." "Tell me what you really think," the white man urged. "One minute I get the feeling that you want to wipe out white civilization, and the next that you are laughing at it."

The Snick worker seemed genuinely surprised, the white man reported later. "It's funny that you should bring that up," the man from Snick replied. "We feel the same way, you know. The white man either wants to rid the world of us, or is laughing at us by making promises or passing laws that he never intends to keep. Some of the Congressmen must say after they pass a civil-rights bill, 'Those niggers will believe anything.'"

The conversation over, the white and the Snick worker went their separate ways, each as angry and puzzled as he was before.

An Advocate of Black Power Defines It

by Charles V. Hamilton

BLACK POWER has many definitions and connotations in the rhetoric of race relations today. To some people, it is synonymous with premeditated acts of violence to destroy the political and economic institutions of this country. Others equate Black Power with plans to rid the civil-rights movement of whites who have been in it for years. The concept is understood by many to mean hatred of and separation from whites; it is associated with calling whites "honkies" and with shouts of "Burn, baby, burn!" Some understand it to be the use of pressure-group tactics in the accepted tradition of the American political process. And still others say that Black Power must be seen first of all as an attempt to instill a sense of identity and pride in the black people.

Ultimately, I suspect, we have to accept the fact that, in this highly charged atmosphere, it is virtually impossible to come up with a single definition satisfactory to all.

Even as some of us try to articulate our idea of Black Power and the way we relate to it and advocate it, we are categorized as "moderate" or "militant" or "reasonable" or "extremist." "I can accept your definition of Black Power," a listener will say to

From the *New York Times Magazine*, April 14, 1968, copyright © 1968 by The New York Times Company.

me. "But how does your position compare with what Stokely Carmichael said in Cuba or with what H. Rap Brown said in Cambridge, Md.?" Or, just as frequently, some young white New Left advocate will come up to me and proudly announce: "You're not radical enough. Watts, Newark, Detroit—that's what's happening, man! You're nothing but a reformist. We've got to blow up this society. Read Ché or Debray or Mao." All I can do is shrug and conclude that some people believe that making a revolution in this country involves rhetoric, Molotov cocktails and being under 30.

To have Black Power equated with calculated acts of violence would be very unfortunate. First, if black people have learned anything over the years, it is that he who shouts revolution the loudest is one of the first to run when the action starts. Second, open calls to violence are a sure way to have one's ranks immediately infiltrated. Third—and this is as important as any reason —violent revolution in this country would fail; it would be met with the kind of repression used in Sharpeville, South Africa, in 1960, when 67 Africans were killed and 186 wounded during a demonstration against apartheid. It is clear that America is not above this. There are many white bigots who would like nothing better than to embark on a program of black genocide, even though the imposition of such repressive measures would destroy civil liberties for whites as well as for blacks. Some whites are so panicky, irrational and filled with racial hatred that they would welcome the opportunity to annihilate the black community. This was clearly shown in the senseless murder of Dr. Martin Luther King Jr., which understandably—but nonetheless irrationally— prompted some black militants to advocate violent retaliation. Such cries for revenge intensify racial fear and animosity when the need—now more than ever—is to establish solid, stable organizations and action programs.

Many whites will take comfort in these words of caution against violence. But they should not. The truth is that the black ghettos are going to continue to blow up out of sheer frustration and rage, and no amount of rhetoric from professors writing articles in magazines (which most black people in the ghettos do not read anyway) will affect that. There comes a point beyond which people cannot be expected to endure prejudice, oppression and deprivation, and they *will* explode.

Some of us can protect our positions by calling for "law and order" during a riot, or by urging "peaceful" approaches, but we should not be confident that we are being listened to by black people legitimately fed up with intolerable conditions. If white America wants a solution to the violence in the ghettos by blacks, then let white America end the violence done to the ghettos by whites. We simply must come to understand that there can be no social order without social justice. "How long will the violence in the summers last?" another listener may ask. "How intransigent is white America?" is my answer. And the answer to that could be just more rhetoric or it could be a sincere response to legitimate demands.

Black power must not be naive about the intentions of white decision-makers to yield anything without a struggle and a confrontation by organized power. Black people will gain only as much as they can win through their ability to organize independent bases of economic and political power—through boycotts, electoral activity, rent strikes, work stoppages, pressure-group bargaining. And it must be clear that whites will have to bargain with blacks or continue to fight them in the streets of the Detroits and the Newarks. Rather than being a call to violence, this is a clear recognition that the ghetto rebellions, in addition to producing the possibility of apartheid-type repression, have been functional in moving *some* whites to see that viable solutions must be sought.

Black Power is concerned with organizing the rage of black people and with putting new, hard questions and demands to white America. As we do this, white America's responses will be crucial to the questions of violence and viability. Black Power must (1) deal with the obviously growing alienation of black people and their distrust of the institutions of this society; (2) work to create new values and to build a new sense of community and of belonging; and (3) work to establish legitimate new institutions that make participants, not recipients, out of a people traditionally excluded from the fundamentally racist processes of this country. There is nothing glamorous about this: it involves persistence and hard, tedious, day-to-day work.

Black Power rejects the lessons of slavery and segregation that caused black people to look upon themselves with hatred and disdain. To be "integrated" it was necessary to deny one's heritage, one's own culture, to be ashamed of one's black skin, thick lips and kinky hair. In their book, "Racial Crisis in America," two Florida State University sociologists, Lewis M. Killian and Charles M. Grigg, wrote: "At the present time, integration as a solution to the race problem demands that the Negro forswear his identity as a Negro. But for a lasting solution, the meaning of 'American' must lose its implicit racial modifier, 'white.' " The black man must change his demeaning conception of himself; he must develop a sense of pride and self-respect. Then, if integration comes, it will deal with people who are psychologically and mentally healthy, with people who have a sense of their history and of themselves as whole human beings.

In the process of creating these new values, Black Power will, its advocates hope, build a new sense of community among black people. It will try to forge a bond in the black community between those who have "made it" and those "on the bottom." It will bring an end to the internal back-biting and suspicious bickering, the squabbling over tactics and personalities so characteristic of the black community. If Black Power can produce this unity that in itself will be revolutionary, for the black community and for the country.

Black Power recognizes that new forms of decision-making must be implemented in the black community. One purpose, clearly, is to overcome the alienation and distrust.

Let me deal with this specifically by looking at the situation in terms of "internal" and "external" ghetto problems and approaches. When I speak of internal problems, I refer to such things as exploitative merchants who invade the black communities, to absentee slumlords, to inferior schools and arbitrary law enforcement, to black people unable to develop their own independent economic and political bases. There are, of course, many problems facing black people which must be dealt with outside the ghettos: jobs, open occupancy, medical care, higher education.

The solution of the internal problems does not require the presence of massive numbers of whites marching arm in arm with blacks. Local all-black groups can organize boycotts of disreputable merchants and of those employers in the black communities who fail to hire and promote black people. Already, we see this approach spreading across the country with Operation

Breadbasket, initiated by Dr. King's Southern Christian Leadership Conference. The national director of the program, the Rev. Jesse Jackson, who was with Dr. King when he was murdered in Memphis, has established several such projects from Los Angeles to Raleigh, N. C.

In Chicago alone, in 15 months, approximately 2,000 jobs worth more than $15-million in annual income were obtained for black people. Negotiations are conducted on hiring and upgrading black people, marketing the products of black manufacturers and suppliers and providing contracts to black companies. The operation relies heavily on the support of black businessmen, who are willing to work with Operation Breadbasket because it is mutually beneficial. They derive a profit and in turn contribute to the economic development of the black community.

This is Black Power in operation. But there is not nearly enough of this kind of work going on. In some instances, there is a lack of technical know-how coupled with a lack of adequate funds. These two defects constantly plague constructive pressure-group activity in the black communities.

CORE (Congress of Racial Equality) has developed a number of cooperatives around the country. In Opelousas, La., it has organized over 300 black farmers, growers of sweet potatoes, cabbages and okra, in the Grand-Marie Co-op. They sell their produce and some of the income goes back into the co-op as dues. Initially, 20 per cent of the cooperative's members were white farmers, but most of the whites dropped out as a result of social and economic pressures from the white community. An offshoot of the Grand-Marie group is the Southern Consumers' Cooperative in Lafayette, La., which makes and sells fruit cakes and candy. It has been in existence for more than a year, employs approximately 150 black people and has led to the formation of several credit unions and buying clubs.

The major effort of Black Power-oriented CORE is in the direction of economic development. Antoine Perot, program director of CORE, says: "One big need in the black community is to develop capital-producing instruments which create jobs. Otherwise, we are stuck with the one-crop commodity—labor—which does not produce wealth. Mere jobs are not enough. These will simply perpetuate black dependency."

Thus, small and medium-sized businesses are being developed

in the black communities of Chicago, San Francisco, Detroit, Cleveland, New York and several other urban centers. CORE hopes to call on some successful black businessmen around the country as consultants, and it is optimistic that they will respond favorably with their know-how and, in some instances, their money. The goal is to free as many black people as possible from economic dependency on the white man. It has been this dependency in many places that has hampered effective independent political organizing.

In New York, Black Power, in the way we see it, operates through a group called N.E.G.R.O. (National Economic Growth and Reconstruction Organization). Its acronym does not sit too well with some advocates of black consciousness who see in the use of the term "Negro" an indication of less than sufficient racial pride. Started in 1964, the group deals with economic self-help for the black community: a hospital in Queens, a chemical corporation, a textile company and a construction company. N.E.G.R.O., with an annual payroll of $1-million and assets of $3-million, is headed by Dr. Thomas W. Matthew, a neurosurgeon who has been accused of failing to file Federal income-tax returns for 1961, 1962 and 1963. He has asserted that he will pay all the Government says he owes, but not until "my patient is cured or one of us dies." His patient is the black community, and the emphasis of his group is on aiding blacks and reducing reliance on the white man. The organization creates a sense of identity and cohesiveness that is painfully lacking in much of the black community.

In helping oneself and one's race through hard work, N.E.G.R.O. would appear to be following the Puritan ethic of work and achievement: if you work hard, you will succeed. One gets the impression that the organization is not necessarily idealistic about this. It believes that black people will never develop in this country as long as they must depend on handouts from the white man. This is realism, whatever ethic it is identified with. And this, too, is Black Power in operation.

More frequently than not, projects will not use the term "Black Power," but that is hardly necessary. There is, for instance, the Poor People's Corporation, formed by a former S.N.C.C. (Student Nonviolent Coordinating Committee) worker, Jessie Norris, in August, 1965. It has set up 15 cooperatives in

Mississippi, employing about 200 black people. The employes, all shareholders, make handbags, hats, dresses, quilts, dolls and other hand-craft items that are marketed through Liberty House in Jackson, Miss. Always sensitive to the development of the black community, the Poor People's Corporation passed a rule that only registered voters could work in the co-ops.

These enterprises are small; they do not threaten the economic structure of this society, but their members look upon them as vital for the development of the black people. Their purpose is to establish a modicum of economic self-sufficiency without focusing too much attention on the impact they will have on the American economic system.

Absolutely crucial to the development of Black Power is the black middle class. These are people with sorely needed skills. There has been a lot of discussion about where the black middle class stands in relation to Black Power. Some people adopt the view that most members of the class opt out of the race (or at least try to do so); they get good jobs, a nice home, two cars, and forget about the masses of blacks who have not "made it." This has been largely true. Many middle-class blacks simply do not feel an obligation to help the less fortunate members of their race.

There is, however, a growing awareness among black middle-class people of their role in the black revolution. On Jan. 20, a small group of them (known, appropriately enough, as the Catalysts) called an all-day conference in a South Side Chicago church to discuss ways of linking black middle-class professionals with black people in the lower class. Present were about 370 people of all sorts: teachers, social workers, lawyers, accountants, three physicians, housewives, writers. They met in workshops to discuss ways of making their skills and positions relevant to the black society, and they held no press conferences. Though programs of action developed, the truth is that they remain the exception, not the rule, in the black middle class.

Another group has been formed by black teachers in Chicago, Detroit and New York, and plans are being made to expand. In Chicago, the organization is called the Association of Afro-American Educators. These are people who have traditionally been the strongest supporters of the status quo. Education is intended to develop people who will support the existing values of the society, and "Negro" teachers have been helping this process over the years. But now some of them (more than 250 met on Feb. 12 in Chicago) are organizing and beginning to redefine, first, their role as black educators vis-à-vis the black revolution, and, second, the issues as they see them. Their motivation is outlined in the following statement:

"By tapping our vast resources of black intellectual expertise, we shall generate new ideas for *meaningful* educational programs, curricula and instructional materials which will contribute substantially toward raising the educational achievement of black children.

"Our purpose is to extricate ourselves momentarily from the dominant society in order to realign our priorities, to mobilize and to 'get ourselves together' to do what must be done by those best equipped to do it."

This is what they *say;* whether they can pull it off will depend initially on their ability to bring along their black colleagues, many of whom, admittedly, do not see the efficacy of such an attitude. Unless the link is made between the black middle-class professionals and the black masses, Black Power will probably die on the speaker's platform.

Another important phenomenon in the development of Black Power is the burgeoning of black students' groups on college campuses across the country. I have visited 17 such campuses— from Harvard to Virginia to Wisconsin to U.C.L.A.—since October. The students are discussing problems of identity, of relevant curricula at their universities, of ways of helping their people when they graduate. Clearly, one sees in these hundreds (the figure could be in the thousands) of black students a little bit of Booker T. Washington (self-help and the dignity of common labor) and a lot of W. E. B. DuBois (vigorous insistence on equality and the liberal education of the most talented black men).

These are the people who are planning to implement social, political and economic Black Power in their home towns. They will run for public office, aware that Richard Hatcher started from a political base in the black community. He would not be Mayor of Gary, Ind., today if he had not first mobilized the black voters. Some people point out that he had to have white support. This is true; in many instances such support is necessary, but internal unity is necessary first.

This brings us to a consideration of the external problems of the black community. It is clear that black people will need the help of whites at many places along the line. There simply are not sufficient economic resources—actual or potential—in the black community for a total, unilateral, boot-strap operation. Why should there be? Black people have been the target of deliberate denial for centuries, and racist America has done its job well. This is a serious problem that must be faced by Black Power advocates. On the one hand, they recognize the need to be independent of "the white power structure." And on the other, they must frequently turn to that structure for help—technical and financial. Thus, the rhetoric and the reality often clash.

Resolution probably lies in the realization by white America that it is in her interest not to have a weak, dependent, alienated black community inhabiting the inner cities and blowing them up periodically. Society needs stability, and as long as there is a sizable powerless, restless group within it which considers the society illegitimate, stability is not possible. However it is calculated, the situation calls for a black-white rapprochement, which may well come only through additional confrontations and crises. More frequently than not, the self-interest of the dominant society is not clearly perceived until the brink is reached.

There are many ways whites can relate to this phenomenon. First, they must recognize that blacks are going to insist on an equitable distribution of *decision-making power*. Anything less will simply be perpetuating a welfare mentality among blacks. And if the society thinks only in terms of *giving* more jobs, better schools and more housing, the result will be the creation of more black recipients still dependent on whites.

The equitable distribution of power must result from a conviction that it is a matter of mutual self-interest, not from the feelings of guilt and altruism that were evident at the National Conference of New Politics convention in Chicago in August. An equitable distribution means that black men will have to occupy positions of political power in precincts, counties, Congressional districts and cities where their numbers and organizations warrant. It means the end of absentee white ward committeemen and precinct captains in Chicago's black precincts.

But this situation is much easier described than achieved. Black Americans generally are no more likely to vote independently than other Americans. In many Northern urban areas, especially, the job of wooing the black vote away from the Democratic party is gigantic. The established machine has the resources: patronage, tradition, apathy. In some instances the change will take a catalytic event—a major racial incident, a dramatic black candidate, a serious boner by the white establishment (such as splitting the white vote). The mere call to "blackness" simply is not enough, even where the numbers are right.

In addition, many of the problems facing black people can be solved only to the extent that whites are willing to see such imperatives as an open housing market and an expanding job market. White groups must continue to bring as much pressure as possible on local and national decision-makers to adopt sound policy in these fields. These enlightened whites *will* be able to work with Black Power groups.

There are many things which flow from this orientation to Black Power. It is´ not necessary that blacks create parallel agencies—political or economic—in all fields and places. In some areas, it is possible to work within, say, the two-party system. Richard Hatcher did so in Gary, but he first had to organize black voters to fight the Democratic machine in the primary. The same is true of Mayor Carl Stokes in Cleveland. At some point it may be wise to work with the existing agencies, but this must be done only from a base of independent, not subordinated, power.

On the other hand, dealing with a racist organization like George Wallace's Democratic party in Alabama would require forming an independent group. The same is true with some labor unions, especially in the South, which still practice discrimination despite the condemnation of such a policy by their parent unions. Many union locals are willing to work with their black members on such matters as wages and working conditions, but refuse to join the fight for open housing laws.

The point is that black people must become much more pragmatic in their approach. Whether we try to work within or outside a particular agency should depend entirely on a hard-nosed, calculated examination of potential success in each situation—a careful analysis of cost and benefit. Thus, when we negotiate the test will be: How will black people, not some political machine downtown or some labor union boss across town, benefit from this?

Black Power must insist that the institutions in the black community be led by and, wherever possible, staffed by blacks. This is advisable psychologically, and it is necessary as a challenge to the myth that black people are incapable of leadership. Admittedly, this violates the principle of egalitarianism ("We hire on the basis of merit alone, not color"). What black and white America must understand is that egalitarianism is just a *principle* and it implies a notion of "color-blindness" which is deceptive. It must be clear by now that any society which has been color-conscious all its life to the detriment of a particular group cannot simply become color-blind and expect that group to compete on equal terms.

Black Power clearly recognizes the need to perpetuate color consciousness, but in a positive way—to improve a group, not to subject it. When principles like egalitarianism have been so flagrantly violated for so long, it does not make sense to think that the victim of that violation can be equipped to benefit from opportunities simply upon their pronouncement. Obviously, some positive form of special treatment must be used to overcome centuries of negative special treatment.

This has been the argument of the Nation of Islam (the so-called Black Muslims) for years; it has also been the position of the National Urban League since its proposal for preferential treatment (the Domestic Marshall Plan, which urged a "special effort to overcome serious disabilities resulting from historic handicaps") was issued at its 1963 Denver convention. This is not racism. It is not intended to penalize or subordinate another group; its goal is the positive uplift of a deliberately repressed group. Thus, when some Black Power advocates call for the appointment of black people to head community-action poverty programs and to serve as school principals, they have in mind the deliberate projection of blacks into positions of leadership. This is important to give other black people a feeling of ability to achieve, if nothing else. And it is especially important for young black children.

An example of concentrated special treatment is the plan some of us are proposing for a new approach to education in some of the black ghettos. It goes beyond the decentralization plans in the Bundy Report; it goes beyond the community involvement at I.S. 201 in Harlem. It attempts to build on the idea proposed by Harlem CORE last year for an independent Board of Education for Harlem.

Harlem CORE and the New York Urban League saw the Bundy Report as a "step toward creating a structure which would bring meaningful education to the children of New York." CORE, led by Roy Innis, suggested an autonomous Harlem school system, chartered by the State Legislature and responsible to the state. "It will be run by an elected school board and an appointed administrator, as most school boards are," CORE said. "The elected members will be Harlem residents. It is important that much of the detailed planning and structure be the work of the Harlem community." Funds would come from city, state and Federal governments and from private sources. In describing the long-range goal of the proposal, CORE says: "Some have felt it is to create a permanently separate educational system. Others have felt it is a necessary step toward eventual integration. In any case, the ultimate outcome of this plan will be to make it possible for Harlem to choose."

Some of us propose that education in the black community should be family-oriented, not simply child-oriented. In many of the vast urban black ghettos (which will not be desegregated in the foreseeable future) the school should become the focal point of the community. This we call the Family-Community-School-Comprehensive Plan. School would cease to be a 9-to-3, September-to-June, time-off-for-good-behavior institution. It would involve education and training for the entire family—all year round, day and evening. Black parents would be intimately involved as students, decision-makers, teachers. This is much more than a revised notion of adult education courses in the evening or the use of mothers as teachers' aides.

This plan would make the educational system the center of community life. We could have community health clinics and recreational programs built into the educational system. Above all, we could reorient the demeaning public welfare system, which sends caseworkers to "investigate" families. Why could we not funnel public assistance through the community educational program?

One major advantage would be the elimination of some of the bureaucratic chaos in which five to ten governmental agencies zero in on the black family on welfare, seldom if ever coordinating their programs. The welfare department, for one, while it would not need to be altered in other parts of the state, would have to work jointly with the educational system in the black community. This would obviously require administrative reorganization, which would not necessarily reduce bureaucracy but would consolidate and centralize it. In addition to being "investigators," for example, some caseworkers (with substantially reduced case loads) could become teachers of budgetary management, and family health consultants could report the economic needs of the family.

The teachers for such a system would be specially trained in a program similar to the National Teacher Corps, and recruits could include professionals as well as mothers who could teach classes in child-rearing, home economics, art, music or any number of skills they obviously possess. Unemployed fathers could learn new skills or teach the ones they know. The curriculum would be both academic and vocational, and it would contain courses in the culture and history of black people. The school would belong to the community. It would be a union of children, parents, teachers, social workers, psychologists, urban planners, doctors, community organizers. It would become a major vehicle for fashioning a sense of pride and group identity.

I see no reason why the local law-enforcement agency could not be integrated into this system. Perhaps this could take the form of training "community service officers," or junior policemen, as suggested in the report of the President's Commission on Civil Disorders. Or the local police precinct could be based in the school, working with the people on such things as crime prevention, first aid and the training of police officers. In this way, mutual trust could be developed between the black community and the police.

Coordinating these programs would present problems to be

worked out on the basis of the community involved, the agencies involved and the size of the system. It seems quite obvious that in innovations of this sort there will be a tremendous amount of chaos and uncertainty and there will be mistakes. This is understandable; it is the price to be paid for social change under circumstances of widespread alienation and deprivation. The recent furor about the Malcolm X memorial program at I.S. 201 in Harlem offers an example of the kind of problem to be anticipated. Rather than worrying about what one person said from a stage at a particular meeting, the authorities should be concerned about how the Board of Education will cooperate to transfer power to the community school board. When the transfer is made, confusion regarding lines of authority and program and curriculum content can be reduced.

The longer the delay in making the transfer, however, the greater the likelihood of disruption. One can expect misunderstanding, great differences of opinion and a relatively low return on efforts at the beginning of such new programs. New standards of evaluation are being set, and the experimental concept developed at I.S. 201 should not be jeopardized by isolated incidents. It would be surprising if everything went smoothly from the outset.

Some programs *will* flounder, some will collapse out of sheer incompetence and faulty conception, but this presents an opportunity to build on mistakes. The precise details of the Comprehensive Plan would have to be worked out in conjunction with each community and agency involved. But the *idea* is seriously proposed. We must begin to think in entirely new terms of citizen involvement and decision-making.

Black Power has been accused of emphasizing decentralization, of overlooking the obvious trend toward consolidation. This is not true with the kind of Black Power described here, which is ultimately not separatist or isolationist. Some Black Power advocates. are aware that this country is simultaneously experiencing centralization and decentralization. As the Federal Government becomes more involved (and it must) in the lives of people, it is imperative that we broaden the base of citizen participation. It will be the new forms, new agencies and structures developed by Black Power that will link these centralizing and decentralizing trends.

Black Power structures at the local level will activate people, instill faith (not alienation) and provide a habit of organization and a consciousness of ability. Alienation will be overcome and trust in society restored. It will be through these local agencies that the centralized forces will operate, not through insensitive, unresponsive city halls. Billions of dollars will be needed each year, and these funds must be provided through a more direct route from their sources to the people.

Black Power is a developmental process; it cannot be an end in itself. To the extent that black Americans can organize, and to the extent that white Americans can keep from panicking and begin to respond rationally to the demands of that organization— to that extent can we get on with the protracted business of creating not just law and order but a free and open society.

The Full and Sometimes Very Surprising Story of Ocean Hill, the Teachers' Union and the Teacher Strikes of 1968

by Martin Mayer

THE TEACHER STRIKES of 1968 seem to me the worst disaster my native city has experienced in my lifetime.

It is always in the interest of those in authority to say in retrospect that a disaster—a war or mine explosion—was inevitable. The belief underlying this report is that what happened in New York in the fall of 1968 was *not* inevitable, and that those who are saying that it was—especially those in the great foundations and in the Mayor's office—are much more to be blamed for what happened than are any of the participants. Great wealth and political leadership carry responsibilities which were not met. At no point did these forces demonstrate any understanding of what was happening in terms other than their own preconceptions,

From the *New York Times Magazine*, February 2, 1969.
Condensation of *The Teachers Strike New York, 1968* by Martin Mayer, copyright © 1969 by Martin Trager Mayer by permission of Harper & Row Publishers, Inc.

and at no point did they exert the authority, leadership or even influence which their status and social roles obligated them to exert.

As an attempt at history, the following narrative concentrates on events and their immediate context, and a certain amount of background should be, as the lawyers say, stipulated·

(1) During the course of political reform in the nineteen-thirties, control of the New York City school system was narrowly concentrated in a central office. In the nineteen-fifties and early sixties, the machinery grew too complicated and too rigid for its purposes, and the system became increasingly unresponsive to both the teachers in the classrooms and the parents whose children were in the schools. The teachers, through trade-union organization, were able to establish countervailing force; the parents were not.

Beginning in 1961, when the State Legislature ordered "revitalization" of local school boards, there was a political drive toward "decentralization" of the system, to make the schools accountable to "the community." As chairman of a local board, incidentally, and as a writer for various publications, I was myself among the leaders of this drive.

In the summer and fall of 1967, formal decentralization proposals were developed by an advisory committee to the Mayor, chaired by McGeorge Bundy of the Ford Foundation, for consideration by the State Legislature in the spring of 1968. No representative of the teachers, the school supervisors, the trade-union movement or the organized parent movement was appointed to the committee.

(2) In the middle nineteen-sixties, the proportion of Negro and Puerto Rican children in the New York schools neared and then passed 50 per cent. The proportion of Negro and Puerto Rican population in the city as a whole, however, is only about 27 per cent, and the proportion of voters who are Negro or Puerto Rican is considerably less than 20 per cent. New York ranks 13th among the nation's 15 largest cities in the proportion of its population which is nonwhite.

Within the schools, Negro and Puerto Rican children are doing substantially less well than mainland white children: At age 12, the gap in accomplishment is more than two years, as measured by standardized tests. It is psychologically very difficult for parents not to blame the schools; and almost equally difficult for people in the schools, who believe they are doing the best they can (and who know that their results are, if anything, a little better than the results in other cities), not to feel a degree of complacency in the face of failure by most of their students.

(3) Most New York City schoolteachers are recruited from the city colleges, which until recently have restricted admission to students from the higher ranks of the city's high schools. Examinations beyond those required by the state have been imposed for a New York City teaching license, and promotion has been possible only through an elaborate system of internal examinations. Much, but not all, of this is required by state law.

The proportion of Negroes and Puerto Ricans among full-time students at the city colleges has been until recently something like 3 per cent. The proportion among the city's teachers is less than 10 per cent (by contrast with 30 per cent and more in other large cities, up to 80 per cent in Washington, D. C.), and the proportion of Negroes and Puerto Ricans among New York school administrators is almost invisible except on the lowest rank, that of assistant principal.

(4) Ocean Hill, the focal point of the teacher strikes, is a border area between the slum districts of Brownsville and Bedford-Stuyvesant, some miles out from downtown Brooklyn. Less than a fifth of its adult population was born in New York City; less than a third completed high school; only two-fifths have lived in the area as long as five years; more than half the households subsist on less than $5,000 a year; about 70 per cent are Negro; about 25 per cent are Puerto Rican. Though there are some blocks of pleasant, owner-occupied private houses, most people live in deteriorating rooming houses and tenements, and much of the area's housing is simply being abandoned by its owners. All the well-known social problems are present. It is a highly discouraging place in which to live and to bring up one's children.

Spring, 1967—Ocean Hill-Brownsville is chosen as a "demonstration district" for an experiment in decentralization

Early 1967 was growing season for plans to decentralize the New York schools, and among those involved in the planning was the Ford Foundation, which was especially interested in projects that would increase community involvement in school administration. The possibility of using Ocean Hill-Brownsville for an experiment along these lines was suggested to Ford by the United Federation of Teachers. Since 1966, the union had been running a project in teacher-parent joint action in the district—picketings and other demonstrations—which had secured the removal of an unwanted principal at a junior high school, and won some special services for that school and for one of the elementary schools that fed into it. The leader of these joint ventures was Mrs. Sandra Feldman, a young teacher, union field representative and civil-rights worker who had been among the organizers of East River CORE.

Meanwhile, a group of social workers and parents affiliated with Brooklyn CORE and with the emerging Council Against Poverty, and led mostly by a white worker priest, Father John Powis of the Church of Our Lady of the Presentation, formed an unofficial "people's board of education" for the Ocean Hill area. Linked by their shared dislike of the Board of Education, and by their common roots in the civil-rights movement, the union-sponsored marching society and the people's board joined forces in early 1967 to plan the liberation of the schools of the area from the heavy hand of the citywide Board of Education.

From the beginning, the two groups had different objectives. The people's board was interested in "community control"—a slogan with no clear meaning, but implying a glorious freedom which "decentralization" somehow lacked—and the union was interested in the expansion of its More Effective Schools (M.E.S.) program, by which very substantial extra sums of money (about $600 additional per child) are invested in elementary schools. M.E.S. is extremely popular with communities where it has been tried, however, so there was no necessary conflict between the participants in what came to be called "the planning council."

In the late spring of 1967, this planning group was recognized by the Board of Education and by the Ford Foundation, which in July put up $44,000 to pay the costs of setting up an experimental "demonstration district" to include the two junior high schools in the area and the five (later six) elementary schools which fed them. (Ford also underwrote similar experiments in the Two Bridges area of the Lower East Side and in the district served by I.S. 201 in East Harlem.)

Summer, 1967—The first split between community and teachers comes with the hiring of a unit administrator

The people's board representatives went into the summer months determined to have their project operative in the fall. They met steadily through the month of July, often with outside groups—from Ford, Brooklyn College, Yeshiva University, the Mayor's office and the Board of Education—in sessions which did not always include the teacher delegates. Among the outsiders at some of the sessions was an old friend of Father Powis's, Herman Ferguson, who had recently denounced the M.E.S. school where he was employed for practicing "educational genocide" and who had been indicted (he was later convicted and is now appealing) for conspiracy to murder N.A.A.C.P. leader Roy Wilkins and Urban League director Whitney Young.

In the absence of any systematic efforts at guidance by the Ford Foundation or the Board of Education (where the man charged to maintain liaison with Ocean Hill took his summer vacation in July), the parent members of the planning council turned increasingly to Father Powis and to Ferguson, who was capable, forceful and extremely hostile to the union. The teacher delegates began to feel uncomfortable at meetings.

As its first step, by arrangement with Ford, the planning council hired a future unit administrator. Several candidates were interviewed by parent representatives and community leaders at sessions to which the teacher delegates were not invited, and the interviewers selected Rhody A. McCoy, a compact, thoughtful, impressive schoolman of 18 years' experience in New York, acting principal of a school for seriously disturbed boys on the West Side of Manhattan.

The teacher representatives on the planning council knew nothing against (or for) McCoy, but they were irked at the procedure and its speed, and a few of them thought there ought to be more than one name proposed to the full panel. Rather frivolously, on the grounds that he was somebody everyone knew. one of the teacher representatives nominated Jack Bloomfield, principal of J.H.S. 271, one of the district's two junior highs. Some of the parents unquestionably felt that the teachers—authority figures in their lives at all times—were seeking to take the project away from them; in quiet moments in Ocean Hill the reverberations of the Bloomfield nomination can still be heard. McCoy's name was quickly approved by the planning council.

Rhody McCoy puts parent representatives on a secret payroll

Among McCoy's first acts as administrator was to authorize checks for sums of $39 to $100 a week for 17 mothers of children in the district's school, most of whom had announced that they were going to be candidates for the parent positions on whatever local board of education was set up as the result of the summer's work. These first payments were made to them as "election consultants." Some weeks after the election, in which 7 of the 17 were declared winners, the category for weekly compensation to the lucky seven was changed to "parent representative." No public announcement was ever made that the parent representatives were being paid.

Payments to the parent representatives declined as the Ford grant ran lower, rose briefly after Ford added another $15,000 in the fall, then declined again. The total up to February, 1968, when the payments stopped, ran to about a quarter of the $59,-000 in the first Ford grants. The grants had been made through Father Powis's church, so McCoy did not have to account to any outside authority. The governing board's public statements became much more radical when the payments ceased.

If poor people are to serve on school boards, they should certainly be paid for their time as part of a published budget. But "community control" is not an intelligent description of a situation in which the community representatives are on a fluctuating and secret payroll controlled by the very staff that they are supposed to be controlling.

The planning council becomes a governing board

After four weeks of day-and-night work, the planning council on July 29, 1967, produced a three-page proposal which took off from a revolutionary preamble: "Men are capable of putting an end to what they find intolerable without recourse to politics. . . . The ending of oppression and the beginning of a new day has often become a reality only after people have resorted to violent means. . . . The following plan . . . is acknowledged to be the last threads of the community's faith in the school system's purposes and abilities."

The plan itself called for the creation of a governing board of 24—one parent and one teacher from each of eight schools, five community representatives to be chosen by the parent members of the board, two representatives of the school supervisors in the district, and one delegate from a university to be chosen by the board as a whole. This board would exercise most of the powers of the Board of Education in the Ocean Hill schools, but its authority over personnel would be very limited—after hiring its own unit administrator, the board could only approve his recommendations of principals for the schools, and would have no functions with relation to the employment of teachers.

Before the Board of Education could react in any way to this document, the planning council held the election for parent representatives. After some house-to-house canvassing to register voters (the Board had not supplied lists of parents), the council advertised the election for Aug. 3 and set up ballot boxes in the schools. Turnout was light, and for the next two days delegates from the council, including the candidates, circulated around the district collecting votes door-to-door. In total, about a quarter of the district's parents voted. The Board of Education never recognized the validity of this vote, but did deal with the resulting governing board as though it had been formally elected.

The elected parent representatives, all mothers, several on welfare, promptly named five community leaders for the board, including Father Powis, Assemblyman Samuel D. Wright, the district's representative in Albany, and the Rev. C. Herbert Oliver, recently arrived from the South and the Southern Christian Leadership Conference to become pastor of Westminister Bethany Presbyterian Church. Oliver, a handsome figure with a resonant voice, whose black separatist beliefs were not yet known, was a neutral in the politics of the area. He was chosen chairman over Assemblyman Wright by a vote of 10 to 6, and the newly formed board got to work on personnel selection.

The governing board hires principals and the split with the teachers grows

Four principalships were vacant in the district, and a fifth vacancy would be created in February with the opening of I.S. 55, a new "intermediate school" (a term which replaces the old "junior high school"). In their proposals, the planning council had insisted on the right to choose any principals who met New York State requirements for such a job, without reference to the city school system's civil-service list. The current list, of several hundred names, contains only four Negroes—and does not expire until 1972.

The Board of Education in August, 1967, applied to State Commissioner of Education James E. Allen for permission to hire principals for Ocean Hill who were not on the list. Allen said no, but ruled the Board could *create* a special category of "Demonstration Elementary School Principal" which could be filled ad lib pending the development of a new exam to license people for such a position. It was this creation of a special category, and removal of the Ocean Hill jobs from the future prospects of those on the normal list, that the Kings County Supreme Court and the lower courts later ruled illegal, influencing the course of the teacher strikes.

The Ocean Hill board met on Aug. 31, and on McCoy's nomination recommended to the Board of Education five men to fill the district's vacancies—among them Irving Gerber, a recently licensed principal who wished to transfer in; Luis Fuentes, a reading consultant from Farmingdale; William Harris, a city assistant principal; and Herman Ferguson, for appointment to I.S. 55 when it opened in February. The teacher representatives felt that they did not know any of these people (except Ferguson, to whom they objected). They also knew that when they had been chosen for the original planning council their colleagues had never expected them to be voting on principals for the schools. Therefore, they announced they would abstain from the vote on the principals, and left the room during the discussion. These actions were unquestionably regarded as a rejection of the principals by some parent and community members of the governing board.

Incidentally, all but one of the principals actually appointed on the governing board's recommendation, then and later, are highly regarded by both the union and by school headquarters. (The exception is Fuentes, who is regarded as emotionally unstable by teachers, by the Bureau of Personnel at the Board of Education and by the members of the local school board for District 1, on the Lower East Side, whom he and his friends held physically captive for some hours one evening in September, in an unsuccessful effort to force them to name him district superintendent.) There is an Alice-in-Wonderland quality about the fact that the U.F.T. in its climactic strike held out for at least the temporary removal of P.S. 144 principal Ralph Rogers, who is universally admired, and of William Harris, whose sense of fairness several union members in the district have special reason to cherish.

September, 1967—The teachers strike the city for their own reasons and Ocean Hill hates them for it

Before anybody could explain to anybody else what had happened at the Aug. 31 meeting to nominate principals, the teachers went out on strike against the whole city on the opening day of the fall term. This 1967 strike, which lasted two wretched weeks and ended with no significant change in the city's original contract offer, was at bottom a protest against Mayor John V. Lindsay's fact-finding technique for resolving labor disputes, but the union's announced goals were educational—smaller class sizes and additional More Effective Schools. "TEACHERS WANT WHAT CHILDREN NEED" was their slogan. Most Ocean Hill parents thought that what children needed was an open school and a shiny new governing board, and that the strike was an abomination.

In retrospect, it seems obvious—indeed, it seemed obvious at the time—that, whatever the merits of the citywide strike, a decent sensitivity to the newly aroused hopes of the people in Ocean Hill should have permitted the union teachers to stay on the job in that district.

Nowhere in the city were more ardent efforts made to keep the schools open through the strike. Letters were sent to the draft boards of male teachers, announcing that the teachers were no longer teaching and should be called up. Traveling militants were brought into the schools to take classes and to scare the teachers on the picket lines. (Ferguson himself ran the training lessons for parents who were going to take over classrooms.) Curses and obscenities were screamed at the pickets from all directions, and some were jostled.

In the aftermath of the strike, the U.F.T. forbade union teachers to become members of the governing board, and joined with the Council of Supervisory Associations (the organization of principals, assistant principals, bureau chiefs, etc.) in a lawsuit to oust the new Ocean Hill principals as illegally appointed.

The impact of this lawsuit within the schools was greater than most commentators have realized. Three of the four new principals appointed that fall were beginners at their jobs, and inevitably insecure. This statement that the assistant principals and teachers did not regard the principals as legitimate or permanent damaged their ability to control what were at best difficult schools. It was easy to believe that anything unpleasant which happened in school had been organized by a subversive staff, and in some instances, probably, the belief was true. The district's teachers were placed in an almost equally difficult position, of course, in their relations with the principals.

The union had not consulted the teachers in the district before joining in the lawsuit. Recently, the union president, Albert Shanker, was asked why the U.F.T. had taken action, especially in the light of its long history of opposition to the principals' licensing exams (the union has always advocated the election of principals by teachers). Shanker said: "Pure pique."

In November, claiming that some of their number had been

harassed (by anti-Semitic insults, among other things)—and that McCoy was not supporting them—all 18 of the district's assistant principals applied for transfer out, leaving the new principals without experienced administrative help in the day-to-day operation of the schools. The governing board, which had never thought about the role of A.P.'s before, now asked the Board of Education for the right to choose its own A.P.'s as it had chosen its own principals. ("The very best principal in the world," a memo from Ocean Hill pleaded a few months later, "cannot operate a school with assistant principals who are not cooperating.") But the Board and Commissioner Allen refused, and new A.P.'s—some of them totally inexperienced—were simply assigned in from the civil-service list.

The New Year, 1968—A flurry of optimism, and grim determination

The start of the second semester, in February, 1968, brought the district a big event: the opening of the new I.S. 55, which was celebrated with gleeful ceremony. The old J.H.S. 178 was converted to an elementary school, ending overcrowding in the district.

Jack Bloomfield, principal of J.H.S. 271, whose relations in the district had disintegrated after his nomination to be unit administrator, was finally granted his request for a transfer out. McCoy wanted to shift William Harris from the now-defunct J.H.S. 178 to J.H.S. 271, because he considered that school his worst problem and Harris his best man. (So did the J.H.S. 178 teachers, nearly all of whom signed a petition asking the governing board to allow Harris to move with *them* to I.S. 55.) The Board of Education would not make the appointment, however, and finally McCoy in desperation simply "recognized" Harris as principal of J.H.S. 271.

Harris, the first male Negro principal of a secondary school in New York, came into an unbelievably chaotic situation. Thirty teachers—a quarter of the staff—had transferred out, and the Board of Education had found only 16 replacements. Five of the six secretaries had left; all the assistant principals were new; and 40 sets of keys were missing. Absenteeism ran from 10 to 25 teachers a day; often there were simply not enough adult bodies in the building to man the classrooms for 1,700 children, let alone chase the kids out of the halls. Fires broke out mysteriously, several every week, and the culprits could not be found. Furniture was thrown from third-floor windows, paint flew around art rooms, vandalism and thievery were everywhere. Harris met grimly with his staff, and they decided they would try to make it work. Somehow.

March, 1968—A court rules against the Ocean Hill principals, but the district supports them

In early March, Justice Dominic S. Rinaldi, Kings County Supreme Court, handed down his opinion in the suit brought by the supervisors' association. He held that the appointment of demonstration elementary school principals in Ocean Hill was illegal under the Education Law.

The next day, Frederick Nauman, a guidance teacher who was U.F.T. chapter chairman for J.H.S. 271 and district chairman for the unit, drafted a letter to Alfred A. Giardino, president of the Board of Education, urging him to appeal the decision and to retain the governing board's principals on the job pending the results of the last possible appeal, because the Ocean Hill experiment was important and would be killed if the principals were removed. Naumann secured 115 signatures, representing virtually the entire staff.

When I visited Ocean Hill that month to write an article for this magazine, I found McCoy working desperately hard with his principals and staff—some white, some Negro—to put a head of steam under a number of new programs in reading, math, Negro and Puerto Rican culture, bilingualism, etc. He had begun small-scale training programs for "paraprofessionals," mothers of children in the district's schools who would, at the end of the programs, become teacher assistants, helping out with reading and math. He was planning for teacher teams, nongraded classrooms, programmed instruction—everything that reputation said might help in a neighborhood where most children were as far behind as they were in Ocean Hill.

I visited four of the district's schools on as many days, and returned to tell McCoy that I had seen a good deal of routine—and some substandard—teaching, and that the schools seemed dominated by a fear of disorder which impeded teaching. He said he knew, that he was working to establish a climate in which teachers could teach, and that once he had the climate he was going to judge who was good and could give help, who needed help, and who ought to be eliminated from the district. It was all intelligent, level-headed—and very sad.

April, 1968—Three shocks, and a confrontation

During April, the district sustained three serious shocks. One was the murder of Martin Luther King, which was followed by assaults on white teachers at J.H.S. 271, some undoubtedly stimulated by an inflammatory notice about the assassination posted on bulletin boards by Leslie Campbell, publicity director of the African-American Teachers Association, who had recently transferred into the district.

Another was a two-day school boycott called by the governing board to support its demand for recognition and for authority over budget and personnel. It proved almost entirely effective.

The third was a fire one afternoon at I.S. 55. It drove everyone out of the building a little after 2 o'clock. At 3, the firemen were still there, and the children were still on the street. A few teachers—there is a dispute about how many, but 10 would seem to be a maximum figure—simply abandoned their classes and went off home, or to their second jobs, or whatever. When the children poured back into the building, coats and other possessions were stolen, fights broke out, and the new school, which had opened less than three months before as the future pride of the community, became the scene of a minor riot.

At about this time, perhaps because of the general level of frustration, perhaps because of these specific events, perhaps because the Ford grant had run out and the parent representatives were no longer being paid—perhaps because it had been planned that way from the beginning—the Ocean Hill board fell under the domination of people who had determined to use it to force what Father Powis likes to call "a confrontation with a sick society."

A frustrated governing board turns on the teachers

Complaints against teachers are endemic to the process of education. Most often, they are ill-founded, the result of childish incomprehension or parental disappointment, and to protect teachers against such complaints and against politically motivated discharge, rules of teacher tenure have been adopted throughout the civilized world. Teachers can still be discharged for malfeasance, but in most school systems it is bloody difficult—most difficult of all, perhaps, in New York. One of the survival skills of a New York school administrator is the ability to slough off bad staff onto other districts, and there are literally hundreds of incompetent (some of them mentally ill) teachers drifting about the school system. Inevitably, Ocean Hill got more than its share of bad teachers.

Ocean Hill administrators were getting complaints about good teachers, too. After all, what's the use of having a home-grown governing board if you can't complain about the teachers?

Like suburban school superintendents, McCoy had only so much time he could put into dealing with parent complaints about teachers. What worried him more were the complaints from his principals about lack of support from the assistant principals the Board of Education had arbitrarily assigned to the district in the fall. Superintendent of Schools Bernard Donovan had transferred out, at McCoy's request, five of these 18 A.P.'s, but McCoy told the governing board that requests to transfer three others had been refused. Someone suggested that the board should simply exclude the A.P.'s from the district.

On March 28 this tactic was rejected, mostly on the urging of Assemblyman Wright, who thought there was a chance to get an effective school decentralization bill through the State Legislature, and that any arbitrary action by the governing board would harm its chances. He proposed that the board announce charges against the A.P.'s and hold public hearings before taking any action, and his motion carried. The next day Wright went back to Albany, the governing board met again, and the motion passed the previous day was rescinded.

At these meetings board members began discussing the possibility of excluding from the district some of the teachers as well as the assistant principals. It occurred to someone that the governing board could make a very big splash in the world by firing a bunch of teachers and administrators and proclaiming that now and forevermore Ocean Hill would make its own decisions about who could and who could not teach in its schools.

But setting up such a confrontation by dismissing teachers was more difficult than the casual observer might think, because Donovan was ready to help McCoy quietly transfer out people he did not want, and had indeed offered to do so. Involuntary transfers are not uncommon in the school system. When McCoy mentioned to Donovan that some teachers were going to have to go, Donovan told him to send along the names with some notion of the reasons why—all in confidence—and the Bureau of Personnel would take care of the matter.

The union, too, was ready to help out. McCoy early in the year had moved to restore good relations with the U.F.T. He went to Manhattan and met at union headquarters with Shanker and Mrs. Feldman and others, to ask what technical assistance the union could give him. A committee was set up, consisting of the chapter chairmen at the schools in the district plus the teacher members of the previous summer's planning group.

Liaison between the committee and McCoy was provided by Mrs. Feldman, who went to his office several times a month. At several meetings in March, McCoy mentioned to Mrs. Feldman that he was under pressure to get rid of some teachers, and Mrs. Feldman said that if he gave the U.F.T. the reasons why he wanted to remove any individual, the union would make no trouble. (Only later was she to learn that four members of the committee formed to help McCoy were among those tagged for removal.)

At no time did McCoy mention to his governing board any of his renewed contacts with the union. (Indeed, the board members learned about them for the first time when Shanker mentioned them on a television show during the strike—at which point the ladies of the governing board got hopping mad.)

*May, 1968—The governing board dismisses the wrong
teachers for the wrong reasons*

Sometime in early March, the Rev. Mr. Oliver appointed a personnel committee of the governing board, with Father Powis as
its chairman (though Mrs. Clara Marshall, a parent representative
and vice chairman of the board, later signed its report). Some
time in early April the report of the committee was ready. It
recommended "the removal from our district" of the one surviving pre-project principal, five assistant principals, and 13
teachers.

Now came the tricky part. If McCoy asked Donovan to transfer
the people the committee wanted out, he would lose most of the
confrontation. McCoy would not have been given all he asked for,
but he would certainly have been given most. (During this period
the similarly organized I.S. 201 complex quietly transferred out,
by informal administrative procedures, more people than Ocean
Hill was seeking to move.) At the same time, the parent representatives, and community representatives like Assemblyman
Wright and Prof. Stephen Lockwood of Brooklyn College (who
had been chosen as the university member of the governing
board), had to be convinced that McCoy had asked for the
transfers, and had been refused.

And the trick was accomplished. To this day, most members
of the governing board believe that McCoy asked to be relieved
of the people whose names were mentioned in the personnel committee report, and got nowhere. Most outside observers think so,
too, either because McCoy told them so (as he did Kenneth
Clark, the Negro psychologist and member of the State Board of
Regents who came to play an active role in the dispute) or
simply because it stands to reason.

In fact, as he has admitted to several university and foundation
advisers to the project—and to me—McCoy never requested
transfer for any of the teachers. (He says it would have been
pointless, because Donovan would have refused.) He could
scarcely claim otherwise to anyone who had been nosing around
the situation. Quite apart from any external evidence at various
hearings, there is the total absence of documents to support a
claim that requests were made. ("Where are his carbons?" Donovan says sourly.)

Despite his apparent cooperation in preparing the confrontation, McCoy seems to have been careful to dissociate himself from the specific action of the governing board. About a week before the dismissals occurred, Father Powis told a meeting of the Coordinating Committee for Community Control that Ocean Hill was about to "fire" 13 teachers, and that McCoy opposed the idea. Certainly, he had nothing to do with the personnel committee report. Two of the teachers whose dismissal was recommended by the committee were identified only as "Mr. Steinberg" and "Mr. Bergen," and any administrator, no matter how inefficient, would at least know the first names of the teachers he was seeking to discipline.

During the weeks before the governing board acted, some trial balloons were lofted to see how people favorably inclined to the experiment would react to an attempt to oust teachers. The most important of them rose on April 26, when members of the governing board met with members of the Urban Coalition education task force. Most of the meeting was devoted to a discussion of the governing board's grievances against the Board of Education. Then, as people were putting on their coats, Father Powis announced: "Next Monday, we're firing 13 teachers"—and everybody sat down again, and listened while Father Powis told of the teachers who had abandoned the children after the I.S. 55 fire and of unspecified "sabotage" by union teachers. John Simon, president of the Taconic Foundation and a lawyer, says that he urged Father Powis to prepare charges against anybody the governing board wished to dismiss; and that Father Powis said: "No. Every time you bring charges, you lose."

Simon recalls asking Preston Wilcox, a former professor of social work who had become a consultant on school decentralization, to go out to Ocean Hill and persuade the governing board to cool it, at least for the period when the Legislature would be considering school decentralization proposals. The matter cannot have loomed large, however, for Wilcox has no recollection of this specific mission.

Then it developed, astonishingly, that the teachers against whom the governing board was acting were not the I.S. 55 teachers who had left after the fire—that some were not even among the incompetents whom any visitor to the district had noted.

Two were U.F.T. chapter chairmen, two others were original participants in the planning council, and the majority were from J.H.S. 271, which was still short of staff and needed everybody it could get. Of the six J.H.S. 271 teachers on the list (the committee report showed seven, but one had recently transferred into an elementary school, which the committee did not know), principal William Harris was willing to certify that two were in fact incompetent—but against the other four he had no complaint whatever.

The committee assured him that the charges against those four had nothing to do with competence, that the members of the committee had been around Ocean Hill longer than Harris and had reason to know these four were bad men and enemies of the demonstration project. The leading figure among the four was Fred Nauman, the U.F.T. chapter chairman who had recently organized the petition to the Board of Education urging the retention of the Ocean Hill principals.

The fact is that the objection to Nauman was simply a generalized rumor of hostility which had been deliberately fed to a few parents. When the time came to present evidence against Nauman, the governing board could produce none. Mrs. Marshall, who signed the personnel committee report, said the other day: "Nauman had been beautiful, one of the best teachers in the school. But after Mr. Harris came in he changed. The parents said that all those awful things were happening and that Nauman knew about them, so he must have had something to do with them. . . ." But Nauman has letters of commendation and thanks from Harris for his work in those first weeks of the new regime at J.H.S. 271, and to this day, neither man has been willing to say a word against the other. Nauman rubbed McCoy wrong, but at bottom he was being discharged from the district for one reason alone: Because he was the U.F.T. chairman, the union would *have* to fight on his behalf. Nauman's presence on the list guaranteed the confrontation.

In the months that followed, a number of supporters of the governing board, especially the New York Civil Liberties Union, insisted that what the board was doing was simply a routine transfer out, which the union blew up to vast proportions as part of its war against decentralization in the State Legislature. There is absolutely no evidence to support this contention. In conversations at the time, Father Powis and others spoke of "firing," and in statements to the newspapers the governing board spoke of "ousting." The report of the personnel committee itself declared: "We feel that we will be condemned by many as having to make this unpleasant recommendation."

Of course, the governing board could *not* fire anybody, because it did not *employ* anybody. Its own headquarters staff were all officially employed by the Board of Education. But it is hard to think of any accusation more likely to damage the future career of an urban teacher than a statement that he is hostile to the legitimate aspirations of Negro parents and children, and is thereby "causing serious danger to our students." The accusation was made against Fred Nauman and at least three others, officially, publicly, without evidence—after an investigation so trivial that it failed to turn up the first names of two of the persons accused. Such behavior can be defended, perhaps, by those who believed in the nineteen-fifties that the Federal Government was right in publicly labeling people "security risks," without evidence. People who opposed McCarthyism in the fifties, though, would not seem to have available to them today the luxury of supporting the action the Ocean Hill governing board was to take on Tuesday, May 7, 1968.

Over the weekend before, Assemblyman Wright had pleaded with the governing board not to take arbitrary action on personnel during the week the State Legislature was to begin its consideration of decentralization bills. Nevertheless, when the governing board met that Tuesday evening in executive session the report of the personnel committee was called up for approval. Professor Lockwood opposed the report, and urged that the board at least call the accused staff before it to talk over the charges before acting. Especially when complaints relate to behavior rather than to competence, he argued, people must be given a right to some kind of hearing. Moreover, if the teachers refused to appear at the meeting, they would be automatically guilty of insubordination. Several of the parent members stirred uneasily while Dr. Lockwood spoke.

Presently, as though on signal, the door to the meeting room burst open and 15 to 20 militants rushed in and ranged themselves against the wall. This was a community board, they said, and they were the community, and they were there to see that the board did what the community wanted. ("At this point," the minutes of the meeting say gallantly and rather glumly, "the community entered the room.") In this atmosphere, the report of the personnel committee was approved, and McCoy was ordered to write letters to the 19, "terminating their services" in the district.

On the poisoned ground of educational failure in Ocean Hill, the governing board had sown the dragon's teeth of personal injustice. And the armed men sprang up.

May, 1968—The union strikes the project

The next weeks saw a succession of premieres of events that were destined to have long runs. Teachers were blocked trying to enter school, police escorted teachers into buildings, parents boycotted schools, residents of the area were arrested, lights burned until 3 in the morning at Gracie Mansion.

Both the governing board and the union began what would be a dreary round of clevernesses. McCoy would admit the dismissed teachers to their classes, then order them to his office; when they did not come, he would dismiss them anew for insubordination. The union would arrange to have its other members wait outside the schools for the appearance of the dismissed teachers, and when their entrance was blocked, the others would all declare themselves locked out. About 350 of the district's 500-odd teachers supported the strike.

McCoy stands pat, and refuses to bring charges against the dismissed teachers

On May 14 the Board of Education appointed Judge Francis E. Rivers, who had recently retired from Civil Court after a long career as one of the city's few Negro judges, to be the trial examiner on whatever charges McCoy might bring. The governing board responded by calling for mediation by state authorities, which Superintendent Donovan accepted; but it turned out that what the governing board meant was mediation of its claims to authority to exclude anybody without giving reasons, not mediation of individual cases.

Donovan brought McCoy and Shanker together, and McCoy assured both men that there were charges aplenty against the six administrators and 12 teachers (the 13th, the one Negro, had been reinstated almost immediately by the governing board). Not all the charges, though, were going to be publishable. For example, one of the men at J.H.S. 271, a man with a family, was shacked up with a girl across the street. McCoy couldn't put that in the public charges ("Indeed not," Donovan murmured), but if the matter came to a hearing it would have to come out, which would ruin the man's life. Shanker agreed that was a problem, and spoke with the teacher McCoy had accused, who roared with laughter and said there was nothing to it and he would happily take his chances at a hearing.

In the end, Shanker continued his demand that McCoy state the governing board's reasons for compelling the transfers, and permit the accused teachers to require the presentation of evidence at a hearing. And McCoy insisted that the community had the right to decide who would and who would not teach in its schools, and that the governing board had forbidden him to present formal charges.

Meanwhile, Donovan was under pressure from Mayor Lindsay (who spoke to him directly almost daily) to get the Ocean Hill staff to accept their removal from the project. He succeeded with the administrators, all of whom eventually accepted reassignment elsewhere, and two teachers also dropped out of the fight. But 10 of the teachers were made of stronger stuff—and their union was striking to support them.

In Albany, the union was riding the gift horse from Ocean Hill to trample the strong decentralization legislation recommended by Mayor Lindsay and by the Board of Regents, and many good liberals assumed this was the purpose of the strike. The Urban Coalition, the Ford Foundation and even the Mayor's office put pressure on the governing board to prefer charges against the teachers and to present evidence before Judge Rivers.

McCoy went to Kenneth Clark and asked him to persuade the State Commissioner of Education to intervene. He assured Clark that he had gone through all normal procedures seeking the removal of the teachers, and that the governing board had finally acted the way it had because all legitimate avenues had been blocked. It never occurred to Clark that McCoy was not telling him the truth.

McCoy at last files charges against some (not all) of the dismissed teachers

On May 25, Donovan put McCoy under orders: Either he would allow the return of the teachers, or he would be fired himself for insubordination. On that pledge, Shanker urged his teachers to return, and they did. McCoy promply suspended six of them on formal charges. And the strike was on again.

By then, the State Legislature had passed the Marchi bill on decentralization, a weaker measure, supported by the union, and the strike could no longer be considered by anyone as a political gesture to affect what happened in Albany. The union was going to see to it that the teachers kept their jobs.

The governing board tentatively accepts, and then rejects, arbitration

The filing of charges made the situation look like a relatively familiar kind of dispute, and the Board of Education was now confident it could be resolved in relatively familiar ways. All parties were summoned to a meeting at the Board for Friday, May 31. Mrs. Rose Shapiro, acting president of the Board of Education, opened the meeting with a statement that nobody was going to leave the building until a settlement had been reached.

And, apparently, a settlement was reached. If the governing board did not wish to go through the usual Board of Education trial examiner's procedure, Mrs. Shapiro suggested, outside arbitration could be invoked and made binding on all parties. The American Arbitration Association was set up to move expeditiously on just this sort of case. Meanwhile, the teachers would go back to work, except for those dismissed by the district, who would be needed at the arbitration hearings, anyway.

A one-page agreement was drawn up and typed, by which the union, Mrs. Marshall of the Ocean Hill governing board and the

Board of Education all agreed to arbitration. Just before it was to be signed, Father Powis objected that Mrs. Marshall could not bind the governing board, and that the language should be changed. The document actually signed, therefore, includes a penciled insertion of the word "consider" before the word "arbitration." Nevertheless, the Board of Education and the U.F.T. left the meeting with the feeling that the fight was over. Mrs. Marshall made an optimistic statement to the television cameras.

The governing board did consider arbitration—and rejected it. To let the Board of Education know its decision, the governing board first called, not Mrs. Shapiro, but the Mayor's office. The strike against the district went on.

June, 1968—Theodore Kheel offers a mediation proposal. The governing board votes to accept it—and Oliver announces it has been rejected

Through Clark, the Ocean Hill governing board now appealed to Commissioner Allen to intervene personally. Allen replied that he could not, because as chief state school officer he had to remain available for any possible appeal process. Instead, he recommended Theodore Kheel, the city's most noted labor mediator.

A meeting was set up at Kheel's law office in midtown Manhattan for Friday, June 7. It lasted several hours, and, again, appeared to be productive. In essence, Kheel's proposal was that he study the cases of the dismissed teachers and make recommendations—not binding in form, but understood to be so in substance. Meanwhile, two of his aides—one white, one Negro—would look at the charges. Those teachers against whom charges seemed flimsy would return to Ocean Hill, at least for the time being; the others would be excluded. Both the governing board and the union were given to understand that a bare majority would be kept out of the district.

The U.F.T. accepted the proposal, though Shanker was concerned about the loss of citywide uniformity in disciplinary procedures, and was less than happy about the apparent sacrifice of six or seven of his people.

The union, the Board of Education, Kheel and Clark all say that the dispute came closer to a solution that weekend than at any other time. In fact, it came closer than they know. On Monday, June 10, the governing board met to consider the Kheel proposal. Assemblyman Wright delivered a furious statement. He had not seen the charges against the teachers before the meeting at Kheel's office, and he was shocked at the insubstantiality of some of them. Decentralization had been wrecked in Albany by these damned discharges, he went on, and the children's school year was being ruined by the resulting strike. He considered Kheel's proposal an honorable and fair way out of the dispute, and urged the board to accept its essentials.

McCoy, who rarely expressed opinions at governing board meetings, and whose image to the outside world was that of a man intent on a fair solution, undertook the reply to Wright. He denounced the Kheel proposal as an establishment trick, and he urged the members of the board to stick to their resolve that these teachers would never again teach in Ocean Hill. The meeting lasted five hours. At its end, the governing board voted 7 to 4 (Oliver in the minority), with four abstentions and four absences (among them, Father Powis), to accept the Kheel proposals.

The next morning, a small committee of the governing board met with the Board of Education, Donovan and the union. Oliver led the group—and at no time did he mention the vote of the afternoon before. Instead, he presented a statement that Kheel was acceptable as mediator, but that the governing board would not be committed to abide by his findings, and that the disputed teachers would never be allowed back in Ocean Hill. At the end of the meeting, he announced to the press—in direct contradiction of the previous night's vote—that the governing board had rejected the Kheel proposals. That evening, with Wright absent and McCoy backing Oliver, the board indeed reversed itself and revoked its own approval of the Kheel proposals. The strike went on.

In the last weeks of the school year, students supervised by Louis Harris's poll-takers interviewed 212 parents in the Ocean-Hill area, and found them in a state of utter disgust. Some 61 per cent thought the schools were worse than they had been before (only 8 per cent thought they were better); 38 per cent thought they would get still worse (only 20 per cent thought they would get better). Negative opinions outweighed positive opinions on the Board of Education (69 per cent to 24 per cent), the unit administrator (44 per cent to 29 per cent), the governing board (47 per cent to 38 per cent). On the specific dispute, 29 per cent supported McCoy and the governing board in their effort to oust the teachers, while 24 per cent supported the teachers, and the other 47 per cent were not sure.

Summer vacation, 1968—The Lindsay appointees to the Board of Education hear what they want to hear

As the school year ended in June, Superintendent Donovan and his staff took the position that the dispute had passed into the hands of Judge Rivers as trial examiner, and that it could be assumed the governing board would abide by any decision reached on the basis of Rivers's report. Oliver and McCoy met with Deputy Superintendent Theodore Lang of the Bureau of Personnel and asked special help in recruiting new teachers for the fall, and the help was given.

Members of the Board of Education were even more optimistic. Under the new Marchi Law, Mayor Lindsay had been authorized to appoint four new members to the Board of Education. Among his first choices in mid-July were William Haddad, a former newspaperman and Reform Democrat who was building himself a new career in the poverty program, and the Rev. Milton Galamison, an independent, easy-going minister of a Brooklyn Negro church, who had sporadically made himself the center of specific civil-rights drives, including two school boycotts in 1963-64 and the People's Board of Education in early 1967. (He had also announced a one-day boycott at seven schools, to support Ocean Hill in May, 1968.)

In different ways, Haddad and Galamison could claim Ocean Hill as their constituency, and both told the Board that their sources said the people out there were ready for compromise and the whole dispute was going to work itself out peacefully. "I've been meeting with McCoy and Shanker," Haddad told one meeting of the Board, "and we're right on the edge of an agreement." This being what the Board of Education wanted to hear, everyone believed it.

The reason Haddad and Galamison thought there was going to be an easy out was, simply, that McCoy—at least by indirection—had told them so. (McCoy denies their interpretation of what he was saying. "If I'd been an outsider listening to me at those meetings," he commented recently, "and the subject had been the weather, I'd have bought an umbrella and galoshes.")

In July, however, McCoy and the governing board had excellent reason to wish to play down the prospects of future conflict. Assemblyman Wright had broken with the governing board over the rejection of the Kheel proposals, and was supporting a neighborhood group called the Committee for Democratic Education that was petitioning for removal of the governing board and new elections. (Oliver seemed to doubt the group's good faith. "Our children," he wrote in a public statement, "have now been stabbed in the back by this belated clamor of those who wish to take our children back to the good old days of educational genocide.")

In the last week of July, Wright formally presented to the Board of Education a petition for new elections. At its Aug. 14 meeting, the Board voted to reject the Wright petition and not to hold new Ocean Hill elections until June, 1969.

From late July on, Galamison met regularly with McCoy and Shanker, often at convivial lunches at which the long-range prospects of the unit were discussed. Galamison's idea was to remove the issue from the narrow focus of 10 teachers to the more general question of what the union could do to make Ocean Hill a model; then the teachers could slip back in (or some would not slip back in) fairly easily, as part of a larger agreement. All the meetings were amicable. Though a majority of the governing board had voted that it would never, never take back any of the teachers who struck the district, or any of the teachers who had been dismissed May 7, McCoy did not warn anyone of the danger of total intransigency on the part of his board. And he never told the governing board about his meetings with Galamison and Shanker.

McCoy alone was in contact with all parties to the dispute. If what he had wanted was a citywide strike, he could not have been more effective in promoting that result.

August, 1968—Judge Rivers orders the reinstatement
of all disputed teachers, and the fat is in the fire

Out in the great world beyond Ocean Hill, the Board of Education was wrestling with the problem of transferring to the city's 30 existing, but formerly powerless, local boards some authority over personnel and budget under the restrictive terms of the Marchi Law, which the Legislature had passed in May. The U.F.T. was, to say the least, concerned about how teachers' working conditions and security might be affected, especially in the light of the Ocean Hill experience.

The workhorses for the Board of Education were Galamison and John H. Lotz, a former telephone-union official and executive of the Health Insurance Plan. Shanker had a long list of grievance procedures he wanted spelled out, and, one by one, Lotz and Galamison worked out provisions satisfactory to the union.

On the Ocean Hill question, Lotz suggested a compromise on numbers—the Board of Education would order the return to the district of four of the 10 teachers who were challenging their transfers (which Shanker had already accepted from Kheel), and maybe 35 or 40 of the 100-odd strikers of the spring who still wished to return to Ocean Hill.

Then, on Aug. 26, Judge Rivers handed down his findings, and denied McCoy the right to transfer out *any* of the 10 teachers.

Even the union was a little embarrassed at the unfairness of the decision. ("*I* could have won cases against at least three of the 10," says one union leader. "The problem is that McCoy and his lawyer don't know how to present evidence.") But now the force of law was behind the reinstatement of all, and Shanker could not yield on any and survive as a union leader. Galamison accepted the need to put all the teachers back in Ocean Hill; the matter was no longer an issue between the Board of Education and the union. It was still, however, very much an issue in Ocean Hill, where the governing board voted not to accept the Rivers findings.

The storm gathers over the city

In the last week of August and the first week of September, that year's crop of college graduates who had just been licensed as substitute teachers returned from their summer vacations, looking for teaching assignments—and found they had none. At the Bureau of Personnel, sympathetic junior assistants told them that although there was a citywide surplus of beginning subs (thanks mostly to draft exemptions for teachers), Ocean Hill still had vacancies. McCoy, whose independent recruiting efforts had mostly failed, took on the new referrals in sufficient numbers to enable Ocean Hill's schools to operate even without any union teachers. Meanwhile, the delegate assembly of the union had voted a citywide strike for the opening of school on Monday, Sept. 9, unless an agreement was reached covering the status of union teachers in all decentralized districts, especially Ocean Hill. Both sides were ready for a showdown.

On Friday, Sept. 6, McCoy and the governing board were scheduled to meet with the Board of Education at the Hotel Commodore. The negotiating committee of the Board of Education had been working hard all day on the details of the contract with the union, and everyone had relaxed with a few drinks at dinner. The members of the governing board were shocked to find some of the Board of Education representatives gently liquored, and the Board members were shocked to find that the governing board, far from listening patiently to explanations of why they would have to take the teachers back, remained bitterly adamant that neither the 10 involuntarily transferred teachers, nor the 100-odd (the governing board thought 200) strikers who wanted to return, would ever again be permitted to darken the door of a school on Ocean Hill.

The totally unproductive Friday-night session was followed by a totally unproductive Saturday meeting with the union (to which several members of the governing board refused to come). Finally, Lotz told the governing board that, if they didn't take back the teachers, the Board of Education would simply close down their schools until they agreed to comply, and might dissolve the district as a separate entity.

Sunday, all the clans assembled, each in its own room, at City

Hall, and Mayor Lindsay met for the first time with the Ocean Hill governing board. They greeted him with a prepared statement, of which the operative sentences were: "Since the legal machinery of this sick society are forcing these teachers on us under threat of closing our schools and dissolving this district, the Board of Education should return to our district any of the teachers who wish to return. Our original decision remains as before. We refuse to sell out. If the Board of Education and the Superintendent of Schools forces them to return to a community who does not want them, so be it."

Members of the governing board remember that the Mayor seemed insulted by this statement, and said it should not be presented to him. He volunteered the help of his assistants in rewriting it, and they went off to edit it into something the Mayor could accept. One member of the governing board says scornfully, "He made it say something that was in his mind, not in ours."

What emerged was a statement to the effect that the governing board would not consent to take the teachers back but would consent to being forced to take the teachers back. As the Mayor phrased it, in reporting to the Board of Education the results of his meeting with the governing board: "They will not seek to prevent their return." When the Mayor was asked about whether the teachers would be assigned to classrooms, he brushed the question aside, leading members of the Board to believe that this crucial matter had not been discussed. In fact, Lewis Feldstein of the Mayor's office had asked McCoy to pledge that the returning teachers would receive normal assignments, and McCoy had done so, not only to Feldstein but also (Feldstein says) to Vincent McDonnell of the State Mediation Service. McCoy said he could not make such a statement publicly, however, without wrecking himself in the district—and he never told the governing board that he had given such a pledge.

The union was waiting in the Board of Estimate room. The Mayor entered and said: "We've settled it." Shanker asked him how he had settled it, and the Mayor said: "They agreed to take the teachers back."

Then the Mayor went downstairs to a televised news conference to announce that schools would be open as scheduled the next day. Oliver told the cameras that the Mayor was misinterpreting the governing board's position. Shanker told the cameras that there was no contract, that he would recommend a strike to the membership, which would vote that night, and that he did not expect the schools to open as scheduled. The vote to call the strike was 12,021 to 1,716.

Neither the Board of Education nor the Mayor was seriously disturbed. There was no major issue still to be resolved between the union and the Board, and they thought Ocean Hill had listened to the voice of reason.

Sept. 9, 1968—School opening day, and the first of the fall strikes begins; it lasts two days

Nearly 54,000 of the city's 57,000 teachers stayed out on the opening day of school, Sept. 9, and pickets ringed the buildings, carrying signs demanding "JUSTICE FOR TEACHERS." The principals, who had been through this sort of thing the year before (and who were even more threatened by possible arbitrary actions of local school boards under a decentralized program), declared in 80 per cent of the city's 900 schools that the failure of teachers to report had created unsafe conditions for children, and the buildings were closed. In Ocean Hill, however, a full complement of staff, nearly all nonunion, reported for work. Because the 100-odd union teachers still assigned to the district did not come to work, Ocean Hill was authorized by Board of Education rules to pay on a per diem substitute basis some 100 extra teachers it had "hired" without approval from (or even notification of) the Bureau of Personnel.

Throughout the day, the union and the Board of Education worked on contract terms in reasonably amicable negotiations. There was, in any event, no disagreement about the Ocean Hill part of the deal: The Board would order the teachers assigned to Ocean Hill to "resume their professional duties," with a wistful offer of voluntary transfer to schools in other districts if they preferred to leave. And the Board agreed to pay for their time on the picket lines the teachers who had struck the district in the spring, a decision which added fuel to the fires on Ocean Hill. The entire grievance procedure of the union contract with the

Board was extended to bind all local school boards and their administrative staffs. In cases where local boards might wish to dismiss teachers, the contract required submission of charges to a panel of arbitrators, whose decision would be binding.

Shanker had also sought an "agency shop," which would require all teachers to pay dues to the union whether or not they were members, and the Board of Education believes that the strike was called more to enforce that demand than for any other reason. No union of municipal employes has such a clause in its contract (though it is an open secret in the labor movement that the city expects to begin granting agency shops in 1969), and the Board was not prepared to give Shanker the triumph of the first agreement of this kind—especially not, as Lotz pointed out at a convivial moment in the negotiations, with Galamison playing piano in the background, as a reward for an illegal strike, one in clear violation of the Taylor Law forbidding strikes by public employes. The binding arbitration clause was offered as a *quid pro quo* in return for the union's temporary abandonment of the agency shop demand.

Agreement on a "Memorandum of Understanding" was reached around 4 in the afternoon on Tuesday, Sept. 10, the second day of the strike. At the Board, leadership in meeting the demands of the teachers had been taken by Galamison, who asked Shanker to give him public credit when recommending the agreement to his members, and Shanker did so gladly: "One of the persons who spent more hours working on a real understanding—and when we have people there who are working we shouldn't go by the impressions given in the newspapers, we should know it—that person is the Rev. Mr. Galamison." William Haddad acclaimed the memorandum as "the first real step toward decentralization."

Shanker offered an olive branch to Ocean Hill with a statement that "McCoy and the governing board are trying to do something in that district." But there were signs that he was less than optimistic that in fact the battle had ended: The motion offered to the membership in settlement of the strike authorized the union's executive board to close the city's schools on 48 hours' notice without further action by the membership, "in the event the agreements with respect to Ocean Hill-Brownsville are broken."

Once this contract was initialed, the governing board's cause was absolutely hopeless. The full coercive power of the state would have to be applied, if the union insisted, to restore the U.F.T. teachers to the Ocean Hill schools. Men like Haddad and Galamison might soon regret what they had said and done (on Wednesday, Galamison, hearing what were to him surprising screams of outrage from Ocean Hill, voted against the contract he had negotiated the day before). But the results could not be changed, and further resistance was certain to be self-destructive. Nobody seems to have bothered to tell the governing board of the drastic change in the status of its dispute with the union. "If you've already got a broken foot," McCoy said the other day, "what difference does it make that you get a broken hand, too?"

Sept. 11, 1968—The teachers return to work, and are terrorized in Ocean Hill

Sandra Feldman went out to Ocean Hill a little before 7 in the morning on Wednesday, Sept. 11, and went directly to McCoy's office. She had always liked him, and she thought he had a "warm, paternal feeling" for her. Her purpose was to plead with him to use all his considerable influence in the district to insure the safe and fruitful return of the union teachers. He was non-committal, but as they sat in his office, with a correspondent from Time, the phone kept ringing and he kept telling callers that, yes, the procedures agreed upon the night before were to be put into effect. Mrs. Feldman, who had done more than her share of demonstrating for various CORE chapters, recognized the syndrome and went off to see what might be going on in the schools.

At J.H.S. 271, a group led by Sonny Carson of Brooklyn CORE, who is widely regarded as terrorist in his inclinations and does nothing to discourage that opinion, had blocked the front door against the returning teachers. Principal William Harris had come out, and with the help of police had escorted the teachers into the building. There he told them, as the other principals were telling the other U.F.T. teachers through the district, to report to the I.S. 55 auditorium for an orientation session with McCoy. When the teachers arrived at the auditorium, they found about 50 Negro men, some wearing helmets, carrying sticks or with bandoliers of bullets who shouted curses at them. The 83 teachers clustered in the center of the auditorium, terrified, and McCoy entered. As he started to speak, choruses of jeers from the men drowned him out, and after a few minutes he left. The lights in the auditorium were then flicked on and off, and the teachers were told from the crowd that if they came back to the district they would be carried out of it in pine boxes. Finally, McCoy returned. If the teachers still insisted on returning to the district, he said, they should report to their schools at 1 o'clock.

The teachers left the auditorium, caucused and decided to go through with what they had come to do. When they reported to their schools again, they found they had been given no teaching assignments and there were no time cards for them to punch. J.H.S. 271 pupils were encouraged to leave the school by some nonunion teachers and members of the governing board. On their way out, they jeered at the union teachers, and, in some cases, maneuvered as though to assault them. Harris locked the teachers into a room for their own protection, and arranged a police escort for them out of the building at 2:15. That afternoon, the Ocean Hill teachers reported on their experiences to the executive board of the union, which exercised the option in the motion which had ended the preceding strike, and called for the city's teachers to walk out again on Friday.

Sept. 13, 1968—The teachers begin their second fall strike (it will last more than two weeks), and Commissioner Allen and Kheel try their hands at a settlement

The explanation from the Ocean Hill governing board was that the community had risen spontaneously in its wrath to keep the union teachers out. The Rev. Mr. Oliver said he hoped the community would do it again. Both the Board of Education and the Mayor's office were paralyzed by the crisis. Though the terrorism on Ocean Hill had obviously been prearranged, there was a strong emotional desire at the Mayor's office to accept the governing board's explanations.

Mayor Lindsay tried to withdraw himself from the situation: On Thursday morning he called Commissioner Allen and begged him to intervene. Allen explained, as he had earlier to the Ocean Hill governing board, that he could not. (The Mayor met with the governing board himself, and they walked out on him.) Then Donovan called Allen and told him that the Board of Education had voted to request his intervention.

Allen agreed to look for an answer. On Friday, Sept. 13, he spoke briefly with some of the participants and then, at 10 o'clock that night, met with Ted Kheel at the Century Association on West 43d Street. Kheel suggested that the solution could be to remove the sources of dispute on both sides—suspend the governing board, and temporarily transfer the 10 teachers to headquarters assignment. That morning, the teachers had begun their second strike.

The next day, which was Shanker's 40th birthday, Kheel invited Shanker to his home in Riverdale and discussed the proposal. After considerable hesitation, Shanker said he thought his negotiating committee might buy it, provided there was a formal agreement that the governing board would not be restored until the 10 teachers were taken back, and that McCoy agreed to take his orders from Donovan.

While Kheel and Shanker were conferring, Mayor Lindsay was facing an angry meeting of parents' associations at J.H.S. 104 near Stuyvesant Town in Manhattan. Among other questions, he was asked how the governing board could be permitted to continue in office after its clear violation of its agreement not to prevent the return of the teachers. The Mayor said he thought the governing board had lived up to its agreement with him— "more or less"—and experienced the first of what were to be several vigorous booings he would receive during the strike. More important, he lost forever any chance to be the guarantor of a strike settlement: The teachers who had been terrorized on Ocean Hill, and all those who spoke to them, would not trust anyone who reacted so calmly to the frightening events of Sept. 11 at I.S. 55.

That first Saturday, Allen announced his first Allen Plan—i.e., Kheel's trade-off of the governing board against the 10 teachers. On the same day, Mayor Lindsay swore in three more new members of the Board of Education—John M. Doar, a former Assistant Attorney General under Robert Kennedy, who had prosecuted civil-rights cases in the South and had come North to be head of the Bedford-Stuyvesant Development Corporation (within whose territory lay most of the Ocean Hill-Brownsville district); Walter W. Straley, a vice president of A.T.&T., and Mrs. Ana Alvarez Conigliaro, a vocal Puerto Rican leader. Almost from the day of his inauguration, the Mayor had been saying that his office should have control of the Board of Education. Now, for the first time, a majority of that board was of his choice. Nobody congratulated him.

The Board of Education suspends the Ocean Hill governing board, and then restores it

The first act of the new Lindsay majority was to follow the Allen directive and suspend the Ocean Hill governing board. The union responded that it would take the paired suspension of governing board and teachers only on condition that the governing board would not be restored until the teachers were in their classrooms —and then added further conditions. The other union teachers the governing board had rejected would have to be guaranteed classroom assignments, union observers would have to be stationed in the schools with power to close them in case of disorder, and the Mayor would have to promise not to approve actions of un-official groups harassing teachers.

The Ocean Hill governing board reacted in fury. Kenneth Clark raged at Commissioner Allen for apparently equating the supposed rights of 10 teachers with the educational hopes of the Negro community.

On Sept. 20, Allen permitted the Board of Education to restore the Ocean Hill governing board. That made Clark (and the ma-jority of the Board of Education) happier, but the net effect was to relieve Shanker of any obligation to accept even the temporary *transfer* of the dismissed 10. Now the union's demand was for suspension of the governing board and *restoration* of all U.F.T. teachers.

The strike becomes a racial conflict

The strike was highly successful, and increasingly nasty. Brushing
off a plea from the Mayor, the teachers' union held a mass meeting in front of City Hall on Sept. 16, with something more than
15,000 teachers and other unionists in attendance. Though
Bayard Rustin and a number of Negro union leaders were present, the crowd was overwhelmingly white. The awkward fact was
that McCoy and most of the governing board were Negro, and
every one of the 10 teachers was Jewish. The Mayor's office had
seen the clash as racial from the beginning, and now began to
say so. And the U.F.T. began to solicit support with the distribution of leaflets reproducing anti-Semitic literature which had
appeared in the Ocean Hill district. As several people have pointed
out, the union gave this stuff infinitely more circulation than its
producers could have dreamed of—and some of it was simply
the ravings of a single fanatic with access to a Mimeograph
machine.*

In Ocean Hill, attendance was light (even with children
brought in from other districts, the schools were never so much

---

* The item for which the union was most severely criticized, however,
was legitimate. It was a report from the independent journal Education
News on a class in which a teacher named Leslie Campbell advocated black
separatism and Molotov cocktails. The leaflet reported the class as an
"actual lesson in J.H.S. 271," and called it an "example of what the Ocean
Hill-Brownsville governing board feels is suitable curriculum." The New
York Civil Liberties Union called these statements "frauds" and "a lie,"
because the class in question had been observed elsewhere in the city. But
Campbell *was* in J.H.S. 271, and he had been hired by the governing board
subsequent to the publication of the report in Education News. So the case
was apparently even stronger than the U.F.T. leaflet indicated.

If one goes a cut deeper, however, it begins to appear that the N.Y.C.L.U.
did unwittingly expose an unfairness in the U.F.T. literature. Campbell was
in the district because he had been punitively transferred from his previous
school. Asked where he wanted to go, he said, "Ocean Hill." Donovan
called McCoy and asked whether he would take Campbell, and McCoy
said, "Sure." Considering who Campbell's friends were in the district, it
would have been almost impossible for McCoy to say no. That the governing board was not united in its affection for Campbell is a matter of
record in its minutes. At the meeting where the dismissal of the 19 was
voted, Mrs. Elaine Rooke, a governing board member sufficiently militant
to be among those indicted by a Brooklyn grand jury in December, moved
to add Campbell's name to the list of those who must go, and got a second
but not a majority. Pity.

as two-thirds full), but all classrooms were manned, most of them by enthusiastic beginners who impressed visitors who were also enthusiastic beginners. Seventy per cent of the new teachers were white, and half were Jewish. Ocean Hill was operating much as its leaders would hope to see it operated if they won their fight. There was no pressure on them to settle. All the pressure was on the rest of the city, where more than a million children were out of school.

Sept. 28-29, 1968—The Mayor settles the strike

The Board of Education kept announcing that schools were open, ordering teachers and supervisors back to them, ordering McCoy and the governing board to receive the union teachers back to their classrooms. Nobody paid any attention. The Board appointed John Doar head of a new negotiating committee.

Accepting, somewhat reluctantly, the Memorandum of Agreement which had ended the previous strike, Doar regarded his mission as one of assuring compliance with law. He had made the University of Mississippi accept James Meredith, and now he would make the governing board of Ocean Hill accept the union teachers. For Shanker, however, the question was one of simple labor-relations obligation. He had taken a grievance, and he had won it, and now the boss was permitting middle management to wreck the agreement in a branch office. Neither man had ever seen anything quite like the other, and personally they got on very well. Between late September and mid-November, Shanker and Doar dined together at least once a week, hashing out their intellectual disagreements on a rather abstract level.

But the schools were still closed. On Sept. 24, reluctantly, the Mayor put himself back in the picture, and the strike began to grind toward settlement. Donovan announced (to the great resentment of the governing board) that he was assigning 37 observers to keep an eye on conditions in the Ocean Hill schools, and that the observers would be backed by police, to make sure the union teachers could return safely. Then the talks with the union broke down over the issue of union observers in the schools, and the power of the observers to close schools. And on Saturday, Sept. 28, all parties adjourned to Gracie Mansion for one of those all-night sessions which have been since the Wagner days part of the disease of labor relations in New York City. Obviously, there could be no retreat from the memorandum which had ended the previous strike. The union teachers were going back. Ocean Hill still manfully opposed their return, but Mayor Lindsay for eight hours wore down the governing board's new lawyer, the peppery civil-liberties specialist William Kunstler. The city was, however, prepared to sweeten the pot by awarding the district as many extra positions as might be necessary to keep existing staff while taking back the union teachers, giving McCoy a unique resource of additional teachers to plan and execute new programs for Ocean Hill children.

And the union won its demand for authority to station observers of its own choice in the Ocean Hill schools, even though the Board of Education was fierce in opposition. Doar insisted that the observers whom Donovan had already stationed in the schools would be all anybody needed. What was required now, he felt, was voluntary compliance by Ocean Hill, which could not be got if the Board seemed to be pushed around by the union. Doar refused to yield to the Mayor on this point, and the negotiations went on to other topics.

By dawn's early light on Sunday, Doar, sitting exhausted in a chair, saw Shanker and state mediator McDonnell and Mayor Lindsay's labor adviser, Harold Israelson—all assuming Doar would give in eventually on the issue of union observers—coming down the stairs together and talking about how the children were going to make up the lost time and the teachers the lost paychecks, and how the deductions were to be taken for the weeks of the strike. Shanker was suggesting that one-third of the teachers' monetary loss be deducted from each of the next three paychecks, to minimize hardship, and Doar suddenly sat up straight and said, "To hell with it; I'm not going to give any more." He thereupon departed. Galamison had left some hours before, as had the Ocean Hill contingent, and Walter Straley remained to sign the new contract for the Board of Education.

Early October, 1968—The schools are open, but
Ocean Hill is riotous. Donovan suspends McCoy and
the principals, and closes J.H.S. 271

A few peace offerings were made in Ocean Hill's direction that Sunday after the deal was closed. Doar stressed that the Board had managed to avoid a situation where union—or even neutral— observers would be empowered to close a school. And Shanker, selling his deal to his delegate assembly, closed with the words: "Now we shall all have to learn to work with Rhody McCoy." The governing board was silent, apparently too shocked to speak.

School opened Monday, Sept. 30, with more than 1,000 policemen in Ocean Hill, an assistant superintendent from school headquarters in each building, and men from the Mayor's office and the union checking up on what was happening. Doar and Galamison went into the schools themselves to see what they could do to keep things cool.

The first week was messy but not hopeless. J.H.S. 271 had a riot with injuries to 10 policemen and an indeterminate number of local and visiting militants, but when it reopened, with Doar on duty in the building, most rooms were reasonably quiet. In the district's seven other schools, more union teachers received classroom assignments every day. But the governing board had voted that the union teachers should not be given classes to teach, and at the week's end Oliver announced the fact to the newspapers. McCoy said he would have to take his orders from the governing board (even though it had been suspended) rather than from Donovan, and Donovan suspended him. Then the principals (with one exception, who requested transfer out of the district) announced that they would have to take their orders from McCoy, and Donovan suspended *them.* The Superintendent ordered the principals to report to school headquarters, rather than to their schools, and McCoy told them to go.

On Wednesday, Oct. 9, with principal William Harris gone, J.H.S. 271 erupted again. Members of the governing board, aggressive teachers and neighborhood militants who had been allowed into the building threatened union teachers, union and Board of Education observers and the assistant principal whom Donovan had told to run the school (a veteran administrator, herself a Negro, she applied for and received transfer the next day). Pupils were encouraged to raise hell in halls, classes and, especially, in the auditorium. Donovan closed the school, and ordered the staff, both union and nonunion, to meet with him in one of the Board of Education offices near Brooklyn's Borough Hall early the next day. McCoy, who had remained at his desk despite his suspension, told the staff to go.

Thursday morning, Donovan met with about 125 teachers from J.H.S. 271, and told them that only they could end the trouble in their school. Either they would learn to get along with one another, or he would bring in a new staff. Albert Vann of the African-American Teachers Association said he thought the teachers would like to talk over their problems by themselves, and Donovan left.

Out in Ocean Hill, the assistant principals who had taken charge of the other buildings assigned union teachers to classes, and the district was reasonably placid—for an armed camp.

Oct. 11, 1968—The Board of Education restores the principals, and Shanker prepares to call another strike

Friday, Oct. 11, the Board of Education held a meeting that was more like a permanent crap game than a session of an official body. Individual members drifted in and out, checking with their constituencies or with the parties to the dispute or making personal phone calls or just walking around. Donovan left the meeting to talk with the J.H.S. 271 teachers, who were meeting down the block. A girl who appeared to be a spokesman for the newly hired teachers rose when Donovan asked for news and said she thought everything was going to work out—and then Al Shanker stepped through the doors at the back of the room and leaned against the wall.

"Why don't you have *him* arrested?" bellowed Leslie Campbell but the other teachers shushed him.

Donovan asked Shanker to leave, and he refused. His people had told him they were concerned that Donovan might push them around, and he wanted to be there to be sure it didn't happen. Donovan explained that it was a private meeting, and Shanker said that he had a right to be at any meeting the

Superintendent held with union teachers. Donovan said icily that he did not equate the post of Superintendent of Schools with that of president of the United Federation of Teachers, and Shanker shrugged. Donovan said that unless Shanker left he would leave, and Shanker stayed.

When Donovan left, Shanker followed, and Donovan stopped him. "What's got into you, Al?" Donovan said. "I don't know that they can work it out, but this is the best chance we've had." Shanker stubbornly insisted that his people might be bullied in his absence. Donovan said he was going to return to the room, and Shanker said that if Donovan did, he would too. Donovan quit, and the two men left in different directions.

The Superintendent returned to where some of the Board were meeting, and reported on his day (mentioning that he had to be brief, for he was to catch a plane for Denver to make a speech). Galamison said he had spoken with the suspended principals, and they had given him a pledge that they would treat all teachers alike, and that all would be quiet at J.H.S. 271. Doar talked to McCoy, who assured him privately that, governing board or no governing board, the teachers would be given real assignments the next day if the principals were restored. You just couldn't ask the Ocean Hill people for a humiliating public promise—"rub their noses in it," as Galamison said.

The members of the Board present at the meeting were furious with Shanker for barging in on Donovan's session with the J.H.S. 271 teachers, and they were in a rush because Donovan had to leave. In this mood, a rump committee of the Board—different accounts speak of four, five or six members, certainly less than a quorum—told Donovan to order J.H.S. 271 reopened and the principals reinstated, as of Monday. Donovan gave a statement to the press, to that effect, and departed for Denver.

What had happened, so far as the union could see, was that the Lindsay-dominated Board of Education had capitulated to Ocean Hill. The principals, still saying they would follow McCoy's directives, were to be reinstated with full power to assign teachers. J.H.S. 271, where children had been egged on to make life impossible for union teachers, was to be reopened with no guarantee of any sort that the same scenes would not occur again. Worst of all, Shanker had not even been given the courtesy of a telephone call to tell him of the decision: He learned about it from reporters who called him for his reaction. His reaction was to set in motion the machinery for calling a third strike,

Before Donovan's plane had set down in Denver, Mayor Lindsay's office had called every possible stopping place in that city to reach him, and to tell him to come home. That day, Oct. 11, was the Black Friday of the school disaster.

Oct. 12-13, 1968—A weekend of hardening positions leaves a conflict without issues

Saturday, Oct. 12, was a day of hardening positions. First thing next morning, Mayor Lindsay called Mrs. Shapiro, in her last innings as acting president of the Board (it had already been leaked that Doar would be elected president the following week, and that Galamison, saints preserve us, would become vice president). The Mayor asked Mrs. Shapiro to call a meeting of the Board for that afternoon. Mrs. Shapiro refused—she had seen enough meetings of the Board to last her quite a while—but she put together a smaller meeting of herself, Donovan, Shanker, Harold Siegel (the secretary of the Board), Israelson (the Mayor's labor adviser) and Deputy Mayor Robert Sweet to gather that afternoon in her apartment on lower Fifth Avenue.

First, though, Donovan, Sweet and Shanker met with Israelson at *his* apartment, and Donovan admitted that he had *not* received a pledge of cooperation from the principals: He had simply told them what they were going to do, and they had not denied it. Nor could he be completely confident of what would be done by the J.H.S. 271 staff, which contained what everybody (including the Ocean Hill administrators and governing board) considered some thoroughly disreputable elements in terms of politics or thuggery. Shanker left in a fury, and after his departure Donovan told Sweet that he felt the Friday announcement that the principals would be returned and J.H.S. 271 reopened had been premature, and that everything should be retained in *statu quo* for at least one more day.

This option was not offered to Shanker, however, at the meeting in Mrs. Shapiro's apartment. Doar, who had been less than enthusiastic about Friday's announcement but had gone along with Galamison, was now arguing that to keep J.H.S. 271 closed after the announcement would be to knuckle under to the union, and would foreclose any chance of the Board's establishing itself as a neutral authority—not only on Ocean Hill, but elsewhere in the city. The most that could be offered Shanker was some kind of public guarantee from Donovan.

Shanker arrived late; he had been discussing the prospective third strike with his delegate assembly. Donovan offered to get on the telephone now, call the seven Ocean Hill principals, and secure from each of them an absolute pledge that the union teachers would be free from harassment and would get teaching assignments. Any principal who would not pledge would not be reinstated.

But the fact is that Donovan was not trying to sell the deal. He was vague about how much leeway the principals would have in assigning union teachers to nonteaching chores. Asked for his personal rather than his official views, he told Shanker that he thought things would be kept cool on Monday and probably Tuesday, but that later in the week hell would probably break out again.

Now Shanker suggested that J.H.S. 271 be kept closed and the principals be kept suspended for just one more day, while arrangements for controlling the reopenings and reinstatements were perfected. He was told that was impossible.

There are conflicting recollections of what happened at this meeting, but it seems that the discussions did move. Shanker was willing to admit that the principals would find it next to impossible to issue public statements that they would assign *all* the union teachers. Donovan offered to make the public statement himself, after talking with them. People began suggesting wordings for Donovan's statement, and Sweet called the Mayor to tell him the situation looked promising.

Then Shanker suddenly shook his head and said it wasn't enough: He was not ready to ask his people to remain on the job on the strength of just a statement by Donovan that third parties had said something or other to him. Sweet suggested that Shanker get his strike authorization and keep it in readiness in case the pledges to Donovan proved delusory, but Shanker had now made up his mind. There could be no question that his people would follow him; the city was in terrible trouble.

Oct. 13, 1968—A secret Sunday dinner meeting produces confusion and catastrophe

One last clear chance remained to avoid catastrophe: The Board of Education could still revoke Donovan's Friday statement about the Ocean Hill principals, and give Shanker and Donovan a day to work out something formal with signatures at the bottom. Having failed to persuade Mrs. Shapiro to call a meeting of the whole Board, Mayor Lindsay got Galamison to call a rump meeting of the seven Lindsay appointees, who came together for dinner that Sunday night, Oct. 13, at Armando's Restaurant in Brooklyn. Sweet and Donovan telephoned them from City Hall. Conscious of all the problems that might follow, both men (Sweet speaking for the Mayor) begged the new members of the Board to abandon Friday's position. Israelson had warned Doar separately that if the union did strike again, any subsequent settlement would be worse, from the Board's and from Ocean Hill's point of view, than what was in the existing contract.

History moves at its own pace; time gallops withal. But one should pause here, at this instant of truly fateful decision, to consider those in whose hands the future of the city was now placed. Six of the seven Lindsay appointees were, in one way or another, intimately connected with poverty programs or with "promoting social change." They were, to be marginally unkind, fundamentally in the resentment business—that is, their function was to push on those who made decisions, not to make decisions themselves. Though it was fashionable to say they had "constituencies," in fact, they did not: They had been elected to nothing and they were responsible to no one except for their performance as spokesmen for positions. Their habit was to deal with issues, not with people. None of the six understood how a big organization runs: the fragility and interdependence of *normal* urban life are things they had no way to think about, because their work dealt entirely with pathologies.

The man who had to run the school system and the man who had to run the city now came to this group, recently placed in brief authority over the one by appointment of the other, and pleaded with them to take the one action that could avoid catastrophe for the city. The six could think about the situation only in terms of slogans and personalities and the positions they had taken. Worst of all, they were to make their decisions in secret, for the Mayor's office would shield them. These pages are the first appearance in print of the fact of the meeting at Armando's Restaurant on the night of Oct. 13.

The seventh man in the group of Lindsay appointees, Walter Straley of the telephone company, had the background and training and position to see how profoundly harmful a new teacher strike would be. For five hours, from 7 to midnight, he hammered at his colleagues to get them to reverse the decision so hastily taken on Friday to restore the Ocean Hill principals and reopen J.H.S. 271 without safeguards for the teachers. He could not budge one of them.

The Mayor on television spoke in agony about Shanker and the teachers' union, about the closing of all the city's schools over a dispute in one of them, about the lack of "moral authority" in the union to do what it was doing. It is no defense of Shanker, who with the third strike of the fall moved his union from a posture of defending its own to a posture of attacking the poor people of Ocean Hill, to say that he was honestly acting in what he considered the best interests of those who had chosen him to make such decisions for them. But it is perhaps a valid defense of the old, supposedly discredited ethnic politics to point out that in a city two-thirds non-Spanish Catholic and Jewish, the political decision to permit the horror of the ultimate teacher strike was taken by a group which did not include a single representative of the two majority elements, and which acted solely on the basis of the ideological bias and self-esteem of its members.

Oct. 14, 1968—The big strike begins. It is to last five weeks

Fewer than 8,000 teachers now voted to commit the union to another strike, but on Oct. 14, 50,000-odd teachers were again out of the schools, demanding now an end to the Ocean Hill project.

This time, the teachers stayed out for five weeks. Though the Board of Education and the newspapers kept making optimistic noises about schools in operation despite the strike, at no time were as many as one-eighth of the city's schoolchildren in school. In September, the union had commanded the sympathy certainly of a majority of the city's residents and perhaps of a majority of parents. By the end of this strike, parents were frantic and furious.

Perhaps it may be noted here without comment that none of the principal figures—not Shanker, not McCoy, not Doar, not Mayor Lindsay—had children in the New York City public schools. And perhaps it should also be noted that all the children of these worthies, and of the teachers, are well-fed at home, while for tens of thousands of black children in New York the free school lunch they now missed was the one good meal they ate.

The Mayor's first reaction to the new strike was to try to nationalize the dispute, and to secure mediation by three figures whose work was fundamentally outside New York—John Gardner of the Urban Coalition, Whitney Young of the National Urban League and George Meany of the A.F.L.-C.I.O. Thought being equal at the Mayor's office to press release, the public knew that the Mayor was trying to gather up this committee at about the same time the Mayor learned that of the three only Young was prepared to serve. The Mayor then put together a more local group, keeping Young, and substituting Harold Israelson and Ted Kheel for Gardner and Meany. Kheel agreed to be a fact-finder only, because there was nothing to mediate.

Meanwhile, the Board of Education had elected John Doar its new president, and Doar had made a few statements which seemed to mean that the Board was, honest Injun, going to try to break a strike by the largest union local in the United States. The response from the labor movement—taken without even consulting Shanker—was quick. At the suggestion of the national A.F.L.-C.I.O. and its Central Labor Council, the custodians' union instructed its members to shut off power and heat and close and lock the schools. In some instances, the custodians thoughtfully changed the locks, so that nonstriking principals and school officials could not get in.

Ocean Hill now went to Federal District Court, seeking an injunction which would forbid its suspension by the Board of Education. The matter was heard by Judge Anthony Travia, who noted with interest that he had all the parties to the dispute in his courtroom. He suggested that they all meet together in his chambers and see if they couldn't work things out, as litigants often do, in pretrial sessions.

The discussion in Travia's chambers on Friday, Oct. 18, set the stage for the eruption of ill-feeling that characterized the last weeks of the strike. Nearly all the governing board attended, sitting suspiciously at the back of the room and glaring at Shanker and Donovan. At this meeting, the governing board for the first time suggested that it might consent to take the teachers back. After all, its new counsel, Morton Stavis, said, the Board of Regents was about to approve new decentralization rules proposed by the Board of Education pursuant to the Marchi Law. Under these rules, a district would be empowered to transfer out anybody without reason, provided only it could find another district willing to accept the transferred fellow. Thus Shanker's teachers could be batted back and forth between, say, Ocean Hill and its friends at I.S. 201. Oliver cheerfully agreed. Thereafter, Shanker, who would have been deeply suspicious anyway, was never willing even to consider any apparent concession offered by Ocean Hill. When Whitney Young announced, the next week, that the governing board at Ocean Hill had changed its mind, and would welcome back the union teachers, Shanker was not even interested.

Mayor Lindsay seeks a simple answer, and everyone gets mad at him

That first weekend of the big strike, Kheel, Young and Israelson met with the people who had been in Travia's chambers, and reported gloomily to the Mayor that it looked like a long strike. Around the city, in an obviously desperate gesture, parents and nonstriking teachers urged on by Galamison broke into some of the schools the custodians had closed. Everywhere, attitudes were growing ever more ugly.

The Mayor decided that the focus of the situation was J.H.S. 271. The Board had made a mistake in reopening it; now the

Mayor would close it. He met with Assistant Chief Inspector Lloyd Sealy, who was in charge of the police in Ocean Hill, and asked how much trouble would result from closing the school by executive order. Sealy said there would be plenty of trouble: People in the district had not been upset when the school was closed before, because they knew that viciousness had been displayed inside it. But now the school was functioning, on the governing board's terms, and closing it would be seen as deliberate, cold-blooded punishment of the community. Still, if need be, his men could control the area.

The Mayor then drove to Brooklyn, where the Board of Education was meeting, and told the Board that he was going to close J.H.S. 271 on his own authority as Chief Magistrate, in hope that this action would end the strike. Some members asked if he objected to their voting on his move, which he did not, though he wanted it understood that he would proceed on his own course whatever the vote was. The Board voted against closing J.H.S. 271, but not, the Mayor thought, passionately. He then returned to Gracie Mansion, called in the television crews, and made his announcement.

Shanker, Commissioner Allen, Kheel, Young and Israelson all learned of the Mayor's action from the news media, and were not amused. The union rejected the Mayor's initiative, and Ocean Hill seethed with feelings of betrayal.

Second week of the big strike—Commissioner Allen produces his second plan

At the monthly meeting of the State Board of Regents in Albany on Thursday, Oct. 24, one of the upstate Regents observed that strikes like this one never got settled publicly—which was what everyone had been trying to do—and that the time had come to settle it privately. By unanimous vote, the Regents asked one of their number, Max J. Rubin, a lawyer who was once president of the New York City Board of Education and had negotiated with Shanker, to go down to New York and check out the union's real demands. Fellow Regent Kenneth Clark volunteered to share the limousine with Rubin, and to look in on the Ocean Hill side of the dispute.

Rubin met for two and a half hours with Shanker at the National Arts Club on Gramercy Park, and Shanker made the offer he would repeat that Sunday night in an hour-long television debate with Doar: the union would drop its demand for removal of the governing board and McCoy and would settle for the status quo of the last day school was open—everybody on Ocean Hill suspended, and J.H.S. 271 closed. This was not, really, much of an offer: with the principals out of the schools and the assistant principals operating under Donovan's orders, little if anything would be left of the Ocean Hill project. Still, it looked like a step forward. Rubin drove back to Albany, found the Board of Regents at dinner, and reported on the substance of his conversation with Shanker.

The next morning Allen read to the Regents a statement he had drafted after the previous night's meeting. It stressed the "long history of oppression" the Negro has suffered, and "commitments we cannot abandon, either as a matter of educational policy or as a matter of conscience." Most of the Regents were not entirely sure what these sentiments meant in terms of the New York strike, but they were touched by the depth of Allen's feeling, and with only minor changes the memorandum was adopted as a Regents' statement. Specifically, Allen proposed that the union teachers go back, that the governing board and McCoy be officially restored to office, that they agree to receive the teachers and give them classroom assignments, and that Allen himself or a designee stand ready to enforce the agreement up to and including the dismissal (not mere suspension) of anyone who interfered with it. The Regents then called a meeting for 5 o'clock that afternoon, Oct. 25, at the Hotel Commodore in New York, with all parties present. The earlier idea of settling the strike privately had been abandoned.

Like most unprepared meetings, the four-way session at the Hotel Commodore went badly, and it ended particularly badly when a group of angry supporters of the governing board entered and shouted curses and obscenities at the union, Board of Regents and Board of Education alike. The Regents had not been exposed to this sort of thing before, and it made an unfortunate impression. Shanker made an unfortunate impression, too, when he replied to a conciliatory statement by one of the parent members of the governing board with a flat statement that he did not believe she was telling the truth.

Anyway, the second Allen Plan was launched—the first having been the one he developed with Ted Kheel back in the spring—and it became a basis for negotiation among the parties. Whitney Young hailed Allen's statement as "a second Emancipation Proclamation."

On Saturday, Oct. 26, Allen and Shanker and Rubin met for three and a half hours in Allen's suite at the Commodore, while the Regent and the Commissioner tried vainly to sell the union leader something which his membership was almost certain to see as a step backward. Listening to Shanker's replies, Allen was especially struck with the union's unwillingness to trust either the Mayor or the Board of Education to enforce an agreement in Ocean Hill, and with Shanker's concern about what might happen elsewhere in the city after the end of the strike.

Third week—Commissioner Allen tries to meet the union half-way with a third Allen Plan and is rebuffed

The following Tuesday, Oct. 29, Allen attempted to remove some of the union's worries with a detailed proposal sufficiently different from what he had said before to qualify as yet a third Allen Plan—and this plan did, indeed, two and a half weeks later, become the centerpiece of the settlement that ended the strike.

In the new plan, the state, instead of being a remote guarantor of peace on Ocean Hill, would be the direct administrator of the project. Allen proposed to put the unit under state trusteeship, with a full-time state trustee supported by a full-time staff of state assistants to assume daily oversight in the Ocean Hill schools. Observers, including union observers, would also be present in the schools, and would report to the trustee rather than to Donovan. The suspension of the governing board would be continued, and McCoy would be reinstated only if he would pledge to follow the orders of the state trustee, regardless of what the governing board (in exile) might say.

Allen called for all parties to accept his new plan by noon on Wednesday, and that morning he met with a very unhappy delegation from Ocean Hill who could not understand why they were so much worse off on Wednesday than they had been on Friday. Ultimately, the governing board decided that it would neither accept nor reject the plan—which meant, functionally, acceptance. The Commissioner's office believes that Shanker, too, was ready to accept—but that his negotiating committee would not go along. They knew Allen only as an antagonist on decentralization and as the author of the previous Friday's emotional statement to the Regents, expressing "commitments" to Negro aspirations.

On Nov. 1, the delegate assembly of the union rejected the Allen Plan as "paper promises." It was the gloomiest day yet.

In despair, the Mayor called for the parties to accept arbitration of the issues—which were not now the return of the teachers (let alone the power of the governing board to exclude teachers without giving reasons), but the right of the governing board to survive and to have the principals of its choice in its schools. There is some reason to believe that Shanker had informally accepted this proposal before the Mayor, who had grown wary, announced it, but in the end, the union, like everybody else, turned it down. The Mayor reacted with a savage attack on Shanker and the union, and an announcement that what Shanker was really doing was seeking to force a special session of the State Legislature, which would almost certainly kill school decentralization in New York.

On Sunday, Nov. 3, Shanker made the announcement Mayor Lindsay had predicted: The union was calling for a special session. With this gesture, Shanker forfeited the support of Negro union leaders, because he had promised them that he would not seek to kill decentralization, an issue to which much of the Negro community has, perhaps unwisely, made a strong emotional commitment. On Nov. 4, Doar, Donovan, Allen, Mayor Lindsay and Joseph W. McGovern, Chancellor of the Board of Regents, issued a joint statement endorsing the Allen Plan and rejecting any possible special session of the Legislature.

Fourth week—The strike turns nihilist

Tuesday, Nov. 5, was election day, and the custodians went back to work in the schools. They remained on the job thereafter, easing the task of those who were seeking to keep schools open. The picket lines grew more abusive of nonstriking teachers. (There probably was, and is today, as much verbal harassment of non-strikers by U.F.T. members as there has been of teachers on strike by parents and community representatives. Many teachers who continued to teach during the strike—including Bernard Donovan's daughter—doubt that they will be able to remain in the schools. They do not, of course, have a union to defend their interests.) In certain areas, most notably Bay Ridge in Brooklyn, the union mobilized mass picketing to prevent the reopening of schools. Sentiment in the city began to change: The teacher strikes had become a bad dream that people hoped to find gone each morning when they woke up, please.

In this fourth week of the strike, nobody in the Board of Education, the Mayor's office or the Commissioner's office could see how it could ever be settled at all. Kheel came around rather wistfully with a scorched-earth plan—governing board, McCoy, principals and all disputed teachers to be removed permanently from Ocean Hill. Shanker was not interested.

The fact was that the strike had gathered its own momentum, and was no longer directed against Ocean Hill. It had become nihilist, an expression of the teachers' distrust of the board, the Mayor and the Commissioner. Max Rubin, surveying the situation with experience as well as distaste, called Allen with the idea that finally produced the settlement—a State Supervisory Commission, an independent instrumentality without the political (or social) interests or obligations of the public officials, which would be created strictly to maintain the rights of the teachers in the New York schools, and which would be empowered to close any school where these rights were violated.

Fifth week—A gimmick and an indirect trusteeship for all city schools bring an end to the strike

Quite independently, the Mayor had called in Shanker, Walter Degnan of the Council of Supervisory Associations and Harry Van Arsdale of the Central Labor Council, and had offered to place in their hands the Chief Magistrate's power to close schools which he had exerted in the J.H.S. 271 fiasco three weeks earlier. Over the weekend before the fifth week, Rubin's proposal coalesced with the Mayor's gesture of despair, and the outlines of the final settlement—state trusteeship for Ocean Hill, State Supervisory Commission for the rest of the city—began to become clear. But another week of hatred in the streets and name-calling on television was necessary before the deal in fact came into being.

During that interval, on Thursday, Nov. 14, the Appellate Division handed down a 3-to-2 opinion upholding Justice Rinaldi's decision that the Ocean Hill principals had been appointed illegally. So the Mayor had something else to give the union: The three principals directly involved in this case would be suspended, supposedly pursuant to rule of law, until the Court of Appeals uttered a final ruling; the other Ocean Hill principals would continue on the job. Though Shanker and the union had no real objection to two of the three principals involved, they had become symbols of the victory the leader could take home to his membership—and of the further defeat that the state trustee would now make Ocean Hill swallow.

Nov. 16-17, 1968—Settlement by exhaustion

Again on a Saturday, Nov. 16, at the end of the fifth week of the climactic strike, everyone in the story gathered at Gracie Mansion—McCoy, Oliver, Father Powis and a few others from Ocean Hill in the front room, the old part of the mansion; the union on the ground floor in the new back wing built for meetings; the Board of Education and the Commissioner in the basement of the new wing, where the Mayor has his office. Ted Kheel was lunching with Kenneth Clark at Le Pavillon, and they were developing a plan by which the Central Labor Council and Clark's research organization could meet together and create a decentralization proposal everyone could live with. Kheel called the Mayor to tell him about the idea, and was informed that a deal was in the making. The two men went up to Gracie Mansion to help out.

Several separate negotiations were in progress. One was between the union and the Board of Education—essentially, Doar, Straley and Donovan—over the contents of the "laundry list," the schedule of longer days and makeup days which would enable children to catch up on missed lessons and teachers to collect missed paychecks. Another was on the composition and authority of the State Supervisory Commission. A third was on the details of Allen's statement establishing a state trusteeship on Ocean Hill.

And a fourth, wholly separate, really not a negotiation at all, was the effort by the Mayor and Allen and their deputies, and Kenneth Clark and Whitney Young, to persuade the governing board to go peacefully, to accept the inevitable and trust Allen's and Doar's and the Mayor's goodwill to build back their influence in the schools of their district. But, since May, the governing board had turned down too many deals infinitely better than this one.

On every issue except its right to live, Ocean Hill had lost. Four of the eight principals the governing board had originally recommended were now to be, at least temporarily, out of its schools; the board itself was suspended and its members were to be forbidden to visit the schools; in addition to the union and Board of Education observers who had caused such offense five weeks before, there were now to be representatives of the State Education Department who had the power to countermand orders from principals or McCoy, on the spot. Any school where union teachers were harassed would simply be closed (as J.H.S. 271 was for two weeks in December). The city—even the Mayor's office—was now prepared to endure a race riot rather than another teacher strike: Ocean Hill's last leverage was gone.

Left with a choice between claiming a sell-out or admitting they had been wretchedly ill-advised and wrong since May, the governing board humanly denounced the agreement as a sell-out, and left. On the way out, Father Powis called: "Hey, baby, now we burn down Brooklyn!" and Whitney Young answered bitterly: "It's a pity—isn't it?—that there are only 2,000 blacks you can get killed on Ocean Hill."

Clark moved down to the basement to be with the Mayor and Allen and Doar, to try to keep a voice for Ocean Hill sounding in the cacophony. Kheel ran upstairs and down, between official-dom and the union, bearing little pieces of paper with clauses written on them. Nobody was keeping track of what had been and had not been settled. The teachers picked at the language of the documents, and Kheel and Israelson patiently rewrote.

Finally there were only two issues left: banning the members of the suspended governing board from visiting any schools in the district other than the one in which the individual member had her own children, and removing from the Board of Education decentralization plan the clause which permitted local boards to transfer teachers out involuntarily, provided only that some other local board would take them.

Clark pleaded that a contract which barred the governing board from its own schools would be an intolerable humiliation. Shanker, in the other room, was adamant: It had been members of the governing board who had made the most trouble in the schools during the previous settlements. The compromise worked out was that there would be nothing in any contract forbidding the governing board access to its own schools, but that Allen would include a statement to that effect in his letter establishing the trusteeship.

Surprisingly, it turned out to be much more difficult to persuade the Board of Education to revise its decentralization plan and withdraw its grant of authority to local boards to transfer teachers to other local boards. Doar absolutely refused to budge on the issue. It dawned on the participants that a lawyer's logic had led Doar to the notion that the whole impact of the troubles since September could be negated if a rule was only allowed to stand, and everyone, including Clark, turned on him angrily. Finally, Doar urged a compromise by which the Board would agree that local boards could not transfer people until after Dec. 31, and his colleagues had him on the ropes. If he was willing to change his document to put a time limit on it, then no issue of principle could be involved. "You're just trying to get me to go along with the union," Doar complained, but he yielded.

If there had been any ambiguity in the union contract which suggested that the Ocean Hill governing board could successfully stage a confrontation on the issue of involuntary transfer, that ambiguity was now gone. Involuntary transfer had been made a grievance, subject to the full grievance procedures—including arbitration. "Pending such decision," the clause concludes, "the status quo of the employe shall be maintained."

Finally, a little after 10 in the morning, some 24 hours after the negotiations had started, the settlement was ready for release. It consisted of two pages of agreements between union and Board, and six pages of a letter from Commissioner Allen. While the city waited to learn whether its agony was over, while the exhausted participants in the negotiations dragged about Gracie Mansion trying to keep awake (Donovan read a detective story), the clerical staff of the Mayor's office took three and one-half hours to type eight double-spaced pages. Nobody's fault, of course: It's the urban crisis.

Why us?

In real life, of course, there is plenty of fault here.

First, blame lies on the foundations and the Mayor's office for their casual acceptance of confrontation techniques. In an article on Ocean Hill in the August-September issue of Interplay, based entirely on information from within the project, Richard Karp wrote that the governing board had dismissed the teachers with the "tacit approval" of the Mayor's office and "the 'establishment.' " Allowing a little for wishful thinking, I think this statement is true. No representative of the Ford Foundation or the Urban Coalition has spoken critically in public—or to me, in private conversation—about the action of the governing board in "dismissing" the union teachers.

Speaking of their April meetings with the governing board—which they had never mentioned publicly until I called to check up on complaints about nonsupport which I had heard in Ocean Hill—the members of the Urban Coalition education task force regretted, not their failure to dissuade the governing board from its suicidal action of May 7 in dismissing the teachers, but their subsequent *success* in convincing McCoy that he would have to prefer charges, thus revealing the arbitrary and deliberately provocative nature of what had been done. Now—*now*—foundation executives are beginning to speak of the troubles they had in the South with projects the Rev. Mr. Oliver was associated with as part of the Southern Christian Leadership Conference. Until now, everybody lay doggo.

The Ford Foundation, which could easily have uncovered the truth about the May 7 action of the governing board, released a pending grant for the benefit of Ocean Hill-Brownsville at the end of May (and moneys from that grant were paid continuously to the governing board and some of its members as individuals through all the suspensions imposed by the Board of Education and the Commissioner).

None of its large collection of big-time white advisers ever warned the governing board that two can play at the game of confrontation, and that in any direct conflict with the labor movement Ocean Hill would take a fearful beating.

Second, blame lies on the Board of Education both for failing to respond to the anguish of the constructive elements on the governing board in the fall of 1967 and for failing to find a reasoned response to confrontation in the spring of 1968. The Ocean Hill governing board was and is a creation of the Board of Education, upon whom the parent body could have mandated compulsory arbitration by simple exercise of its rule-making powers.

Decentralization is a viable idea only if the plan includes arrangements for some higher authority to assume effective trusteeship over a seriously erring local board. The simplest and least painful way to enforce such a rule would have been to announce that unless the Board of Education was convinced that all teachers in Ocean Hill would be protected against the sort of casual injustice that had been perpetrated on May 7, the Bureau of Personnel would refuse to assign to the district new teachers to replace those who were surely going to leave. This option was available at least until July.

Later, when the new school year opened, the disorders of the first week and the union's response to them gave the Board of Education a clear choice between keeping the schools closed on Ocean Hill or watching Shanker close them everywhere in the city. Inertia, as usual, won, penalizing 1,150,000 children, rewarding and encouraging the terrorist elements in Ocean Hill—and ultimately, of course, leaving the governing board much worse off than it would have been if the Board of Education had lowered the boom at once and announced that the Ocean Hill schools were going to be closed until the governing board cooperated in the reinstatement of union teachers.

Third, blame falls on Mayor Lindsay, whose drive to politicize the school system has been quite exclusive of any thought of the reaction such politicalization might provoke—and whose devotion to his Urban Task Force has left him increasingly at the mercy of a secret service which gains rewards to the degree it can convince its chief that his state is insecure.

In the controversy over decentralization, the Mayor insisted on treating the teachers as just another pressure group, rather than as the only adults who spend all day in schools. In the spring, when the Ocean Hill situation blew up, the Mayor used his influence to work against decisive action to control and localize the dispute—and in the fall he panicked, saying increasingly harsh things about the union in public and offering increasingly grave concessions in private.

Underlying the climactic strike was the ugly fact that the teachers' union was not prepared to accept the Mayor's word, or even his signature on a document, as a pledge of his future actions. Not until the three-man State Supervisory Commission had been created to police the agreement—meaning that the teachers would not under any circumstances have to deal with Mayor Lindsay or his appointees if they felt their rights had been violated—would the union agree to end the strike.

At the interface between the white world and Ocean Hill stood Milton Galamison and Rhody McCoy, assuring everybody that everything was going to be all right—which was just what they had been saying, most inaccurately, for months. I have the feeling from browsing around Ocean Hill that this time they may have been right. The neighborhood was not at all happy about the games its children had been encouraged to play around J.H.S. 271, and the parents of the children were probably eager in October to see peace return to their schools.

"I can see why Shanker struck the first two times," said one of the most important Negro figures in the Ocean Hill unit. "Though you wouldn't expect it, because I'm out here and I'm loyal to this experiment and to these people, I even sympathize with him. But that last strike was just a horror."

Through all this tortuous course, one must take account of the extraordinary figure of Rhody McCoy. For six months McCoy kept saying different things to different people. He was against the original confrontation, but helped set it up; while appearing to favor arbitration of the dispute, he opposed even the Kheel recommendations at meetings of the governing board; throughout the summer he was discussing future joint ventures with Shanker while urging the community to continue its total intransigency to the return of Shanker's people; maintaining his image of professionalism and exclusive interest in education, he did not stop the terrorism of the first Wednesday; during the strikes (and in the weeks following the final settlement) he was the source of any number of inflammatory statements and helped set up situations which would reveal what he called (correctly) the "degrading and humiliating" terms of the deal that had ended the strike—but each time one of his actions or statements made trouble he could and did give a plausible explanation in terms of the demands upon him from "the community."

McCoy has an odd locution for his most disruptive statements: They are almost always put in the mouth of some anonymous other. Speaking about the radicalization of the governing board, for example, he said recently, "When a mother sees her own kid failing, she thinks it's her fault or the kid's. When she sees a whole *class* of kids failing, then she begins to think the whole system is designed to keep black children down." The listener can come away from that statement believing either that McCoy himself thinks the school system is a deliberate conspiracy against Negroes, or that he sympathizes with the violent if misdirected feelings of naive women.

A foundation officer said the other day that he wished he could get some confidence that he knew the real McCoy. Members of the governing board would not be so clever about it, but sometimes they share the same view. McCoy keeps his pipe in his mouth, speaks slowly and not often—sometimes militantly, sometimes moderately, always intelligently. In Christmas week, I challenged him with some of the inconsistencies detailed in this narrative, and finally he said: "Everybody else seems to have a public posture and a private posture. Why shouldn't McCoy?" There is, I think, an answer to this, but I'm damned if I know what it is.

In the end, I suspect, what went wrong was that the fall's second strike was too successful—it was actually *popular*. A member of the Board of Education says almost seriously that he believes Shanker called the climactic strike because he wants to be Mayor—and that if he ran he would win.

The enormous turnouts at the teachers' rallies—5 and 10 times the size of the crowds that the followers of Ocean Hill could muster—ultimately persuaded the union that it could in effect refuse to deal with the elected Mayor of the city, and that it could dictate public policy on the continuance or abandonment of the Ocean Hill experiment. The strike revealed a shocking quantity of racist sentiment in the city, among more teachers than one would have expected—especially given the leadership the teachers had chosen for themselves.

For Al Shanker was the leading integrationist in the New York labor movement. He marched in Selma, served on the steering committee of the Conference for Quality Integrated Education, and led the union's executive committee to a 30-to-2 endorsement of Mayor Lindsay's civilian review board to hear charges against the police. Not long before Ocean Hill blew up, Shanker proposed a civilian review board to deal with complaints against teachers from parents who found the existing disciplinary structure unresponsive to their anger.

Teacher lunchrooms were better integrated than any others I have ever seen, and Negroes probably felt more at home in the teachers' union than in any other white institution in the city. On the real issues that must be resolved in the city's schools, the U.F.T. as an organization was by no means unsympathetic to the Negro position.

But there were no real issues in the strikes—just slogans. What is ultimately disgusting about the teacher strikes and the public officials who failed to prevent them is that words like "community control" mean no more in dealing with the complex of relationships between school administrators and parents than words like "quality education" mean in dealing with the inadequate teacher training and severe multiple deprivations which combine to produce so much wretched work in our slum schools. On words like these, people who knew no better created a confrontation.

During the course of the crisis, a member of the Mayor's Urban Task Force told a meeting of architects that he thought the strikes would be good by showing people how important education is. One can, perhaps, be a little more precise about the impact of the teacher strikes. They accelerated the flight from the city's schools—and indeed from the city itself—of those who can afford to leave. They made companies which had thought of establishing themselves in New York decide to shun the city. They poisoned the wells of human decency which did exist in this cosmopolitan and sophisticated metropolis, which the Mayor only three years ago called "Fun City." And they will very probably reduce to the condition of a Boston or an Alabama, or some mixture of the two, a school system which was wretchedly ill-organized and weakly led but relatively alert intellectually and by no means so completely ineffective as it has become fashionable to say—and which was almost the only real hope the city could offer for the future of hundreds of thousands of Negro and Puerto Rican children.

The Call of
the Black Panthers

by Sol Stern

SAN FRANCISCO

IN EARLY MAY, front pages across America carried the illustrated story of an "armed invasion" of the California Legislature by a group of black men known as the Black Panther Party for Self-Defense. What actually happened that day in Sacramento was something less than the beginning of a Negro insurrection, but it was no less important for all that: The appearance of the gun-bearing Panthers at the white Capitol was a dramatic portent of something that is stirring in the Northern black ghettos.

By any yardstick used by the civil-rights movement, the Panther organization is not yet very important or effective. The Panthers' political influence in the Negro community remains marginal. The voice of the Panthers is a discordant one, full of the rhetoric of revolutionary violence, and seemingly out of place in affluent America. But it is a voice that ought to be studied. Like it or not, it is increasingly the voice of young ghetto blacks who in city after city this summer have been confronting cops with bricks, bottles and bullets.

The Panthers came to Sacramento from their homes in the San Francisco Bay Area not to "invade" or to "take over" the Legislature, but simply to exercise their right to attend a session of the Legislature and to state their opposition to a pending bill. The bill was, and is, intended to impose severe restrictions on the carrying of loaded weapons in public—a practice not prohibited by present law so long as the weapons are unconcealed. Since the Panthers have been in the habit of carrying loaded weapons at rallies and public meetings, they regarded the legislation as aimed at them in particular and at black people in general. The only thing that was unusual about their lobbying junket is that they brought their loaded guns with them.

The Panthers arrived in hot, dry, lifeless Sacramento and descended on the Capitol with M-1 rifles and 12-gauge shotguns cradled in their arms, .45-caliber pistols visible on their hips, cartridge belts around their waists. Up the white steps and between the classic marble pillars they marched, in two columns, young, black and tough-looking in their leather jackets, boots and tight-fitting clothes. As they marched grimly down the immaculate halls, secretaries and tourists gaped and then moved quickly out of the way. By the time they were halfway down the corridor, every reporter and cameraman in the building had gathered; they stayed in front of the Panthers, moving backward, snapping pictures as they went.

The Panthers, though all were experts on firearms legislation, did not know their way around the building; they followed the reporters and cameramen who were backing toward the legislative chamber. Instead of veering off toward the spectators' galleries, the group flowed right into the Assembly, past guards who were either too startled or simply too slow to stop them.

Actually, it was the photographers, moving backward, who were the first to move through the large oak doors at the rear of the chamber. The Speaker, seeing the commotion, asked the guards to "clear those cameramen." By the time the legislators realized what was happening behind them, most of the group of cameramen and Panthers had been moved out of the chamber. Outside in the corridor, the guards took some guns away from the Panthers—but since the Panthers were not breaking any law, they had to return them. The Panthers read their statement of protest to the reporters and television cameramen, and left. That would have been all, except for a car that broke down.

A Sacramento police officer spotted the armed Panthers at the gas station at which they stopped for repairs, and sent out a hur-

232 • *Sol Stern*

ried call for reinforcements. This time, the Panthers were arrested on a variety of charges, including some stemming from obscure fish-and-game laws. After they had been in jail overnight, the Sacramento District Attorney changed all the charges; 18 members of the group, now out on bail, await trial for disrupting the State Legislature—a misdemeanor—and for conspiracy to disrupt the Legislature—a felony.

As lobbyists, the Black Panthers are not very effective; but then, the Panthers did not really care much whether the gun bill passed or not. Their purpose was to call attention to their claim that black people in the ghetto must rely on armed self-defense and not the white man's courts to protect themselves.

The adventure at the Capitol assured the passage of the gun legislation, however, and it will soon be signed into law—welcome news to Bay Area police chiefs, who have been frustrated ever since the Panthers first started carrying their loaded weapons in public. In Oakland, across the bay from San Francisco, the police have not waited for the new legislation; they regularly arrest armed Panthers, usually on charges of brandishing a weapon in a threatening manner. The Panthers insist that this is merely harassment, but they have tactically retreated and usually now leave their guns at home.

For the Panthers, their guns have had both real and symbolic meaning—real because they believe they will have to use the guns, eventually, against the white power structure that they charge is suppressing them; symbolic because of the important political effects they think that a few blacks, openly carrying guns, can have in the black community.

"Ninety per cent of the reason we carried guns in the first place," says Panther leader Huey P. Newton, "was educational. We set the example. We made black people aware that they have the right to carry guns."

Only seven years ago, when the head of the Monroe, N.C., chapter of the National Association for the Advancement of Colored People proposed that Negroes should shoot back when armed bands of white rednecks start shooting up the Negro section of town, he set off a furor in the national civil-rights movements and turned himself into a pariah. Robert Williams, eventually charged with kidnapping in what his supporters insist was a frame-up, ultimately left America for Cuba and then China, a revolutionary in exile. It was a short time ago; much has happened in black America since the simple proposal of armed self-defense could provoke so much tumult.

The Black Panther Party for Self-Defense was organized principally by 25-year-old Huey Newton and 30-year-old Bobby Seale. Newton looks younger than his years, is tall and lithe, with handsome, almost sculptured features. His title is Minister of Defense, while his darker and more mature-looking friend, Seale, is the chairman. The Minister of Defense is preeminent because, they say, they are in a condition of war. "Black people realize," Newton says, "that they are already at war with the racist white power structure."

Being at war, they are reluctant to give out strategic information about the internal workings of their organization. As they put it, quoting Malcolm X: "Those who know don't say and those who say don't know." Outside estimates of their membership run anywhere from 75 to 200, organized into small units in the various black communities in the Bay area. Each unit has a captain; the captains, along with Newton, Seale and a treasurer, make up an executive committee which sets basic policy for the entire organization. The Panthers get out their message of armed self-defense to the black communities through a biweekly newspaper, and on Saturdays there are outdoor street rallies.

On a sunny Saturday at the end of June, two such rallies were scheduled. The first was on San Francisco's Potrero Hill, at a nearly all-black housing project composed of decaying World War II barracks that should have been torn down years ago. Desolate and windy, the project overlooks an industrial section of the city jammed between Potrero Hill and the Bay. It is an ugly and depressing place.

By the time Huey Newton and Bobby Seale arrive from the other side of the Bay, there are about 30 young blacks milling around at the rally site, a dead-end street which serves as a parking lot in the middle of the development. Newton and Seale do not seem disappointed at the turnout. Seale turns over a city garbage can, stands on it and announces that the rally will begin. A half-dozen curious children come running over as the bloods gather. Some women poke their heads out of windows overlooking the street. There is not a white face in sight, nor a policeman, unless someone in the crowd is an undercover agent.

Seale explains the Black Panther Party for Self-Defense and the significance of its name. It was inspired, he says, by the example of the Lowndes County Freedom Organization in Alabama, which first adopted the black-panther symbol. That symbol, Seale says, is an appropriate one for black people in America today. "It is not in the panther's nature to attack anyone first, but when he is attacked and backed into a corner, he will respond viciously and wipe out the aggressor."

Seale then introduces the Minister of Defense; Huey Newton provides a 15-minute capsule history of the Negro struggle in America, and then begins to relate it to the world revolution and to the example of the people of Vietnam. "There were only 30 million of them," Newton says of the Vietnamese, "but first they threw out the Japanese, then they drove out the French and now they are kicking hell out of the Americans and you better believe it, brothers." Black people can learn lessons from the fight of the Vietnamese, Newton continues; black people in America also must arm themselves for self-defense against the same racist army. "Every time you go execute a white racist Gestapo cop, you are defending yourself," he concludes.

When Seale returns to the garbage-can platform, the crowd is already with him, shouting "That's right" and "You tell it" as he speaks.

"All right, brothers," he tells them, "let's understand what we want. We have to change our tactics. Black people can't just mass on the streets and riot. They'll just shoot us down." Instead, it is necessary to organize in small groups to "take care of business." The "business" includes among other things "executing racist cops."

Graphically, Seale describes how a couple of bloods can surprise cops on their coffee break. The Negroes march up to the cop and then "they shoot him down—voom, voom—with a 12-gauge shotgun." That, says Seale, would be an example of "righteous power." No more "praying and bootlicking." No more singing of "We Shall Overcome." "The only way you're going to overcome is to apply righteous power."

Seale tells the young crowd not to be impressed by the fact that Negroes are only an 11 per cent minority in America. "We have potential destructive power. Look around at those factories down there. If we don't get what we want, we can make it impossible for the man's system to function. All we got to do is drop some cocktails into those oil tanks and then watch everything go."

No one in the crowd questions the propriety of the Black Panther program. One man says that it sounds O.K. but it's all talk and the trouble is that, when it's time for action, "most of the bloods cut out." Seale says that's true, but "we have to organize."

While a few of the bloods take membership applications and give their names to the local captain, Seale and Newton jump into a car and race across the Bay Bridge to the second rally in Richmond, 20 miles away on the east side of the bay, just north of Berkeley. Only the surroundings are different: It is a ghetto of tiny homes and rundown cottages with green lawns and carports. The rally is held on the lawn of George Dowell, who joined the Panthers after his brother Denzil was shot and killed by the police. Denzil Dowell's body was riddled with six shotgun pellets. The police say he was shot trying to escape after he was caught breaking into a store. The Panthers and many of the people in the neighborhood say simply that he was murdered.

During the rally George Dowell patrols the fringes of the small group, carrying a loaded .30-.30 rifle. Another Panther stands on the Dowell roof, demonstrating the loading of a shotgun with a 20-inch barrel—a gun which Bobby Seale tells the group he recommends highly.

Driving away from the rally, a tired Huey Newton jokes with a pretty girl who is his date that evening. She is a member of the Panthers, and has her hair done African style. She says that Richmond reminds her of Watts, where she grew up; the people in Richmond, she adds, are very warm and friendly. Newton agrees.

Asked whether the talk at rallies about killing cops is serious, Newton replies that it is very serious. Then why, he is asked, stake everything, including the lives of the Panthers, on the killing of a couple of cops?

"It won't be just a couple of cops," he says, "when the time comes, it will be part of a whole national coordinated effort." Is he willing to kill a cop? Yes, he answers, and when the time comes he is willing to die. What does he think is going to happen to him?

"I am going to be killed," he says with a smile on his face. He looks very young.

To Oakland's chief of police, Robert Preston, the Panthers are hardly worth commenting upon. "It's not the police but society that should be concerned with groups such as this," said Preston, displaying a cool response to the Panthers that perhaps masks a deeper concern. On second thought, Preston said: "They have on occasion harassed police and made some efforts to stir up animosity against us, but they are not deserving of any special treatment. They have made pretty ridiculous assertions which don't deserve to be dignified by anyone commenting on them."

Some of Preston's men on the beat were less reluctant to voice their gut reactions to the Panthers. One of them issued a series of unprintable epithets; another, giggling, suggested, "Maybe those guys ought to pick their best gunman and we pick ours and then have an old-fashioned shoot-it-out."

Despite Huey Newton's fatalism, the Panthers are not simply nihilistic terrorists. When confronted by the police and placed under arrest, as they were in Sacramento, the Panthers have so far surrendered their guns and submitted peacefully. If cops are to be shot—and there is no reason to question the Panthers' willingness to do this—it will be part of a general plan of action they hope will force revolutionary changes in the society. The Panthers see the white cops in the ghetto as a "foreign occupying army" whose job is to prevent that change by force.

Reflecting on the outbreaks in Northern ghettos recently, Huey Newton said, "They were rebellions and a part of the revolutionary struggle, even though incorrect methods were used. But people learn warfare by indulging in warfare. That's the way they learn better tactics. When people go into the streets in large numbers they are more easily contained. We ought to look to historic revolutions such as Vietnam and learn to wear the enemy down. The way to do that is to break up into groups of threes and fours."

The Panther program calls for the black community to become independent and self-governing. The Negro community in which the Panthers held their second rally that Saturday is an unincorporated part of Contra Costa County; the Panthers are organizing a petition drive that would put the question of incorporation on the ballot. If they should succeed, they will accomplish by legal means one of the goals for which they say they are ultimately willing to engage in violence—removal of the white man's government from the black community.

Like most revolutionaries, the leaders of the Black Panthers do not come from the bottom of the economic ladder. Huey Newton could have escaped from the ghetto, if he had wanted to. He went to the integrated and excellent Berkeley High School, and eventually spent a year in law school. Bright but rebellious, he had numerous run-ins with the authorities (he always remembers them as "white authorities") in high school before he finally was graduated, to go on to Merritt College, a small, rundown two-year institution on the fringes of the Oakland ghetto. That was in the early nineteen-sixties, when Merritt had become a kind of incubator of Negro nationalism.

Both Newton and Seale, who also attended Merritt, remember the time as an exciting period of self-discovery for scores of young Oakland blacks. They would cut classes and sit around the nearby coffee shops, arguing about the black revolution, and reading the classics of black nationalism together.

Both Seale and Newton joined their first organization during that period: a group called the Afro-American Association, which advocated black nationalism and stressed Negro separateness and self-improvement. Seale and Newton both became disillusioned with the group because they felt it did not offer anything but some innocuous cultural nationalism. (The group still functions, led by a lawyer named Donald Warden, whom Seale and Newton scoffingly refer to as a "hard-core capitalist.")

After they had left the Afro-American Association, there was a period of political uncertainty for both Seale and Newton. At one point, Newton was tempted to become a Black Muslim; he had great respect for Malcolm X, but could not "accept the religious aspect." There was also a period of "hustling on the streets" for Newton and frequent arrests for theft and burglary. "But even then I discriminated between black and white property," he says.

Eventually came a year in the county jail on an assault-with-a-deadly-weapon conviction. In jail, again, there was the confrontation with white authority. Newton led riots and food strikes —for which he was placed in solitary confinement. In Alameda County at the time this constituted a unique and degrading form of punishment. The solitary cells were called "soul breakers" by the Negro prisoners. Each was totally bare, without even a washstand. The prisoner was put into it without any clothes and slept on the cement floor. In the middle of the cement floor was a hole which served as a toilet. The prisoners did their time in blocks of 15 days, after which they were allowed out for a shower and some exercise before going back in again.

Newton took it as a challenge. The "white bulls" were out to break him, and he had to resist. He made sure that when they opened the door to his cell he would be doing push-ups. It was also a time for thinking, since there was nothing else to do.

"I relived my life," he says. "I thought of everything I had done. And I realized some new things in that jail. I viewed the jail as no different from the outside. I thought about the relationship between being outside of a jail and being in, and I saw the great similarities. It was the whites who had the guns who controlled everything, with a few Uncle Tom blacks helping them out."

For Newton, as for Malcolm X, the prison experience only confirmed his hostility to the white world and made him more militant. Outside, Newton and Bobby Seale hooked up again and began to talk about the need for a revolutionary party that would represent the black masses and the ghetto youth unrepresented by other civil-rights groups.

"We began to understand the unwritten law of force," says Bobby Seale. "They, the police, have guns, and what the law actually says ain't worth a damn. We started to think of a program that defines and offsets this physical fact of the ghetto. I view black people in America as a colonial people. Therefore we have to arm ourselves and make the colonial power give us our freedom."

San Francisco's Hunters Point riot of last summer galvanized Newton and Seale into action. They viewed the disorganized halfhearted attempts of the Negroes to fight back against the cops as a waste. A new strategy was needed. After the riots they moved around the Bay Area talking to groups of bloods and gangs from the ghettos. The young bloods would ask Seale and Newton: "Tell us how we are going to do something. Tell us what we are going to do about the cops." The answer was the Black Panthers.

"The dream of the black people in the ghetto is how to stop

the police brutality on the street," says Bobby Seale. "Can the people in the ghetto stand up to the cops? The ghetto black isn't afraid because he already lives with violence. He expects to die any day."

To someone who is not black, the issue of police brutality and police malpractice in the ghetto cannot be disposed of by checking a sociologist's statistics or the records of police review boards. It remains, an unrecorded fact that lurks in unlit ghetto streets, in moving police cars, in the privacy of police stations. It is recorded in the eyes of the young Negroes at Black Panther rallies who do not even blink when the speaker talks of "executing a cop"; it is as if every one of them has at least one memory of some long-unpunished indignity suffered at the hands of a white cop.

To these young men, the execution of a police officer would be as natural and justifiable as the execution of a German soldier by a member of the French Resistance. This is the grim reality upon which the Panthers build a movement.

To the blood on the street, the black man who can face down the white cop is a hero. One of the early tactics of the Panthers was the "defense patrol." Four Panthers, armed with shotguns, would ride around in a car following a police car in the ghetto. If the police stopped to question a Negro on the street, the Panthers with their guns drawn would get out and observe the behavior of the police. If an arrest was made, the Panthers would try to raise the money to bail the Negro out.

On the basis of such acts, new members were recruited, taught the rudiments of the law on search and seizure, the right to bear arms and arrest procedure, and introduced to the standard works of militant black revolution: Frantz Fanon, Malcolm X, W. E. B. DuBois, Marcus Garvey. Currently, Panthers are reading and digesting Mao Tse-tung's Little Red Book. Seale and Newton admit that the rank and file of the Panthers, many of whom are members of street gangs, are not sophisticated politically, but insist that they are "wise in the ways of power."

To Newton and Seale the identification with world revolution is a serious business. They see the United States as the center of an imperialist system which suppresses the worldwide revolution of colored people. And, says Newton: "We can stop the machinery. We can stop the imperialists from using it against black people all over the world. We are in a strategic position in this country, and we won't be the only group rebelling against the oppressor here."

If the Panthers are no more than a tiny minority even among militant Negroes, it does not seem to affect their revolutionary fervor. Theirs is a vision of an American apocalypse in which all blacks are forced to unite for survival against the white oppressors. Newton puts it this way: "At the height of the resistance they are going to be slaughtering black people indiscriminately. We are sure that at that time Martin Luther King will be a member of the Black Panthers through necessity. He and others like him will have to band together with us just to save themselves."

In the meantime, all is not smooth among the black militants. The Panthers have had running feuds with other black nationalist groups, one of them a Bay Area group which has also used the name "Black Panthers," and which has been attacked by Newton and Seale for its overly intellectual approach and for its unwillingness to carry guns in the open. "Cultural nationalists" is the epithet that Newton and Seale use for black nationalists who they claim never try to develop grass-roots support in the ghetto community, but are content to live in an intellectual milieu of black nationalism.

In turn, the Panthers have been criticized for their provocative and public actions by other black militants. One Negro leader in the area said privately, "These cats have just been playing cowboys and Indians." But opinions among black leaders are sharply divided on the subject. When asked about the Panthers on a recent trip to the Bay Area, H. Rap Brown, the new national chairman of the Student Nonviolent Coordinating Committee, had only favorable things to say about them. "What they're doing is very important," said Brown. "Black people are just beginning to get over their fear of the police and the Panthers are playing an important role in helping them to surmount that fear." (Eleven days ago, Brown was arrested on charges of inciting Negroes to riot in Cambridge, Md.)

How does the ordinary, nonpolitical Negro respond to the Panthers? Consider, not because he is representative, but for the quality of the reaction, 22-year-old Billy John Carr, once a star athlete at Berkeley High School. Carr lives in Berkeley's

Negro ghetto, has a wife and child now, and tries to keep his family together with sporadic work as a laborer. He has never been a member of any political organization and knows the Panthers only by reputation. Of the Panthers he says: "As far as I'm concerned it's beautiful that we finally got an organization that don't walk around singing. I'm not for all this talking stuff. When things start happening I'll be ready to die if that's necessary and it's important that we have somebody around to organize us." The Sacramento incident clearly won the Panthers grudging respect and put them on the map in the ghetto. Recently, when traditional civil-rights organizations and Negro politicians in California organized what they called a "Black Survival Conference," the Panthers were invited to speak and got an enthusiastic response.

Are the Panthers racists? Both Huey Newton and Bobby Seale deny it. "Black people aren't racists. Racism is primarily a white man's problem," says Seale, perhaps begging the question. Whatever the root causes of American racism, there *are* Negroes in the society who simply hate whites as a matter of principle, and would commit indiscriminate violence against them merely for their color. The violent rhetoric of the Panthers—which pits the black man against the white cop—undoubtedly fans such feelings. Yet the fact is that the Panthers, unlike certain other black nationalist groups, have not allowed themselves to indulge in baiting the "white devil." They are race-conscious, they are exclusively "pro-black," but they also seem conscious of the dangers of simple-minded antiwhite hostility.

Though the Panthers will not allow whites to attend their membership meetings, they have had friendly relations with groups of white radicals in the area. They participated in a meeting with leaders of the San Francisco "hippie" community, in which common problems were discussed. The hippies had been concerned about trouble with young Negroes in the area who were starting fights and harassing the hippies. "We went around and told these guys that the hippies weren't the enemy, that they shouldn't waste their time on them," says Newton.

The Panthers' relations with the local chapter of S.N.C.C., which has a number of whites in it, have been friendly. Terry Cannon, a white member of the editorial board of The Movement, a newspaper affiliated with S.N.C.C., and long a Bay Area activist, sees the Panthers' initial action as necessary. "The Panthers have demonstrated something that was very much needed in Northern cities," says Cannon. "They have effectively demonstrated that the black community is willing to defend itself."

Though they claim to have started chapters in Los Angeles, Harlem and elsewhere in the North, the Panthers remain pitifully small in numbers and their organizational resources meager. Frequent arrests have brought severe financial strain in the form of bail money and legal fees—and police harassment is certain to continue. If the Panthers increasingly "go underground" to escape such pressures, they will find it that much more difficult to broaden their contact with the rest of the black community.

But to write off the Panthers as a fringe group of little influence is to miss the point. The group's roots are in the desperation and anger that no civil-rights legislation or poverty program has touched in the ghetto. The fate of the Panthers as an organization is not the issue. What matters is that there are a thousand black people in the ghetto thinking privately what any Panther says out loud.

The Black Studies Thing

by Ernest Dunbar

ITHACA N.Y.

THE BLACK girls, cooperative at Cornell University is a large frame
house on Dearborn Street close to the campus. Nearby are other
frame houses occupied by private families, white families. Until recently, the glass panel of the co-op's front door had the word
"Wari"—Swahili for "home"—stenciled across it; now the door is
freshly painted and unobtrusive among the others. Inside, a record-
player booms the earthy chants of Aretha Franklin. Each of the 13
black girls who live in "Wari" has a "natural" hairstyle. One of
them, Gayla Cook, a sloe-eyed sophomore from Cleveland, pours
wine into a sauce for the chicken dish she is preparing. Potato salad
and rice, spiced with hot condiments, will accompany the chicken.
Cornbread, warm and fragrant, waits atop the stove.

Aretha Franklin gives way to Ray Charles's evangelical moans as
a group of black male students stomp in, shaking the snow from their
shoes. There is a lot of palm-slapping and cool badinage ("Hey baby,
what's happening?"). A tall, black, bearded youth slumps on the
living-room sofa, relaxed yet intense, surveying, questioning. He is
19-year-old Ed Whitfield, Cornell '70, a math major from Little
Rock's Central High School, where he graduated fifth in a class of
600. Why is he at Cornell? "I thought I'd make one last swipe at
America before I gave up on it."

It is a weekend, and later in the evening the house is jammed with
black youth, moving and grooving against the insistent Motown

*From the *New York Times Magazine*, April 6, 1969, copyright © 1969
by The New York Times Company.

rhythms pulsing through the darkened rooms. Some of them drift back to the kitchen to pick up on the chicken and potato salad, others sit transfixed in the small television room, gazing at the tube. Mixing easily among the Cornell students are young members of Ithaca's small black population.

Ithaca (population: 29,750) seems an unlikely setting for a black uprising. Implanted amid the bucolic hills, gorges and lakes of Tompkins County, the town is a snowy, Rip Van Winkle-esque retreat from the hustle, pollution and distractions of New York's larger urban centers. But Ithaca's 2,000 native blacks are not the people making waves. The restless ones live in Cornell University dormitories, in rooming houses or in apartments outside the town. They are among some 250 blacks studying with 14,000 white students at Cornell. Though the university has long had a few black athletes—among them its famed 1937 All-American, Jerome (Brud) Holland, now president of Virginia's Hampton Institute and a member of Cornell's board of trustees—until recently blacks were about as abundant on the campus as Nepalese.

TODAY, the small but growing contingent of black students gets more than its share of attention from Cornell administrators, faculty members and many white students. In a process that is being duplicated on campuses across the nation, university executives and deans are undergoing a painful self-examination that is part of a new learning process in which the black students often do the teaching.

Last year, Cornell blacks kept the head of the economics department barricaded in his office for seven hours to protest an allegedly racist classroom statement by a visiting economics professor, tussled with campus policemen who were trying to keep some of them out of the economics office and roughed up a reporter and photographer for The Cornell Sun who tried to take pictures of the incident. They have demanded separate living facilities and classes and challenged the credentials of some Cornell professors and the relevancy of their courses. In February, Gary S. Patton, a sophomore member of Cornell's Afro-American Society, grabbed President James A. Perkins by the collar and yanked the startled administrator from a microphone as he was explaining to an audience of 800 why the university would not sell its stock in banks that did business with South Africa.*

Ironically, the Cornell black revolt is linked to Perkins's arrival at the university's helm. A tall, ebullient man who had been vice president of the Carnegie Corporation and before that vice president of his alma mater, Swarthmore College. Perkins recalls: "When I came to Cornell in 1963, I discovered there was an average of six or seven black students per class, or only about 25 out of a total enrollment of 11,000. That had been going on for decades, and I suspected it was not an accident—that there was a quiet quota. I later discovered there was no quota, but neither was there an affirmative interest in increasing that number, and in this area, where there are few Negroes, without a special recruiting effort that's the kind of situation you get."

The Philadelphia-born Perkins, a Quaker, came from a family with a strong interest in the problems of race and was chairman of the board of trustees of the United Negro College Fund. (He is also a board member of the Chase Manhattan Bank, one of the institutions whose investments in South African commerce were under fire from students at Cornell.) With his trustees' backing, he decided to provide the "affirmative interest" that would increase the number of Negroes at Cornell. There were two significant hurdles. One was money, since the poorer blacks required twice as much financial aid as white scholarship students. The other was entrance exams. Blacks tended to score lower on the Scholastic Aptitude Test given college applicants, but Perkins, then also chairman of the board of the Educational Testing Service, which conducts the test, suspected that there were shortcomings in these examinations that reduced their ability to predict the performance of students from "disadvantaged" backgrounds. (The SAT involves two exams, one verbal and one mathematical. The maximum possible score for each is 800. At Cornell, the average scores are between 600 and 700.)

With a $250,000 grant from the Rockefeller Foundation, Cornell began in 1965 to bring in black students whose SAT scores averaged only 450 to 550. "It wasn't that we didn't substitute anything for these deficiencies," says Perkins. "We put great reliance on personal interviews and visits with these students, as well as on what their principals and teachers said the students were capable of doing."

Much of the screening was done by Dr. Gloria Joseph, a black sociologist who is a Cornell assistant dean of student affairs. Dr. Joseph, a tall, soft-spoken woman who wears her hair swept back in a bun, says: "I look for a sense of responsibility and self-discipline in the students I interview. For example, if a girl is the oldest child in her family, is often acting as a parent by taking care of her young siblings, and is *still* near the top of her class, that says something to me even if her SAT is only 400. I don't care about the clubs they belong to in high school, I want to know what they have *really* done! Let's face it, a lot of these tests are set up to conform to the middle-class white experience. They sometimes fail when it comes to testing blacks.''

As an example, Dr. Joseph cites a widely used intelligence test for children about 5 years old. It contains sketches of two women: one the Hollywood stereotype, with a straight, turned up nose and thin lips; the other with a flat nose and thick lips. The child is asked to choose the prettier face. While both faces are white, the latter one—the one the child is not expected to choose as prettier—has Negroid features. "This shows," says Dr. Joseph, "that our society feels that by the age of 5 a child should have internalized the white concept of what is prettier. But in these days of 'black is beautiful' little black kids won't pick that picture of the straightnosed type."

THE Cornell experiment proved the correctness of Perkins's hunch on the imprecision of traditional testing procedures when applied to black youths from poorer circumstances. Black students who came to Cornell with SAT scores as much as 200 points below the average performed well. As a result, Cornell's trustees voted special funds for the Committee on Special Education Projects, an expanded recruiting, guidance and counseling program administered by Dr. Joseph. While COSEP includes a few Puerto Ricans, American Indians and members of other minority groups, most of its students are black. "In about five years' time," observes Perkins, "we will have gone from a total enrollment of 25 black students to somewhere around 400."

But the presence of the COSEP students at Cornell was to raise issues that went far beyond anything the university envisioned. Many of the newcomers are from such black Northern ghettos as Harlem, Cleveland's Hough, Los Angeles's Watts and Chicago's South Side as well as from the urban and rural South, and they reflect the experiences and concerns of those communities. They also reflect their generation's determination not to let a college degree trap them between the black community and white society, fleeing one and being rebuffed by the other. The key word in any conversation with a black student at Cornell—as at other universities—is "relevant." They say they want an education that relates to the black American's special problems so that, upon graduation, they may employ their new skills and knowledge to alleviate the ghetto's desperate condition.

Earl Armstrong, a biochemistry senior and a founder and former president of the Afro-American Society, expresses a view encountered again and again among Cornell's blacks. "We've always questioned why we were brought here," he says. "I think they want to get us into this 'mainstream' thing. They figure that after four years up here in this isolated world, you'll go back and fall into your $200,000-a-year job and never think twice." Why should that be of concern to the university? "Because they'd rather have us like that," says Armstrong, "than like Malcolm X."

One black student quotes Perkins as having once told them that he wanted white students to become accustomed to blacks and blacks to become adjusted to the kinds of whites they would meet in the business and professional world. Some blacks view this as evidence that, at best, their function is to help condition young whites to what blacks are like and, at worst, their role is to submit to a kind of brainwashing that will "whiten" blacks for their role in a postgraduate white society.

"The problem we did not foresee when we started this program is the problem the country did not foresee," says Perkins, "that is, the problems that have arisen out of the great drive for Negro identity, out of black separatism and out of growing militancy. These came with the increase in numbers. As soon as black students were numerous enough here, they no longer felt themselves a lost people. They did not wish to lose themselves in the largely white student body so they decided to combine."

In 1966, the second year of the COSEP program, some blacks organized the Afro-American Society at Cornell. The organization lists its objectives as these: "to initiate and support programs which aid in the dissemination of factual material concerning the history of black people," and "to initiate and support programs which are devoted to the eradication of the social, economic and psychological conditions which blight the lives of black people." Membership in the society is open to "all students of Afro-American descent," but may with special approval be conferred on "any Cornell student who expresses a desire to join."

The creation of the Afro-American Society sent shock waves through the Cornell faculty. "There were many people here, white liberals and even radicals, who felt they had been fighting for integration so long, and they just couldn't turn themselves around that fast," says one professor. "They had been fighting fraternities for refusing to admit blacks and Orientals, and now they saw themselves faced with what looked like a very familiar pattern of discrimination—this time by blacks.''

Despite such faculty discomfort, however, the society was accredited. Then last year a group of black coeds requested that the university set up a cooperative house where they could live together. They argued that they were not at ease in the dormitories and that some of their customs were misunderstood by their white dorm-mates. A black girl said that a white coed living on her floor had complained to university authorities that she smelled a ''pungent'' odor coming from the black coed's room and believed it to be marijuana smoke. According to the black coed the ''pungent'' odor was caused by her straightening her hair with a hot comb. (Hair-straightening, by the way, is on the decline among Cornell's black coeds. One senior recalls that there were no girls with ''naturals'' in her freshman and sophomore years, but today the cropped style is worn by many blacks, men and women alike.)

The university provided the cooperative house for the black coeds who requested it (the majority of the school's 100 black girls still live in dorms or apartments), and though the Ithaca representative of the American Civil Liberties Union looked over the arrangement, no complaint was filed. Officially, the house is for COSEP students, which would include the few Puerto Ricans, American Indians and whites enrolled under the program, but in fact, the 13 girls who live in ''Wari'' are black. Similarly, 15 black male students live together in Elmwood House, a university-owned structure that had been occupied by white coeds who vacated it when they grew too small in number to maintain it. It should be pointed out that many Cornell students live off campus as residential restrictions increasingly relax. Many also live in fraternity houses. Once the center of Cornell social life (70 per cent of the university's alumni joined fraternities), Greek-letter organizations are playing a steadily shrinking role. Until recently, they chose their members on racially or religiously exclusive criteria. While there are still ''Jewish'' or ''Protestant'' fraternities at Cornell, some of them have taken in a black or two under administration pressure to desegregate; two have black presidents, each one the only black in his group. Most of the fraternities, however, remain virtually all-white.

AS the housing problem was eased through the establishment of the black residences, another issue came to the fore. A large number of Cornell's blacks asked for a program of Afro-American studies, arguing that much of traditional teaching either ignores the role of the black in the development of the country or, affected by the institutional racism endemic in American society, has distorted history, sociology, political science, economics and other subjects to accommodate a biased white perspective. Last September, Cornell set up a committee of eight faculty members and seven students from the Afro-American Society to outline such a program, with the university pledging to initiate an Afro-American studies course by the fall of 1969. In an unprecedented move, the university accepted nominations by the black students for the post of program director.

In November, however, a dispute developed within the Afro-American Society; one faction headed by Earl Armstrong, then the group's president (he was replaced by a "chairman," Ed Whitfield, in February), was challenged by the followers of the society's vice president, Marshall John Garner, an engineering junior from Akron. The Garner group said the Armstrong faction was too much in the pocket of the administration and argued that the only meaningful black-studies program was one entirely under the control of blacks.

At a student-faculty committee meeting convened in December to interview a candidate for the Afro-American studies directorship, about 40 members of the society suddenly entered the room and announced that the blacks on the committee were no longer authorized to represent the group and that the committee itself no longer had the sanction of the society. The black-studies program, they said, was to be an autonomous program run by blacks.

In the next few weeks there occurred a day-long series of demonstrations and counterdemonstrations on campus that included a singing, dancing, bongo-beating performance by black students outside Perkins's office and a wild melee in a dining hall as black students walked on the tables during a meal. Though 1,000 white students signed a letter of protest, no immediate disciplinary action was taken.

Finally, a group of black students came to the president's office for a session that Perkins describes as "semi-polite." "I just explained to them that the setting up of an autonomous black college granting its own degrees was impossible," he says. "The Afro-American studies program, the headquarters for it, the taking on of a black director for it, the hiring of more black professors [there are fewer than a dozen blacks among Cornell's 2,200 faculty members], the employment of a black psychiatrist—which some students wanted— were all things we were willing to do, but an autonomous black college was out of the question."*

In January, Cornell agreed to establish an Afro-American studies center, setting aside $175,000 for the purpose. Beyond this there is wide disagreement and uncertainty. The black students wanted the center to be a degree-granting institution with a director able to choose his own staff independent of the university's department heads. The administration, on the other hand, specified that the center would *not* be a degree-granting unit (its students would continue to be enrolled in one of the schools or colleges of the university) and, while the center would offer courses for credit, the divisions of the university would have to determine whether the credits were acceptable.

Afro-American or black-studies programs have been defined differently in the institutions, from Harvard to Stanford, where they are being shaped, most often in response to black student requests. Usually the program includes a core of courses that deal with African history (not just the colonial experience or Africa as a reflection of Europe's history but also pre-colonial African empires and societies), the history and sociology of the blacks in America, the analysis of other multi-racial societies in which blacks live, political science courses that may consider the black impact on America's urban politics, African and Afro-American art and dance and African languages. At some universities, related courses already being given are regrouped and new topics added to make up the new curriculum. At a few institutions, a top-to-bottom reconstruction is under way.

At Cornell, several new Afro-American courses were created, even while the controversy was raging. Last year, the black author-playwright-actor Julian Mayfield gave a seminar on Negro writers of the 20th century; a white Cornell economics professor, Douglas Dowd, lectured on the economic development of the urban ghetto, and a course on black literature was taught by another white professor, Daniel McCall. A black poet and author, Don L. Lee, is teaching a freshman humanities course this year; Cleveland Sellers Jr., a former organizer with the Student Nonviolent Coordinating Committee is lecturing on black ideology, and Michael Thelwell, a writer and, like Sellers, a black, teaches a seminar on black literature and its cultural roots.

---

*The Department of Health, Education and Welfare recently notified colleges that they risk losing Federal support if they allow all-black dormitories or exclude whites from black-studies programs. What effect this ruling might have on Cornell's plans is uncertain.

THOUGH approaches differ, many educators have recognized the academic validity of Afro-American studies and the failure of most universities to deal adequately with the subject in the past. The report of a faculty subcommittee exploring the possibility of creating an Afro-American curriculum at Harvard noted:

"In the current period of rapid social change and upheaval, where the oppression of American blacks and the consequences of that oppression are among the most salient domestic events of our time, Harvard has important intellectual obligations. Unfortunately, in its neglect of Afro-American affairs, Harvard has tended to be a microcosm of the larger society.

"It is our feeling that an undergraduate emphasis on Afro-American studies can best be carried out within the framework of one of the traditional disciplines. However, ample precedent does exist, as can be seen in the Latin American, East Asian or Russian studies programs, for an interdisciplinary focus on a particular subject matter." Acting on the subcommittee's recommendation, Harvard has established an Afro-American studies program leading to a B.A. degree.

Dr. Charles Hamilton, a black professor of political science and head of the graduate program in urban studies at Chicago's Roosevelt University (as well as the author, with Stokely Carmichael, of the book "Black Power"), says: "It's very clear in my mind that Afro-American studies are a legitimate field—because the development of blacks has been different from that of any other group in America, because of the impact of slavery, because of the size of the black population and because of our post-slavery experiences.

"When you propose a *black* studies course, people say you're a 'separatist,' yet here at Roosevelt University we've had a Jewish cultural studies major for over 20 years. You can get a bachelor's degree in that!" The Jewish studies program, Hamilton explains, quoting from Roosevelt's catalogue, is for "students who have careers or career plans specifically related to educational and social service in the Jewish community, and students who would like to secure a knowledge and appreciation of Jewish culture."

Prof. C. Vann Woodward of Yale's history department agrees: "Insofar as Afro-American studies mean a form of academic attention to the black part of our population, its history, its experience, I think there is a logical case for it." Yale's own program will not be operative until this fall, though a student can take related courses now. As at Harvard, a Yale student will be able to get his B.A. in Afro-American studies, though there will be no separate department or staff for the program.

As many universities attempt to put together black studies programs, they, like Cornell, are running into an academic whipsaw. Since the basic impetus for black studies came from black students, not faculty members, black collegians are striving to retain a say in what the programs will contain and who will teach them; some are adamant about autonomy for Afro-American departments. In the view of the most militant blacks, no white professor is really qualified to teach black studies because he has not had the experience of growing up black in America and because, they say, white professors collaborated in the academic distortions that the students are now trying to correct. Other blacks feel that some whites might qualify but that they are few in number. At Cornell and other schools, some black students are demanding courses from which white students would be barred on the ground that they lack sophistication and would slow up classes while black instructors explained what blacks already know about ghetto existence, or that in the presence of whites black students would be inhibited about delving into the most sensitive—sometimes embarrassing—areas of the black experience, such as crime, illegitimacy or leadership deficiencies.

AMONG scholars, the reaction to black demands is mixed. Yale's Woodward, a Southern-born white, says: "I don't believe in a color qualification for teaching. That's neither possible nor desirable. The fact is that there are not nearly enough Negroes trained and qualified to meet the need in these programs. As for autonomy or things like student control of the budget, I'm strictly against that. Fortunately there are no such demands at Yale."

Dr. Martin Kilson, a black assistant professor of government at Harvard who was on the subcommittee that recommended the establishment of an Afro-American program, says: "Of course it's possible for a white to teach these courses. If he can't, he can't teach anything else. If whites can't teach about black culture, we should all stop studying foreign cultures of any kind—Chinese, Irish, whatever. The American black is not a Yoruba, but he assumes he can study Yoruba even though it is a *foreign* culture to *him*. These kinds of demands are ideological and political arguments, not pedagogical positions, and I just don't see any proof for them."

Kilson also opposes autonomy for black studies departments or permitting a student role in policymaking. "Students are still *students*," he says, "and that means they are not intellectually disciplined or trained people. Students must be trained by people who are. Otherwise these black-studies programs will be just a kind of revivalist situation where the repetition of the experiences that each black kid has had will give him a sense of cathartic gain or of therapeutic value, but this will not be an intellectual process. It'll really be a kind of group therapy."

ROOSEVELT'S Hamilton vigorously disagrees. "To me, autonomy for the black-studies department is perfectly acceptable," he declares. "After all, many other departments already have it. I'm willing to give it to the same degree as my political-science department has it." Nor is Hamilton frightened by the specter of student participation in policy or hiring. "I believe it is possible (and black students are paving the way) for students at certain levels—say, upperclassmen—to participate in some meaningful way in the hiring of faculty. As chairman of the urban-studies program here, I've made it a policy not to hire anybody until he's come and given a seminar to our upperclassmen. I'd be a fool to hire him if they were against me.

"I'm going to Columbia University," says Hamilton who's to join that institution in September as a professor of government and holder of a special chair in urban studies, "and I lectured there. If the students had been opposed to me, I'm sure Columbia would not have taken me on." Hamilton thinks the uproar over Afro-American studies is partly racial in origin. "I believe many faculty people are reacting to the fact that these are pushy *black* students who are taking the initiative. And some are afraid that what we'll have is courses like 'Chitlins 101.' But I think they are over-reacting. I know most of these students are *very* serious—oh, we have a few who are shuckin' and jivin', and for them, black studies may be a substitute for fraternities—but most of them are quite serious and they are not going into this to spend four years just shuckin'."

At Cornell, administration and black students agree that the crucial role for determining the content and thrust of the proposed Afro-American center will be played by its director. The man who seems destined for that post is James Turner, a young black who grew up in Brooklyn's Bedford Stuyvesant ghetto. Turner, 29 and a doctoral candidate in sociology at Northwestern University, is an activist. Last year he led a takeover of the Northwestern bursar's office during a black student protest. Turner believes that the Cornell Afro-American center must break new ground. "If you are still tied to the old disciplines," he says, "you are denying the validity of the new. The black students and I feel there are other relevant criteria. Don Lee is more relevant to our concerns than some guy who studied Florentine art history. Why is Latin more valuable than Swahili, Hausa or Arabic? Latin is a dead language. The people who can best judge these things, I believe, are the people most related to the problem, namely, black people.

"Certainly there are white men like Herbert Aptheker, who has the original papers of W.E.B. Du Bois and is one of the long-standing scholars in the field, who might be invited to lecture or do research at the center. Other white scholars like the British writer Basil Davidson or George Shepperson, who teaches African history at the University of Edinburgh, would also be invited in. But there are some whites, like historians Kenneth Stampp, Stanley Elkins and C. Vann Woodward, with whose work we would find question."

The issue of who controls the black-studies program is tied to "the question of black peoples' effort to define themselves as a valid part of mankind," says Turner. "When the N.A.A.C.P.'s Roy Wilkins says we ought to 'learn what the white boys learn,' he forgets that we would not have had [Supreme Court Justice] Thurgood Marshall or Dr. Charles Drew [the inventor of the blood bank] if they had accepted the law or medicine as the white boys learned it. The law of Marshall's student days was segregationist law, the ethical medicine of Drew's school era assumed the inferiority of black people, that black people did not deserve first-class medical service. Marshall and Drew came to their professions from a different angle of vision, and so do we."

Why focus the drive for black studies at predominantly *white* universities? "At this historical juncture," argues Turner, "that's the contradiction we're forced to live with, since the Negro universities are controlled by conservative whites or by Negroes who think like them. Thus Harvard can readily come out for black studies but Howard can't. Yale can mount an Afro-American studies course but North Carolina A. & T. can't. Duke University can but Shaw University can't. Look, think about this: at a time when the black community is in desperate shape for doctors and dentists, Howard is recruiting more and more whites for its dental and medical schools. Upwards of 60 per cent of its incoming dental-school students are white!

"Secondly, black students at white universities have had more experience with the realities and contradictions of American life than have students at all-black schools, so they are the ones who begin to raise these questions.

"Finally, we use the institutions as best we can. After all, young Africans went to the London School of Economics, Cambridge and the Sorbonne to get the tools to win *their* freedom. We have to do the same thing."

Turner says those who view black studies as essentially separatist "totally misunderstand the position of our struggle. We want to provide space so that blacks can follow their own options as to where they want to go as long as they are not impinging upon anybody else's options. People who say blacks can't sit at a table together or take a room together, if they wish, are robbing us of our freedom of expression. We are not saying where anyone else can sit."

THE black demands for educational reform have caused a great deal of soul-searching within the Cornell faculty. Opposition to some of the proposals exists but has been muted. So far, most of the university's professors seem inclined to follow President Perkins's lead.

Among the occasional dissenters is Dr. Allan P. Sindler, a professor of government and a member of the academic-policy committee of the College of Arts and Sciences, the committee which must approve all new courses. Sindler says: "The black students seem to be saying two things at the same time: 'We are part of this community' and 'We do not want to be part of this community.' Many white faculty members and students are bewildered. They also think a double standard of behavior is being applied to the blacks. And, of course, some feel the central *educational* questions involved in these courses have not been really looked at."

Sindler admits to a measure of ambivalence about the black students' propositions. "I am sympathetic, with reservations, to their requests for all-black classes in certain areas," he says, "and perhaps a certain amount of subterfuge may be necessary at this stage, like classes that would not be held under university sponsorship. I feel some uneasiness about this, but I hope this is a stage we'll pass through."

Like Cornell's administration, Sindler believes the director of the Afro-American center will be a key to the resolution of the controversy. "The job calls for extraordinary qualities: a man who can relate to the black students and has their confidence, and at the same time has the qualities the Cornell faculty respects. He will be occupying the middle ground, and that is always difficult. I was once the only Jew in the department at Duke University, so I have some sensitivity to the position of a black professor who feels dual allegiances, to the community and to the school. It's a very difficult role to play.''

Dr. Donald Kagan, professor of ancient history, is concerned about what seems to him to be a segregationist trend at Cornell, and he is critical of the administration "for not being honest and aboveboard" in its handling of the whole affair. Kagan, who's resigned to join the Yale faculty this fall ("I hope they will handle the problem better there"), was also, until recently, a member of the academic-policy committee with Sindler.

"At one point," he recalls, "we were asked to approve two courses in which we all understood the students would be black. It was not spelled out, but we all understood what we were being asked to agree to. I opposed but was outvoted 5 to 1, and the black students went away thinking that the courses would be segregated. Later, the university backed out on that one and when the classes were actually held, they were not all-black. The black students felt, understandably, that they had been double-crossed. I felt they should just have been told in the beginning. 'No, we are not going to do it.' ''

Like Sindler, Kagan is re-evaluating some of his views. "Originally, I was against a black housing co-op for girls," he says, "but I've changed my position on that. I now feel that some blacks will feel so uncomfortable and so alienated in communities so different from what they've ever known as to interfere with their educational possibilities. I'm prepared to bend all kinds of feelings to avoid that. You cannot bend on the classroom, but you can bend on where kids live. Because, in fact, we already do, all over the place. There's a Young Israel House, and all these Jewish kids observing the same dietary laws live together. I don't like that one, either, but the fact is it seems to be necessary. It also seems necessary for some people to live in these stupid fraternities. We aren't moving on *that*, so a black co-op is understandable in view of all the other stupid things we do.''

KAGAN is candid about his low rating of Perkins's performance: "I think he is handicapped in the same way that most whites are handicapped—they have never known any black people as *people*. I consider myself less handicapped than my colleagues. I grew up in a ghetto, in Brooklyn's Brownsville, and I went to a junior high school that was 55 per cent black. I was in classes with black kids. I played basketball with black kids, and although blacks and whites rarely get to the point where they can call each other *friends,* by God, I had daily contact with black people up until the time I was 18 years old. And I happen to know things that my colleagues here don't know. I know black people are *people,* which implies that they can be bastards, too. They can be smart and dumb, they can be pushing improperly or they can have a legitimate demand. I don't think Perkins has that kind of experience. He's flawed, like most whites, in his capacity to understand these things.''

Douglas Dowd, the white economics professor, believes that certain subjects can be taught only by a black faculty. "I'm not saying that a white professor should not teach black students," Dowd explains, "it depends upon the subject matter. If the subject matter is such that the black students care deeply about it because it affects *their* lives and implies policy changes—doing something about something—then I think it has to be a black guy who teaches it.

"I'll give you an example. Last semester I taught a course on the economic development of the ghetto. During the semester I asked a black economics professor, Robert Browne of Fairleigh Dickinson University, a friend of mine, to come up and talk to my class and other blacks who cared to sit in. He had all the *bona fides,* the black kids knew about him—that he was 'black' in his thinking and so on. He started by saying that the ghetto is not a viable economic unit, that you really can't talk about the economic development of the ghetto in isolation—if you're going to talk about changing it, you have to first change a lot of other things, for the problem is really a political and social one. Black people have to get themselves together politically and culturally before they can make these economic changes. The black students all agreed with Browne and later they asked me, 'How come you didn't tell us that, Mr. Dowd? but, in fact, I *had* been saying just that, over and over, using exactly the same words. But they didn't hear it, coming from *me.* They must have thought, 'It's just another one of those white bastards telling us we really can't do anything about the ghetto.'

"When you talk about faculty that is functional and productive, the real criterion for a teacher, you have to talk about people who have the confidence of the student, and sometimes race affects this. In teaching technical or natural-science subjects, it does not make any difference, but all of the social sciences involve ideology, and there it *does* make a difference who teaches it."

At the two black co-ops at Afro-American Society headquarters at 320 Wait Avenue, in the dorms and apartments where they live, black students are continuing to debate the pros and cons of what they are trying to achieve at Cornell. Told that a white professor had been critical of Cleveland Sellers' "Black Ideology" course because it did not include readings from the statements of men like the N.A.A.C.P.'s Roy Wilkins or the National Urban League's Whitney Young, Ed Whitfield, the society chairman, replies: "A course in black ideology doesn't necessarily include everybody's ideas. My assumption would be that people already know what Roy Wilkins thinks. If Sellers had titled his course 'Colored Ideology,' then Wilkins would fit in, but this is *black* thought, and that's a different thing."

White student reaction to the black revolt ranges from the stanch sympathy of Cornell's Students for a Democratic Society to vocal opposition from some white athletes and fraternity members. In March, 200 members of S.D.S. and the Afro-American Society disrupted interviews by recruiters for Chase Manhattan Bank and forced the bank's representatives to cancel campus talks with prospective applicants. But other groups of white students have taken at least two advertisements in The Cornell Sun to complain about disorders and call upon the administration to act firmly to restore calm.

Stan Chess, the 21-year-old editor of The Sun, whose editorials have frequently been critical of the Afro-American Society, says: "A lot of people here feel that the university is disregarding white students in its dealings with the blacks, and that much of what the administration does is being done under an implicit threat by the black students."

Chess, a senior from East Meadows, L. I., says that tension has grown in relations between Cornell blacks and whites. The whites feel blacks will keep on demanding until it reaches a point where the university says "no," he believes: "I feel that if the administration said 'no' now, it would get the backing of a majority on this campus."

CORNELL'S white faculty members reflect some of the hardening attitudes surfacing in the student body, but an accurate reading of faculty opinion is difficult to obtain. Though there is a faculty council made up of all 2,200 teachers, its monthly meeting seldom attracts more than 300. But the black protests, S.D.S. confrontations and an incipient strike by research assistants recently brought a lessening of the faculty passivity. At a lengthy meeting of the council March 12, Provost Dale R. Corson appealed to the 600 faculty members present to involve themselves in the resolution of the mounting problems facing the university: "The issues are so complex and they pervade the whole fabric of the university so completely that no one can hope to sit in Day Hall [the administration building] and have adequate wisdom to deal with all the problems at the dizzying rate at which they arise." He added an ominous warning: "The faculty must not stand aloof from a series of actions that possess the potential for the university's destruction."

Part of the impetus behind the provost's call was a challenge to Cornell's student-faculty disciplinary board by six blacks who had twice refused to appear before the board to answer charges stemming from last December's demonstrations. The blacks questioned the board's composition (it has no black members), its jurisdiction (the defendants said their actions were political) and its morality as an instrument of an institution whose vestigial racism the Afro-American Society was attempting to combat.

At a third meeting of the disciplinary board, eight black faculty and staff members presented a brief of "concern" urging the board to defer action and requesting the society to "seek an acceptable forum in which to present its case."

Though the six students did not appear at the third board meeting, 150 of Cornell's 250 blacks did attend and this show of support, the black faculty brief and the pleas of some white faculty members persuaded the board to postpone a decision.

The action of the student-faculty board, like that of the extraordinary faculty meeting, illustrated the labyrinthine complexity of the Cornell upheaval and the difficulty of trying to steer a consistent course in the swift-moving waters of today's campus scene. For in postponing a decision, the board appeared to be recognizing its own lack of legitimacy.

And while the faculty council approved a resolution that said "alleged student violations must be processed through the existing adjudicatory system," it passed another that "reaffirms the common responsibility of students, officers and faculty to re-examine periodically the philosophic, moral and social principles by which the university is guided and the procedures and existing code of conduct in light of changing circumstances." To many Cornell blacks, as well as to some whites, the latter resolution meant that the faculty was acknowledging that the present disciplinary setup lacks validity. Ten days ago, however, the Faculty Committee on Student Affairs, which has been working since last June on revisions in the student code of conduct, issued a report that reaffirmed the competence of the disciplinary board in the case of the six blacks who had refused to appear.

Confusion is found in the administration as well as the faculty. After the incident in which a student grabbed a microphone away from President Perkins as he was explaining why Cornell could not sell its stocks in banks doing business with South Africa, Lewis Durland, the university treasurer, disclosed that the stock had been sold months earlier. The data on the sale had been in the treasurer's report to the trustees (Perkins confessed: "I never read those reports") and Durland, who had been away when the incident occurred, said he was unaware of what the fracas was all about.

THE hassle over who will teach or be admitted to classrooms and the tactics of confrontation have partially obscured what may be the most significant development in Afro-American studies on any college campus in the country. As the Cornell program has evolved, with agreement between faculty, administration and the Afro-American Society, the university will create an institute of black education and research that will go beyond the usual black history and culture courses to the establishment of a full-scale professional school designed to equip its graduates to meet the needs of the black community as black people see them.

According to James Turner, who is virtually certain to head the institute, the new concept will be broader than a black-studies department or program or the Afro-American center Cornell contemplated in January. The Cornell institute's program will be designed to complement technical courses in medicine, engineering, city planning, agronomy and law offered by Cornell's professional schools, adding "a commitment or value orientation" to equip blacks comprehensively and at an accelerated pace to meet the demands of the black ghetto. "We've sat down and isolated the needs," Turner says. The institute would draw upon qualified scholars inside and outside the university, whatever their race, though the emphasis would be on those who have the confidence and ability to teach the representatives of the black community.

A key part of the proposed institute will be an urban extension center in Harlem or some other metropolitan black community, in which several other universities might also participate, where students enrolled in the Cornell Afro-American Institute would spend a year living and working with the problems of the ghetto. Says W. Keith

Kennedy, Cornell's vice provost: "Assuming we can assemble the necessary faculty, a student could graduate from the College of Arts and Sciences with a major in Afro-American studies by June, 1971."

James Turner adds: "It is our intention to do more than give psychic refurbishment to blacks who have suffered the ravages of racism. We must give them a purpose for service, focusing not just on individual achievement but on creative, productive work that benefits the whole black community."

SO the controversy bubbles on under the seemingly tranquil surface of the Cornell campus. Black students meet in the house at 320 Wait Avenue and talk about refinements in the proposed program. Visiting black scholars and whites knowledgeable about black affairs come to the campus to lecture. At Day Hall, members of the administration huddle with department heads and influential members of the faculty, discussing the challenges of the proposed black institute.

In the days to come, Cornell's problems will probably be shared by many academic institutions, including some that have hastily erected black-studies programs which lack an organic link to the black community. But for the once somnolent institution "high above Cayuga's waters," the age of innocence has given way to an experiment that may provide an important key to the solution of America's racial dilemma.

Odyssey of a Man—and a Movement

by Paul Good

JOHN LEWIS, former chairman of the Student Nonviolent Co-ordinating Committee in the days before black power, is 26, but he looks years older. He was among the first to sit-in, to be clubbed down on Freedom Rides, to be trampled at the Selma bridge. He has been in jail 40 times, in the White House six times and these experiences have aged him. A few civil-rights leaders, including some who recently gathered in an urgent summit meeting as the tempo of race violence quickened in places like Tampa and Cincinnati, have experienced similar travail. But in the present welter of racial bitterness and threat, Lewis's experience uniquely illustrates important realities—not because he is singular, but because in his leadership role the part of Southern Black Everyman was played out to a melancholy conclusion.

As a boy Lewis chopped cotton on white man's land in Alabama and at 16 he was a Baptist minister, seemingly destined for a lifetime of preaching the gospel in a good black suit to "amening" old ladies and drinking their lemonade from dime-store pitchers on sunbaked rural Sundays. Then the movement intervened and he found himself preaching civil rights to Catholic nuns in Wisconsin and downing martinis with Westchester liberals. For five years the movement became his life, he helping to

From the *New York Times Magazine,* June 25, 1967, copyright © 1967 by The New York Times Company.

shape it, it molding him. And suddenly one night, a year ago, it was all over.

On the night of June 24, 1966, both Lewis and the movement he epitomized reached the symbolic and literal end of the road in Canton, Miss. No formal announcement was made that something was over in American life. To the public at large, Canton was just another stopping place on the Meredith March, that meandering trek through Mississippi begun after James Meredith tried to demonstrate that a controversial Negro could walk safely through the state and, for his temerity, was shot near the town of Hernando, Miss. (Meredith, his temerity undiminished, announced just a few days ago that he would resume his walk this weekend.) A few weeks before the march began, Lewis had been defeated by Stokely Carmichael for re-election as S.N.C.C. chairman. But beyond the fact of lost leadership, there would be deeper loss in Canton.

The march that arrived there had been plagued by disunity almost from the start with S.N.C.C. and CORE generally on the militant side, the N.A.A.C.P. blaring at them in bourgeois tones from the other side, and Dr. Martin Luther King's Southern Christian Leadership Conference somewhere in the middle. The press had harped on the differences until they seemed a stigma instead of a reflection of the natural economic and philosophic divisions among 25 million people in different stages of social development. During the march, the fusion of two words, black and power, had further divided blacks and antagonized whites the country over.

The marchers reached Canton on June 23. That evening Mississippi lawmen routed them when they tried to set up tents at the McNeil Elementary School, still segregated, like most Mississippi schools, 12 years after the U. S. Supreme Court decision. The Federal Government had reacted to this with legalisms, chiding march leaders for having broken state law by trespassing on school grounds. Law, after all, was law, even in a state where law, very often and despite the work of Congress and the Court, was not law.

The logic might be fuzzy, but in the hardening racial context of 1966 the Washington message seemed clear: America was a country tired of confronting its conscience. A majority of white people were sore from probes into racial nerves. The political emphasis was on image, not reality. Something that flared briefly in the national soul, a confession of racial guilt and a penitential urge toward reform, was now feeble.

A mantle of common cause still was draped over the march but it was slipping fast on that night of the 24th when men, women and children who had been clubbed and tear-gassed the previous evening returned to the school again in protest. But the leadership—split over black power, nonviolence and its judgment of the prevailing American mood—had decided against new confrontations in an acrimonious council. The knowledge of disunity was in the dark air as people stood and waited for their leaders on ground made soggy by state troopers who had opened water pipes in a final act of petty harassment.

The people wanted to do something, but no one knew what. The chunky form of Lewis rose on a shaky box. "Fellow freedom fighters," he said, "The whole man must say no nonviolently, his entire Christian spirit must say no to this evil and vicious system. . . ."

Even as he spoke, listeners sloshed away. The speaker's credentials were in order, but his time was out of joint. He spoke the old words of militant love, but the spiritual heart of the movement that for years had sent crusaders up and down American roads, trusting in love, was broken and Lewis had become that most expendable commodity, a former leader. It was not so much that he was losing his audience; the audience was already lost.

"That night in Canton I felt like the uninvited guest," Lewis says in a choppy Alabama accent. "It's hard to accept when something is over even though you know things have to change. In the beginning, with the sit-ins and Freedom Rides, things were much simpler. Or we thought they were. People just had to offer their bodies for their beliefs and it seemed like that would be enough, but it wasn't. By the time of Canton nobody knew what would be enough to make America right, and the atmosphere was very complicated, very negative."

About a month later the front page of The New York Times carried the headline:

LEWIS QUITS S.N.C.C.;
SHUNS BLACK POWER

The headline's partial truths fitted the rationale of a white society that had tolerated racial injustice for a century, yet denounced "black power" in a day. At the same time, some in the society were paying sentimental homage to the good old days when Negroes faced fire hoses and police dogs with beatific smiles. Moderates lamented. If only Carmichael hadn't raised his raucous voice or Dr. King had stuck to nonviolence in the South instead of messing with Chicago housing or Vietnam. The rationale comforted Americans who had never been black, since it subtly shifted blame from oppressor to oppressed. Lewis, it followed, was a victim of his own kind.

Today he works for the Field Foundation, which supports civil-rights and child-welfare programs. He lives in a one-room apartment in Manhattan's crowded Chelsea district, an area of urban renewal and civic decay where civil rights are guaranteed but human destinies are often circumscribed. The apartment walls bear mementos from his life in the movement—a photograph with Senator Robert Kennedy, a Kenyan antelope-skin drum from an African tour and, next to it, a snapshot of two water fountains in an Alabama courthouse that shows a big electric cooler labeled White and a dinky bubbler marked Colored. The picture leads Lewis to talk about his origins as he sits on a day-bed, his face habitually serious, his manner somewhat formal, befitting a properly brought up Southern boy.

Lewis was raised in Pike County, Ala., in a family with six brothers and three sisters. The landscape is red clay and green pine, the population 60 per cent white and the rest black. Pike and its county seat of Troy exist on a hard-scrabble economy of cotton, lumbering, peanuts, cattle and credit.

"When I grew up, white kids went to high school, Negroes to training school," he says. "You weren't supposed to aspire. We couldn't take books from the public library. And I remember that when the county paved rural roads they went 15 miles out of their way to avoid blacktopping our Negro farm roads."

He also remembers watching Tarzan movies from the segregated balcony, he and his friends identifying with the tribesmen and cheering them on against Tarzan. These memories of clay roads dusty in summer and gluey with fall rain, of books denied and movie heroes with bones through their noses are only about a dozen years old. Yet many white Americans are impatient when Negroes don't forget all this promptly or when their recent past makes them wary of present white promises and advice.

Somehow, Lewis became converted to (some would say hooked on) nonviolent love early in life. He is not sure why.

"My mother is a good Christian but nonviolence was never a family topic," he says. "Sometimes my father wanted me to do chores instead of go to school, and I'd hide out to get the school bus. He'd catch hold of me later and he wasn't nonviolent."

Lewis was already a teen-age preacher when the civil-rights gospel began spreading over the South. In 1957, he tried to apply to all-white Troy State College. His mother, fearful, wouldn't sign the papers. The classic ingredients of black American drama that so often ended in tragedy were beginning to mix: a boy moved to rebel against injustice, parents fearing the unknown content of change more than the reality of oppression.

In a broader American tradition, the cornball tradition of the poor boy who leaves the farm to struggle for an education in the big city, Lewis obtained a work scholarship at the all-Negro American Baptist Seminary in Nashville. Working as a janitor and pursuing a bland ministerial education, he encountered a transcendant personality in another student, James Lawson. A pacifist who had served time as a conscientious objector, Lawson is the generally unheralded spiritual father of the movement's belief in nonviolence and was a major influence on Martin Luther King.

"Lawson didn't talk much about demonstrations," Lewis recalls. "But he philosophized about keeping in harmony with the Christian faith until Christ's example wasn't something remote anymore. Your flesh could suffer like Christ's out of love. This was a strong current in the Nashville Student Movement that evolved into S.N.C.C. in 1960. You have to understand this to understand what S.N.C.C. was in the beginning."

By 1960, the Montgomery bus boycott was four years in the past. But aroused black emotions still were searching for direction and Nashville was the center of the ferment, particularly among young people filled with both urgency and frustration as they watched their slow-moving elders.

"When I'd come home and preach civil rights," says Lewis, "my mother would say: 'Preach the Bible, preach the Scripture.'

She'd talk about my 'call,' and I'd say, 'Mama, if I'm called by God, why can't *I* do what He tells me to preach?' "

Lewis was arrested half a dozen times during the 1960 sit-ins, but that was only a prelude to the 1961 Freedom Rides. For many veterans of the movement, those days were a combination of Dickens's French Revolution (". . . the best of times . . . the worst of times . . .") and America's own frontier days. The risks were so grave, the rewards to the spirit so satisfying that it was difficult for many participants, and impossible for some, ever to adjust to the prosaic tasks of black political and economic organization. Lewis himself may be a victim of that fearful glory.

It seems a very long national time ago when CORE sponsored 13 volunteers who left Washington, D.C., on two regularly scheduled buses heading into the territory of Jim Crow. It was May 4, 1961, only six years ago. One bus was burned in Anniston, Ala., and riders were beaten at other stops. The atmosphere was murderous.

"CORE called off the rides as too dangerous," Lewis recalls. "Robert Kennedy was Attorney General and he wanted a cooling-off period. The Nashville Christian Leadership Council—an affiliate of Dr. King's Southern Christian Leadership Conference—said it was suicidal. A group of mainly young people decided we had to go on. On Wednesday morning, May 18—no, May 17—three young ladies and seven guys left Nashville for Birmingham. Eight Negroes and a white young lady and a white boy, Jim Zwerg was his name. All those names come back of people you never see again."

They were arrested in Birmingham, went on a hunger strike and two days later, in the predawn hours, were driven by the police to the Alabama-Tennessee line and dumped out near the town of Ardmore. "It was still dark. We didn't know if whites were waiting to welcome us, so we hunted up the railroad tracks because colored families always live by them. There was an old Negro couple in a shack, scared to death, but they took us in.

"At first light, the old man went out to get some food. He went to half a dozen stores, buying a little bread, a little milk and baloney in each one so as not to arouse suspicions. We called Nashville to send a car, talking in a kind of code. You know, 'Pick up the packages in Ardmore.'

"A boy—Leo Lillard; he lives in Brooklyn now and I just spoke to him the other day for the first time again—drove down and we started back to Birmingham to get another bus. A bulletin came in on the car radio with the exact highway we were on and saying we were going to Birmingham. We were plenty frightened. But we took side roads and managed to get into the city."

On the morning of May 20 the bus reached the apparently empty Montgomery terminal. Scores of whites, hidden in doorways, rushed out and in the absence of protective Federal presence or local police (the terminal was half a block from police headquarters) they went to work. Lewis was knocked unconscious for 45 minutes. As he came to, an Alabama official served him with a court order barring integrated travel.

The battered riders regrouped, although black and white elders again counseled against continuing. With some Northern reinforcements, including a cool New Yorker named Stokely Carmichael, they took the bus to Jackson. There were more beatings, arrests and sentences to the state penitentiary.

"I came out very disturbed that America had left it up to a few students to do what had to be done," says Lewis. "But I was still convinced that nonviolence was the right way. The whole idea of beating people into submission should have died out with the early Christians and Romans. You're not submitting when you're a victim of violence. You're exerting a much greater force."

Each year of the movement has had a special flavor. After 1961, characterized by improvised daring, 1962 was largely a time of regrouping to plan attacks on the monolith of Southern segregation. In Mississippi, a campus-sized Civil War erupted when James Meredith enrolled at Ole Miss with the legal backing of the N.A.A.C.P. and an army of U.S. marshals. The nation at large was outraged by the violent Mississippi defiance and white public opinion outside the South allied emotionally with the movement. In 1963, a year of horrors as well as hope, the magnetism of epic change in the making drew Lewis from Fisk University, where he was studying philosophy, into permanent action.

The S.N.C.C. chairmanship fell vacant and he was elected unanimously. He became titular head of an organization already in flux, its original Southern element stirred by Northern recruits. Bohemianism was rubbing shoulders with old-time religion; nonviolence ·was alternately a creed and a tactic. Black Southern youth who saw salvation in the right to vote heard disillusioning Northern tales of ghettos that generations of black ballots could not vote away. Lewis was the embodiment of a deep paradox. Here was a young man of rural courtliness and moral high-mindedness, a square even, leading a group that generally disdained bourgeois manners and morals as just another American hangup.

His cherished concept of nonviolence passed through one crucible after another. Soon after his election, Mississippi N.A.A.C.P. leader Medgar Evers was murdered. Demonstrations in Birmingham made police dogs and fire hoses synonymous with Southern repression, the orgy of white violence culminating in the Birmingham church bombing that killed four Negro girls. Lewis—only three years off an Alabama farm—was called to the White House with other civil-rights leaders for emergency meetings with President Kennedy.

Despite violence and sluggish Federal reaction, the movement in 1963 drew hope from press and television coverage which dramatically presented a modern morality play to the nation. Good was clearly black people, marching lamblike and singing hymns; evil was the white face that spat and sneered. In August, the March on Washington struck an exultant chord. Lewis, for all the innate contradictions between himself and S.N.C.C., was God's angry young man in the original speech he prepared for the march:

"We will march through the South, through the heart of Dixie, the way Sherman did. We shall pursue our own 'scorched earth' policy and burn Jim Crow to the ground—nonviolently."

The tone so upset white liberal sponsors like Walter Reuther and Negroes like Roy Wilkins, that the program at the Lincoln Memorial was held up until Lewis changed it to:

"If we do not get meaningful legislation out of this Congress, the time will come when we will not confine our march to Washington. We will march through the streets of Jackson . . . Danville . . . Cambridge . . . Birmingham. But we will march with the spirit of love and with the spirit of dignity that we have shown here today."

By 1964, President Kennedy was dead and the Johnson Administration, convinced that Federal inaction would bring internal disorder and international obloquy, pressed for a civil-rights bill to open up public accommodations. Negroes following Dr. King in St. Augustine sought to spur passage by inviting racist excesses as they sang "God Will Take Care of You" into the teeth of white mobs. The bill passed but many Negroes thought such nonviolence a singular way to lobby for legislation in a democracy. That spring Lewis was unanimously re-elected S.N.C.C. chairman. S.N.C.C. and CORE decided to attack the stoutest segregationist bastion, Mississippi, and planned the Freedom Summer of 1964 to send volunteers into the state.

They cast a net of conscience over American youth and gathered in a mixed bag—young people wise and witless, God-inspired and beat, reformers and social renegades. The catch recalled the self-descriptive words written by an abolitionist 100 years before: "We are what we are. Babes, sucklings, obscure men, silly women, publicans, sinners and we shall manage this matter just as might be expected of such persons as we are. It is unbecoming in abler men who stood by and would do nothing to complain of us because we could do no better."

The press was beginning to prove itself an undependable chronicler in depths beyond the episodic. With few exceptions, it observed with fascinated repulsion the surface aspects of volunteers' beards or black boy-white girl pairing instead of digging deep into the social and economic cul-de-sac into which America's history had forced black men throughout the country. Adult newsmen—attitudes slightly corpulent and bedeviled by their mature anxieties over careers, sex and money—were suspicious of and, in turn, scorned by volunteers going their lean, instinctual way, indulging their sexual vigor, making progress and mistakes with the same reckless abandon, with nothing much at stake. Except possibly their lives.

After three rights workers were murdered in Neshoba County, F.B.I. Director J. Edgar Hoover arrived in Jackson to decry what he called an "overemphasis" on civil rights, declaring his bureau "most certainly" would not offer protection to volunteers. Such sentiments had a traumatic effect on Negroes in general and S.N.C.C. members in particular since they were under the gun. S.N.C.C. skepticism about American justice became institutionalized. Many white "friends" deplored the attitude, but they had not been there.

Lewis skipped around the country fund-raising, and, he concedes, often losing touch with troops in the field. Meanwhile, the independent Mississippi Freedom Democratic party ran into the facts of political life at the 1964 Democratic convention in Atlantic City. The regular Mississippi Democratic party historically had disregarded non-discriminatory laws when choosing delegations and had disloyally backed Republican and Dixiecrat nominees.

But when the M.F.D.P. sought to unseat it, columnists and commentators warned that the movement was naively seeking a moral solution to a political problem. President Johnson confirmed their judgment by ordaining a "compromise" that tossed two at-large seats to the rebels while seating the regulars. Negroes were left to ponder: If morality and politics were mutually exclusive, then why go on with hymn-singing forbearance? Atlantic City was a milestone on the movement's road to final disillusion in Canton.

By 1965, though Lewis was still doggedly following his star of brotherhood through nonviolence, many in S.N.C.C. weren't following him. The John Lewis who on March 7 led a band of black people across the Selma bridge toward Montgomery bore little relevance to his own organization. Trudging toward a motley posse of helmeted men, Lewis wore a light coat, dark suit, shirt and tie, and had a bedroll neatly slung over his shoulders. He looked like a minister leading his Sunday School class on a jolly outing. But anyone watching who knew Lewis might have bled for him, since he made no secret of the fear he felt that faith could not quiet.

The first truncheon cracked his head in the same spot as the blow that felled him on the Freedom Ride, and he slumped to his knees with a concussion. America saw it all on television and was predictably, though momentarily, appalled. But many Negroes in S.N.C.C. thought that John Lewis was a Christ-loving damn fool to have crossed that bridge.

"I felt after Selma that it was my last demonstration," Lewis said later. "We're only flesh. I could understand people not wanting to be beaten anymore. The body gets tired. You put out so much energy and you saw such little gain. Black capacity to believe white would really open his heart, open his life to nonviolent appeal was running out."

Faster than he knew. Lewis was re-elected chairman of S.N.C.C. in 1965, but this time there were many opponents, Carmichael among them. A massive deterioration of white credibility in Negro eyes was taking place and Lewis could no more prevent it than nascent black nationalism could take credit for it. White conscience seemed to need black sacrifice to stimulate it, and often lapsed when black militancy insisted on human prerogatives beyond the letter of the law. White conscience, many Negroes were concluding, was a sometime thing.

The Voting Rights Act of 1965 passed. Whites predicted a black wave. But figures showed that in five Deep South states, only 60 of 418 counties had a potential Negro voting majority. Nothing less could break racist control and experience would demonstrate that in only a dozen of those counties could barriers of tradition and economic intimidation be surmounted.

S.N.C.C. limped through a desultory year in 1965, frustrated and edgy with black-white internal tensions. It needed revitalization but John Lewis could not provide it. The body *was* tired.

"I came to believe that maybe the scars of racism couldn't be erased in my lifetime," he says. "But some people inside S.N.C.C. were moving into a fantasy world where mountains had to be moved right away. They were filled with self-righteousness and closed themselves off from anyone who disagreed. The ideal of nonviolence came under question. But as far as I was concerned, with a goal of the world community at peace with itself, methods had to be consistent with the goal. Maybe I was at fault because I couldn't adapt. But I couldn't."

"Some old S.N.C.C. veterans still respected him," says John Wise, now S.N.C.C.'s executive director. "But a lot of new ones didn't have that feeling. The old day of love was gone."

S.N.C.C. began last year by denouncing the draft and the Vietnam war, and Lewis concurred. Despite the fact that Negroes were overrepresented in Vietnam and underrepresented on draft boards, the position assured S.N.C.C.'s continued unpopularity on the American scene. Lewis himself was the first Negro in Alabama history to be granted C.O. status. The Justice Department successfully intervened in his case after an obdurate local board chairman told Lewis: "But *we're* all Baptists and *we're* not C.O.'s."

S.N.C.C. still was receiving White House invitations in 1966 and Lewis planned to participate in the June conference President Johnson had scheduled under the title, "To Fulfill These Rights." He went to a preliminary meeting in March under the impression that the conference and pending civil-rights legislation would be discussed.

"But all the President wanted to talk about was Democratic losses in the coming Congressional elections," says Lewis. "He kept saying, 'I need your help, you have to help me.' It was embarrassing. Consensus. He must have used that word a dozen times. But there wasn't any consensus anymore. Why should all Negroes think alike? And who could be patient seeing the war getting bigger and the poverty program tightening up?"

What had begun simply with a bus ride was foundering on domestic and foreign complexities. On April 21, 1966, in Nashville, Lewis was defeated for re-election by Carmichael in an atmosphere charged with racial polarity. Lewis had favored a black-directed movement, with whites taking their place inside it. Carmichael sought the essence of insularity that had characterized the political battles of other minority groups. When the Irish in New York, for example, had originally formed their political organizations, Italians and Jews were not invited in. Whether the analogy was valid could be debated, but the notion that Negroes, in the best American tradition, had to do for themselves, by themselves, was not as radical as it was made to appear.

Carmichael's cry of "Black Power" caught the nation in a mood of rearoused racism. White Chicagoans were furiously opposing open housing, and new civil-rights legislation that would affect North and South was bogged down in Congress. The press pounced on Carmichael's careless rhetoric and establishment Negroes like Roy Wilkins equated Black Power with Nazism.

The movement, like a gem scored for cutting, had long been ready to come apart and Black Power supplied the final tap. Bitterness among all parties accompanied the split, and John Lewis decided his role was no longer effective. He resigned from S.N.C.C.

"Part of it I can see now was ego," he says. "Losing the election hurt. Part of it was Canton, reviving all the white violence and making black people so disillusioned. But mostly it was the bitterness all around that turned me. Some people wanted retaliatory violence. But even as a practical measure, how many people are you going to attract to a program based on violence? It might deliver some quick solutions, but in the long run it debases you. I felt I owed an allegiance to a higher principle than S.N.C.C. It was as simple as that."

The consequences weren't simple. He was charged with running out. His highest S.N.C.C. salary had been $40 a week and he was broke. The limited life of a church pastor no longer would satisfy. During years when other young men were perfecting educations or starting careers, he was sitting-in, going limp, getting jailed. As it did for many movement veterans, it all made peculiar reading on a job resumé.

The Field Foundation offer meant leaving the South and Lewis took a long train ride up to New York, the kind where the landscape of a young man's country and his years slips by. "It was lonesome, leaving the movement," he says. "I kept thinking, 'Where am I going, and why, why?' But I also felt liberated. I thought it was ordained because there was nothing left for me to do in the movement. And truthfully, it was good to be going toward a real job and to know that for the first time I'd be earning enough to send something home to my family."

Today, Lewis is learning to live with ambivalence. When Tampa Negroes riot after police shoot a black suspect, he feels he should be on the scene. But he is puzzled over what he or anybody else can do as the racial climate seems inexorably to worsen. Lewis is proud of S.N.C.C.'s accomplishments when he was chairman but painfully aware of its failures and its present debilitated condition.

The organization he left is now a small, embattled group of about 50 young pariahs struggling to stay alive. The only offices still functioning are in New York, Washington, Atlanta and San Francisco, and while there is brave talk of programing, the programs are not much in evidence. Carmichael—swashbuckler of Black Power—has been replaced by Rap Brown, an experienced Southern field organizer but an unknown quantity as leader. Persons close to S.N.C.C. believe that Carmichael had become too hot for even S.N.C.C. to handle if it wanted to maintain liaison with other black and white civil-rights groups. Lewis does not know Brown well. Those who do say he is philosophically a Black Power militant but determined to be less visible and vocal than Carmichael. But the question of his qualities may be academic. Without a power base, alienated from most white liberals and a target of opportunity for forces out to squelch any sign of black self-assertion, S.N.C.C. in its present form has a limited life expectancy.

Looking back on the year since that night in Canton, Lewis sees a steady growth of reaction in the North and South—the election victories of Lester Maddox in Georgia and Lurleen Wallace in Alabama, the defeat in New York of a police review board, the virulent press campaign against Dr. King's Vietnam position.

"The Vietnam debate lets a lot of plain racism come out as patriotism," he says. "The Government is contradictory, telling oppressed black men not to be violent in the streets while it carries out the terrible slaughter in Vietnam and finances it with money it should be spending to get things right at home.

"Black conditions in the rural South are desperate. In Mississippi, Negro faith in the democratic process is being strained. The Johnson Administration has been out to break the Freedom party ever since Atlantic City, deliberately using programs like Head Start to lure people away from their first hope for political independence and back under the white thumb. And at the same time, Vice President Humphrey takes the arm of Lester Maddox to show there is Democratic consensus."

Not long ago, Lewis returned home for a visit. After all his wanderings, the illusion of permanence moved him—the house of concrete blocks with its wide breezy porch looking out on his father's fields and a pecan grove.

A few things in Pike County had changed for the better and it was satisfying to know he had played a part. His parents were voting for the first time, albeit for white-picked candidates, and his brothers were taking books from the library. But they still attended segregated schools and no jobs were available except the old ones, like bagboy in the local A&P. Most of the men would eventually go North, following the established pattern. One 24-year-old brother married early, has four children and lives in a rented shack.

"He works cutting pulpwood," Lewis says. "That's all there

is. No factories and nobody to build them. The only wealth is land and the good land stays in white hands. He's going to be working hard for nothing the rest of his life."

Lewis felt stymied by these realities. He looked into white Southern faces and saw no spiritual change, only grudging retreat from the old authoritarianism under pressure of law whose enforcement depends on the white national mood.

While he cannot conceive of Negroes slipping back as they did after Reconstruction, he is fearful that the opportunity for the creation of the "beloved community" of black and white together is being lost to bitterness. Black hopes would be again betrayed. On his way back to New York, he rode the integrated bus from Troy to Montgomery, and at the terminal he walked to the spot where he had been beaten on that Saturday morning in 1961. He says he stood there, letting his memory flow back and forth over all that had happened since then. He had taken his various beatings dry-eyed. But in that moment, John Lewis almost cried.

Dr. King's March on Washington, Part II

by José Yglesias

THE DAY AFTER Lincoln's Birthday none of the leaders in the Atlanta headquarters of the Southern Christian Leadership Conference had read President Johnson's speech, at the Lincoln Memorial, likening himself to the Civil War President. Johnson had said that, like Lincoln, he, too, was "sad and steady." Martin Luther King Jr. simply laughed when he heard this and guessed the President was looking for some sympathy for the mess he had gotten himself into in Vietnam. On Lincoln's Birthday, Dr. King and his staff had spent the entire day in a planning meeting on the Poor People's Campaign to begin in April in Washington, and for this reason, no doubt, had little attention or sympathy to spare for the President. In fact, their plans are calculated to disturb whatever peace of mind the President enjoys these days.

Not all of the campaign plans are known—nor will be, since prior knowledge might allow the Administration to upstage them in the dramatic confrontations that may become necessary—but the original announcement last December was disquieting enough. President Johnson replied that he hoped the 3,000 followers Dr. King expects to bring to Washington will be acting constructively,

From the *New York Times Magazine,* March 31, 1967, copyright © 1968 by The New York Times Company.

not disruptively. Dr. King had warned that they might tie up transportation in Washington, jam the hospitals, boycott schools and sit-in at Government offices in "a last desperate demand to avoid the worst chaos, hatred and violence any nation has ever encountered."

The President does not have the consolation that the demonstrations will confine themselves to the domestic situation. The Administration will be scored on the issue of the war, too. Dr. King for a long time now has been prominent in the peace movement, and although at first he attacked the war on the basis of national priorities—that we were mistakenly making it the first order of business—he has since made clear that his opposition is also a moral one, one which he would maintain were there no other problems at home to tackle. His thinking permeates the entire staff of S.C.L.C., as I found after a day of speaking to those in the Atlanta office. "This war is being used by the American establishment," says the literature of the campaign, "against the poverty-stricken people of Vietnam and the poor people here at home."

I had, in fact, heard that during the original discussions last fall on the Poor People's Campaign, one member had held out for a long time for concentrating their activities on bringing the Vietnam war to an end. When I saw King on my second day in Atlanta, I asked him how S.C.L.C. had finally unanimously decided on a Poor People's Campaign—how, specifically, the advocate of peace demonstrations had been won over. King explained that although the cost to the nation of wiping out poverty had not been reduced to a dollar figure, the war in Vietnam—"this unjust and immoral war," as he always characterizes it—cannot be waged if the campaign's demands are met. "That is what convinced those who wanted a peace demonstration."

King and his colleagues have come to believe that war and poverty are inseparable issues and, in another context, he has said that it may well be the job of the American Negro "to reform the structure of racist imperialism from within." Consequently, to demand that the country use, in their words, "the $70-billion it spends annually for war" to create jobs and wipe out the ghettos seems to him the best way to end the war. ($70-billion was the total defense outlay for 1967, according to Federal budget figures submitted to Congress in January; of this sum, $20.5-billion was for Vietnam. Estimates for fiscal 1968 put the defense total at $76.5-billion.) In any case, the black audiences in Alabama to whom he spoke during the next two days caught the message, for his denunciation of the Vietnam war always brought one of the most enthusiastic responses.

Besides the twin issues of the war and poverty, one other fact had become clear about the demonstrations by mid-February: they were not to be a weekend affair. Sitting in the Rev. Andrew Young's office—he's Andy to everyone, though executive director of S.C.L.C. and perhaps as important as Dr. King in formulating policy—I heard Mr. Young say to an inquirer on the phone, "Listen, we don't have a cutoff date, but I figure that by the end of June we will have gotten some response or all of us will be in jail." All 3,000 recruits, for whom workshops in nonviolent techniques were to begin this month, will be committed to the probability of jail sentences. Not just for one offense but for the many they may feel morally compelled to commit to force Congress to act.

That they are willing to go to jail is nothing new for civil-rights demonstrators, nor even that they are willing to disrupt the normal activities of a city. This is what they did in Montgomery and Birmingham and Selma. But in the past they demonstrated, almost without exception, for the implementation in behalf of the Negroes of rights promised to all Americans. Now the nature and content of the demonstrations have changed: they are not going to Washington, as in 1963, to support proposed legislation; they are not speaking for blacks alone but for all poor people, and they will not be following a line of march benevolently set out for them and protected by a generally approving Administration.

Faced with the general demands of the campaign—everything from jobs and a guaranteed income to medical care and decent homes and quality education for all—a Rip Van Winkle from the thirties might well come up with the old rhetorical question: "Do you think the world owes you a living?" From King's followers he would get for reply a resounding yes. As he puts it, they are out to get an Economic Bill of Rights. The tactics are nonviolent and the tone of the language in S.C.L.C. literature is moral, but the substance of the demands is revolutionary for America: class demands dramatically expressed through other than the orderly democratic process.

In a question-and-answer form the Atlanta headquarters has prepared for its campaign workers, the question is asked: "Why would you disrupt or dislocate Washington, D.C.?" The answer is militant: "Poor people's lives are disrupted and dislocated every day, and we want to put a stop to this."

When Young put the phone down, I asked if S.C.L.C. wasn't getting into radical, working-class politics. He looked puzzled. "I don't know about that. I am doing what I joined the ministry to do," he said, and quoted Jesus about preaching the gospel to the poor.

He admitted that until now the main objectives of the civil-rights movement had been ones that most benefited middle-class Negroes. "The people who marched in the demonstrations and got beaten to desegregate restaurants and hotels can't take advantage of those gains," he said. "They can't afford them. Now these people are saying, 'What about us?'" And Young was the first of those I was to meet in the next few days to paraphrase Gandhi to describe one motive for the Poor People's Campaign: "There go my people—I must hurry and catch up with them, for I am their leader."

A few minutes later, in Dr. King's office on the other side of a thin partition, an office no larger than Young's and much more cluttered, I asked King also if he hadn't abandoned moral issues for the class struggle. He was in shirt sleeves and had leaned back in his chair, one arm raised, tapping his head lightly with his hand, a favorite position with him. Now he leaned forward and spoke directly, a manner I was to find customary with him, so that interviewers seldom have to rephrase questions; he responds to the tone and level of the question but also, as if fulfilling a personal need, to implications that at first do not seem implicit in the question: an intellectual curiosity that gives the effect of total sincerity.

"In a sense, you could say we are engaged in the class struggle, yes," he said. He explained that the gains for which the civil-rights movement had fought had not cost anyone a penny, whereas now—"It will be a long and difficult struggle, for our program calls for a redistribution of economic power. Yet this isn't a purely materialistic or class concern. I feel that this movement in behalf of the poor is the most moral thing—it is saying that every man is an heir to a legacy of dignity and worth."

Although we went on to talk of other things, this question remained with him, and I heard him the next night, at a church in Birmingham, expand on it. There he continued with a discussion of the parable of the rich man and the beggar Lazarus. Lazarus had not gone to heaven simply because he was poor, King argued, nor the rich man to hell because he was rich. "No, the rich man was punished because he passed Lazarus every day and did not see him. . . . And I tell you if this country does not *see* its poor—if it lets them remain in their poverty and misery—it will surely go to hell!"

In his office, however, I quoted to him a New York radical who had said that Dr. King's political problems derive from the fact that his present support comes from middle-class Negro churches and organizations: they would oppose his new tack. Has there been opposition?

He shook his head. "When we began discussing this thing last fall, we expected there would be opposition—from the timid supplicants and from the ultramilitants." He shook his head again. "In a sense, you could say we are waging a consensus fight. The Harris Poll recently showed that 68 per cent want a program to supply jobs to everyone who wants to work, and 64 per cent want slums eradicated and rebuilt by the people of the community —which means a great many new jobs."

Just as in 1963 the majority desired action on civil rights for the Negro, he said, so did most people now agree that poverty has to be wiped out. I pointed out that the 1963 March on Washington had the cooperation of the Kennedy Administration, whereas President Johnson's reaction to the Poor People's Campaign was negative. Most people do not know, he replied, that the initial reaction of the Kennedy Administration was also negative; it was only after Kennedy had his aides talk to them and find out their plans that the Administration's attitude changed.

A few minutes earlier, I had told Young that everyone was saying that King, after the December announcement, could surely no longer get an appointment at the White House, and Young had answered, "He has never looked for one." Propped on a shelf in King's office, in so unfavored a position that it had to compete with every object in the room for attention, was a copy of the famous photograph of King and President Johnson talking privately. Had the Johnson Administration made any overture? Like Young, King said no.

Negroes prominent in one of the Washington Government departments had made inquiries about plans for the campaign. King did not know whether these were feelers—an attempt on the part of the Administration to learn their plans—or simply interest on the part of individuals who in the past have supported the civil-rights movement. "I can assure you and them that we will never destroy life or property and if the demonstrations become violent, if the people who come to Washington do not abide by nonviolence, we shall call them off. We may be greeted by violence—I cannot guarantee you that we won't—but we will never respond with violence," King said.

After a pause, he added, "Nevertheless, we may have to break perfectly reasonable and just laws to call attention to the situation."

What reasonable and just laws?

"Well, I think a law that doesn't allow 15 people to come into this office and camp here is just and reasonable," he said with a smile. (Fifteen people in King's office would not have room to sit.) "But we may have to break such laws."

The demonstration will be low-keyed at first, he explained. The core of recruits—those 3,000 who will act as marshals for the thousands they hope will come to Washington for the weeks of demonstrations—will attempt to present to Congressional committees and Government departments general demands to meet the crises of the cities and rural communities. Only at this stage will the campaign outwardly resemble orderly civil-rights demonstrations, though the arrival in Washington of the demonstrators was still being discussed in February—a dramatic act is what they were looking for. Since they are not going to Washington in support of some particular bill they themselves will have drawn up, the presentation of demands may be symbolic in themselves, such as the announced jamming of hospitals with people seeking medical care.

The reasons for not presenting detailed legislation are tactical. They believe that if the campaign is tied to specific bills they may, in Andy Young's words, be building in failure. Their job is to mount a massive, militant demonstration of poor people's needs—the wiping out of slums, the creation of jobs through government spending on, say, the rebuilding of cities, immediate guaranteed incomes, the extension of medical services and quality education for everyone; in effect, to spend the annual $70-billion allotted "for war" to insure that the poor break out of the cycle of poverty and discrimination they believe the system now imposes on them. Finding legislative solutions is the job of the Administration and Congress.

King shows a certain impatience with those who want them, at every turn, to come up with specific programs. In his last book he pointed out that there is no dearth of programs—from his own of 1964 entitled a "Bill of Rights for the Disadvantaged" to those of many agencies, organizations and individual social scientists. "Underneath the invitation to prepare programs," he said, "is the premise that the Government is inherently benevolent —it only awaits presentation of imaginative ideas."

One lesson from past civil-rights demonstrations the Conference people consider applicable is that of the Selma march in 1965. The voting-rights act, they were told, could not be passed. It was not a practical measure to demand. Yet a massive, militant demonstration persuaded the Administration and Congress to find a solution. The apocalyptic tone of this spring's demands is justified: beyond these demonstrations looms a summer of violence in the cities. The Conference does not promise to head it off— or to provide a safety valve—and it is almost as if, the need being so large, it cannot risk talking specific legislation without being accused of either.

"I am not optimistic about the immediate response of Congress," King said. "But you can say that the goal of this campaign will be to expose Congress. We will escalate the campaign on the basis of the response we get."

One plan that everyone, including King, is very taken with is that of building a shanty town in Washington, a symbolic picture of how the poor live in many areas but also a historic reminder of the bonus marchers of the thirties. They will first build it on public property, expecting that they will be run off from a succession of sites until they end on private property belonging to a sympathizer. King hopes the demonstrations will end with a march in Washington similar to 1963's but lasting for at least three days.

I had been discussing projected actions with Young earlier, trying to learn how they were specifically organizing each, and it had seemed to me that they were in flux and largely unorganized. "What, for example," I asked, "will you do if the hospitals to which you take people do accept them and give them all a medical checkup?" Young said that in that case they would call for people everywhere needing medical treatment to come to the hospitals; as things happen they will improvise their responses.

King confirmed this and, to overcome my misgivings, pointed out that during the Selma march they had never planned their actions more than one day in advance. They simply met every night and decided about the following day. "We're aware that to a degree we're riding on the forces of history and not totally shaping things."

"For two years we have been discussing philosophy," King said, a favorite diagnosis of his for what he considers the inaction lately of black organizations. In speeches I was to hear him give, he put it differently: "We have been bogged down in the paralysis of analysis." In his office, he nodded to himself and said, "I believe that this action will create new alliances, wake new forces."

King doesn't initiate criticism of the Black Power movement. I asked him if he still would say, as he did in his book, "Where Do We Go From Here: Chaos or Community?", published last year, that Black Power is a slogan without a program. He nodded, and I asked him if he'd read the book by Stokely Carmichael and Charles Hamilton, "Black Power: The Politics of Liberation in America." Each time he had taken it with him on a plane, he said, someone had talked to him at such length he had not been able to read it, but a colleague had informed him that the book proved his point that the Black Power people have no program of action.

The 10 per cent of whites in S.C.L.C.'s staff of 100 were, in the main, hired when the issue of black separatism was raised, but King is in sympathy with many of the points that Black Power leaders make. In the hive of tiny offices in the Atlanta headquarters, there are still posters advertising its recent cultural evening entitled "Black Is Beautiful." The organization's newspaper then in the planning stage was to be called Soul Force. In one office there are even posters of Che Guevara. All staff members become wary when one asks whether they believe the Black Power people will join them in Washington.

King believes that they will, once the action begins, for Black Power leaders do not want senseless riots either, he says, and he only criticizes them because they do not have a program to channel the anger of the black people into positive actions. "I tell you, many more riots of the kind we had last summer," he said, "and we shall be in danger of a right-wing takeover of the fascist type!"

This was something of a passionate outburst with him, and he added, more calmly, a statement he again made during the next two days: "Riots increase the fears of the whites and relieve them of their guilt." He usually expands this statement to explain that the Conference program is militant if only because it allows the whites—or, in the case of the Poor People's Campaign, the privileged—no out. The recruits are going to Washington to bear witness and by their presence to make ugly facts of American life visible in the capital.

Some of the new alliances he hopes for were only tentative in February. But there were hopeful signs. S.C.L.C. was a month late with plans but had already made contact with the poor in Appalachia, the New York Puerto Rican community, and with Mexican-Americans and Indians. King took pride in this. I said, "You can't say that you're in civil rights any longer."

He smiled. "But you can say I am in human rights."

His secretary, Dora McDonald, cut our interview short; it had already run a half-hour beyond schedule and had followed on the heels of a formal interview, with photographers shooting all the while for a mass-circulation magazine. King had arrived at the office three hours late because each time he tried to leave home a long-distance call delayed him. I told him I'd read several years ago that his wife had declared that five years from then there would be a big change and their lives could go back to normal. "She wouldn't put a date on it now," he said.

Outside his office, in an alcove of the narrow corridor, where King's unflappable secretary tries to tighten his expanding schedule, her phone seldom showing less than two blinking lights, we listened to Andy Young report on a call from a friend in Washington. The Black United Front, "a S.N.C.C. operation," had discussed the Poor People's Campaign and decided to support it. A break that was hard to believe because the King organization made only one unnegotiable demand of the campaign's supporters: nonviolent response to any action of the authorities.

That night I walked about the campus of a Negro college in Atlanta with a black intellectual committed to the Black Power movement. "Well, did you talk to De Lawd?" he asked. "Did you talk to De King?"

I told him King was persuasive and impressive, and informed him about the reported decision of the Black United Front. The latter puzzled him, as it did me, but not the observation that King was persuasive. "I'm sure he is," he said, with a touch of dismay, "I'm sure he is."

We looked in at a meeting protesting the killing last February of three Negro students on the campus of State College at Orangeburg, S. C., and he led me out because the attendance was so disappointing. To make him feel better, though not solely for that reason, I told him I suspected that some of the people in King's Atlanta office only went along with nonviolence as a tactic and that others more likely were Black Power advocates. "Oh, sure, they are," he said. "They make a point of hiring ex-S.N.C.C. kids. It's some kind of paternalism."

Most young people are attracted to Black Power, he said (a point S.C.L.C. leaders had also made), but they have not had any real experience of struggle. "They haven't paid their dues to the movement," he said. He couldn't blame them if they didn't turn out to every meeting—he was sick of meetings himself—for what could you do, for example, about the Orangeburg murders? What the hell could you do?

We had walked into a new restaurant and there were many whites there, though it was in a black neighborhood, a phenomenon that was unthinkable in the South I had known. "The jazz club I go to often has more whites than blacks," he said, restively. "It's begun here, too. They're running after the black chicks. Soon there'll be intermarriage."

As if to confirm our talk about S.C.L.C. personnel, a young man I had seen at the Atlanta headquarters came over to greet my companion and stayed a while. He didn't seem to know any more about the April plans than I had been able to find out.

"They're all worried about what might happen," he said. "I mean, they can't tell *what'll* come off."

I said King would call it off if the demonstrators returned violence for violence.

"Man, *he* can't call it off!" he exclaimed. "You can't call off things like that no more!"

Despite their put-down tone about King and their wariness about his proposals, young blacks do not ignore him. They have not written him off, as have white theorists of the black movement in the last year. Young people recognize in him that courage they demand of themselves, just as white Southerners, conversely, still hate and fear him despite their surprised respect for him, a fact that became evident the next morning at the airport.

In order for King to cover in two days all the areas in Mississippi and Alabama where the campaign was to be launched, he had rented a plane from a private charter service. The service's office man and I were the first there, at 6:30, and he looked at me with great curiosity; as soon as he learned I was not on the King staff, he confessed that the job had been passed on to them by a larger company that had been afraid to take on Dr. King. "We don't care about all that," he said, his way of dissociating himself from civil-rights quarrels, "but we told our pilot, if there's any trouble any place you land, just take the plane out on the runway."

It was a twin-engine Cessna with room for nine, including the pilot and copilot, and both were needed because it was a rainy, overcast day. Before the pilot took off into the white mist, he turned around to King and asked him if in his travels he had ever met Timmy Brown, who plays for the Philadelphia Eagles. "I don't believe I have," King said. The pilot said he and Timmy had both been raised on the same Indiana farm and he was going to write his folks to tell Timmy he had been flying Dr. King around. King simply smiled, taking the pilot's friendliness at face value.

With King were Bernard Lee, a personal assistant who worries about arrangements and tapes King's speeches; Hosea Williams, in charge of voter registration for S.C.L.C. and now assigned to the Poor People's Campaign; an Associated Press man, and two film-makers shooting the campaign for Public Broadcasting Laboratories. They were all worried about the weather, and Hosea Williams, a chunky man with a smiling face, was reminded of a bumpy flight the previous week. The hostess had asked him if he were frightened and he'd said, "Not me—I'm a Presbyterian!"

King, a Baptist, enjoyed that, and, instead of opening his briefcase, he half turned in his seat and talked with Williams and Lee during most of the flight, while the film men worked their hand-held camera and portable sound equipment. Williams said that the news of the Black United Front's support had to be checked because he'd heard that while they endorsed the objectives of the April demonstrations, they still couldn't go along with the tactics. King nodded soberly.

(Later, Young confirmed that the Black United Front had voted to endorse the campaign, support it with food and housing for delegates and leave the question of participation to the decision of individual followers—a decision that pleased the King organization.)

I asked about the Orangeburg incident, and King said he had issued a statement about it. "Terrible, terrible," he said. Only two weeks earlier he had married Cleveland Sellers, the S.N.C.C. field secretary who had been wounded at Orangeburg while watching from the sidelines. "That's a lovely girl he married," Williams said. King agreed: "A beautiful girl." Williams found it funny that the only witness Sellers brought to his marriage ceremony was a white friend. King laughed: "Oh, he's a *white* black nationalist!"

In a moment they were reminiscing. "What was the name of that sheriff in Monroe, Georgia?" King asked. "He was the meanest man—meaner than Jim Clark [Selma's ex-sheriff], I believe. Something about a Negro wearing a hat drove him crazy. *'Take off that hat, boy!'* " And King laughed with his whole body, like a man who trusts his feelings.

Before we left Atlanta we knew we might have to land at Jackson, Miss., and not Vicksburg, because of the weather, and Lee had called ahead to let them know. But it was not until the last moment, while still flying through clouds, that the pilot decided on Jackson because its radio beam could lead him into the field. Leon Hall, S.C.L.C. leader in Mississippi, was waiting at the airport; so was a man, presumably from the State Sovereignty Commission, the agency set up by the Legislature in 1956 to keep check, among other things, on "potential agitators." The man photographed our every move, occasionally darting forward for individual closeups; he also carried a clipboard with a pad and made notes.

No one paid any attention to him except Hall. "You ought to work for us," Hall said, pointing a finger at him. "I don't know if you're a good photographer, but you sure can take them fast." The man followed us to Edwards, Miss., site of the Mount Beulah Conference Center, a former Negro college now owned by the Delta Ministry, a project of the National Council of Churches, but none of the 32 leaders of black organizations who had responded to Dr. King's call bothered about him or about several other men who looked like police or F.B.I. agents. The black leaders were to meet in the dining hall to hear King, Andy Young, who had arrived the night before and Hosea Williams; then they were to decide whether they would back the campaign. It was a crucial meeting for King, but you could not tell it from the relaxed, happy way in which he greeted old friends.

Walking to the dining hall, the Rev. Henry Parker told me: "I'm prejudiced, I have known Dr. King a long time and respect him. But I don't know about this campaign. The people here are interested in practicalities now—they have been on lots of demonstrations, there's nothing new about them. You know, I could show you black people here in Mississippi just starving to death, their children dying of worm infestation."

At the dining hall Andy Young decided it would be best if the film men and newsmen were not at this meeting, so discussion could be unconstrained. (There was also some worry about the reaction of black nationalists.) We waited at another building and were joined by a white Southerner from The Jackson Daily News, whom everyone had taken for an unfriendly policeman; his editor had called him at 6:30 that morning and told him to cover the meeting. "I wonder how he knew," the A.P. man said, "there's been no publicity about it." The reporter had no idea.

Three hours later hunger drove us into the dining hall. An elderly Negro woman was speaking. "I like that—going to Washington to get money in our pockets," she said. "But let's not forget about other things while we's getting the money. They're running black people off the land here, making it so we can't have any." The meeting had been good: there had been no objections to the campaign and it was expected the leaders would now go back to their organizations, obtain approval and begin recruitment of those to be trained for Washington. King left happy, his car followed by four others with State Sovereignty Commission and F.B.I. men riding in them.

The children of the junior high school at Edwards, all black, were out in the street waiting for him and he had only time to get out of his car and walk up and down to greet them. A thrill ran through the rows of children—one heard it as a collective intake of breath—and they clapped and moved toward him, their faces beaming. The same was to happen when he walked into the Alabama meetings at Birmingham that evening, at Selma next morning and Montgomery that afternoon. He turns the most distracted gatherings into a unified mass, their applause for him pride in themselves.

The weather and the long meeting in Edwards made it necessary to cancel a flight to Eutaw, Ala. (for the pilot and copilot, one less check of the plane for bombs) to visit the tent city of people thrown off the plantations, and to miss an afternoon meeting in Birmingham with business leaders. (In the few minutes he spent at the Jackson airport, King called Dora McDonald, got her reports and dictated three letters.) There was only time to reach Birmingham's Gaston's Motel, a historic headquarters for civil-rights demonstrations, for dinner. King took no more than a cup of coffee and listened to Albert Turner, S.C.L.C. leader in Alabama, tell about the men King had missed that afternoon. "They're ready, they're interested, but you got to open the gates." King decided to see them after the meeting, no matter how late.

He opened the gates at a packed church that night in Birmingham, as he was to do in Selma and Montgomery the next day. They were singing when I got there, the minister calling to each row in turn to walk down the aisle to the front where the collection baskets had been placed before the pulpit. The choir and the audience sang to rhythmic clapping as the marching people dropped their contributions into the baskets and returned to their seats:

Great day for me,
Great day for me!
Oh! Oh! Oh! Oh!
I am so happy
I'm gonna be free!

When King spoke, they called out their agreement in words—
"Oh, yes!"; "Yessir!"; "That's the truth!"—or with murmurs and
sighs, a chorus to his rhetoric. His humor is varied and their
responding phrases and laughter always caught his tone. Ironic
—"When black folks can't get jobs, it's a social problem; when
whites can't, it's a depression; with the black man it's welfare,
with the whites, subsidies." Sarcastic—"This country has social-
ism for the rich, rugged individualism for the poor." Just plain
funny—"Governor Wallace and his wife are 'Sister and Brother
Wallace.' "

After the meeting, a white woman reporter from a Birmingham
paper asked me if I thought King would bring off his Washington
demonstrations. "He just might," I said, considering it a conservative statement after the enthusiasm of the meeting. "I don't
think so," she replied. "I know the Negro people of this city
and they just aren't interested."

I repeated this to another white woman later, a Southerner
whose looks and accent made it seem a miracle that she had
devoted the recent years wholly to the civil-rights movement. To
my surprise, she said, "It's going to be hard. You know, the
movement has never won anything really. Things aren't the same;
they're worse."

I said that with so many people who had nothing to lose, it
should be easy to accomplish.

"You see, sometimes poor people don't know how bad off they
are," she said. It pained her to say this and to see my disappointment, so she explained: "I am thinking of the woman who was
sitting next to me at the meeting—did you see her? She was
amen-ing and saying she'd go to Washington with Dr. King while
he spoke, but when the meeting was over, she put a hand on my
arm and said, 'Missy, can you help me out with the bus fare
home?' Of course, I gave it to her and she said, 'Missy, I knew
you was a kind white lady.' "

She thought that over a moment and made an effort to be positive. "But we're going to do it," she said. "We've got to do it. I believe this is the last chance this country has to put things right nonviolently. Otherwise, it's just going to explode in the worst way."

Flying back to Atlanta the next afternoon, everyone was relaxed on the plane, including King. He had spoken twice that day. At the Atlanta airport there would be an hour before he caught a plane to Detroit (to hear Aretha Franklin, the singer, in her first hometown concert), and he expected to spend it going over correspondence and dictating letters to Dora McDonald, who has never bothered to figure out how many hours a week she works. He would also call his wife. The next day, Saturday, he would fly to Chicago to talk to his staff there and give a speech. Sunday morning he would preach at the regular service of the Ebenezer Baptist Church in Atlanta, where he shares the pulpit with his father. In the afternoon he would leave for Miami for week-long seminars with a group of Negro ministers on urban leadership problems, a project for which S.C.L.C. had received a Ford Foundation grant.

But in the plane to Atlanta he was especially happy because Montgomery, quiescent in the movement lately, had responded the most enthusiastically of the four places he had visited. Hosea Williams was happy because he had obtained such a large contribution at Montgomery. It seemed an augury that all the thousand arrangements before April would go well, and it led Hosea to reminisce about the Georgia plantation where he was reared, just one plantation away from Marvin Griffin's, Governor Wallace's running mate.

I asked Hosea where the plantation was, and he called out over the plane's engines, "Attapulgus!"

Dr. King clapped his hands and laughed when he saw my quizzical look. "*Nobody* knows where that is—it's a suburb of Chitlin Switch!"

Seeing King in that mood, the film men took out their equipment, and I remembered to ask Hosea if I had heard right at the meeting when he said he had been in jail 42 times. "That's right," he said. I asked King how many times he'd been in jail. He believed it was 19, but he wasn't sure. Hosea talked about the times he had been really frightened. King said he had been frightened twice. There was the time he was marching through Chicago for open housing while people jeered and threw rocks: "It was then I faced the inevitability of death for the first time." The other time was in Philadelphia, Miss., where the three young civil-rights workers, James Chaney, Andrew Goodman and Michael Schwerner, had been murdered in the summer of 1964. With a colleague, the Rev. Ralph Abernathy, he was speaking at a meeting there, and Sheriff Lawrence Rainey, one of the principal suspects in the triple killings, stood right behind him on the platform.

King laughed as he recalled the moment when he had said that the people were behind them in their fight and Rainey had growled in his ear: "That's right. I'm right behind you!" King shook his head at the thought. "Well, it came time to pray and I sure did not want to close my eyes! Ralph said he prayed with his eyes open!"

Everyone in the plane laughed and then slowly stopped and became quiet. The film men put away their camera and sound equipment; they were *cinéma vérité* men and they knew they could not hope to catch a better sequence that day, just as I felt that I had the key to Dr. King's style: praying with his eyes open is what he does all the time.

"No Man Can Fill Dr. King's Shoes"— but Abernathy Tries

by Paul Good

MORNING DAWNED gray in Memphis April 5. Dr. Martin Luther King Jr. had been dead 11 hours, and in the same Lorraine Motel where he was fatally wounded, a squat black man with a broad, dolorous face dictated his speech of accession to the presidency of the Southern Christian Leadership Conference. The Rev. Ralph David Abernathy did not look like a leader at that moment. Numb from lack of sleep, jowls unshaven, he spoke haltingly as some staff members gathered around to help while others drifted off to their private griefs.

"The assassination of Martin Luther King Jr. has placed upon my shoulders the task—" he began. "No, make that 'the awe-some task.' The awesome task of directing the organization which he established, which has given—what do we say here—'hope'? So much hope to the black people—to the oppressed people of this nation. Even after 15 years of sharing the struggle with Dr. King, I—I tremble as I move forward to accept this responsibil-ity. No man can fill Dr. King's shoes."

A few weeks later in Selma, Ala., Abernathy was leading

S.C.L.C.'s Poor People's Campaign to Washington. He wore two strands of yellow and white African beads. An armband reading "Mississippi God Damn" circled the sleeve of his blue denim jacket. Sweating under the glare of television lights, his expression tragi-comic, Abernathy wagged his head and declared to a black church audience:

"Don't ever get it in your mind it was Martin Luther King's dream only. It was Ralph David Abernathy's dream too. So no need of asking me to be Martin Luther King. I never tried to preach like him and he never tried to preach like me. I've been Ralph David Abernathy for 42 years and each time I look in the mirror in the morning I look better and better. I have two little girls and a boy, and they tell me I'm the sweetest daddy in the world and they wouldn't swap me for Lyndon Baines Johnson. So we better get adjusted to each other. I'm not gonna be anybody but Ralph Abernathy and, Lord knows, with me you're gonna have hell on your hands."

The contrast in attitude from uncertain to bombastic was a measure of the dilemma Abernathy faced as he replaced a revered Negro martyr: how to assert himself while keeping fresh the King legend. For nearly 15 years, he had labored in the shadow of Dr. King. The substance in that shadow eluded the public eye although those close to the movement always understood that Dr. King and Abernathy had achieved a unique human symbiosis. Together the two Baptist ministers had begun the 1955 Montgomery bus boycott. Together they helped found S.C.L.C. For a dozen dangerous and exhilarating years they marched, preached and were jailed together as they cracked the monolith of Southern racism. S.C.L.C. Mobilization Director Hosea Williams, a goateed former truck driver, describes the relationship this way:

"They were just the greatest team, and Ralph was the unsung hero of the civil-rights movement. Martin wouldn't make a decision without him. He trusted Ralph like he trusted Jesus. And Ralph ran interference for Martin, going out to meet a hostile audience so he wouldn't have to, and most times turning it around for Martin. Ralph gave him confidence, security, a strong soul to lean on. On the other hand, he gave Ralph his brilliance, his eloquence and intellectual depth, that charisma the white press is always talking about. Look, he had to be a terribly powerful man to develop this kind of association with the *most* powerful spirit of our times.

"And it showed two days after Martin's death. The S.C.L.C. staff went into a retreat in Hampden, Ga. You read all these press lies about us arguing over nonviolence. It never happened. We were just crushed. And then Ralph talked to us. He was militant and nonviolent and filled with substance. The staff was rising from their chairs as Martin finished and we hoisted him up on our shoulders. There's the dissension you hear about."

He stopped.

"Did I say Martin? I meant Ralph. We all do that sometimes. It touches him."

To the public at large, there seemed no confusion of identity. Comparisons between the two men were inevitable, and on the surface all they revealed were differences. Abernathy is a thoroughly black man where Dr. King was light-skinned. Dr. King's speech was polished, his bearing poised and his intellectuality apparent. There is an earthiness about Abernathy from his thick Alabama accent to the informality of his words and gestures. "Bearish" is an adjective commonly applied to him; it fits a voice that sometimes growls and arms that encircle friends in ponderous hugs. Dr. King, for all his radical assault on American racism, was cast in a sophisticated Negro mold that many white Americans found reassuring; it even flattered their own liberal self-image to accept him and his dream. But for many of these same people, it is jarring, threatening when black man Abernathy emerges from the shadows to sloganeer:

"Dr. King wanted to reel and rock and shake the nation until everything fell into place. But under this leadership we're going to turn it upside down and right side up."

"Right side up" often gets lost to white listeners in the rush of applause from blacks. So do the similarities between the two men. Like most social revolutionaries (including Stokely Carmichael), they came from middle-class families. Abernathy's father had the most prosperous Negro farm in Marengo County, Ala., and his 12 children never lacked for food or education. Abernathy eventually earned a master's degree in sociology, an academic notch below Dr. King's Ph.D. in philosophy. Both men became masters of the homily early in their ministries. Dr. King's ran along more erudite lines (Bryant's "Truth, crushed to earth, shall rise again," or Carlyle's "It seems that God sits in His heaven and does nothing"), with Abernathy favoring more homely observations ("If everything is moving smoothly in your life, you aren't doing anything," or "We spend too much time trying to make a living rather than trying to make a life"). But the transcendent similarity between Martin Luther King and Ralph Abernathy lay in their shared belief that militant nonviolence could bring salvation to black and white America.

Their friendship had begun in Montgomery before the epic bus boycott and their nonviolent philosophy grew with it. The vehicle for carrying that philosophy into action was a wondrous machine called the Southern Christian Leadership Conference. No one could be certain precisely how it worked. A ministerial staff grew by accretion around Dr. King and Abernathy, and decisions evolved through group debate with Abernathy's intuitive judgments a strong influence on Dr. King's final authority.

Beyond the inner circle, S.C.L.C. was and is an exercise in organized chaos. The quality of a largely volunteer office and field staff varies wildly, the delivery of telephone messages is a sometime thing and if anyone has ever been dismissed for incompetence, no one can remember who. But through the zeal of its collective leadership, variable support from Southern black churches and financial help from Americans of conscience, it not only survived from its founding in 1957 but achieved some remarkable victories, like the Voting Rights Act of 1965.

However, all past movements—Birmingham, St. Augustine, Selma—were only preludes to a present infinitely more complex and dangerous than confronting a peckerwood sheriff or shifty registrar. The Poor People's Campaign was planned to probe the essence of the American system, to see whether it could make a massive material and spiritual readjustment to change the lives of its poverty-stricken millions and construct a rational future where base poverty would not coexist with stupendous wealth. Shortly before his death, Dr. King confided to intimates his fear that America might not be able to respond to S.C.L.C.'s nonviolent call for change, that it might have to burn. The prevailing national mood, he felt, was to view with alarm the prospect of a few thousand white, black and Indian poor demonstrating in the capital, but to regard with equanimity 35 million poor spread throughout the country.

Still, the staff carefully prepared position papers for Congressional perusal on welfare reforms, a guaranteed income, agriculture practices. Dr. King, aware that nonviolent militancy could be volatile, achieved an accord with Stokely Carmichael and his Black United Front in Washington. Carmichael's forces would not participate in P.P.C., but neither would they disrupt its nonviolent course.

While Carmichael's rejection of nonviolence as an outmoded and discredited weapon precluded any coalition with S.C.L.C., the *entente* demonstrated Dr. King's accelerating search for a *modus vivendi* with militants. His plans for mass civil disobedience in Washington if officials proved unresponsive were decried by organizations like the Urban League and N.A.A.C.P. He was laying his immense prestige on the line, chancing a violent accident or deliberate sabotage that could come from either left or right. Then on the eve of the test, he was gone and the leadership he had willed to Ralph Abernathy was inherited in a moment of peril.

Two former staff members, both mature men still dedicated to S.C.L.C., rallied to Abernathy's side. But their evaluations of him differed. One said: "If Ralph tries to cut the mustard by himself, he's going to fail. He lacks Doc's all-round abilities, and he's going to have to rely heavily on the staff to see him through. He can't dominate the situation as Doc did, and he must adjust to that fact."

The other said: "The man who held the staff together was Ralph. Dr. King never put out the fires when there was conflict. He'd say, 'Ralph, you do it.' And Ralph would. He has the kind of personality that cuts through disagreements and resolves them. Intellectually, he was far behind Dr. King, but in terms of native intelligence he was way ahead."

As the caravans of the poor started rolling toward their present encampment in Washington and whatever destiny awaits them, the dimensions of Abernathy became a national concern. What was he really like? What had he done? What would he do?

The Rev. Ralph Abernathy's West Hunter Street Baptist

Church in Atlanta is bright and handsome with polished pine pews filled for the 10:45 Sunday service by a well-dressed black congregation. The ladies' hats are floral bourgeois masterpieces. The usherettes wear lime green dresses and little white gloves. Abernathy is leaving for Mississippi in the afternoon to lead a Poor People's march out of Mt. Beaulah next day. He has already baptized new church members at the 7:30 service, beginning a long day. Now his children have come to hear their daddy preach before he goes away. Donzaleigh Avis, 7, is radiantly beautiful with lustrous black hair and her father's soft brown eyes in a tan face. She examines herself in a mirror in the rectory office and, complimented, replies: "I look gross."

The service begins with the processional hymn, "We're Marching to Zion," and before his sermon on "A New Heaven and a New Earth," Abernathy announces that at 3 P.M. he will perform a marriage, the groom a legal counsel for S.C.L.C.

"The news has gotten out," he says, "that when I put you together, you stay put."

The congregation smiles. There is obvious affection between them and their pastor.

His sermon is mostly concerned with the Poor People's Campaign. A listener who has often heard Dr. King preach begins the game of comparisons and then abandons it. Abernathy sets his own rough-hewn style.

"The life of a Christian is a hard life," he preaches. "You must get ready to live dangerously for God. Because if a man has not found something he's willing to die for, then he's not fit to live. . . . Do you know what I'm talkin' about? We're goin' to Washington and we're saying to the President and the Congress, 'We're goin' all the way. We'll bring in all our rats and roaches and we're gonna build a shantytown and call it the City of Hope.' Now some of you middle-class Negroes *don't* seem to know what I'm talkin' about. But let me tell you—you only got out of there about a week and half ago yourself."

Later, when the choir sings "Take My Hand, Precious Lord, Lead Me On," Abernathy raises a hand to his glistening eyes.

The air is turbulent between Atlanta and Jackson, Miss. As the DC-8 falls and rises like a wayward elevator, Abernathy sips a glass of milk and reminisces about the tragedy.

"I had thought they would kill us together," he says. "I never thought the day would come I'd live without Martin. But he always told me they would get him first.

"We had started out of the motel room together, and I went back to get some shave lotion. Before I could put it on, I heard it. I was the first one to him. I patted his left cheek. I said, 'Martin, Martin, this is Ralph; everything's going to be all right.' He knew I was there. He looked at me but he couldn't talk. Still, I'm certain he tried to talk to me with his eyes. He gave me a good, long, solid look as if to say, 'See, Ralph, didn't I tell you it would happen this way?' "

The plane is over Alabama, a state Abernathy says he loves despite its racist antecedents. Childhood was apparently secure and happy.

"I never farmed," he recalls. "I was always reading and writing, and my father gave up on me early as far as the farm went. A stern, wonderful man. I taught Sunday school at 10, but he didn't believe in boy preachers. Still, I knew deep down I would one day end up preaching, I just had to have a platform ready-made. I'm a preacher and I love to preach."

Preaching brought a pulpit at the First Baptist Church in Montgomery, a short while before Dr. King was called to the Dexter Avenue Baptist Church there. Their friendship was already established that day in 1955 when Mrs. Rosa Parks refused to give up her bus seat to a white woman and became the catalyst for America's racial reformation.

Abernathy recalls how the Montgomery bus boycott began with a phone call to him from a Pullman porter named E. D. Dixon protesting Mrs. Parks's arrest. Abernathy talked to Dr. King and together they organized the boycott. Each was preoccupied with his religious duties and neither wanted the leadership. Each suggested another man, but at the meeting that organized the Montgomery Improvement Association (the precursor to S.C.L.C.), Dr. King's choice declined and nominated Dr. King. It was amicably agreed on, and Ralph Abernathy took the secondary role as director of programing.

Although he was destined to remain in that secondary role, Abernathy would be the first to be arrested, his home and church destroyed by bombs. But the glory of international renown and a Nobel Peace Prize went to Dr. King. Was there never a twinge of envy during all those years of marching in his shadow?

Abernathy shakes his head.

"You have to understand one thing. We were so honest with each other. No decisions were ever taken without him asking my thinking and vice versa. My wife, Juanita, and Coretta—Mrs. King—couldn't understand it but that's how we worked. I never tried to duplicate him or steal the show. In press conferences, he'd take all the questions without referring any to me. We just tried to be ourselves and to help each other."

I remember how a former staff member, analyzing the present staff around Abernathy, told me of the camaraderie created by memories of perils and triumphs shared. At the same time, he pointed out that there were often personality clashes between Hosea Williams, militant-minded and only tactically nonviolent, and the Rev. Andrew Young, the S.C.L.C. executive vice president, who had been spiritually and intellectually close to Dr. King. He mentioned the Rev. James Bevel, another member of that inner group, a brilliant tactician with his own highly individual visions of what must happen to America. Could Abernathy control them and prevent a schism now that the unifying presence of Dr. King was gone?

"I'm nothing new to them," he says. "Most of us have been together a long time now. So far, nobody's gone."

Is he convinced that Stokely Carmichael's pledge not to interfere with the P.P.C. in Washington will be honored?

"I love Stokely," Abernathy says. "He's a wonderful guy. A real, likable personality. A brilliant young man. I may disagree with individuals like him on strategy, but not on goals. All I know is we will remain nonviolent."

The plane slips and lurches toward a landing. A down-draft brings it perilously close to trees. Even the stewardess—especially the stewardess—looks frightened. Abernathy smiles at his uneasy seatmate.

"O ye of little faith," he says. "Course, maybe it's easier for me. I know the Man who owns the airspace."

There is a welcoming committee of Negroes at the Jackson Airport who sing: "Who's our leader? Aber-*na*-thy!" Before, the refrain had ended, "Martin Luther King!" A fast press conference has been called. The press and television, it seems, have been sniping at the P.P.C.: The Montgomery Advertiser has called Abernathy an "unprincipled and unspeakable bum"; N.B.C.'s Sander Vanocur has been harping on disorganization and hinting at failure. Abernathy is tired now and cranky, and when someone reports that a newspaperman has bet that he will be late for the conference, he growls: "I'm not running a movement for the press."

A TV reporter tells him there has been some "criticism" that the campaign has lost its impetus. Heralded plans for a mule caravan and a Freedom Train appear to be disintegrating.

"The trouble with the press," Abernathy replies, "is, if you try to make things logical, you're always gonna be wrong. A movement moves with the spirit, not with some organizational table."

Abernathy falls into a deep sleep as we drive through the night to Mt. Beulah, a former Negro junior college outside Edwards that currently is operated as a training center by the militant Delta Ministry. He is still foggy as he enters the meeting hall. The hall is crowded, the ancient wooden balcony seeming to sag under the weight of black youngsters, but for all the crowd the applause for him is mild. Hosea Williams warms up the audience for Abernathy with freedom songs, just as Abernathy used to warm them up for Dr. King with preaching:

> *If you miss me from the back of the bus*
> *And you can't find me nowhere,*
> *Come on over to the front of the bus,*
> *And I'll be riding up there.*

For a moment, it seems like the old movement of the early nineteen-sixties with its infinite hope. An elderly black man in a cast-off Army jacket and baggy pants claps along, not knowing the words but his eyes shining, and old black women, come in from Mississippi shacks, stomp in time. But it is not the old movement. Now there are black boys in African regalia, some wearing earrings, and girls stunning in their natural hair, and P.P.C. marshals with the armbands reading "Mississippi God

Damn." (The official explanation is that God will damn Mississippi unless the state straightens out, but more direct renderings are acceptable.)

The young people, in particular, watch Abernathy closely as he begins to speak, judgment in their eyes. He has come wide awake, loose before this audience, teetering as he slowly builds the intensity of his speech, sometimes plucking at the tails of his suitcoat like a boy reciting.

"They freed us as slaves and promised us 40 acres and a mule. I haven't got my mule. You haven't got your 40 acres. But we're going to Washington to get our mule and 40 acres—plus interest," he tells them.

The audience applauds, then cheers when he says:

"I'm nonviolent, and I don't care much about boxing. But we say to white America: 'We want our black champion back.' We say: 'If you don't want Cassius Clay, then get a white man and let him beat him.' "

That hits the button with the kids and they explode. He follows by talking about the stewardess who served him on the plane, pointing out that she is little more than a waitress. "But the white man gives a white girl like her some dignity," he says. "He dresses her up fine, and gives her a fancy title. But when they put our women in a restaurant, they dress 'em up to look like Aunt Jemima."

This time, the balcony shakes. The press still is rankling him and he good-naturedly chides a TV cameraman about the Sander Vanocur criticism. Inconveniently, the cameraman is from another network.

"You know," he continues, "the press asks me, 'Well, what bills do you want written in Washington? It's not my job to write bills. My job is to raise questions. Eastland makes $30,000 a year to write 'em, and if he hasn't got enough sense to write a good bill, he better learn. But even though it's not my job, lemme tell you somethin'—when they do write the bills they got to write them to *my* satisfaction."

By the time he finishes, Abernathy appears to have won over most of his audience. It is a process he must repeat over and over in the days ahead.

Early next morning, Andy Young stands in a pale sunshine watching the poor people gathering for the short march into Edwards and then the bus ride on to Selma and, eventually, Washington. They have the patience of the poor as they stand with cardboard suitcases and bulging paper bags on a street called Medgar's Way in honor of the slain Mississippi civil-rights leader, Medgar Evers. Young, a bright and courageous man in his mid-30's, left a New York job with the National Council of Churches in 1963 to come South and attach himself to Dr. King. Few persons loved or admired Dr. King more, but now he says:

"At this time, Ralph might be the better man to identify with Negroes. He can get on easily with the militants; his attitude is right. The brothers in the street, or out here, remember things he says, even when they don't know his name or who he is. With Dr. King, it was often the other way around. His language and concepts sometimes sailed over their heads. Ralph can talk the language."

Abernathy appears in blue work denims and heavy brogans, with "Mississippi God Damn" encircling his arm. Another march is about to begin—like so many they had led together. How did he feel?

"It still really hasn't hit me. It hasn't sunk in. I've been so busy, so little sleep. . . . It might sound hard, but there hasn't been time to let myself go. I know what I'd like to do is walk into those pine woods over there and talk to him, commune with him. You share so many agonies, and this morning just to talk to him again would feel good."

He moves to a pair of mules donated by a local black farmer to lead the march. They are promptly named Eastland and Stennis after Mississippi's Senators.

"Come on, Stennis," Abernathy says, grasping the bridle. "Let's go."

The march moves down dirt roads fragrant with sprays of honeysuckle and mimosa, past ramshackle houses where black families cluster, watching, waving. The motion of a march going forward revives memories of simpler days in the movement, when political and economic complexities were not so apparent, and when physically moving forward produced the illusion you were getting some place. Edwards is a stark little town with a few cafes and gas stations. Local Negroes and a few hard-eyed whites have congregated for the big event. Five years earlier—even four years—Abernathy might have been mobbed for what he says from the mule cart:

"That mule there is named Eastland. I didn't know why. Then I found out he's old and forgetful, and he don't even want to carry his part of the load. The other's Stennis. They gave me the task to lead him. Now, Stennis is still full of life. But he's so stubborn. He wanted to get off the road to eat grass. I said, 'All these years, you been leading us around, but today, thanks be to God, we're leading you.' "

Even after the speech has ended and the buses have pulled out, the black people of Edwards are standing around, smiling at one another, shaking their heads over what that preacher Abernathy said.

En route to Selma by car, Andy Young drives part of the way, with Abernathy beside him, while Hosea Williams and Abernathy's white secretary, Terry Randolph, sit in the back. Abernathy goes out of his way to introduce her at all rallies, although S.C.L.C.'s integrated staff is anathema to many black militants. The conversation in the car revolves around church stories; scripture is quoted back and forth—and some tales not found in scripture.

Williams, an enthusiastic if erratic singer, tells how he used to sing his own version of the Lord's Prayer during worship, to the delight of the doting aunt who raised him. Then he entered the Army. Three years later, on his first Sunday home after discharge, the deacon called on him to perform, while his aunt sat beaming. But Williams found his voice register had changed, and he decided to flee after croaking a few notes.

"There was that pot-bellied nigger deacon waiting for me to go on," he says. "And there I was, so ashamed, crawling out of the church on my hands and knees so nobody would see, and my poor old aunt wondering where I went to."

Abernathy laughs along with his two assistants, alleged antagonists in a power struggle. Later, the talk turns to Washington and a questioner reminds Abernathy that for the last two years of Dr. King's life he had never once been invited to the White House by President Johnson. At the same time, conservative

Negroes, like Whitney Young of the Urban League, were regular visitors, were named to commissions and were consulted. Was Abernathy disturbed by this Administration favoritism?

"Oh, no," he replies. "There are lots of paper leaders. But to be a real leader, you have to have people in back of you. If some of these paper leaders want to lead people, let them get out and lead. It never bothered Martin that the White House didn't invite him. He was glad not to go and get compromised for a bunch of tea and cookies. And I feel the same way. It's just another handout.

"Also, you take the way Senator Kennedy and Governor Rockefeller supplied the planes to carry Coretta to Memphis and bring back the body. We're appreciative for what they did. But it takes more than kindness to solve our problems, and attending to the burial of Martin Luther King is not enough to determine who will be the next President of the United States. Kennedy people have already asked me for an endorsement, but I turned it down. I'm not giving any endorsement until I hear somebody's poverty program in detail. And if I hear the right program, this year S.C.L.C. may come out with a political endorsement for the first time in our history."

In Selma, where three S.C.L.C. supporters were murdered in the campaign that produced the Voting Rights Act and where Abernathy and Dr. King shared a jail cell for three days, officials try to limit the march. They back down when Abernathy tells them to get a few hundred jail cells ready because all the marchers are going ahead anyway.

That night, at a church rally, a trumpeter plays a solo, "How Great Thou Art," in tribute to Dr. King. The church where he had preached is silent as the notes pour forth, reverential but laced with a current of blues. Abernathy's face is grim as he begins to speak. He manages a few sentences, but when he tries to refer to Dr. King, the delayed reaction at last hits. His mouth opens, but no words come out. The audience understands and waits. A slow minute goes by—then two, while fat tears run down his cheeks.

An old man in a front pew chants: "Jesus has all power. . . . Lord, keep us together." "Amen," people respond. Finally, it passes and Abernathy says: "It has been so lonely since he went away. But with your help and with God's help we have made up our minds we are going on until victory is won."

It is not so emotional two days later in Boston. Abernathy is making his first Northern excursion. The occasion is a $100-a-plate luncheon at Northeastern University, which raises $15,000 for S.C.L.C. Those gathered include former Gov. and Mrs. Thomas Peabody, university Brahmins, some latter-day Abolitionists and a sprinkling of middle-class Boston Negroes.

Abernathy is good and late, and he enters preceded by a squad of Boston black militants called the Youth Alliance Patrol. They have come uninvited, but Abernathy blandly accepts their presence. Some carry weighted canes and walkie-talkies, and the leader is swathed in fabric of African design revealing only his eyes, so that he looks a cross between Rudolph Valentino and the Mummy's Revenge. The sensation in the dining room is obvious but it is quickly smothered by proper Bostonian *noblesse oblige*.

Abernathy has brought with him a written speech he had recited the day before at a Y.M.C.A. luncheon in Atlanta. It is a speech without soul—not really a bad speech, but a boring one —and he reads it badly. Its pleas for economic justice and its reiteration of the nonviolent creed all are predictable, and even Abernathy seems bored reading it. He tries an ad lib:

"Unless my mind fails and my tongue cleaves to the roof of my mouth, I will not disappoint you and I will not let America down."

The applause is mild.

A line that always gets a good response in Southern black churches, no matter how often it is used, concerns Bull Connor, the public safety commissioner of Birmingham in 1963, who became a symbol of villainy through his use of police dogs and fire hoses against demonstrating Negroes. "With the knife of nonviolence," Abernathy says, "we took Bull Connor and turned him into a steer."

The diners are not amused.

And when he ends by saying, "Let us walk together, children. And don't get weary. 'Cause there's a great camp meeting in the Promised Land," the lack of response indicates they may choose to miss the meeting.

S.C.L.C. and what is left of the movement obviously are not going to be the same with Abernathy. The bullet that killed Dr. King halved a whole made up of two compatible personalities and left the leadership shorn of an image that had been building for 15 years. What may not be obvious is that Dr. King today would be as much a captive of the times as Abernathy is.

It may not strike certain whites—or Negroes—as seemly when Abernathy puts on African prayer beads instead of a clerical collar, taunts white boxing prowess and does not rebuff the attention of swathed black militants with loaded canes. But Dr. King was being moved in the same direction. Dr. King's prestige would confer a distinction on the deeds, while Abernathy's lack of identity suggests to some that he is pandering to extremists and indulging in demagoguery.

An exquisite and sinister sense of timing removed Dr. King in the moment he had made a peace, of sorts, with Stokely Carmichael, and at the same time had issued a black challenge to the Federal Government and the white nation at large. With the strongest leader removed, a lesser leader like Abernathy elevated and would-be leaders encouraged to make their bids, nascent black unity could get lost in the shuffle. Small wonder that black suspicions run deep over who really pulled the trigger in Memphis. Many Negroes are convinced, while offering no proof, that the C.I.A. murdered Malcolm X just as he was moving to forge a oneness of blackness. They do not consider it outlandish that Dr. King might have paid the same price for striking a bargain with Stokely Carmichael.

Abernathy plainly lacks—to use the vogue word—charisma. At least, for white people. But this may no longer be relevant, and the disdainful white sniff sensed in the air of the Boston luncheon could work to his advantage. He is a thorough-going, straight-talking black man of intuitive intelligence and acquired authority in moving black people. No other black man in America today has his experience or his credentials.

How well he will use his background is impossible to predict, and it is unfair to expect miracles of demonstrated leadership in seven weeks. Past performance may provide some measure and an impartial evaluation comes from John Doar, a former civil-rights trouble-shooter with the Justice Department and a legend in his own right.

"I saw him frequently in the Selma campaign," Doar says, "and while I never sat in on the S.C.L.C. councils, his public judgment always seemed good, tough and sensible. He did not equivocate but said what he thought. He was committed to substantial changes in existing institutions through nonviolence. I felt he had compassion and considerable feeling for the little people of the South he was trying to help."

Today, Abernathy's public voice still is uncertain because he is trying to be all things to all people, black and white. But his character suggests that he will settle on something close to that image he sees in the mirror, each day looking better and better to him. How good it looks to old-time allies of S.C.L.C. and those blacks still under the spell of Dr. King is something else. Clearly, he is more at home among Southern black people than he is among blacks or whites in the North.

Muddying any judgment about him is the fact that he has been physically exhausted since April 4, making nonstop public appearances, sometimes contradicting himself, occasionally undermining through blunders the image of dependable leadership he must create. When police attacked marchers in Marks, Miss., for example, he rushed to announce that three marchers had been killed. It proved untrue.

Part of the problem here is that his staff, however loyal, is not protecting him as it did Dr. King from the pitfalls of continual public exposure. He needs an occasional shield, and an occasional respite from making all declarations in the name of S.C.L.C.

Even care for his physical safety has been slack. Two weeks ago, at the Jackson, Miss., airport, he was left alone to park the staff car, and was subjected to verbal harassment from police— and even from a drawling parking-lot attendant. The potential for a dangerous incident was obvious. Dr. King would never have been exposed to such a danger.

This problem probably will be resolved in time as his new role solidifies and staffers make the necessary mental transition, transferring their past solicitudes from Dr. King to Abernathy.

Inside his own organization, he certainly wields unchallenged authority. He is in control of the Poor People's Campaign as well as anybody can control such an amorphous undertaking. Because he is a tougher administrator than Dr. King—who could never bring himself to chastise, much less fire, anybody—Abernathy may reduce S.C.L.C.'s organizational chaos. Inevitably, there will be staff changes. No one will leave until the Poor People's Campaign ends, out of loyalty to Dr. King and dedication to the ideals that brought them to S.C.L.C. in the first place. S.C.L.C. is not General Motors, and no board-of-directors battle is raging. But when a leader like Dr. King goes, balances are upset, not so much along moderate-militant lines as in the more subtle area of personality.

The final question is: Can S.C.L.C. under Abernathy survive as a black force for nonviolence in American life? One crass impediment is money. S.C.L.C. is spending vast sums on the Poor People's Campaign with no guarantee they can be readily replenished. In the past, Dr. King's fund-raising magic always worked miracles of loaves and fishes; Abernathy's skills are untested. Much will depend on his acceptability to the whites who provided the largest share of past financing.

But more critical to S.C.L.C.'s future is what will happen in Washington. Without a significant victory, survival will be difficult. Southern blacks are getting tired of marching miles while change in their lives is measured in millimeters. Most Northern blacks have long regarded nonviolence as an aberration of Southern Christers and are cynical about Washington's ability to respond to the peaceful lobbying of the poor.

So the answer to the question does not rest with Abernathy of S.C.L.C. but with the American essence now being tested in Washington. The Congressional and executive reaction to the Poor People's Campaign—if it reflects the white American majority—indicates that white America has learned little about blacks and less about itself in the past decade of civil-rights activity.

A recent photograph in the New York Times showed anti-riot troops being trained at Ft. Gordon, Ga. Some of the units are probably on call for Washington duty today, should the poor people demonstrate. The photograph depicted a group of "enemy" demonstrators being assaulted by antiriot troops. Lest there be any confusion in identity, the mock enemies carried a placard. The slogan it bore was not "Black Power" or "Up the Vietcong." It was the title of a hymn that Dr. King and Ralph Abernathy had sung a thousand times together and that the President of the United States had quoted twice in an address to Congress:

"We Shall Overcome."

"We Can't Cuss White People Any More. It's in Our Hands Now"

by Walter Rugaber

JACKSON, MISS.

THE CROWD gathered in Charles H. Griffin's campaign headquarters in Jackson on the night of March 12 exuded satisfaction and relief. Griffin had just won a Congressional seat in a special election, and Mississippi's white Democracy had thus turned back the first serious challenge by a major Negro candidate in 88 years. Then something unheard-of occurred. Charles Evers, the Great Nigra Peril himself, walked in the door, calmly signed the guest book and strode up to his victorious opponent. Griffin had sufficient presence of mind to flash a cordial smile as he shook hands. "Congratulations," said the loser. "I'll do anything I can to help you. Just remember, we're all Mississippians." The startled whites applauded.

Charles Evers had lost to Griffin by a 2-to-1 margin. Still, he didn't *feel* like a loser. "Do you realize," he asked later, "that 43,000 Negroes voted who never would have before, and that we came out and challenged the entire political system of Mississippi? You watch us next time. We're going to take every sheriff we run. The local school boards are up, and we're going to take some of them, too."

Yes, this is Mississippi. No, Evers was not just dream-talking. A decade after virtually being run out of the state, five years after his younger brother Medgar was slain from ambush, Charles Evers has made a fair start—though only a start—on turning Mississippi around. He has launched Negro registration drives and follow-up election campaigns that provided the first breaks in Mississippi's lily-white government. He has organized tight, tough economic boycotts in some of the South's most hard-bitten areas, winning Negro advances in employment and the desegregation of public facilities. And he has made of himself, as politician and businessman, a symbol of what the Negro can aspire to, even in rural Mississippi.

Just how far Evers has come was indicated in the special election to fill the 10-month unexpired Congressional term of newly elected Governor John Bell Williams. It took place in the Third District of southwestern Mississippi, which includes the capital city of Jackson; an estimated 64 per cent of the voters are white. In the Feb. 27 primary, the white vote was split among six white candidates, and Evers—on leave from his post as state field secretary for the National Association for the Advancement of Colored People—led the field. In the runoff, the white vote united against him.

But Griffin will have to run for the office again in the fall, and for a time Evers considered opposing him. The state House of Representatives rushed through a change in the election law —aimed directly at Evers—calling for a runoff if no candidate achieved a majority in the general election. The bill died in the Senate, and Evers does not plan to make the race, but the widespread support the measure had gained underlined the impact of the Evers threat.

The events of the last few months have done nothing to diminish his position. On May 21, Evers was one of some 40 Negroes named to participate in the state Democratic convention—the first of their race since 1876. He was also elected chairman of the Jefferson County Democratic executive committee. The next day, he announced that he would serve as state co-chairman of Senator Robert F. Kennedy's Presidential campaign. (He was with the Senator in Los Angeles when Kennedy was shot June 5.)

One morning early this month Evers was elected a delegate to the Democratic National Convention—and resigned the same afternoon, arguing that he could not be "used as a pawn" by a state party leadership fundamentally unreconciled to change. Only four Negroes had been named to the state's 68-member delegation to Chicago.

But Evers will be in Chicago this month, a much more visible figure than he would have been as a member of the state delegation. He is expected to provide the cutting edge for a challenge to that delegation by a coalition of Negroes and white liberals. And the Mississippi challenge is expected to serve in turn as the cutting edge for similar challenges from several other Southern states. Those who recall the emotional confrontation over the seating of the Mississippi Freedom Democratic party at the 1964 convention will recognize the potential dramatic impact of a more broadly based and determined challenge this year. It will be all of that and more, if Evers has his way.

Charles Evers is a big, husky man whose voice and manner can slip suddenly and easily from gentle humor to stinging condemnation. He was born 45 years ago in Decatur, a country town in east-central Mississippi which he remembers as "a very small, quiet place" with relatively few Negroes and hence "not too much violence." The Evers family, which ran a funeral home and a lumber contracting business, was successful and well established in the Negro community there. Charles and Medgar grew up with distinctly different personalities.

"They were brothers," an acquaintance recalls, "but that's about as far as it went." Medgar was gentle and easy-going and usually took pains not to offend others. His brother is blunt and direct, and there is hardly a toe—black or white—that he has left unstomped. But for all the disparity, the two shared a fierce antagonism toward white supremacy. It was an essential bond.

Each day they walked two miles to the Decatur Consolidated School. "We never understood," Charles says, "why the white kids could ride by in their big, yellow, shiny bus while we sloshed through the mud. That disturbed us. Although we were a little more fortunate than many, we never did feel any different than other Negroes, and Medgar and I always said, when we got grown, we'd change it."

They went off to high school in nearby Newton and roomed there with a white woman who ran a small restaurant where Charles worked. "She taught us a lot that we learned about white people. She was always kind to us—she was like a mother to me. I remember they had separate entrances to the restaurant, and every chance I'd get I'd go in the white side. Since I worked there, I wouldn't be questioned too much about it. I wanted to see how it was so different."

Mrs. Payne tried to explain things:

"Charles, that's just the way Mississippi is. The colored have their side, and the whites have theirs."

"But ours is so dirty."

"Well, you just have to keep it clean."

The brothers remained entirely unconvinced. There were many such incidents, all part of the dreary business of growing up black in the rural South. Most young Negroes learned their "place," but Charles and Medgar resisted the process with a particular intensity.

"We weren't going to let anything or anybody stop us," Charles says. "I think it really dawned on us the time they killed a friend of my father's. They drug him out and hung him to a tree. Our parents rushed us back in the house, but we could hear everybody yelling and hollering. We were just kids, but I remember it just as good as if it was the day it happened."

In 1941, after completing the 11th grade, Charles volunteered for the Army serving in the Pacific. He then finished high school in Newton and in 1950 received a degree in social science from Alcorn A. & M. College, a Negro institution in Lorman. After a year in Korea with his reserve unit, he moved to Philadelphia, a small town 23 miles north of Decatur, where he took over his family's funeral parlor and started a hotel, a restaurant, a taxicab service and a gas station.

Philadelphia was about as tough then as the world found it a decade or so later when three young civil-rights workers were murdered there. But Evers and his brother, who had graduated from Alcorn to work for an insurance company in which the family had an interest, began their civil-rights agitation. They would assemble four or five Negroes in a deserted pasture or an out-of-the-way barn and enroll them in the N.A.A.C.P. The membership cards came back from New York in unmarked envelopes, and one of the brothers would secretly deliver them.

In 1954, the N.A.A.C.P. decided to hire a full-time staff worker for the state. The brothers easily agreed that Medgar was the more diplomatic, and he moved to Jackson for $3,000 a year. Charles stayed and even gained brief popularity over radio station WHOC as Mississippi's first Negro disc jockey. But he found himself more and more isolated in Philadelphia.

The town's segregationists began to apply various pressures: his Negro employes were threatened, lawsuits were filed, credit was more or less impossible to obtain. And in 1957, Charles left the state. He arrived in Chicago with a new Ford, $2 in cash and the driving ambition which even today feeds an active set of ulcers.

During the day he carried sides of beef at Swift & Co. At night he worked as a washroom attendant at hotels in the Loop. On weekends he tended bar at a little tavern on California Avenue. In just two years he had the money to start his own cocktail lounge, and later he opened a second.

Evers owned the jukeboxes at both places, an impertinence that greatly offended the Chicago syndicate. Medgar telephoned one day early in June, 1963, and cautioned his brother that big city hoodlums could be quite as unpleasant as Southern sheriffs.

"I thought I got you out of trouble down here," Medgar laughed.

"Don't worry about me," Charles replied, "you just take care of those rednecks down there."

Medgar was shot a few nights later.

"We made an agreement when we were boys," Evers says. "If anything happened to either one of us, the other would carry on [with the civil-rights effort]." Evers confronted the N.A.A.C.P.'s national leadership and more or less demanded his brother's job. "I wasn't going to let anybody mess up what he had done. I knew nobody else could do [the work] like I could." In the tense, emotional aftermath of Medgar's assassination, there was no particular resistance; he took over two days before Medgar's burial at Arlington National Cemetery.

It is practically impossible to compare the performance of the two brothers. Mrs. Ruby Hurley, southeastern regional director of the N.A.A.C.P. and an associate of both men, recently mused: "The times were so different; the personalities were so different."

Medgar's tenure coincided with the South's most militant resistance to desegregation—the days of Emmett Till and Mack Charles Parker, of the White Citizens' Councils and the State Sovereignty Commission. Medgar did some work on voter registration and employment opportunities for Negroes, mainly in Jackson and the Delta region; but as Charles observes, "His work was much harder than mine. He spent a lot of time just trying to keep Negroes alive." Within a few years of his appointment, Charles had the advantage of a more relaxed climate and a series of important Federal laws and court decisions. But the actual implementation of advances in such areas as education and employment posed a major challenge.

Charles Evers built his organiaztion in southwestern Mississippi almost entirely on an N.A.A.C.P. base. He established local branches in each county, attended most meetings and played a major role in choosing officers and setting policy. Today, the branch presidents serve as his leading deputies and the members make up his main field force. There is little significant opposition evident among Negroes in the area.

They had been battered for decades by an unusually rigid pattern of oppression, and Evers found almost no indigenous civil-rights movement in the area. "This was the worst section of Mississippi as far as violence was concerned," he said, "and maybe that gave them the feeling that I wasn't pretending, I wasn't joking, I wasn't doing it for publicity." Evers is proud of the organizing he did and regularly insists upon his status as an insider, a neighbor more than a civil-rights leader.

"Everybody likes to know what's going to benefit him," he said. "I'd always go to the ministers first and try to get their support. We'd more or less show them what it would do in their behalf in uniting their church: the more progressive you are and the more leadership you show, the more people will cater to you. We'd show them it's their duty, it's their God-given duty, because they had been chosen to be leaders.

"Then I'd go to the common Negroes, the laborers, the maids, the unemployed. You start, for instance, with the welfare. Everybody wants to know about the welfare. The conditions, really, are what we work on. In any community, a man can go in and start cussing the welfare or cussing the school system, and he's going to get some support."

One of Evers's key weapons was the boycott, and he proved himself a superb tactician—organizing local Negroes to stay away from white stores until the black community's demands were met. The white merchants fought him bitterly, but sooner or later they capitulated and extended major gains. In Natchez, for example, he not only got a signed agreement but also insisted that the Board of Aldermen formally ratify it. The boycott led to such steps as the desegregation of a hospital and the employment of Negroes as clerks, cashiers, policemen, deputy sheriffs and salesmen. Similar advances were won after boycotts in Fayette, Port Gibson and other towns.

The campaigns were strict and unyielding, but Evers rarely missed a chance to show off a better side. Once he sat back and allowed an "outsider," young and sharply militant, to lash the white leadership. Then Evers quietly led the Mayor aside and offered the town a choice: "Work with me—or that wild youngster over there."

But after a bomb injured a local N.A.A.C.P. leader in Natchez, Evers himself blew up: "We're not going to take it any longer. We're not going to start any riots, but we've got guns and we're going to fight back. I may be fired [from the N.A.A.C.P.] for saying this, but that's what we're going to do."

Despite such angry talk, the Evers view of Mississippi's whites is uncommonly optimistic, as in the following exchange:

"You've often said you think Mississippi will be way ahead of the country some day [in race relations]."

"I know so."

"A lot of people would think that means you think the white people are basically your friends."

"They are. They really are. They just don't know any better now. They don't hate us for any reason other than because we're black."

"That's enough, isn't it?"

"Well, once you convince this rascal that black is nothing dirty and there's nothing disgraceful about it, he's going to change. Once we stand up to them and let them know that we can do whatever they can do, they're going to start accepting us. And once we get them to accept us, we're going to be on our way."

For Evers, the transition from civil rights to politics was natural and inevitable. The way to solve the Negro's problems was to get rid of the people responsible—"the board of supervisors that's responsible for welfare, the mayor who allows police brutality, the sheriff who administers it, the constable and justice of the peace who arrest you falsely and judge you falsely." The way to get rid of them, he preached, was to register and to vote.

Registration, of course, must be the first step. There are a variety of techniques an organizer can use, and Evers has used most of them—staging marches and rallies, sending workers out on door-to-door canvasses of Negro neighborhoods. Essential to the effort are his records for each area listing the names of those Negroes who have registered and those who require more encouragement.

An Evers election campaign begins with the selection of qualified candidates, for he has found that Negroes will not vote for just anyone with a black face. Then a coordinator is appointed for each district, and workers are selected to drive people to the polls. As Negro voters appear there on election day, their names are checked off. At noon and again at 4 P.M. each district makes up a list of those who have failed to vote, and workers make special visits in an effort to coax them out.

This now goes on, to a greater or lesser extent, in six southwestern counties. In three—Jefferson, Claiborne and Wilkinson—Negroes have a majority of the registered vote. In three others —Adams (Natchez), Copiah and Franklin—whites still hold the edge. Soon Evers hopes to move effectively into Yazoo, Warren (Vicksburg) and other counties to the north.

The political program requires tireless pump-priming by Evers himself. His speeches are an awesome blend of reprimand and forgiveness, mockery and cajolery; he threatens and he pleads. "You've got to do it yourselves," he tells audiences. "We can't march anymore. We can't picket. We can't cuss white people anymore. It's in our hands now."

One night during last summer's campaign, Evers spoke at the Mt. Zion Baptist Church in Rodney, a village deep in the Mississippi backwoods. The church is a simple structure with unadorned windows, crude wooden benches and a picture of Jesus on the wall. At the back there is an inadequate window fan and a jug of drinking water with a porcelain dipper hanging on the

wall above it. A clock gave up at 1:45 one day, and the light
bulbs flicker in their dangling sockets. More than 100 Negroes,
most of them in workclothes, were waiting when Evers walked in.

"On Aug. 8," he said sternly, "you all voted for the white
man." A murmur of protest went up from his audience. "Yes,
you did," Evers insisted. "We read the returns. You, the Negroes
in Rodney, didn't care enough. Or maybe you didn't know. But
we can't make that mistake again. You are the ones who can keep
denying yourselves decent homes, decent jobs, decent schools. It
ain't never going to change until you send some of our own
people down there to represent us at the courthouse."

At a planning session in Lafayette Evers told his drivers: "I
don't want you to haul a single Negro who gets in your car and
starts talking about how he 'ain't gonna vote for no niggers.'
Put him out right there." Then he turned to lash more formidable
enemies: "If we find out that one of these preachers is up in his
pulpit campaigning for a white against a Negro, he can't preach
in this county anymore. We want our ministers to do right. If
we find out they're doing wrong, they're going to go."

Criticism of his sometimes heavy-handed methods tends to
center on his team of about 65 Negro youths, variously described
as "a goon squad," "The Black Hats" and "The Defenders." The
group's sole purpose, Evers insists, is protection. Whites often
harass Negro rallies in the South, and the Federal Bureau of
Investigation has warned Evers repeatedly of assassination plots
cooked up against him by hot-eyed haters in the Ku Klux Klan.
(He owns a small arsenal of weapons and almost never ventures
out without a gun.) In this year's Congressional campaign, an
Evers bodyguard exchanged shots in Jackson with a white youth
in a passing car.

But many have seen the Evers "army" jostle Negroes entering
stores under boycott, and some shoppers have had their packages
knocked to the street. Evers points out that the boycotts all had
the ardent support of the Negro community at large, and he sol-
emnly denies any knowledge of strong-arm tactics in enforcing
them. Yet such dismaying incidents have occurred—though they
had little to do with the decisions of thousands of Negroes to
boycott white stores for months at a time.

A man who has worked with both Evers and his critics says of
such tactics, "Philosophically, of course, I disapprove of it. But

I think he's getting results, and maybe you need a little benevolent dictatorship."

Evers is no less a success as a small-town entrepreneur. Few civil-rights leaders are as openly and happily in pursuit of the dollar. In Fayette, Evers built a modern grocery store, a lounge, a radio repair shop, a ballroom and a liquor store, all contained in an attractive complex which he named the Medgar Evers Shopping Center. (He has also helped organize "cooperative" groceries, shares of which are held by Negroes, at Natchez, Port Gibson and Hazlehurst.) He maintains a home in Jackson for his second wife (an early marriage ended in divorce) and three daughters; a fourth daughter is married. He commutes the 77 miles to his home when he can, but he is found most often at his Fayette shopping center, which includes a small apartment at one end.

"Good day, ladies," he chirps to customers. "Come right in, come right in." He sweeps to the front of his Fayette grocery to peck both women on the cheek. "We've got a lot of wonderful buys around here today." He waves his arm at the brightly lit shelves. "Come on back here and let me show you some pork chops." It goes on like that for hours.

But some of the most bitter criticism of Evers has stemmed from his performance as a businessman. His affluence is in strong contrast to the economic status of so many well-known civil-rights leaders who are poorly paid ministers or professionals. Even more to the point, there is the fact that he profits from the civil-rights movement: his customers are often the same people he has organized, and it seems to some observers that he opened his stores in unseemly proximity to the time when white competitors were being hit by the boycotts he had initiated.

"The trouble with Charles," one critic contends bluntly, "is that he's something of a hustler. He's not putting everything out on the table any of the time, and he always has an eye out for things that will help Charles as much as the movement." Even friendly observers have their doubts. "He didn't call those boycotts to make a buck for his stores," said one. "The cause-and-effect relationship just isn't there. But he sure didn't hesitate to utilize them. I think he would have been better advised not to have done it."

"I don't have to boycott the white man to get business," Evers retorts. And it is true that, though boycotts in the area have been over for years, his Fayette shopping center is as jammed with customers as it ever was. "People have to look at my background and see I've been a businessman all my life. That's why I've been able to go out and confront and fight discrimination and segregation. I was independent, and I lived off what the Negroes did for me and not what some racist, some bigot, handed out. If we had more Negro leaders as independent businessmen, they could fight harder and it would be less likely for them to be bought off by the power structure."

The Evers approach to life has sometimes alienated civil-rights leaders; he has little appreciation for the niceties of corporate association activity. For example, when the nation's most prominent rights leaders hurried to Mississippi for the 1966 James Meredith march, Evers said that he hoped the demonstration wouldn't "turn into another Selma, where everyone goes home with the cameramen and leaves us holding the bag." A militant-minded critic recalled this broadside some months later and noted dryly that "the only Negro I've seen on television in Mississippi lately has been Charles Evers." Evers used to delight in dismissing groups such as the Student Nonviolent Coordinating Committee as "those boys running all over the country looking for glamour and glory."

Of late, though, Evers has been less abrasive. In a recent interview, for instance, he remarked that "if America would straighten up and do what she's supposed to do" there would be no need for S.N.C.C. or its black power philosophy. Until then, presumably, the need remains. "Everybody's not as patient as Medgar and I happen to have been." And though he sometimes implies that the N.A.A.C.P.'s national leadership doesn't understand the hard realities of Mississippi, he avoids any direct criticism.

Local Negroes seem overwhelmingly loyal to Evers. They refer to him as "the big boss," and some recall times before 1963 as "B.C.—before Charles." A wiry, middle-aged workman in Port Gibson says, "We're going to take good care of him; he's done more around here than any of us ever thought of." A local clergyman says, "There are a lot of problems with Charles, but the people want him."

One of the problems, some critics feel, is Evers's great popularity itself. They say that the N.A.A.C.P. local structure is built almost entirely around Evers and that other Negroes have little chance to share the responsibility. The loss of Evers, they warn, would mean disaster. One astute Negro, commenting on the still slow political progress, put it this way:

"I think some of the Negroes just *want* to vote for the white man. He puts some gravel in somebody's driveway, and—you know—who can argue with gravel? . . . Evers didn't do his homework. They didn't do the kind of citizenship education that ought to be done. Evers tried to do it all by himself. That's one of his shortcomings. I like Charles—you just can't tell him a goddam thing. And you know, maybe if I was in Mississippi under them circumstances you couldn't tell me anything either."

"I may suggest certain things, and usually my suggestions are carried out," Evers says with an easy laugh, "but I certainly don't tell people what to do. We have adult education classes, poverty programs, we try to get people jobs, we talk about the issues at meetings and everybody is supposed to get up and say what they think—I don't know what else you can do. When you lose the spoke out of a wheel, you weaken it; but I don't think it would stop the wheel from turning." That, of course, depends on the number of spokes there are.

Though he has at least his share of critics, Evers has begun to forge a unity among Negro groups that seems unmatched anywhere in the South. The Freedom Democratic party, for example, a militant Negro organization that has often been opposed to the Evers approach, lent its support in the Congressional race.

Evers is convinced that growing political unity and sophistication will lead not only to local victories in counties where the Negro is in a majority but also to effective alliances with progressive whites on a statewide basis. Four years from now, he says, there will be a Negro running for Lieutenant Governor to test the liberal strength. He acknowledges that it will prove a difficult course even if Mississippi's Negro registration climbs above the one-quarter level at which it now stands.

"Negroes haven't learned to trust each other yet. Many of them think Negroes can't do the job. They say to me, 'Mr. Evers, Negroes have never done this before.' We have been taught all our lives to be servants, and that this is the white man's world, and that he's supposed to make all the laws and all the rules.

The Negro mind has to be freed, too, and it will be. Too many have died for this, too many have suffered for this, we have worked for this too long."

For years, the civil-rights movement in general has been turned outward—toward Congress, the white liberal and national opinion in general. Now there are signs in the North of an inward turn, a separatist movement. Evers, too, has an inward direction—but of a very different kind, one that includes not only the individual problems and needs of the Mississippi Negroes but of their segregationist neighbors as well.

"We in Mississippi," he says, "white and Negro, are going to have to work out our own problems." For those who believe that only the outside world can hold the state's racial terror in check, it must be disconcerting and more than a bit offensive to hear Evers suggest, as he often does, that even an arch-foe such as Senator James O. Eastland will eventually come around.

"I believe in proving a point and letting it go," Evers says. "Once you get what you ask for, then there's no point in hanging on and hanging on and just wearing it out. I definitely believe in working with white people if they want to work on a man-to-man basis. There's no point in anybody fooling themselves. I don't care how much the black power boys scream, I don't care how much the Ku Klux Klan screams, we can't get along without each other. They may as well realize that unless we do these things together we're all going to be in a continuous turmoil."

There Is No Rest
for Roy Wilkins

by Martin Arnold

"IN MY YOUTH, goddammit, the newspapers did not call a Negro
woman a beauty. A Negro man was called a black—a good word
now but not then—and a rapist and a clown. There *were* no
demonstrations and parades. Who the hell did it? Who got them
to allow the demonstrations? What is allowed today is affected by
today's climate—the opportunities opened up for the kids by the
people taking part in the civil-rights fight 20 years ago and
more."

Slender, stoop-shouldered, the slight bulge of his years pushing
out from under his neat gray tweed vest, Roy Wilkins, still dedicated, still rebellious, was sitting before a television set, watching
Richard Nixon inaugurated as President of the United States.

In his 69th year, when a man should be resting, Wilkins is still
enduring what the 19th-century black abolitionist Frederick
Douglass called the "awful roar" of struggle. Only now, to his
great surprise, the "awful roar" is often sounded by some of
his own people, the blacks who are young and militant—and he is
the target. So, like a pontiff, a man of great vanity and com-
manding influence, he takes what he considers the long view of
history. He issues biting encyclicals against those blacks who
would exchange his theology of integration for separatism and

who, in the process, would tear down his church, the National Association for the Advancement of Colored People. There is no rest for Roy Wilkins.

Wilkins had received two invitations to attend the Nixon Inauguration; but in the style and code of black politics, a black leader simply does not go to the inauguration of a Republican President—not if he is to retain any following or any power. And if there is one thing Roy Wilkins understands, it is power.

He watched Nixon being sworn in on television, sizing him up, trying to get a reading of Nixon the President, as opposed to Nixon the Vice President and Nixon the Presidential candidate— all the time letting those watching with him know that he is a man accustomed to sizing up Presidents.

"This inaugural's full of squares, full of lawyers. There are no swingers there like me," he said. He mocked the fact that President-elect Nixon had actually arrived on time for his inaugural concert the previous night: "Kennedy was never on time; Johnson was always comfortably late."

Someone asked him if he could pick up the telephone and get President Nixon on the other end. "I wouldn't say that," he replied. "With a President you don't do that unless he himself has put you in a special category—one known to the White House switchboard and the President's appointments secretary. With Kennedy or Johnson, I had no difficulty getting to them, either in person or on the telephone."

The point was made, and if emphasis were needed, one could look on his desk and see, dated three days previously, a "Dear Roy" letter from Lyndon Johnson thanking Wilkins for "the selfless friendship you gave me throughout my Presidency." (On Inaugural Day, as one of his last official acts, Johnson awarded Wilkins the nation's highest civilian award, the Freedom Medal.)

Wilkins turned back to the television set. An aide noted the sparsity of black faces at the inaugural. "This is an integrated crowd," Wilkins retorted. "What *you* want is a Jim Crow crowd." When "The Star-Spangled Banner" was played, Wilkins sang along—and he tapped his feet in time as the Marine band saluted the new Republican President with "Hail to the Chief."

By April Wilkins was not so casual about "hailing the Chief." Clifford L. Alexander Jr., a black, had felt forced to resign as chairman of the Equal Employment Opportunity Commission, citing Nixon's "lack of support." There were indications that the Nixon Administration would allow more flexible school desegregation guidelines—as a sop to Southern Republicans.

By July, Wilkins was speaking in most un-Wilkins-like terms. The new school guidelines were "almost enough to make you vomit." The selection of Warren Burger as Chief Justice of the United States was a disappointment. And the proposed elevation of Clement F. Haynsworth Jr. to the Supreme Court "was a deadly way of negating completely the legislative victories won through the hardest effort by the nation's minority of black citizens."

Was a new, tougher, more militant Roy Wilkins surfacing? Was the old man trying to recapture some of the youthful militant support he had lost? Most observers thought otherwise. What was emerging was not a new Wilkins, but a new enemy: the Nixon Administration. During the Kennedy-Johnson years, the N.A.A.C.P. had functioned more or less as an arm of the Democratic party. Neither Kennedy nor Johnson had entirely pleased Wilkins, but they were, he felt, at least on his side, and they were headed in the right direction.

The black youths who were marching in the streets were not old enough to recall that Wilkins had talked tough before—during the Eisenhower years, for example. Now—as then—he suits his tactics to his enemy. For the Democrats he held out the carrot; for Nixon he is brandishing the stick.

He told this year's N.A.A.C.P. convention in Jackson, Miss., that the organization was confronted with "a hostile Administration that doesn't mean us any good." He would attack.

The young militants who had disrupted the 1968 convention in Atlantic City were not among his listeners this year. They had left the organization or, in the words of one N.A.A.C.P. leader, they had been "purged." The remaining Young Turks, as they call themselves, pledged their "respect and allegiance" to the leader—if Wilkins was not all he should be, at least he was in the fight against Nixon.

Had he gone even further on other issues—such as supporting black dormitories for black students—he might have been able to regain some support from the militant black youths. But Wilkins really does not care for such support, and in his perspective on history, that kind of support is not very important. So in June, as if to make that point very clear, he ended his lecture at the C.W. Post College commencement this way: "Knuckling under to raucous demands for blanket amnesty for those detained for acts of trespass, violence and destruction is not a contribution to the development of fiber in white or black youths." Once again, he spoke out against the concept of "non-negotiable" demands by black militants. He would fight, but he would fight his way, on his terms.

Wilkins is a politician in the cause of civil rights and, like all successful politicians, like Nixon, he has mastered the mechanics of power. "The Negro has to be a superb diplomat and a great strategist," Wilkins once said. "He has to parlay what actual power he has along with the goodwill of the white majority. He has to devise and pursue those philosophies and activities which will least alienate the white majority opinion. And that doesn't mean that the Negro has to indulge in bootlicking. But he must gain the sympathy of the large majority of the American public. He must also seek to make an identification with the American tradition."

Following this blueprint, Wilkins became the chief advocate of the use of constitutional means to achieve black civil rights. In the American tradition, he involved Presidents, legislatures and the courts in the construction of the logical and legalistic engine that is integration. Wilkins considers himself the architect.

The outstanding monument to the Wilkins method is the 1954 Supreme Court decision that overthrew the doctrine of "separate but equal" facilities in public education. It is, he believes, the greatest American public document since the Emancipation Proclamation. "It is very rare for a person in the civil-rights movement—actually in it—to live to see so many of his goals in sight."

Yet the black revolution is a formless, changing movement. The chief enemy of 1954, the bigoted Southerner, has been replaced by the bigoted Northerner—the landlord, the union leader, the schoolteacher, the college dean and now, in Wilkins's view, the national Administration. Angry young militants demand black separatism instead of integration; they opt for violent demonstrations in lieu of court proceedings. The establishment, the entire system, has come under attack—and for many young blacks, that includes Wilkins and the N.A.A.C.P.

"Integration as a talking point is dead," a prominent young

Negro journalist says. "Black people are trying to work out our own problems. We're putting down white help, not seeking it, like Wilkins does."

Another young Negro writer, his eyes flashing in anger, ostracizes Wilkins as an "Uncle Tom" and adds: "We consider integration not productive at this time, certainly not compared to the concept of black people being totally independent."

The rage against Wilkins reached a new peak last spring with the groundswell of black activism in the nation's colleges. He refused, for example, to tie in the Vietnam war with the civil-rights movement, and he denounced black students for bringing guns onto the Cornell campus. Today, he still threatens to challenge in the courts the concept, espoused by black students, of separate black dormitories and courses of study. "If the country gives racial control to a dormitory or an art center," he says, "finally everything in the country will be racially controlled and we'll be right back at the point where we started."

A young black intellectual shouts, "Betrayal." Wilkins, he says, "has done the worst thing any black man could do. By not supporting the students, he has let the white man use him. The white press, public officials, they point to Wilkins and say, 'See, he agrees with us.' Wilkins has made himself irrelevant to the blacks. Worse, he is helping our enemies."

Roy Innis, national director of the Congress of Racial Equality, insists that the student demands express a legitimate need for "black identity, self-awareness and togetherness." And he calls for Wilkins to "withdraw from the stage" and leave the struggle he helped launch to younger men. Wilkins doesn't even bother to note that CORE, under Innis's direction, has become virtually nonexistent as a national civil-rights group—but such attacks cannot but strike deep.

Wilkins tries to respond to his critics with a cool, understated disdain. He stares ahead, as if at a vision only he can see, and runs his long, slim fingers slowly back and forth across his face. "I am sorry to say I have not had too much contact with the young black militants," he will comment. "I have talked to their groups and such, but I imagine they don't think too much of me. And I'm not too excited about their suggestions for solving problems." Are Detroit and Newark any better for the Negroes now after the rioting? Clearly, he says, the answer is no. He is asked

about the new hospital and new garbage collection program in
Watts: would they have come without the riots? "Perhaps not
so soon. They are good things, but they are small things. Tokenism." Rioting has changed little for the blacks, he feels—except
perhaps to harden the white backlash. He adds that the moderate
black is strongly against violence and separatism, and that the
moderate black is the average black.

The Wilkins way, he insists, is the right way: "The whole
point of the N.A.A.C.P. was to establish the Negro as a legal
entity, with the rights and privileges of a citizen. Who did that?
We did that. We are still doing that. Who goes into court in some
small Southern city because a colored woman is earning only $1
an hour doing the same work a white woman gets paid $2.50 an
hour for? We do, every week, almost. Judicial rights and legislative approval, that's our continuing fight."

Wilkins believes that the country—even the Nixon Administration—can be moved by negotiation, by litigation, by the black
man's increasing voting power and by public pressure, carefully
nurtured by Wilkins's pronouncements which increase in decibel
count only to keep up with the needs of the moment.

"Of course, there wasn't any real need for Roy to blast off
at Johnson," a friend says. "Not that the Johnson Administration
was perfect, but it was pretty well committed to eliminating segregation and doing something about the blacks. This Administration, on the other hand, may become more committed as Roy
sounds off. Rioting certainly wouldn't get very far with this group
in Washington."

Wilkins's response to his critics often exhibits a philosophical
schizophrenia of sorts. He bends a bit in the direction of the
young militants, snaps back, bends again: "Negro people, particularly the youth, are outraged, angered, frustrated. They do
not want to crawl. They want to run, and so do I. But civil rights
do not automatically give a man the esteem of his fellows, and
the young Negroes must realize that they also need this esteem."

The realization has not come, however, and the attacks have
grown ever sharper. Even within his own N.A.A.C.P., criticism
of Wilkins's leadership and policies has become the daily fare of
the pioneer activist and friend of Presidents.

The career of Roy Wilkins is, in its way, a classic black example of the Horatio Alger syndrome that so enrages his young

critics. His father, William, was born and raised on a share-cropper farm in Holly Springs, Miss., where he went to Rust College. For all his better-than-average Negro education, the elder Wilkins "drove mules and plows" before he fled Holly Springs in 1900 "because he was considered a troublemaker, who didn't like the way Negroes were treated." In St. Louis, where Roy was born on Aug. 30, 1901, his father went to work as a foreman in a brick kiln. When Roy was 4, his mother died, and he went with his younger sister and younger brother to live in St. Paul with an aunt and uncle, Mr. and Mrs. Samuel Williams. (His sister died in 1927 and his brother died in 1941.)

For "the great sum of $85 a month," Williams was the private carman on the private railroad car of the president of the Northern Pacific Railroad. He taught Wilkins that if a Negro wanted to get ahead, he had to be educated and neat, have learning and clean fingernails. Wilkins attended the integrated Mechanic Arts High School, a block from the State Capitol; he was editor of the school newspaper. At the University of Minnesota, Wilkins majored in sociology, supporting himself as a Pullman car waiter, redcap and slaughter-house worker. He was also night editor of the school paper, The Minnesota Daily, and editor of a black weekly, The St. Paul Appeal.

While still a student, Wilkins became secretary of the local N.A.A.C.P. chapter. And the lynching of a black in Duluth prompted him to enter the university's oratorical contest with a strong antilynching speech that won first prize. After receiving his B.A. degree in 1923, he immediately went to work for The Kansas City (Mo.) Call, a leading black weekly, and soon became its managing editor.

In 1931, Wilkins left The Call and came to New York to work for the N.A.A.C.P. "One of my first jobs was to go South to investigate the conditions among Negroes who were working to build the levees on the Mississippi River. They made 10 cents an hour. Two dollars and fifty cents a day was tops, for a Caterpillar driver, and you know how many Negros had those jobs.

"I lived in the camps and earned 10 cents an hour. We tried to sneak pictures of the work. You didn't say you were from the N.A.A.C.P. It would have meant being lynched.

"It used to be that picketing, except for a labor cause, was against the law. [In 1963, Wilkins was arrested while picketing a Woolworth store in Jackson, Miss., along with the late Medgar Evers, who was shot from ambush just 12 days later.] We went to court over that, and won the right for these kids to march and picket now. I understand their impatience. I share it, but they should have some idea what it has taken to get them their right to raise hell. And before there's a final victory, it will take more than just loud talk."

In his office, which is spare like the man himself, Wilkins leans back in his chair. The walls are beige, the motif early American. It looks as if it had been decorated with little thought, slapped together in a hurry—the office of a man secure in his power with no need for plush-carpet trappings. He points to several automobile models he has made. "I'm a fast-car buff. Maybe if the kids knew that, they'd like me better. I like a car that can handle, that has an easy-steering wheel. I like a car that goes when it's supposed to go. My wife has got a Plymouth Barracuda. I put a four-barrel carburetor on it. I drive a black TR-3. It's 8 years old. It's my only recreation, my only hobby."

Wilkins enjoys words—long words, old words, words not in common usage (he will speak of the "dandelion spread of segregation" or refer to his problems as "nettles"). He slips them into his conversations, his speeches, his news conferences. "If you went to school," he'll tell a puzzled reporter, "you should know what it means." When a book of his writings was published, he sent a copy to a black journalist with this inscription: "Every sentence a gem, Tom." The journalist isn't sure the comment was in jest.

The love of words finds expression, too, in a variety of writing projects: speeches, a weekly newspaper column appearing in 44 papers and frequent editorials for the association magazine, Crisis. Some of the editorials—such as that which denounced demands for segregated black enclaves on campus—are quoted in the national white press, often on the front pages.

A man of aloof charm, Wilkins has few friends, many acquaintances. Of course, the 14-hour day he normally spends on the job allows him little time for purely social matters. But he also has the kind of mind that is more concerned with specific detail and subjects of consequence than with the fuzzy generalizations that make up so much of what passes for social intercourse. He is quickly bored. He is also a man who seems to like his loneliness, his isolated pinnacle.

In 1946 Wilkins underwent stomach surgery for cancer, and he has since refrained from the cigars and occasional cocktail he once enjoyed. He has an inner will, and is generally tougher than his fragile appearance would suggest. Though he is several inches shorter than 6 feet, one has the feeling he is in fact a tall man—he is so slender, except for the small paunch, and his movements are so graceful.

He and his wife, the former Aminda Badeau (a social worker), live in an apartment in Queens. They have no children, and Wilkins's only living blood relative is a nephew, Roger Wilkins, a 36-year-old attorney who works in the field of urban affairs for the Ford Foundation.

"We are good friends," the younger Wilkins says, "but he is not a substitute father to me. Sometimes I know he looks upon me with fatherly pride, but our relationship is not a give-and-take relationship. I don't ask advice and assistance, and he doesn't offer it.

"He is this type of man: Once when Vice President Humphrey wanted to appoint me to a civil-rights committee, he called my uncle and asked him if he should. The answer was prompt: 'No, you should not appoint him.' My uncle didn't want to be compromised. Another time, when I had just gotten out of law school, a member of a very prominent law firm called him and asked him, 'Do you have a nephew named Roger?' He said he did. When the man asked him if I should be hired, he said, 'Well, how do you usually judge people you are going to hire? Judge Roger the same way, hire him or not, as you would anyone else.' And then he hung up. He is a very proud, courageous man, and I love him."

Roger Wilkins, like so many young black leaders, does not always agree with his uncle's actions and attitudes. But he says, "I wouldn't think of trying to change his beliefs. He was in civil rights before I was born."

Wilkins was elected N.A.A.C.P. executive secretary (the title is now executive director) on April 11, 1955, following the death of Walter White. The organization is the oldest (founded in 1909) and the largest (450,673 members as of December,

1968) and richest ($3.2-million income last year) civil-rights organization in the country. It is run, in theory, by a 60-man board of directors. Most of the board members are in their 60's, and they include old-line white liberals, such as Walter Reuther, who were fighting the civil-rights battles 20 and 30 years ago and whose loyalty is to Wilkins. The Young Turks charge (without proof) that the association loads its annual conventions in Wilkins's favor by paying poor blacks "to come up from the South and vote at meetings to keep Roy in control." True or not, board or no, the N.A.A.C.P. is in fact run by Wilkins alone.

The financial strength of the association today is in part the result of a Government ruling four years ago that contributions to its educational and legal programs were tax-exempt charities. That decision started a flood of gifts from philanthropists in general, the Ford, Rockefeller and Carnegie Foundations in particular. Such big-money sources provided somewhat over half of the N.A.A.C.P.'s income last year. The remainder came from the members—from dues (ranging from $2 a year to a $500 lifetime membership), from the local chapters (which raise money at cake sales and rallies) and from subscriptions (at $1.50 a year) to Crisis, which is published 10 times a year.

The N.A.A.C.P. is the only black organization of national influence that has not suffered financially—or lost other, less tangible support—because of the tensions between blacks and Jews, who in this country make up a large share of the politically liberal community. The association's money—other than the foundation funds—has traditionally come from blacks who constitute at least 90 per cent of the membership, not from white liberals.

Since N.A.A.C.P. counsel (now Supreme Court Justice) Thurgood Marshall argued the school desegregation case to a successful conclusion in 1954, the association's membership has nearly doubled. But the figures are somewhat misleading. Many of the 1,300 branches of record are wholly inactive. And even among active branches, the percentage of membership participation is sometimes minimal. The Harlem branch, for example, is the largest in the country with 7,000 members—but no more than a few hundred generally show up for the monthly meetings.

As Gloster B. Current, director of the branches, will admit, the association is middle-class oriented. "The typical branch official," Current says, "has a relatively secure income, probably as a minister, doctor or lawyer, is a churchgoer and belongs to at least one fraternal organization."

In the South, members are either professionals and their families or laborers, who are poor by white standards but middle-class by Southern black standards. In the North, Midwest and West, most members are schoolteachers, sociologists and up-and-coming black politicians.

Wilkins denies it, but the whole structure is held together by the force of his personality and the love that the members have for him. "Roy is in demand every night of the year," says John Morsell, the assistant executive director. "If he let himself, he could be speaking to chapters 365 nights a year. The members want to see him, touch him, hear him. There's nothing else that really holds them. We don't give money to local chapters. We can't really make them do things. It's just Roy Wilkins. They'll do it for him."

The tone of the New York headquarters, where Roy reigns, is brisk, businesslike, quiet. An occasional youth in a cowboy hat or an African dashiki can be seen in the corridors, but the staff consists in the main of neatly dressed black women—not in mini-skirts—and black men in three-button suits, button-down shirts and striped ties.

Wilkins is constantly away from the office on his travels in pursuit of the money and influence to fuel his civil-rights machine. Recently he had a two-week schedule that took him to South Carolina, Indiana, Washington, D. C. (twice), New Jersey, Illinois, Texas, Virginia, Pennsylvania and Georgia. Yet his presence hovers over the office whether he's in town or out.

He is not so popular with his staff as with the association's members. "I think of him as a very distant man," says a former N.A.A.C.P. executive. "He is sort of a figure rather than a human being. I had no personal human contact with him. A lot of the workers were afraid of him. I never heard anyone say they loved him or held him in awe."

Within the last few years, the split between civil-rights traditionalists and the new breed of black militants has brought turmoil to the organization. Many younger N.A.A.C.P. members and staff feel that the Wilkins methods are no longer effective, that the organization has become a *de facto* arm of a go-slow

Federal Government. This split has not been a source of pride to Wilkins. And like any strong man faced with a revolution from within, he has moved to squash it, firmly, before it squashes him.

Last summer, at the association's 59th annual convention, 600 youth delegates asked to form an autonomous and more militant organization. The proposal was denied, and the youths staged a walkout.

In the ensuing controversy, Chester Lewis, a 40-year-old Wichita, Kan., attorney, resigned from the association's board. "I was completely fed up. I felt the association no longer was relevant to the needs of the black people. We need viable black power, and the severest critic of black power is Wilkins."

More recently, an article in this magazine produced another crisis between the young and old in the association. The article, written by a young white N.A.A.C.P. staff member, Lewis M. Steel, charged that the Supreme Court was not a libertarian body, that it only attacked the "overtly obnoxious" discrimination patterns in the country and thus helped maintain the status quo. Twenty-five members of the association's board met the following day, while Wilkins was returning home from Europe aboard an ocean liner, and voted unanimously to discharge Steel without a hearing. The entire legal staff, including its chief, Robert L. Carter, quit in protest. Wilkins supported the decision.

The future of the N.A.A.C.P. depends in large measure upon who succeeds Wilkins. The matter has apparently been given little thought, and even less has been done to bring a potential successor into the association's power structure (one of the few ways in which the organization is not run exactly like a large corporation). Most speculation centers around Criminal Court Judge William Booth, formerly Human Rights Commissioner under Mayor Lindsay, and Edward McClellan, a bright, articulate former policeman, who is the N.A.A.C.P.'s urban program director for the Chicago area. But as one member says, "Roy doesn't believe he's going to die, so why worry about a successor?"

Wilkins says he is planning to strike out in new directions to develop leadership and economic power in the city slums, where the association is weakest. He admits that the N.A.A.C.P. has a lot of catching up to do. "We were, very frankly, caught off guard. We were geared up for programs of opposition—telling people,

'Don't let the white man do that to you'—and when the barriers started falling, we were not ready to make a shift. Our problem is that we offer the young people nothing spectacular." He admits that other, more militant, leaders do.

The N.A.A.C.P. effort to compete for the young people involves placement of urban program directors in major cities to work in the ghettos. Their assignment: to find new black leadership, to train black urbanists. It has recently approved local branch sponsorship of low-income housing.

The N.A.A.C.P. is also planning a massive legal attack, supported by peaceful demonstrations if necessary, against what Herbert Hill, its labor director, calls "organized labor's racial stranglehold" on hiring practices. The particular target is the building-trades unions, which Wilkins has called "the last bastion against the employment of Negro workers as a policy."

The Federal Model Cities program is the first target. The N.A.A.C.P. will attempt to halt the program unless more minority workers are employed in the building of model cities. Similar efforts will be made to stop all housing built with Federal, state or city funds where such discrimination is practiced.

How successful these efforts to "up-date" the organization will be remains to be seen. The necessity for some action is underlined by Dr. Kenneth Clark, the distinguished black psychologist: "The problem is the N.A.A.C.P. and Wilkins are not doing the job now. The work they did in the past brought us to the point where the urban crisis has become uppermost in importance. But the N.A.A.C.P. is not solving that crisis. Neither are the so-called militants. Who is? I don't know the answer, but I think Wilkins and the N.A.A.C.P. will have to find the answer or become irrelevant."

One thing is certain: as long as Roy Wilkins remains in his post, part of the organization's "relevance" will be its connection and, if possible, cooperation with the white power structure.

On that day last winter when President Nixon was inaugurated, after the Chief had been Hailed, Wilkins turned away from the television set and spoke briefly of the new man in the White House, a man he looks upon with little favor. Yet Wilkins was somewhat optimistic: "I tend to believe the times will shape him. Nixon knows about the problems of the black people, the oil people, the textile people. He cannot help but know about every element of the American people. He may not speak their precise language, but he knows all about them."

Wilkins is not so sanguine now. He is tightening his belt for the battle. Perhaps with some pushing and speaking out and some new lawsuits, Nixon can be moved. Maybe 1970 will produce a more liberal Congress, particularly if the war in Vietnam continues. Maybe, if everything works just right, and the old Wilkins machine is running smoothly, it's just possible that in four years Wilkins will be willing to accept a "Dear Roy" letter from Dick Nixon. It doesn't look likely now, but with two men who have mastered the mechanics of power, it is possible.

Meanwhile, the fight for the unsegregated world will go on. "When it's won," Wilkins says, "the youths who are marching now will realize that there's going to be beer, and double-headers with the Yankees, and ice cream, and mortgages and taxes, and all the things that the whites have in their world, and tedium, too. It's not going to be heaven."

A Strategist Without a Movement

by Thomas R. Brooks

LAST SPRING, leaders of New York City's black communities met with leaders of the United Federation of Teachers to discuss school decentralization. They met at the request of Bayard Rustin, executive director of the A. Philip Randolph Institute and just about the only man in town who could call such a meeting and get it.

The group wrestled with the problems that have since divided the city so bitterly; surprisingly, as one participant put it, "We worked out a proposal [for decentralization] to which all could subscribe." But when the black spokesmen returned to their organizations seeking endorsement, each called back saying, in effect, "Our people say, don't talk to Whitey. It's no go."

Some seven months later, when it seemed as though the whole school mess would land in the laps of the State Legislature and one wing of the U.F.T. was pushing a hard line on the strike, Rustin met with Central Labor Council president Harry Van Arsdale, U.F.T. president Albert Shanker, a group of black trade unionists, and other prominent members of the New York labor establishment. Alarmed Negro spokesmen already had been after Rustin to exert a moderating influence on the U.F.T., which was on a collision course with the black community over school decentralization. As Whitney Young of the Urban League told me, "We all felt it important for Bayard to work on Shanker."

A delegation headed by Van Arsdale, and including Rustin, then met with the U.F.T. negotiations committee "to express the labor movement's concern about [black-white] polarization." Rustin spoke both of his support of the U.F.T.'s fight for teachers' rights—he and A. Philip Randolph, retired head of the Brotherhood of Sleeping Car Porters, were the only Negroes of national prominence to back the union—and of the hatred building up within the black community for the union and all its works. With a restrained lyricism, Rustin made a plea for a settlement that could pave the way for reconciliation between black parents and unionized teachers.

As a result, Rustin has been credited with helping to bring about a nonpunitive settlement of the teachers' strike and with exercising a restraining influence upon the U.F.T. since school resumed.* Shanker denies that this is so; but he did tell me, "Bayard did help moderate the situation, because we were aware of how he put his head on the block."

Aside from defending due process for teachers in his column, which appears every other week in The Amsterdam News and 34 other Negro newspapers throughout the country, Rustin gathered together a group of black trade unionists to do likewise in full-page newspaper advertisements. "You'd think we had committed a heinous crime," Rustin told me, "from the insulting telephone calls, vulgar letters and general denunciation in the press we received from a number of black people."

Within black leadership circles, Rustin has been faintly praised for his role in the school conflict—"Whatever sanity Shanker has shown, Bayard had something to do with it" (Whitney Young)—and loudly damned—"Bayard has no credibility in the black community" (James Farmer). Some believe that he has forever cut himself off from black people, especially the young militants; others are not so sure. Eleanor Holmes Norton, a passionate civil-libertarian lawyer with the American Civil Liberties Union, put it this way: "I'm one of the few calling herself a black mili-

---

* Within the labor movement, Rustin is also credited with forestalling an outburst of black anger that might have led to a black-white split within the city's trade unions.

tant who considers that Bayard still has something to contribute to us." Mrs. Norton is convinced, however, that Rustin must change course, "cut away from the current old-fashioned and machine-driven labor movement." Sad to say, she added, "Bayard is attached to old radical forms rather than to building new radical institutions."

"Rustin?" snapped one angry young militant. "He's No. 4 Uncle Tom." (The others, in uncertain order, are the N.A.A.C.P.'s Roy Wilkins, Randolph and the late Martin Luther King. Whitney Young, possibly because his Urban League is a source of money for black projects, appears to be in favor with black militants.)

Elegant, urbane, with a large, high-cheekboned face, expressive beneath a bushy shock of gray hair, Rustin plays a unique role in our politics. He is to the labor movement, to liberals and religious groups what Whitney Young is to corporate executives, the foundations and the business world—contact man, go-between and interpreter of the Negro movement. As organizer of the 1963 March on Washington, which brought more than 200,000 blacks and whites together in the major civil-rights demonstration of our time, Rustin came on the intellectual and political scene as the most articulate strategist of the drive for Negro equality. As a pacifist, a Socialist, an early advocate of street demonstrations and marches, Rustin enjoyed a range of relationships that strengthened his position as chief tactician of the civil-rights coalition. As Dr. John Morsell of the N.A.A.C.P. said, "Almost no one is able to work with such a diverse body of people as Bayard." That ability is Rustin's greatest source of power and influence.

Rustin's standing with the older elements of the coalition— those labor and liberal forces that first grouped around the New Deal and which showed surprising staying power in the latest election—has never been higher. Rustin is an honored guest at trade-union conventions and banquets and a speaker eagerly sought by the Anti-Defamation League, the American Jewish Committee, the Jewish Labor Committee and black universities. Last year, he was named chairman of the executive committee of the Leadership Conference, a civil-rights lobby of 115 organizations, at the suggestion of Wilkins. When Vice President

Hubert H. Humphrey came to New York City during the election campaign for the traditional noon-time garment center rally, Rustin was one of two companions riding in the candidate's car.

At one time, Rustin was consulted on nearly every major project planned by the Student Nonviolent Coordinating Committee (Snick), which a few short years ago was the most militant wing of the Negro movement and as such has since been supplanted by the Panthers. In the early nineteen-sixties, Rustin was clearly something of a hero to the young militants in CORE and in Snick. As Tom Kahn, then a young, white student at Howard, recalls Rustin's influence on Stokely Carmichael and others: "Bayard gave them a sense of being radical as well as being Negro. It was something emotional. There is this quality of Bayard's—a certain fiery anger in him, like DuBois had. Bayard gave them a glimpse of radicalism that had status and prestige behind it. It was in his voice, his accent. DuBois was a cigar-smoking, cane-carrying gentleman with radical ideas. And to them Bayard was something like that."

The polarization that has now set in between blacks and whites at almost all levels of discourse has cut Rustin out of New Left and black militant circles almost entirely. In intellectual terms, for example, Rustin commands the attention of the readers of The New Leader, Commentary and, say, Partisan Review, while he has lost that of the swingers' Village Voice and of the pop guerrillas' New York Review of Books. Ever fickle, intellectual fashion has taken up Eldridge Cleaver and dropped Rustin. He has lost luster among WASP's, at least those who favor black capitalism, Negro self-help and separatist tendencies. "It's not Bayard's fault," said Arnold Aronson, secretary of the Leadership Conference, "it reflects a trend." In fine, a dedicated integrationist, Rustin is a strategist suddenly without a movement. His people—black and white—appear to be drawing back on either side of a deepening chasm.

For a man in essentially an uncomfortable position, Rustin is remarkably relaxed. Although he has parted politically, though not personally in all cases, with many of his former colleagues, Rustin is singularly free of bitterness and recrimination. Whenever I mentioned an old comrade-in-arms with whom Rustin has publicly quarreled, he said, "Oh, we still talk." His incessant cigarette-smoking is the only sign of the nervous energy bottled up in an athlete's build, imperceptibly thickening mid-waist at 58. His office, a large corner room on the sixth floor overlooking Park Avenue South and 21st Street, is sparsely furnished. Across from his desk hangs a great black-and-white photograph of the people massed in front of the Lincoln Memorial on Aug. 28, 1963, along the mall toward the Washington Monument rising in the background. There is a warm, evocative head-and-shoulders picture of Martin Luther King and another showing King on the podium, delivering his "I-Have-a-Dream" speech. On the wall over the low bookcase is a hastily sketched street map of Memphis, showing the route of the memorial march for King last April, and in the lower left corner of the map is Rustin's police pass. It's a very effective piece of natural art.

"This period will pass, too," said Rustin, looking rather like a mahogany-skinned Cesar Romero and waving his left hand, a cigarette between the first two fingers, and a good-sized onyx ring on the little finger. We were talking about black militants, black capitalists and the present state of the Negro movement. Rustin, who speaks with a slight sibilance caused by a broken upper molar, smashed by a chain-gang guard, added, "Withdrawal is nothing new for the Negro. Back in the eighteen-forties, the free Negro came to believe that we couldn't make it here, so a fair number left for Liberia. Then, after 1877, when Union troops were withdrawn from the South, the Negro internalized his problem and we had Booker T. Washington telling us: 'Don't worry about voting rights, look to yourself.' After 1918, we had Marcus Garvey's 'Back-to-Africa' movement and today you find the same syndrome—great expectations, a worsening of economic and social conditions, and a turning inward and toward Africa."

Toward the new, young black militants, Rustin displays a certain ambivalence. "It's not that we don't need militance," Rustin told me, "but that we need militants who can tread that thin line, and not go over to where militance causes reaction."

Rustin, too, is impatient with the young's politics, or rather, lack of politics. "Anybody," he said, "can say to white people, 'Roll over, we don't need you.' But that is not a political expression. The alternative to politics is to cop out and talk about hair, about what name you want to be called, and about soul food. Wearing my hair Afro style, calling myself an Afro-American, and eating all the chitterlings I can find are not going to affect Congress."

While conceding that King's murder has created a despair that turns the young to violence, Rustin remains firm in his belief in nonviolence. "Three courses are open to Negroes who are incapable of advocating nonviolence," he said. "They can end up in jail. They can end up in exile. They can end up shot— and probably by Negroes." He is particularly alarmed by new tendencies toward violence within the Negro community. "There are no parallels in our past to the Panthers," he said. "The Muslims did not bother anyone not in their sect. We now have the Panthers and some in CORE who resort to threats against individuals and against anyone in the movement who doesn't agree with them. They can exercise a veto power over the center." This prospect disturbs Rustin profoundly.

He draws on his cigarette. "If the coalition cannot be reconstituted and rebuilt, what is the alternative? Certainly not Negroes running back to their ghettos. Anybody who wants to build more businesses in the Negro ghetto, anybody who wants to rebuild the Negro ghetto can go ahead. But all you shall have secured is the institutionalization of two Americas—segregated and unequal."

What would he suggest? "I would urge young Negroes who want to go into business to work their way into General Motors; to work their way into steel production; to work their way into those enterprises in America which produce real money, and are not being wiped out either by big business or by cybernetics."

Rustin hasn't much use for black capitalism, an idea which "makes everybody feel good. Nixon picked it up. CORE picked it up. But I would never advise the young to open a small grocery store. The A&P people own acres and acres of land on which they grow peas. They simply back up their machinery into the pea patch and in 15 minutes the peas are in the can and labeled. So, if we are going into business we have to think straight: A&P can move next door any day and put our little shop out of business." He added, "I'm all in favor of Negroes opening co-op stores and shoe shops in Harlem. Negro youngsters ought to see Negroes owning businesses. That's good for psychological reasons. But what the Negro community is going to discover is that the Negro businessman will ultimately be a businessman before he is a Negro, just as white businessmen are businessmen before they are white. The black-capitalist stuff essentially is going to benefit only a small class within the Negro community."

"Political alliances are needed," Rustin argued, "to achieve all the programs that will solve poverty for all Americans. The Negro will gain nothing economically in this nation simply because he is a Negro. One-tenth of the population cannot go to Congress for the billions which are needed for jobs, for new transportation facilities, new roads, new hospitals, new libraries. Negro youngsters will not be truly educated until there is a plan whereby every person capable of going to school—from public school through the Ph.D.—gets his tuition and books free and a salary for going to school. We must have free and better medical care for everybody. And a guaranteed income for all who cannot work, or who are too old to work. To get these things, we must go with other like-minded people: the labor movement, Catholics, Protestants, Jews, liberals and students. Together we must create a political force and a political alliance, or an atmosphere which makes that alliance possible."

But it isn't only black militants that have copped out of the alliance; Rustin believes that white liberals are equally if not more culpable. "The majority of whites," he told me, "are taking the Kerner Report as a call merely to examine their individual attitudes. All over the country people are beating their breasts crying *mea culpa*—'I'm so sorry that I am a racist.' If that is all —just that Americans are racist—then the only answer would be to line everybody up, all 200 million of us, line up 200,000 psychiatrists, and we'd all lie on couches for the first 10 years trying to understand the problems and the next 10 years learning how to deal with them.

"Still the fundamental problem," Rustin added, "will not be solved by sitting around examining our innards, but by getting out and fighting for institutional changes." He recalled that while working with the N.A.A.C.P. some years ago to integrate the University of Texas, he ran into a battery of arguments against letting Negroes in: They would be raping white girls; they did not wash; they were dumb and could not learn; they ate with their fingers. "These attitudes were not destroyed because the N.A.A.C.P. psychoanalyzed white students or held seminars to teach them about black people. They were destroyed because

Thurgood Marshall got the Supreme Court to rule against and destroy the institution of segregated education. At that point, the private views of white students became irrelevant."

Rustin, however, is not optimistic about the possibilities for change. "We're going to get more black rage and white fear," he told me. "The burning of the ghettos and the vote for George Wallace have the same root—the economic and social inequities of this country. People have TV—and cars—but everyone believes they've got six months before the bottom falls out." The white worker fears that the black worker will take his job; the black fears that he won't have a job because of the white worker's efforts to defend *his* job. Still, Rustin is not so naive as to believe that black anger will be disarmed merely by jobs, decent housing and a good education. "Every Negro in the nation," he told me, "could be provided with those things, and we would still have a revolt because Negroes want, deeply and sincerely, to share in the decision-making process." What has happened instead, Rustin said, is that "this society is systematically teaching them that it will respond only to tactics of desperation and violence.

"This is the tragedy of a society which will not make basic changes but will vote promises and token concessions—so long as rioting goes to point X. When Negroes rioted in Chicago, Mayor Daley gave them $8 sprinklers so that they could take showers in the streets; when Negroes rioted in New York the establishment made a Negro head of the Harlem police precinct." But when rioting reaches X plus one, Rustin predicted, "We are in trouble, for then there will be the most vigorous repression. Then there will be vigilantism. Even more important, you cannot repress one-tenth of the population, no matter how badly elements of it behave, without threatening the civil liberties of everyone in the nation. Where there are not civil liberties, we cannot make social progress. That I believe is the problem before us."

Rustin remains an integrationist, despite strong currents in the opposite direction within the black community—and despite white intellectuals and white liberals who approve of such trends on the grounds that this is what black Americans want. "There's no need to hold a finger to the wind to find out what people think, then agree with it," Rustin told me, adding, "Spokesmen ought to educate their people."

This is what impresses me about Rustin—aside from his dedication to justice and to nonviolence as a way of life—he is willing to go it alone. He shares with two of his heroes—Norman Thomas and Randolph—a quality of moral engagement, a passion for truth no matter the consequences, and a generous anger. Something of this comes through in his style, so highly articulate when compared to the monosyllabic sloganeering of the young militants. You catch it in his speeches,* as in his recent comments on the current rise in black anti-Semitism before a conference of the Anti-Defamation League of B'Nai B'rith: "For the things which must be done, I request the understanding, the cooperation and the aid of Jews. I do so knowing that there is Negro anti-Semitism and knowing how Jews must feel when they hear some Negro extremists talk. To hear these young Negroes speaking material directly from 'Mein Kampf' must bring up terrible memories, shocking inner turmoil. But in these times of confusion I recommend to Jews what I do for myself in times of confusion. I go back and read the Jewish prophets, fundamentally Isaiah and Jeremiah. And I want you to know that if every Jew in the United States—not just a minority of extremists—called me a black nigger, and said we don't need you to speak out against anti-Semitism in Poland, we can handle it ourselves, I would not stop speaking out against anti-Semitism in Poland. I would continue to speak because I could do no other, because Isaiah and Jeremiah have taught me to be against injustice wherever it is, and first of all in myself . . . remember that the issue never was, and never can be, simply a problem of Jew and gentile or black and white. The problem is man's inhumanity to man. . . ."

* Rustin is one of our great extemporaneous speakers. He rarely uses a prepared text, and often jots his notes on backs of envelopes, the odd scrap of paper, or even on match folders. While most speakers can manage a line or two of poetry, Rustin is the only one of many I've heard who could break out in song. And this only once in my acquaintanceship. At the Norman Thomas Fund "Rededication," Rustin, gripping the podium with both hands, his head thrown back and looking as I imagine Old Testament prophets must have looked, opened with "No More Auction Block," and closed with "Oh, Freedom." It was magnificent, evoking a silence that seemed to last and last until shattered by applause and bravos and tears.

Rustin's vision is essentially radical, but with a conservative bias. As a mutual friend said to me, after listening to Rustin demolish an opponent in a debate, "Bayard always comes on from the left to move you to the center." Rustin is one of the few radicals I know who, almost instinctively, grasps the wisdom of Alexander Herzen, who once wrote, "An end that is infinitely remote is not an end, but, if you like, a trap; an end must be nearer—it ought to be at the very least, the laborer's wage or pleasure in the work done." As a strategist, Rustin is a firm believer in the morale-building, forward, cumulative thrust of victories, even small victories. As he put it recently, "The slogan ought to be, 'Integration where possible, and improvement where integration is not immediately possible.'"

Rustin strongly identifies the Negroes' interests with the trade-union movement. "Not a single bill affecting the poor, including the civil-rights legislation, could have got through Congress without the labor lobbyists in Washington. If Negroes all over the country were making the $2 an hour minimum wage demanded by the A.F.L.-C.I.O., we would have in our pockets each year more money than has been spent to date on the whole war on poverty. And, all the war on poverty could not do for the *Lumpenproletariat* what trade unions have done by organizing over two million of the working poor."

Such views, of course, give bite to James Farmer's crack, "Bayard's commitment is to labor, not to the black man. His belief that the black man's problem is economic, not racist, runs counter to black community thinking now." And it is true that Rustin is more a product of the radical movement than he is of the Negro movement as such.*

When I first met Bayard Rustin he was singing folk songs at a Yipsel (Young People's Socialist League) party back in the late nineteen-forties. For the more romantic among us, Rustin epitomized the radical as a man of action, just as Dwight MacDonald, then editor of Politics, epitomized the radical as a man of thought. Rustin, as I recall, had recently returned from 30 days on a North Carolina chain gang and his exposé in The New York Post

---

* While Rustin is very much a loner, his political kitchen cabinet comprises author Michael Harrington; his associate director, Norman Hill; administrative secretary, Rochelle Horowitz, and Tom Kahn, executive director of the League for Industrial Democracy.

helped bring on the abolition of the chain gang in that state. He had been arrested for participating in the first Freedom Ride—The Journey of Reconciliation by bus through the upper South to test enforcement of the 1946 ban on discrimination in interstate travel. Rustin and George Hauser, then staff secretaries of the Fellowship of Reconciliation, originated the test. Rustin, then in his middle 30's, had already lived several radical lifetimes—as a Communist, a pacifist and anti-Stalinist radical.

Rustin was born on March 17, 1910, in West Chester, Pa., a community of "some 15,000 when I was growing up" roughly 20 miles west of Philadelphia where the Quakers had relocated many black freedmen before the Civil War. Rustin was raised by his grandparents; to this day he thinks of his four aunts as "sister-aunts." His grandfather's father was a slave in nearby Maryland. His grandmother was two-thirds Delaware Indian, and had been raised by Quakers. Rustin's grandfather worked for the Elks and catered on the side. "His turtle soup was known all over the country," Rustin recalls, "and we lived on party leftovers," a rich diet of soups, *pâtés,* lobsters and cakes and pies. A legacy of Rustin's upbringing is his crazy tastes—he is "a gourmet who loves pig knuckles," as a close friend put it. Nonviolence was something Rustin learned from his Quaker grandmother, although the family was brought up within the African Methodist Episcopal Church.

Young Bayard attended a segregated grade school and an integrated high school, where he played left guard on the football team. He was a track star, a champion in tennis, and class valedictorian. (Rustin no longer plays tennis or any other sport but, believe me, a walk with him is exercise.) After graduation, he went to Wilberforce in Ohio, left for Cheyney State Teachers College in Pennsylvania where he got a better scholarship and then came to New York City where a "sister" taught in the public schools. He attended City College nights. Somewhere along the line, he picked up an elegant diction, with a clipped quasi-British cadence, which is now so much a part of him that he is often taken for a West Indian. If one listens carefully, however, one can detect the Philadelphian, or Eastern Pennsylvanian in his accent in "ou" words like about.

To earn money, Rustin sang with Leadbelly and Josh White at Cafe Society Downtown. Friends treasure two rare recordings

Rustin made for the Fellowship of Reconciliation 15 years ago. One features Bayard, a countertenor, singing Elizabethan and folk songs; the other, James Farmer narrating and Rustin singing spirituals and protest songs. Rustin plays the piano, harpsichord, lute, lyre and guitar. He sometimes entertains friends with a talk on the history of Negro music and how sorrow songs led to jazz. A tea-drinker, Rustin likes Scotch when on the rounds of his favorite Harlem bars.

Rustin joined the Young Communist League in 1936. "They seemed the only people who had civil rights at heart," Rustin now explains. "The party played a very active role in most civil-rights cases, like Scottsboro." During the Stalin-Hitler Pact, Rustin was asked to form a committee against discrimination in the armed forces. The day afer Hitler turned East, Rustin was called in and told to dismantle the committee. He refused, and decided to quit the party and managed to do so just before it expelled him.

When in the early forties A. Philip Randolph organized his first March on Washington, threatening to bring hundreds of thousands of Negroes to Washington unless fair-employment practices were instituted in the nation's defense industries, Rustin volunteered to work with Randolph and became youth organizer for the march. As a conscientious objector Rustin might have chosen to go to a work camp during the war, but since only religious objectors enjoyed that privilege, Rustin chose protest and went to jail in 1942. He served 28 months. While in prison, Rustin's adherence to the tenets of nonviolence was severely tested on numerous occasions. He is, after all, a large man and it isn't easy for the physically strong to restrain themselves when attacked. Yet Bayard stopped a giant bloodthirsty Southerner dead in his tracks by offering the man a chance to clobber him.

After the war, Rustin gravitated toward civil-rights activity rather than radical civil protests. Immediately following his chaingang experience, he worked wih Randolph on the Committee to End Discrimination in the Armed Forces. When President Truman ended such discrimination with his famous executive order, Randolph dismantled the committee. Rustin and the "Young Turks," however, wanted to keep it going until the last vestige of discrimination was gone and until protestors who had refused to register for the draft were released from jail. When Randolph wanted a press conference at 4 in the afternoon to announce his decision, Rustin called it for him and then called one of his own for 10 that morning, at which he roundly denounced Randolph. "That was a dirty trick," Rustin ruefully concedes. "We're getting some of the same medicine today from the young people." As a result of his oneupmanship, Rustin did not see Randolph for several years. "When I finally did," Rustin told me, "Mr. Randolph rose from behind his desk, came toward me with his hand out, saying, 'Well, Bayard, where have you been?' "

In 1955, after Martin Luther King became leader of the year-long bus boycott by 42,000 Montgomery Negroes, he received a wire from author Lillian Smith saying, "There's a young man in New York with whom you should be in touch." Rustin was soon off for Montgomery.

The Rev. Ralph T. Abernathy later said, "Rustin was wearing blue jeans, his hair looked funny, but that fellow sure could work." Rustin quickly displayed the knack he has of grasping the essentials to any larger scheme of success. He soon discovered that the group had nothing in the way of a motor pool for transporting people to and from work. Asking himself where Negroes thereabouts would have some economic independence and cars, he went to Birmingham and solicited the needed automobiles from black steelworkers.

Rustin did research for King, sat in on all the major strategy meetings, drafted the plan for what became the Southern Christian Leadership Conference, and in general acted as King's man in the North. When King was indicted in 1960 on charges of perjury in connection with his income tax returns, Rustin as director of a defense committee raised $150,000 to fight the case and win it.

Later that year, Rustin, acting for King and Randolph, organized civil-rights demonstrations outside the Democratic and Republican convention halls (18,000 picketed the former, 10,000 the latter). Adam Clayton Powell, "for Powell reasons," as someone once put it, or perhaps because he wanted to forestall the demonstration at the Democratic Convention, sent word to King that he would publicly attack Rustin's character unless King fired Rustin. "If there's going to be a mess," Rustin told King, "I'll go away," which he did in the interest of harmony.

For a time, Rustin was at rather loose ends. Rumors were circulated in the Negro community that he was a draft-dodging

Communist. Just about the only respected Negro leader who kept up his relationship with Rustin was Randolph, who simply said, "I will not hear that discussed in my presence." Rustin's reputation was at such a low point that Roy Wilkins would not allow Rustin to sit in on the early planning conference for what became 1963's March on Washington—even though the whole project had been Rustin's idea in the first place. Randolph proposed that Rustin direct the march; others vetoed the notion, insisting that Randolph serve as director. Randolph agreed to do so only on the condition that he could name his own staff. The leadership agreed. Randolph promptly named Rustin organizer of the march.

The success of the march made Rustin. When the Rev. Milton A. Galamison's 1964 school boycott for desegregation appeared to be failing, Rustin was called in to save it; when also that year the Mississippi Freedom Movement party delegates arrived at the Atlantic City convention demanding seats, Rustin was called in to help work out a compromise, which ultimately led to the seating of an integrated delegation to this year's convention; when worried Democrats wanted to discourage "let's-go-fishing" reactions to the 1968 election campaign among black voters, they turned to Rustin, who launched a counterdrive within 10 key black communities.

If Rustin's greatest strengths are as a strategist, tactician, and, to a lesser extent, as political analyst and philosopher, his greatest weakness as a spokesman is his lack of a mass base. Rustin has either gone it alone or attached himself to another—A. J. Muste, in his earlier pacifist days; Randolph, off and on for almost 30 years; and King.

Since Randolph—always "Mr. Randolph" to Rustin despite the length of their filial-like relationship—retired last year as president of the Brotherhood of Sleeping Car Porters, Rustin has increasingly been "sitting in" for him on boards and delegations within the civil-rights movement and elsewhere.

Most recently Rustin sat in on an Urban Coalition delegation to then-President-elect Nixon. The question is whether Rustin will be seated permanently within the upper echelon of the civil-rights movement when Randolph retires from active political life.

Meantime, Rustin has created an institutional base for himself. He set up in 1965 the A. Philip Randolph Institute and its tax-free sister, the A. Philip Randolph Education Fund, backed, in part, by the labor movement and by foundation grants for specific projects. Rustin obviously could not go on forever operating out of a hat, or out of his apartment in the I.L.G.W.U Penn Station South housing cooperative.

Rustin, however, has by no means lost touch with the street Negro. When he organized the Memphis march to commemorate King's death, the first thing he did was to see the young toughs who had "messed up" an earlier march organized by King. Rustin made them marshals, responsible for the security of the march. No one was to be let through to the speaker's stand unless he had a pass; when Walter Reuther arrived, saying he had an invitation from Rustin, the youths said, "Show it." Reuther did not have it with him so the youngsters sent one of their number to the stand to see "if it's O.K. with Mr. Rustin."

When I asked Rustin, "What next?" he said, "President Nixon must understand that we are all for unity, for binding up the wounds. But it cannot be done with billy-clubs, or Mace, or because President Nixon wants it done. We'll have no peace in this nation until we bring the *Lumpenproletariat* into the working classes—and into a social-and-economic program that does away with the inequality between the haves and the have-nots. Then we shall be together."

Part 3

EPILOGUE:
THE ASCENDANCY OF
POLITICAL ACTION

AS BLACK protest became less confrontational, concerted political action emerged as a workable alternative. The implications of this growing black political power for the nation's politics have been most strikingly manifested in the Democratic Party by the two campaigns of Jesse Jackson for the Presidential nomination. The perceptive 1971 article by Andrew Greeley, a white specialist in the role of race and ethnicity in American life, speculates about the kind of gains that would result from the addition of a black to a national ticket.

For a Black Vice President in 1972

by Andrew M. Greeley

IT IS NEXT summer and the Democratic party has just nominated on the third ballot Edmund Sixtus Muskie as its candidate for the Presidency of the United States. In one of the God-awful hotels along Collins Avenue in Miami Beach, Muskie and his advisers are agonizing over the question of the Vice-Presidency. If it looks as if there is a possibility of a fourth party, made up of dissident left-wing Democrats, Muskie will have to secure his left flank and the Vice-Presidential candidate must be someone who will appeal to the liberals, the young, and the blacks—Senator Tunney or Senator Stevenson, or, just possibly, Mayor Lindsay. If, on the other hand, the left flank seems reasonably safe, the obvious thing for candidate Muskie to do is to follow the 1960 strategy of John Kennedy and seek out a presentably liberal Southerner, such as Georgia's Jimmy Carter. Thus, a year before the event, it appears that the Vice-Presidential nominee will be either a young Northerner or a liberal Southerner.

At least the traditional political calculus would dictate such a presentation of alternatives. But though these times are not quite as extraordinary as commentators such as Frederick Dutton would have us believe, they are still extraordinary enough. Muskie and his ad visers ought to consider a third possibility: the nomination of a black man for the Vice-Presidency.

The Senator will remember in his Collins Avenue suite that he said quite candidly back in September, 1971—and this is fact, not scenario—that he did not think the country was ready yet for a black Vice President, though he thought that it *ought* to be ready. But after touring the country for almost a year, analyzing survey data, and listening to the deep longing of Americans for reconciliation, candidate Muskie finds himself in a position where he must reappraise his judgment: maybe the country is much more ready for an integrated Presidential ticket than he had thought in September, 1971.

It would have to be a rather special kind of black man. His credentials in the black movement would have to be impeccable; and yet he would also have to be the sort of person who could appeal to the white American majority as a representative of that vast number of Americans, both white and black, who believe in reconciliation and brotherhood which transcends—though by no means eliminates—racial, religious, social, ethnic and geographical diversity.

There are a number of such potential black Vice-Presidential candidates available. The one who comes most obviously to my mind is Andrew Young, the black Southern Christian Conference leader who ran well in the Atlanta Congressional district last year. An articulate, persuasive person with strong TV presence, Young is a man who simply refuses to hate, no matter what the provocation. He is one of the most remarkable and impressive human beings I have ever met, though he is by no means the only man who would fill the bill. The imaginative political strokes are many.

(1) A black Vice-Presidential candidate would have tremendous symbolic impact on race relations in the United States. Men do not live by symbols alone. You can't eat symbols, live in them, or take them as medicine. But man is still a symbol-creating animal. He orders and interprets his reality by his symbols, and he uses the symbols to reconstruct that reality. A black moderate running for Vice President would be an extremely powerful symbol of the possibility of achieving racial justice and harmony in American society. A symbol by itself, of course, would not create either justice or harmony, but it might create an atmosphere in which justice and harmony (by which, of course, one means *relative* justice and *relative* harmony) would become possible.

(2) A national ticket made up of a Polish-American and a black American might go a long way to polishing the tarnish off Ameri-

ca's international luster. Is there another major (or, for that matter, minor) nation in the world which would have racial integration in its two highest positions? And such integration at that. A Polish ethnic for President and a black man for Vice President! It would say a great deal to the rest of the world about the possibilities of cultural pluralisms.

(3) A black Vice-Presidential candidate would reinforce the possibly flagging black loyalty to the Democratic party. A more serious threat to the Democrats than a black separatist party would be an organized or unorganized black movement to "go fishing" on Election Day. The Democratic party may as well face the blunt fact that probably more than one-fifth of its regular voters are black. At some time in the not too distant future it will have no choice but to nominate a black Vice President. Indeed, if the Democrats lose in 1972, I wonder if they would ever win again without a black man on the ticket. In 1972, the Democrats may still have a choice—they could still do for reasons of political statesmanship what they will in the near future have to do for reasons of political necessity.

(4) Not only would a black Vice-Presidential candidate almost automatically guarantee the support of the liberal wing of the Democratic party and most of the young activists, it would also appeal quite strongly to the large majority of the voters under 25 who are not activists but who would still be powerfully moved by such a vigorous and imaginative stroke on the part of the Democratic leadership. The youthful enthusiast could not say that the Democrats offered nothing new and provided no meaningful alternative to the Republicans.

An integrated Presidential ticket could have a profound impact on the political behavior of many young people under 25. Frederick Dutton and others quite correctly note that the young are more likely to describe themselves as political "independents." However, such scholars as Seymour Lipset and Everett Ladd have pointed out that, there is nothing particularly unusual about this phenomenon. The 20's are years of "sorting out" such things as religious and political affiliations. Young people are always more likely to be "independents" than their elders, and even more so in times of crisis. However, the fundamental political experiences of their 20's shape political affiliations for the rest of their lives. The permanent Democratic majority since 1932 is in substantial part the result of a "generational experience" of those who came of political age during the New Deal. An integrated national ticket in 1972 might be a fundamental and "shaping" experience for those who will vote for the first time in that election. It is worth remembering that the number of new voters in 1972 will be the largest in history and probably the largest that will ever be. A black Vice-Presidential candidate could go a long way toward winning the permanent allegiance of many of these new voters to the Democratic party—just as Franklin Roosevelt won their parents and grandparents 40 years ago.

THERE are two principal objections to this strategy: one from the left and the other from the right: The left-wing objections would be that a black moderate running for the Vice-Presidency would be one more example of "tokenism," and would in fact be an attempt on the part of white America to "co-opt" blacks. Those who would offer the objection are capable of making a great deal of noise but have relatively few voters at their disposal. The Vice-Presidency may be only a "token," but it is a pretty damned big token and one that was not available to American Catholics for more than a century and a half, and is not available to American Jews even today. Furthermore, a moderately militant black candidate would be far more representative of black America than would be an extremist. The extremists may get the media coverage, but they no more represent a vast majority of black Americans than Tony Imperiale represents Italian-Americans or George Wallace represents WASP Americans.

Besides, political symbols are two-edged swords. For just as an integrated ticket would co-opt blacks for the cause of the Democratic center, so it would necessarily commit the Democratic center to the cause of blacks in a more profound way than it has been committed in the past.

A far more serious objection, from the point of view of a professional politician, would be the argument that the American people are not ready yet for a black face in the chair of the United States Senate. If one believes, as apparently do many political commentators, that the American population is fundamentally "racist," then this objection may be conclusive, but I would argue that, as in so many other matters, the commentators know nothing about the people whom they so glibly describe. The most recent Gallup polls show that almost two-thirds of the American population said that it would not object to voting for a "qualified" black candidate for the Presidency—a substantially higher proportion than were willing to say they would support a Catholic candidate for the Presidency in 1958. If Americans are ready to assert that they would accept a "qualified" black for the Presidency, *a fortiori*, they would be willing to accept a black Vice President.

The commentators—and perhaps the candidates' advisers, too—may well respond that people are simply not telling the truth to the Gallup interviewers. Maybe they are not, and maybe again they are. Certainly the Gallup interviews about a Catholic candidate in the late fifties were quite precise predictors of what happened in 1960. The Gallup data do not necessarily indicate that the public is ready for a black Vice President, but at least the Gallup data suggest that the public *might* be ready and this is a possibility that between now and the summer of 1972 ought to be explored at great length.

Actually, whether the majority of Americans are bigots is hardly a very fruitful way of posing the question of whether the time is right for a black Vice-Presidential candidate. Practically all of us are capable of bigoted responses under certain circumstances and, as the work of Robert Coles has showed, even the most prejudiced of us are capable of nonprejudiced responses under other circumstances. The critical question is what sort of circumstances are most likely to appeal to that aspect of our personality which is not prejudiced. The Gallup data create the possibility that the right kind of black candidate, saying the right kinds of things on a television screen, would not only not be a liability to the Democratic party, but might be a very strong asset.

Americans—even the most prejudiced Americans—pride themselves on their "fairness." The very clever appeal of the Kennedy clan in the West Virginia primary made "fairness" to a Catholic candidate the central issue in a state where anti-Catholicism would, under normal circumstances, have put the Kennedys at an extreme disadvantage. Americans—even the most prejudiced Americans—are also proud of what they think to be the "enlightened," "progressive" attitudes of American citizens. (I will not argue at this point with the contention that the attitudes are not in fact enlightened or progressive; I'm simply asserting that Americans like to think of themselves as enlightened and progressive.) An argument that the black Vice-Presidential candidate represents a dramatic, imaginative and creative breakthrough in interracial relations from which the whole world would learn would not be without considerable appeal.

Such an approach might be unduly devious. However, there is, I suspect, an approach which no one could call devious; there is a deep hunger in American society at the present time for reconciliation. The plea of the young woman with the placard to President Nixon—"Bring us together again"—echoes, unless I miss my guess, the powerful, pervasive and profound sentiment in American society. People are tired of violence, hatred, anger, shooting, name-calling demonstration and other forms of "extremism." Mr. Nixon's political past, and indeed his political instincts in the present, make it impossible for him either to resonate or respond to this appeal for reconciliation. Part of Senator Muskie's attractiveness may well be the Lincolnesque aura of being a great reconciliator. A candidate who chooses a black running mate in the name of reconciliation combined with social progress will, unless I miss my guess, touch deep wellsprings of the American political symbol system. The very boldness and daring of such an attempt to "bring us together" would make a deep impression on middle America.

Furthermore, the symbol of the pluralist ideal runs strong in the American political and social imagination. Those of us who are intellectually sophisticated are likely to dismiss as Fourth of July imagery the rhetoric of a "nation of nations" and the theme of citizens of different nationalities, races and creeds joining together in a common enterprise while still maintaining their own diversity. It is true that reality does not fully live up to the symbol (it never does), but that the symbol persists in the face of so many obvious failures proves it is a powerful symbol. Cant is rarely something that has no meaning at all; it is rather the overuse or the abuse of something that has a great deal of meaning for many of those who hear it; the line between a valid symbol and cant is a thin one, though most people are better at drawing it than we intellectuals are inclined to concede. A skilled campaigner could touch profound and vigorous resources in the American political personality by appealing to the theme of unity among diversity—a theme which would be correctly reinforced by an integrated national ticket.

I HOPE I am not misunderstood. I am not suggesting that there ought to be a black Vice President as a means of smoothing over the causes of unrest in the United States. In any event, I do not think that unrest can be smoothed over. What I am saying is that most human beings have a deep need for some kind of social order, stability and harmony, that this need is especially profound in American society at the present time—probably no less profound for blacks than for whites.

The healing of wounds, the ministering of reconciliation is not, in my judgment, a dispensation from the obligation in work for social progress. On the contrary, it is, I think an absolutely essential prerequisite for further social progress. Unless I misread completely the survey data on racial attitudes of the American public, the average citizen by no means is opposed to major social restructuring of the society. Indeed, data collected by the University of Michigan would indicate that the majority of Americans are willing to pay a 10 per cent increase in their income taxes in order to eliminate problems which cause urban riots.

The American public, I suspect from reading the survey data, is far more favorably disposed to racial change than its leaders and its social commentators are prepared to acknowledge. But this readiness to accept major social change at the present time, it seems to me, cannot be activated for politically constructive purposes unless the public is persuaded that there is in the midst of rapid social change some underlying fundamental harmony and order. A black Vice-Presidential candidate like Andrew Young on the television screen would unleash all kinds of positive and constructive forces within the American political system. It would not satisfy those who believe the society can be reformed only by first destroying it, but they are a tiny fraction of the population, no matter how vehement and articulate they may be. A Presidential ticket which powerfully symbolizes the possibility of both change and harmony, both justice and reconciliation, both militant loyalty to one's own community and a sense of brotherhood for one's fellow human beings, regardless of race or religion or geography or social class, would be extraordinarily attractive to a vast majority of Americans, no matter what their color.

It is a calculated risk, of course, for Muskie or for any Democratic nominee; it might blow up, it might give Mr. Nixon four more years in the White House on a silver platter.

But it also might be one of the most enlightened and creative political ploys of American history. A bicentennial celebration presided over by a Polish-American President and a black Vice President is something that this nation would not soon forget.

Suggested Reading

Alan B. Anderson and George W. Pickering, *Confronting the Color Line: The Broken Promise of the Civil Rights Movement in Chicago.* Athens: University of Georgia Press, 1986.

Inge Powell Bell, *CORE and the Strategy of Nonviolence.* New York: Random House, 1968.

John Bracey, August Meier and Elliott Rudwick, eds. *Black Nationalism in America*, Indianapolis: Bobbs-Merrill, 1970.

Taylor Branch, *Parting the Waters: America in the King Years, 1954–1963.* New York: Simon and Schuster, 1988.

Clayborne Carson, *In Struggle: SNCC and the Black Awakening of the 1960's.* Cambridge, Mass.: Harvard University Press, 1981.

Stokely Carmichael and Charles Hamilton, *Black Power: The Politics of Liberation in America.* New York: Random House, 1967.

David R. Colburn, *Racial Change and Community Crisis: St. Augustine, Florida, 1877–1980.* New York: Columbia University Press, 1985.

William R. Corson, *Promise or Peril: The Black College Student in America.* New York: Norton, 1970.

Angela Davis—An Autobiography. New York: Random House, 1974.

E.U. Essien-Udom, *Black Nationalism: A Search for an Identity in America.* Chicago: University of Chicago Press, 1962.

Sara Evans, *Personal Politics: The Roots of Women's Liberation in the Civil Rights Movement and the New Left.* New York: Knopf, 1979.

Adam Fairclough, *To Redeem the Soul of America: The Southern Christian Leadership Conference and Martin Luther King, Jr.* Athens: University of Georgia Press, 1987.

James Farmer, *Lay Bare the Heart: An Autobiography of the Civil Rights Movement*. New York: Arbor House, 1985.

David J. Garrow, *Bearing the Cross: Martin Luther King, Jr. and the Southern Christian Leadership Conference*. New York: William Morrow, 1986.

Peter Goldman, *The Death and Life of Malcolm X*. 2nd ed. Urbana: University of Illinois Press, 1979.

Lorraine Hansberry, *The Movement: Documentary of a Struggle for Equality*. New York: Simon and Schuster, 1964.

Lewis Killian and Charles Grigg, *Racial Crisis in America: Leadership in Conflict*. Englewood Cliffs, N.J.: Prentice-Hall, 1964.

Julius Lester, *Look Out Whitey! Black Power's Gon' Get Your Moma!*. New York: Dial Press, 1968.

David L. Lewis, *King: A Biography*. 2nd ed. Urbana: University of Illinois Press, 1978.

C. Eric Lincoln, *The Black Muslims in America*. Boston: Beacon Press, 1961.

Doug McAdam, *Political Process and the Development of Black Insurgency, 1930–1970*. Chicago: University of Chicago Press, 1982.

The Autobiography of Malcolm X. New York: Grove Press, 1964.

August Meier, Elliott Rudwick and Francis Broderick, eds. *Black Protest Thought in the Twentieth Century*. Second Edition. Indianapolis: Bobbs-Merrill, 1971.

August Meier and Elliott Rudwick, *CORE: A Study in the Civil Rights Movement*. New York: Oxford University Press, 1973.

Aldon D. Morris, *The Origins of the Civil Rights Movement: Black Communities Organizing for Change*. New York: Free Press, 1984.

Robert J. Norrell, *Reaping the Whirlwind: The Civil Rights Movement in Tuskegee*. New York: Knopf, 1985.

Report of the National Advisory Commission on Civil Disorder. Washington, D.C.: U.S. Government Printing Office, 1968.

Cushing Strout and David I. Grossvogel, ed. *Divided We Stand: Reflections on the Crisis at Cornell*. Garden City, N.Y.: Doubleday, 1970.

Nancy J. Weiss, *Whitney M. Young, Jr. and the Struggle for Civil Rights*. Princeton: Princeton University Press, 1989.

Howard Zinn, *SNCC: The New Abolitionists*. Boston: Beacon Press, 1964.

Index

Abernathy, Ralph, 127, 351, 293, 311
Activists, civil rights, 12; Northern, 145; in South, 10–11
AFL-CIO, 33, 75, 348
African-American Teachers Association, 208
Afro-American Association, 237
Afro-American societies, 22, 244–247, 257, 258, 260
Afro-American Studies, 249–255, 259–261
Alabama delegation at 1964 Democratic party convention, 89–90, 96, 163, 275, 279–280, 290
Albany, Georgia, 10, 11, 97, 105
Alexander, Clifford L., Jr., 326–327
Allen, Ivan, Jr., mayor of Atlanta, 141
Allen, James E., 176, 191, 201–223. See also New York City; Ocean Hill–Brownsville experiment.
Allen, Ralph, 50–51
American Arbitration Association, 190
American Civil Liberties Union, 144, 340
American Federation of Labor–Congress of Industrial Organizations, See AFL-CIO.
American Jewish Committee, 341
American Scholar, 105
Amsterdam News, 41, 340
Anti-Defamation League of B'Nai B'rith, 341, 347
Anti-discrimination laws, in South, 7
Anti-discrimination movement, 68
Anti-poverty act and program, 16–17, 145
Anti-semitism, 347. See also Ocean Hill–Brownsville experiment.
A. Philip Randolph Education Fund, 353
A. Philip Randolph Institute, 339, 352
Aptheker, Herbert, 254
Armstrong, Earl, 247, 249

Arnold, Martin, 128
Aronson, Arnold, 342
Association of Afro-American Educators, 160–161
Atlanta, Georgia, 142–143, 146, 280–284, 286; police, 141
Atlanta student movement, 149

"Back-to-Africa" movement, 343
Barnett, Ross, governor of Mississippi, 38
Beyond the Melting Pot (Glazer and Moynihan), 133
Bigelow, Albert, 146
"Bill of Rights for the Disadvantaged," 283
Birmingham, Alabama, 5, 76, 97, 105, 267–268, 279, 290; "battle of," 66–67; integration ferment, 62–65; racial explosion, 68; white violence, 269
"Black Is Beautiful," 20, 284
Black militants. See Militants.
Black Muslims, 7, 13–14, 18, 26, 36, 66, 69, 130, 164, 237, 344; religion of protest and rebellion, 37–45
Black nationalism, 21–23, 105, 135, 146
"Black nationlists," 147; reject integration, 120, 289. See also Negroes.
Black Panthers, 18–22, 127, 130, 149–151, 230–234, 342, 344; program, 235–242
"Black Power," 3, 9, 14, 19–21, 127, 130, 136–137, 140–144, 152–161, 164–168, 262, 273–275; protest movement, 3–4, 16, 284–286
Black Power: The Politics of Liberation in America (Carmichael and Hamilton), 284
Black studies, 243–261
Black United Front, 285–286, 288, 298
Booth, Judge William, 336
Boutwell, Albert, 69

Boycotts, 4–5, 12, 57, 62, 120, 125, 156–158, 318–323; bus, Montgomery, 8, 266–273; economic, 42; schools, 278
Brandeis University Center for the Study of Violence, 137–138
Branton, Wiley, 58
Brown decision, 4
Brown, H. Rap, 18, 155, 240, 274
Browne, Robert, 257
Bunche, Ralph, 42
Bundy, McGeorge, 170
Bundy Report, 165
Burger, Warren, 327

Cambridge, 255
Camus, Albert, 141
Cannon, Terry, 241–242
Canton, Mississippi, 26–27, 56, 263–264, 273–275
Carmichael, Stokely, 18–19, 141–144, 149–155, 263–275, 286, 296, 298, 301, 308, 342
Carnegie Foundation, 334
Carter, Jimmy, 356
Carter, Robert L., 336
Central Labor Council, 339
Chaney, James, 293
Chappell, Fred D., sheriff of Sumter County, Georgia, 46–52
Charles, Ray, 243
Chase Manhattan Bank, 245, 258
Chess, Stan, 258
Chicago, 160–163, 259; housing, 265; riots, 346. *See also* Riots.
Children, Negro, reasons for marching, 96–105
Civil disobedience, 4; mass, 15–16
Civil Liberties Union, New York, 204
Civil rights, 37, 60, 76, 310, 325–329, 330–345, 341–350; activists, 5; agencies, 112–113; agitation, 315–318; bill, 270; demonstrations, 136–137, 279–283; diminishing importance, 125; evolution into social movement, 123; Field Foundation, 265; laws, North, 7; leaders, 262–266; national, 232; revolution, 18; struggle, 113
Civil Rights Acts, of 1964, 11, 123; of 1957 and 1960, 47, 55, 97, 105, 117
Civil Rights Leadership Conference, 10, 15
Civil rights legislative program, 4–10, 15, 18, 60–72, 112, 116, 119, 164, 272–273; national, 16; progress, 118
Civil rights movement, 5–8, 14, 107–111,

146–147, 154, 291, 295, 323–324; middle class, 281–282, 287; nonviolent, 114; Southern, 145; split, 140
Clark, Jim, 100–103, 288
Clark, Kenneth B., 27, 45, 129, 184–223, 337
Clark College, 37
Cleaver, Eldridge, 342
COFO, 12, 26–27, 57, 79–81, 86–88, 93–94, 158–159
Coles, Dr. Robert, 105, 147, 360
Collins, E. K., Mississippi state senator, 90
Columbia University, 253
Commentary, 342
Committee on Special Educational Projects, (COSEP). *See* COSEP.
Committee to End Discrimination, 350
Communists, lack of influence on Negro groups, 120, 144, 146
Conant, James Bryant, 109
Congress, U.S., 12, 70–72, 116–117, 282–283, 299, 324, 338, 344–345, 348
Congress of Racial Equality (CORE). *See* CORE.
Cook, Gayla, 243
Coordinating Committee for Community Control, 185
CORE, 9, 12, 14–16, 20–21, 26, 40–41, 57, 61, 79, 82, 128, 152, 158–159, 172, 200, 263–270, 329, 342–344; forming of, 4–5
Cornell Afro-American Institute, 260
Cornell University, 243–261
Corson, Provost Dale R., 258
Council of Federated Organizations (COFO). *See* COFO.
Council of Supervisory Associations, 178
COSEP, 246–248
Cox, Courtland, 150
Cox, Rev. B. Elton, 61
Current, Gloster B., 334–335

Daley, Richard A., mayor of Chicago, 346. *See also* Chicago; Riots.
Davidson, Basil, 254
Deacons for Defense and Justice, 125
Democratic party, 21, 27, 86, 163, 327, 356, 358; in Alabama under George Wallace, 163; losses, 273; in Mississippi, 90–91
Democratic party convention of 1964 (Atlantic City), 12, 16, 93–94, 122, 148–149, 314; compromise proposed, 94; credentials committee, 89

Demonstrations, 62, 65, 74, 97–98, 282; Birmingham, 67–69; leaders, 72; trauma of, 105; Washington, 70–71
Dennis, David, 57
Desegregation, 30, 36, 68–69, 77, 318; lunch counters, 8; schools, 77, 117, 351
Detroit, 155, 156, 160
Devine, Mrs. Annie, 94
Direct action, 5, 8–12, 15–16; in Birmingham, 62–63; but nonviolent, 66; economic and social problems, 12; movement, 96–106; organizations, 10. *See also* Nonviolent direct action.
Dirksen, Senator Everett McKinley, 71–73
Discrimination, 3–6; 16, 45, 58–59; efforts to eliminate, by Federal courts, 76; in Birmingham, 65; in Mississippi, 7; in organized labor, 19; in public accommodations, 75–76; in public transportation, 77; residential, 77, 118
Doar, John M., 202–203, 205–207, 210–211, 219, 221–223
Domestic Marshall Plan, 164
Donaldson, Ivanhoe, 150
Donovan, Bernard, 182–183, 189–193, 202–212, 215–224. *See also* New York City; Ocean Hill–Brownsville experiment.
Dorrough, Charles M., mayor of Ruleville, Mississippi, 86
Douglass, Frederick, 325
Dowd, Douglas, 250, 257
Dowell, Denzil, 235
Dowell, George, 235
Drew, Dr. Charles, 254
DuBois, W. E. B., 6, 161, 239, 254, 342. *See also* W. E. B. DuBois Clubs.
Duke University, 254, 255
Dunaway, R. M., 46, 49, 51
Dunbar, Leslie W., 55
Durland, Lewis, 260
Dutton, Frederick, 356

East Asian studies programs, 251
Eastland, Senator James O., 27, 38, 303–305, 324
Ebenezer Baptist Church, 292
Ebony, 22, 116
Economic Bill of Rights, 279
Economic Opportunity Act, 123
Education News, 204
Educational Testing Service, 245
Election campaigns, 313; electoral activity, 156; mock, 94–95

Elkins, Stanley, 254
Equal Employment Opportunity Commission, 326–327
Evers, Charles, 128, 313–323
Evers, Medgar, 269, 313–317, 332
Extremist groups, Negro, 66, 308

Fair Employment Practices Commission (FEPC). *See* FECP bill.
Fairleigh Dickinson University, 257
Family - Community - School - Comprehensive Plan, 165, 167–169
Fanon, Frantz, 140–141, 239
Fard, W. D., 38. *See also* Black Muslims.
Farmer, James, 4–5, 9, 340, 348–350
FBI, 80, 270, 290, 320
Federal fair employment practices agency created, 11
Fellowship of Reconciliation, 350
FEPC bill, 41, 75
Ferguson, Herman, 173, 176, 177–178
Field, Stephen R., 59
Field Foundation, 265, 274
Fisk University, 140, 268
Ford Foundation, 170–174, 189, 224, 333–334; grant, 292
Forman, James, 145–146, 151
Franklin, Aretha, 243
Freedmen's Bureau, 117
Freedom march, 19. *See also* Meredith, James.
"Freedom Now," 10
"Freedom Primer," 85–86
Freedom Riders, 29–30, 34–36, 42, 62, 151
Freedom Rides, 11, 25, 97, 146, 262–264, 267, 271, 349; in Alabama and Mississippi, 9. *See also* Journey of Reconciliation.
Freedom schools, 27, 121; Ruleville, Mississippi, 79–88
Freedom vote campaign, 86
"Freedom walks," 44

Galamison, Rev. Milton A., 193–200, 206–215, 352
Gandhi, 4, 145, 280; Gandhian techniques, 4–5
Garner, M. J., 249
Garvey, Marcus, 239, 343
Gary, Indiana, 161, 163
General Motors, UAW sit-down strike against, 32–33

Ghettos, 17, 26, 107, 115, 118, 269, 278, 346; black, 12, 20–21, 155–156, 165; "internal" and "external" problems, 157; Northern black, 230; racial, 77; riots, 108–112, 136. *See also* Riots.
Glazer, Nathan, 133
Goldman, Eric, 25
Goldwater, Senator Barry, 90
Green, William, 33–34
Greenberg, Jack, 43
Greensboro, North Carolina, 3, 25
Gregory, Dick, 69
Grigg, Charles M., 157
Guerrilla warfare, 20–21; tactics, 121

Haddad, William, 193–194
Hall, Leon, 288–289
Halleck, Charles A., 71
Hamilton, Charles V., 127, 251, 253, 284
Hamer, Mrs. Fannie Lou, 27, 91, 94, 122
Hanes, Arthur J., mayor of Birmingham, 68
Harlem, 107–109, 116, 121, 165
Harlem Youth Opportunities Unlimited. *See* HARYOU.
Harrington, Michael, 348–349
Harris, Jesse, 145
Harris, Louis, interviews by his poll-takers, 192
Harvard University, 105, 141, 147, 149, 251, 252, 254
HARYOU, 45
Hatcher, Richard, mayor of Gary, Indiana, 161–163
Hauser, Dr. Philip M., 78
Hayden, Tom, 121, 146
Haynsworth, Clement F., Jr., 327
Henry, Aaron, 74, 90, 122
Hick, James, 41
Hill, Herbert, 118–119, 337
Hitler, Adolf, 40
Holland, Jerome (Brud), 244
Hollander, Edward S., 57
Holloway, Lucius, 49, 51
Hoover, J. Edgar, 50–51, 270. *See also* FBI.
Howard University, 150–151
Humphrey, Hubert H., 72, 275, 333, 342
Hurley, Mrs. Ruby, 316–317

Ideology of accommodation, 21; revolutionary, 15
Industrial Union Department, 75
Industrial Workers of the World ("Wobblies"), 144

Innis, Roy, 165, 329
Integration, 6–7, 23, 325–329, 346, 348; black nationalists reject, 120; ferment over, 62–63; "irrelevant," 145; Muslims oppose, 38; public school, 22; token, 137; viewed as denial of blacks' heritage, 156–157
Italian Americans, 359

Jackson Daily News, 289
Jackson, Mississippi, 160, 312, 316, 327, 332
Jackson, Rev. Jesse, 158. *See also* Operation Breadbasket.
Jazz. *See* Soul, music.
Jenkins, Herbert, Atlanta police chief, 141
Jewish cultural studies, 251
Jewish Labor Committee, 341
Jim Crow, 31, 267, 269, 326
Johnson, President Lyndon B., 11–12, 15, 90–94, 271, 299, 305, 326–330; administration, 269, 275, 282; Negro loyalty to, 122, 124; reaction to Poor People's campaign, 281; speech at Lincoln Memorial, 277
Johnson, Paul B., 55
Jones, Joseph Charles, 48, 51
Joseph, Dr. Gloria, 245, 246
Journey of Reconciliation, 348
Justice Department, 47–51, 55–59, 160, 272; civil rights division, 61, 68

Kagan, Dr. Donald, 256
Kennedy, President John F., 15, 30, 40, 59, 72, 147, 269, 326–327, 356; administration of, 65, 77, 281
Kennedy, Robert F., 30, 60–64, 68, 109, 267, 306, 314
Kennedy, W. Keith, 260
Kheel, Theodore, 191–195, 202, 215–221
Killian, Lewis M., 157
Kilson, Dr. Martin, 252
King, Rev. Edwin, 92
King, Dr. Martin Luther, Jr., 9, 15–23, 27, 41, 62–68, 71–78, 91–97, 120–149, 155–158, 181, 240, 262–265, 289, 290–311, 341–351; leadership, 7; at Selma, 11; SCLC established, 5–6. *See also* Civil rights; SCLC; Selma, Alabama.
Ku Klux Klan, 39, 69, 97, 110, 212, 320, 324. *See also* Civil rights.
Ku Klux Klan Act, 117
Kunstler, William, 206

Labor Department, report on Negro unemployment, 119
Ladd, Everett, 358
Latin American studies programs, 251
Lawrence, David L., 89
Lawson, James, 266
League for Industrial Democracy, 348
Lee, Bernard, 287
Lee, D. L., 250, 254
"Legalism," 7-9, 12
Lehman, Herbert H., governor of New York, 42
Lewis, Chester, 336
Lewis, John, 98, 127, 147, 152, 262-276
Lincoln, Abraham, 66, 74-75, 277
Lincoln, Dr. C. Eric, 37
Lincoln Memorial, 70-71, 269, 277, 343
Lindsay, John V., mayor of New York, 173, 189, 191, 193, 196-226, 356. *See also* New York City
Lipset, Seymour, 358
Little, Malcolm. *See* Malcolm X.
Little Red Book (Mao), 239
London School of Economics, 255
Los Angeles, 108, 109, 111, 125. *See also* Riots; Watts riot.
Lotz, John, 195-196
Lowndes County Freedom Organization, Alabama, 234
McCall, Daniel, 250
McCarthyism, legacy of, 144
McClellan, Representative Thompson, 57
McComb, Mississippi, 146
McCormack, John W., 71-72
McCoy, Rhody A., 173-209, 214-224
MacDonald, Dwight, 348
Maddox, Lester, governor of Georgia, 275
Madison County, Mississippi, 55-56, 60
Mahoney, Bill, 150
Malcolm X, 14-15, 39-41, 69, 136, 143-146, 152, 167, 233-239, 247. *See also* Civil rights; Muslims.
Malcolm X Speaks, 140
Mansfield, Senator Mike, 71
Mants, Bob, 148
Maoists, 120
Maoist Progressive Labor Movement, 146
Mao Tse-tung, 155, 239
March, Poor People's, 299
Marches, night, 96
Marchi Law, 193, 195, 215
March on Washington Movement (1941), 4
March on Washington (1963), 11, 15, 26,

112, 123, 147, 269, 281-283, 341, 350. *See also* Civil rights.
Marshall, Burke, Assistant Attorney General, 61, 68
Marshall, Thurgood, 15, 42-43, 254, 334, 346
Martin, Homer S., 35
Mathews, Z. T., sheriff of Terrell County, Georgia, 46-51
Matthew, Dr. Thomas W., 159
Mayfield, Julian, 250
Meeley, Fred, 147
Meredith, James, 19, 138, 205, 262, 322
Meredith March, 263, 268
MFDP. *See* Mississippi Freedom Democratic party.
Militants, 65-66, 77, 121, 155, 178, 272, 307, 327-329, 340, 342-343; nationalist, 127; nonviolent, 298; ultra, 281. *See also* Civil rights; Violence.
Minnis, Jack, 148
Mississippi, 105, 116, 121, 138, 268-275, 287; challenge to political system, 312-324; Congressional delegation, 94; cooperatives, 159-160; regular delegation, 89-94
Mississippi Freedom Democratic party, 12, 16, 27, 89-94, 116, 122-124, 271, 275, 314, 323
Mississippi Freedom Summer Project, 148
Mississippi, University of, 205
Model Cities Program, 337
Montgomery Advertiser, 302
Montgomery, Alabama, 102, 106, 112, 268, 279, 290; bus boycott, 58, 295, 300. *See also* Boycotts; King, Dr. Martin Luther, Jr.
Montgomery Improvement Association, 5, 300
More Effective Schools (M.E.S.), 172
Morgan, Charles, 144
Morgan v. Virginia decision, 5
Morsell, Dr. John, 335, 341
Moses, Robert, 12, 141, 149
Mount Beulah Conference Center, 289, 302
Movement, 241-242
Moynihan, Daniel P., 134
Muhammad, Elijah, 38-39, 40. *See also* Black Muslims, Malcolm X.
Muskie, E. S., 356, 357, 361, 362

NAACP, 7-10, 15-26, 36-44, 54, 66, 69, 75, 79, 119-120, 128, 173, 232, 254, 258, 268-269, 313-323, 326-341, 345;

NAACP (*cont.*)
59th annual convention, 35; largest civil rights organization, 42; technique of legalism, 7, 9, 12. *See also* Civil rights; CORE; SCLC; SNCC.
NAACP Legal Defense Fund, 5, 40–42
NAG (Nonviolent Action Group), 150
Nashville Christian Leadership Conference, 267
Nashville Student Movement, 149, 266
National Association for the Advancement of Colored People (NAACP). *See* NAACP.
National Conference of New Politics Convention, 162
National Council of Churches, 289, 304–305
National Economic Growth and Reconstruction Organization (N.E.G.R.O.), 159
National Teacher Corps, 166
National Urban League, 18, 120, 164, 258
Negroes, children march, 27, 96–105; college student sit-down strike, 28; constitutional rights, 8–9; deprived of participation in Democratic party, 94–98; discrimination in public accommodations, 58, 76; disfranchisement, 86; economic and social problems, 118–119, 123; equality, 35, 62; extremist groups, 66, 298; gains, 118; in ghettos, 107; legal and social status, 118; in Muslim movement, 40; integration into American life, 119; "internal colonialism," 141; Los Angeles, 109; middle class, 150, 281; militants, 65–69, 77; nationalism, 120, 237, 272; national problems, 74–75; passive resistance movement, 35; potential violence, 110; psychological makeup, 129–138; racial confrontation, 45; reconstruction suffrage, 86; rights, 29–30, 278–279; self-hatred, 129, 132–136; social thought, 6; students, 37; subculture, "positive sense of identity," 14, 130; unemployment, 7, 119; voting rally in Georgia, 46–52; voter registration drive in Mississippi, 56–58; Washington demonstration, 70. *See also* Black Muslims; "Black Power"; Civil rights; Militants; Nonviolent Direct Action.
Neshoba County, Mississippi, 270
Newark, 155, 156
New Leader, 342
New Left, 155, 342
Newton, Huey P., 232–241

New York City, 160, 169; riots, 346; school system, 170. *See also* Lindsay, John V , Ocean Hill–Brownsville experiment.
New York Civil Liberties Union, 186
New York Post, 338
New York Review of Books, 342
New York Times, 25–28, 62, 65, 70, 74, 89, 93, 264–265
New York Times Magazine, 29, 37, 79, 107, 116, 149, 169, 230, 262, 277, 294, 312, 325, 338, 339
New York Urban League, 165
Nixon, Richard, 325–338, 353, 361, 362
Nonviolent direct action, 3, 4, 13, 62, 102, 105, 120, 127, 265–272, 286, 310, 347, 349; demonstrations, 133; organizations, 18; philosophy, 301, 303; protest, 145; techniques, 25–26
Norman, David, 61
Norman Thomas Fund, 347
Norris, Jessie, 159
North Carolina Agricultural and Technical College, 25, 28, 254
Northeastern University, Boston, 307
Northwestern University, 253
Norton, Eleanor Holmes, 340–341

Ocean Hill–Brownsville experiment, 22, 127, 171–229
Office of Economic Opportunity, 17
Oliver, Rev. C. Herbert, 176, 187, 192, 193, 201, 224
Operation Breadbasket, 157–158, 248–249. *See also* Jackson, Rev. Jesse.

Parker, Charles Mack, 317
Parker, Rev. Henry, 289
Parker, William, Los Angeles police chief, 110
Parks, Mrs. Rosa, 300
Partisan Review, 342
Patton, Gary S., 244
Paul, Alice, 31–32, 34
Patch, Penelope, 48, 51–52
Patterson, Floyd, 69
Perkins, James A., 244–247, 249, 255, 256, 257, 260
Police, 11, 239; brutality, 109, 123. *See also* Riots.
Poll-tax, 58
Poole Elijah. *See* Muhammad, Elijah.
Poor People's Campaign, 23, 280–287, 295–303, 309–310; Corporation, 159–160; in Washington, D.C., 127.

Powell, Congressman Adam Clayton, 41, 43, 136, 351
Powis, Father, 173–174, 181, 185–187, 191, 221–222
Poverty, 15–16, 111, 127, 278–279, 298; campaign against, 123, 124; mass, 116; war on, 348
President's Commission on Civil Disorders, 166
Pressure-group tactics, 154; bargaining, 150
Preston, Robert, 236

Racial Crisis in America (Killian and Grigg), 157
Racism, 40, 45, 74, 129–130, 138, 241, 262, 272, 275; American, 3–5, 107, 110, 112, 162; black Muslims, 66; cancer of, 113; condescension, 107; contamination, 113; crisis, 46–47; domestic, 16; extremists, 65; perpetuates itself, 113; police, 109; Southern white, 137, 295
Radicalism, 342; agrarian, 122; Russian students of, 146
Radical right, 120
Randolph, A. Philip, 4, 15, 125–126, 340–341, 347, 350–352
Rauh, Joseph L., Jr., 90–91
The Rebel (Camus), 141
Reconstruction, 276; Acts, 117; amendments, 4; Negro suffrage, 86
Registration, *See* Vote.
Rent strikes, 125, 156
Republic of New Africa, 22
Reuther, Walter, 42, 75, 269, 334, 353
Revolution, Negro, 116–117, 122, 154–157, 161; protest phase, 125; revolutionaries, social, 296; revolutionary demands, 279; revolutionary regeneration in American society, 121, 124
Revolutionary Action Movement (RAM), 18
Ricks, Willie, 139, 150
Riots, 108–109, 187, 285; form of "community suicide," 129; ghettos, 136. *See also* Ghettos; Violence.
Roberts, Gene, 127
Robinson, Jackie, 69
Rockefeller, Nelson A., governor of New York, 306
Rockefeller Foundation, 245, 334
Roosevelt, Mrs. Eleanor, 42
Roosevelt, President Franklin D., 4, 32, 359
Roosevelt University, 251, 253
Ruleville, Mississippi, 27, 79–89

Russian studies programs, 251
Rustin, Bayard, 5, 15–16, 123–124, 204, 339–353

St. Augustine, Florida, 97, 105
Sacramento, California, 230–232, 241
Sasser, Georgia, 26, 46–47
SCLC, 9–11, 23, 41, 66, 71, 78–82, 97, 101, 158, 176, 263, 267, 290–310, 351; Atlanta headquarters, 277–279, 284–287; Birmingham campaign, 26; established, 6. *See also* King, Dr. Martin Luther, Jr.
Schwerner, Michael, 293
Schwerner, Mrs. Rita, 92
SCOPE, 123–124
Scottsboro, 350
Seale, Bobby, 233–241
Segregation, 36, 55, 58, 156; banned in schools, 37, 66, 75; Birmingham, 67; de facto, 118–119; de jure, 118; demonstrations, 44; in North, 3–5; public transportation, 77–78; residential, 118; unconstitutional, 43–44. *See also* Discrimination.
Segregationists, 23, 65–66, 104; bigotry, 113; critics, 80; resistance, 66
Sellers, Cleveland, 250, 258
Selma, Alabama, 27, 96–106, 112, 120, 142, 146, 262, 271, 290, 294, 305, 309, 322; Camp Selma, 100–101; march, 11–12, 279, 283–284. *See also* King, Dr. Martin Luther, Jr.
"Sensorimotor intelligence," 316–317
Separatism, 21, 154, 325, 342; black, 284; cultural, 127; racial, 3; separatists, 23. *See also* Civil rights.
Shanker, Albert, 178–179, 183, 189, 190–228, 340. *See also* New York City; Ocean Hill-Brownsville experiment.
Shaw University, 254
Shepperson, George, 254
Sherrod, Charles, 47–48, 51, 148
Shuttlesworth, Rev. Fred Lee, 68
Sindler, Dr. Allan P., 255, 256
Sit-ins, 4, 42, 48, 62, 97, 125, 264, 278; failure, 12; Mississippi, 130; Southern college students, 8
Smith, A.P., sheriff of Holmes County, Georgia, 58
Smith, Scott B., 145
SNCC, 9, 10, 12, 18–26, 47–48, 79–82, 97, 103, 122–124, 127–128, 139–153, 159, 240–242, 262, 275, 285, 286, 322, 342. *See also* Civil rights.

Sorbonne, 255
Soul Force, 284
Soul Story, 127
South Africa, 260
Southern Black Everyman, 262
Southern Christian Leadership Conference (SCLC). See SCLC.
Southern Consumers' Cooperative, 158
Southern Regional Council, 26, 143
Southern Regional Council's Voter Education Project (Atlanta), 55, 158
Stampp, Kenneth, 254
State Board of Election Commissioners, Mississippi, 94
State Sovereignty Commission, Mississippi, 289–290, 317
Stell, Lewis M., 336
Stennis, Senator John, 73, 304
Stokes, Carl, mayor of Cleveland, 163
Student Non-violent coordinating Committee, 250
Students for a Democratic Society (SDS), 121, 146, 258
Summer Community Organization and Political Education. See SCOPE.
Supremacists, white, 40, 56–57
Supreme Court, United States, 15, 45, 58, 60, 327–328, 334, 346; decision of 1954, 7, 35, 37, 43, 55, 63–66, 75–77, 112. See also Desegregation; Integration.
Sutherland, Elizabeth, 144

Taft-Hartley Act, Section 14b, repeal of, 123
Teacher strikes of 1968, 169-229. See also New York City; Ocean Hill–Brownsville experiment.
Teachers' Union, 172–229.
Terrell County (Georgia) Board of Voter Registrars, 47
Thelwell, Michael, 250
Thomas, Norman, 347
Till, Emmett, 317
"To Fulfill These Rights," 273
"Tokenism," 21, 26, 40, 45, 66, 117, 122, 137
Tougaloo College, 92
Truman, President Harry S., 30, 350
Tunney, Senator, 356
Turner, Albert, 290
Turner, James, 253, 254, 260, 261
Tuskegee (Alabama) Civic Association, 5

United Automobile Workers (UAW), 32–35, 75
United Federation of Teachers (UFT), 172–228, 339–340
United Negro College Fund, 245
United States Steel, 40
"Uncle Tom," 13, 135, 238, 329, 341
University of Edinburgh, 254
University of Michigan, 362
University of Mississippi, 66
Urban Coalition, 224; delegation, 352; education task force, 158, 189
Urban League, 16, 40–41, 298, 306, 341. See also Civil rights.
Urban Task Force, 225, 228

Van Arsdale, Harry, 339–340
Vanocur, Sander, 302–303
Vietnam War, 16, 234, 265, 272, 275–279, 283, 329, 338; opposition to, 146, 149
Village Voice, 342
Violence, 17–18, 74, 136–138, 141, 154, 296; against SNCC, 146–147; apostles of, 120; race, 262; repression, 155–156; retaliatory, 20, 273–274; on West Coast, 117; white, 269. See also Civil rights; Nonviolent direct action; Watts riot.
Vote, 12, 55–56, 70–72, 90–92, 97–102, 116, 161–162; denial of, 75–77; discriminatory procedure, 93–94; tests, 59, 61
Voter registration, 19–20, 117, 123–124, 142, 287; campaign, 26–27; drive, Tuskegee, Alabama, 150; tests, 79–80, 87
Voting Rights Act of 1965, 11, 117, 123, 272, 283, 297

Wagner Act, 32, 34
Walker, Wyatt Tee, 124
Wallace, George C., governor of Alabama, 68, 163, 291, 346, 359
Wallace, Lurleen, 275, 291
Ware, Bill, 146, 147
Washington, 277–280, 285, 290; march on, 70–74, 295–298, 310
Watts riot, Los Angeles (1965), 27, 107–109, 116, 155, 235, 330
W. E. B. DuBois Clubs, 120
West Virginia, 360
Where Do We Go From Here: Chaos or Community? (King), 284
White Citizens' Councils, 7, 45, 317
White, Walter, 333

Whitfield, Ed, 243, 249
Wilkins, Roger, 333
Wilkins, Roy, 18, 40–44, 75–76, 128, 173,
    254, 269, 273, 325–342
Williams, John Bell, governor of Mississip-
    pi, 313
Williams, Hosea, 287–289, 292, 295,
    301–305
Williams, Robert, 232–233
Williams, Robert F., 17–18
Wilson, Woodrow, 31, 34
Wise, John, 272
Wise, Rabbi Stephen S., 42
Woodward, Prof. C. Vann, 251, 252, 254
World War I, 32
World War II, 7; first use of nonviolent
    direct action,
Wretched of the Earth (Fanon), 140

Yale, 251, 252, 256
Yale Law Journal, 59
Yipsel, 348
Young Communist League, 350
Young, Israel House, 256
Young Left, 120–121, 122–123
Young People's Socialist League (Yipsel).
    See Yipsel.
Young Rev. Andrew, 279–304, 357, 362
Young Turks, 327, 334
Young Whitney, 18, 215–216, 222, 258,
    306, 340–341
Youth Alliance Patrol, 307

A Note on the Editors

AUGUST MEIER teaches history at Kent State University. Born in New York City, he studied at Oberlin College and Columbia University, and taught at three black colleges—Tougaloo, Fisk, and Morgan State—as well as at Roosevelt University, before coming to Kent State. He is the author of *Negro Thought in America, 1880–1915*. The late Elliott Rudwick taught both history and sociology at Kent State University. Born in Philadelphia, he studied at Temple University and at the University of Pennsylvania. He served as a consultant to the U.S. Civil Rights Commission and the Kerner Commission. His books include *W.E.B. Du Bois: Propagandist of the Negro Protest* and *Race Riot at East St. Louis, July 2, 1917*. Meier and Rudwick co-authored *From Plantation to Ghetto; CORE: A Study in the Civil Rights Movement; Black Detroit and the Rise of the UAW*; and *Black History and the Historical Profession*. John Bracey teaches in the W.E.B. Du Bois Department of Afro-American Studies at the University of Massachusetts, Amherst. Born in Chicago, he studied at Howard University, Roosevelt University, and Northwestern University. He has taught at Northern Illinois University and the University of Rochester. He is the author of numerous articles, co-editor with Meier of the microfilm series *Black Studies Research Resources*, published by University Publications of America, and co-editor with Meier and Rudwick of *Black Nationalism in America*.

375